Social Construction and Social Work Practice

Social Construction and Social Work Practice

Interpretations and Innovations

EDITED BY

STANLEY L WITKIN

Columbia University Press   *New York*

Columbia University Press
Publishers Since 1893
New York   Chichester, West Sussex
Copyright © 2012 Columbia University Press

Library of Congress Cataloging-in-Publication Data

Social construction and social work practice : interpretations and innovations /
[edited by] Stanley L Witkin.
p. cm.
Includes bibliographical references and index.
ISBN 978-0-231-15246-4 (cloth : alk. paper)—ISBN 978-0-231-53030-9 (ebook)
1. Social constructionism. 2. Social service. I. Witkin, Stanley L, 1947–II. Title.

HM1093.S63 2011

361.201—dc22   2011012093

Columbia University Press books are printed on permanent and durable acid-free paper.
This book is printed on paper with recycled content.
Printed in the United States of America.

c 10 9 8 7 6 5 4 3 2 1

References to Internet Web sites (URLs) were accurate at the time of writing. Neither the
author nor Columbia University Press is responsible for URLs that may have expired or
changed since the manuscript was prepared.

Contents

Contents

Foreword

Stanley Witkin, whose career path has led him from the ideological and methodological inclinations of positivism and modernism to the penchants of social constructionism, has put together a book that begins with that journey but quickly branches out into a rich and compelling accounting of what social constructionism means for social work theory, practice, and pedagogy. A central constructionist notion is that words, images, and ideas constitute the world for us; words do not reflect what is "real," as modernists and positivists would have it. In that spirit, Witkin makes it clear at the outset that disparate theoretical and ideological allegiances and preferences will value different kinds of information, concepts, and ideologies and will, therefore, lead to different kinds of talk and practices. In the case of social constructionism, however, what practitioners do in their routines, how they relate to clients, and the "tools" they use are always emerging from the dialogues, the conversations, and the interactions with individual clients and colleagues. That assumption, he says, gives us "greater freedom to respond to the nuances and particularities of the situation" (see Chapter 1).

Importantly, and clearly within the purview of a social constructionist ethos, Witkin writes in a style that is accessible and conversational. The late pedagogue of freedom, Paulo Friere, wrote of the contrast between "banking education" whereby the oppressor, however well-intentioned, stifles true engagement and conceals the students' power and wisdom from them through the use of foreign or strange concepts and theories. Liberating education, on the other hand, regards "dialogue as indispensable to the act of cognition which unveils reality" (Friere, 2001, p. 83). It is in this spirit that Witkin has compiled this book. He has brought together contributors to this volume who know the importance of discourse and dialogue, and it is reflected in their writing, their teaching, their practice, and their understanding of social work.

Over the years, Jerome Bruner (1990) has written of the critical distinction, both in professional discourse and in ordinary conversation, between the paradigmatic and the narrative, or, more simply, between theory and story. We know a lot about the paradigmatic; it reigns supreme in our education, and professions, including social work, aspire to it. In its most developed form, it is a logical, scientific, formal, even mathematical system of explanation. But books like this one bring to social work a much needed corrective to the paradigmatic ambition, and help put practice, research, and teaching in social work back in the niche where it can acknowledge, appreciate, affirm, and, most importantly, act in the daily world of clients. The significance of this book to the social work profession cannot be overstated. Students, teachers, and researchers will find here an abundance of ideas and practices to leaven the work that they do on behalf of clients and in the service of social justice.

Dennis Saleebey
Professor Emeritus
School of Social Welfare, University of Kansas

References

Bruner, J. (1990). *Actual minds, possible worlds.* Cambridge, MA: Harvard University Press.

Freire, P. (2001). *Pedagogy of the oppressed,* 30th anniversary ed. New York: Continuum.

Preface

I have been fortunate during my career to know many bright, interesting people. Building relationships and engaging in conversations with these folks has enriched my personal and professional life and has been a continual source of ideas and inspiration. About 10 years ago, one of those people (Dennis Saleebey) and I decided to make sure that we (and others) would have the opportunity to continue these conversations on a regular basis. We instituted a small, annual gathering in Vermont where participants could take part in two and a half days of dialogue about social construction and other "postmodern" perspectives (see Witkin and Saleebey, 2007, for additional information). As we hoped, these gatherings have generated many stimulating conversations and connections with interesting people from all over the world. Some of them constitute the contributors to this book: social work scholars-practitioners for whom social constructionist ideas have informed and enhanced their practice.

Anyone who has published an edited book knows that it is a collaborative enterprise. The current text is no exception. Coordinating the efforts of 11 talented authors from six countries requires mutual patience, flexibility, and conscientiousness. I was fortunate in working with a group who exemplified these qualities. Therefore, my first acknowledgement and note of thanks goes to them. Their ability to translate social constructionist ideas into creative practices and to express those translations in ways that are accessible to readers gives this book its potential to contribute to the corpus of knowledge about social work practice.

In addition to the chapter authors, there are many others, past and present, whose intellectual curiosity, perspicacity, wisdom, friendship, enthusiasm, and support have contributed to my ability to conceptualize and carry out this project. Without diminishing the contributions of those not mentioned, I want to particularly acknowledge Dennis Saleebey, Roberta Iversen, Mirja Satka, Mary Katherine O'Connor, Jan Fook, Katherine Tyson-McCrae, Ann Weick, Adrienne Chambon, and Allan Irving. Their friendships and ongoing dialogues have been an invaluable resource and wellspring of ideas. Brenda Solomon, Susan Roche, and Susan Comerford, colleagues in the social work program at the University of Vermont, have been collaborators in the development and delivery of a social constructionist–oriented curriculum and steadfast supporters of this work. The many students who have taken my classes (voluntarily and not) over the years made the need for such a book visible to me. The many colleagues and friends from the Global Partnership for Transformative Social Work, the umbrella organization for the previously mentioned gathering, have been an enduring source of intellectual enrichment and an antidote to the sometimes numbing effects of an overly corporatized academic life.

I am fortunate to have a daughter, Shana Witkin, who holds graduate degrees in social work and English. Her review of my writing has combined an understanding of social work practice with the uncompromising "blue pencil" of a skilled editor. A special acknowledgement of gratitude goes to my wife, Fran Joseph. Her insightful editorial assistance, constructively critical commentary, and unwavering support have added immeasurably to this project. I thank her, too, for teaching me how to laugh for no reason. Finally, I want to thank Lauren Dockett of Columbia University Press for taking on this project and her support throughout its completion.

For many, social construction has an aura of mystery. What does it mean when we say something is socially constructed? Are we saying that it is not real? Sure, one can grasp that preferences, fads, and the like are socially constructed, but what about "things" like poverty, depression, and violence? Don't try to tell social workers these are "only" socially constructed! Such questions are understandable and I hope that readers will find satisfactory responses to them. What I also hope they will find is that practicing from a social constructionist perspective does not discount people's pain and suffering nor the conditions or actions that contribute to them. Rather, I believe that the practices described in the following chapters demonstrate the potential for increased sensitivity and creative ways of addressing such issues.

Powerful cultural and social forces maintain our customary ways of understanding the world. Challenging well-entrenched beliefs or assumptions can be unsettling; however, the rewards can be great. Please accept this invitation to accompany the book's contributors on their journeys through meaningful and useful practice.

Reference

Witkin, S. L., and D. Saleebey (Eds.) (2007). *Social work dialogues: Transforming the canon in inquiry, practice, and education.* Alexandria, VA: Council on Social Work Education.

Social Construction and Social Work Practice

Beginning the Journey

STANLEY L. WITKIN

Humans cannot live alone. To envision human life is to envision relationships. Our beliefs and feelings, what we find pleasing or displeasing, beautiful or ugly, right or wrong, are all products of social relationships. This, in a nutshell, is the guiding principle of social construction. Since the mid-1980s, I have spent much time exploring, discussing, playing with, and trying to live in accord with social constructionist ideas and sensibilities. I have been fortunate to teach in a program in which social construction is a primary theme of the curriculum. This has given me relatively free reign to teach about and from a social constructionist framework. It has also afforded me the opportunity to observe how students take up these ideas and what excites, puzzles, angers, and intrigues them about this form of sense making. The idea for this book sprang from these experiences.

One of the more challenging aspects of social construction is its nonprescriptive stance. Although different practices can be judged as more or less congruent with social constructionist ideas, no particular collection of methods or techniques *is* social constructionist practice. For students entering a graduate program in a profession like social work, this position may be contrary to what they were expecting or hoping, can feel threatening, or may even be considered an abrogation of the program's responsibility to them. Simply put, many, if not most, students to varying degrees (and I might add that I was no different as an MSW student) want to be taught techniques they can readily apply to various problems. This desire is not surprising given the considerable responsibility they will bear as social workers. They will encounter people in great need, people who have been marginalized by society, people who are in pain, who are angry, scared, and confused. In many cases, their professional judgments will have a significant impact on the lives of these people. In such circumstances, being taught methods and techniques, what to do in given situations, provides a level of comfort and sense of competence that is highly appealing.

In addition to the anxiety associated with the uncertainty about the "right" way to respond to problems, practice tends to be thought of as constituted primarily of techniques or specific interventions. For instance, a behavioral approach might be described as skills training, desensitization, self-monitoring, and the use of rewards. These techniques are reasonable responses to how problems are understood—for example, as responses to reinforcements and punishments. Criteria used for identifying positive change (e.g., increases in the frequency of targeted behaviors) and their assessment (e.g., monitoring of frequency counts) are consistent with the approach. This gives the approach coherence and intelligibility. It would not make sense, for example, for a behavioral practitioner to treat superego or transference issues with a behavioral procedure. In this case, the "nature" of these problems, that is, the way they are construed and understood, invites psychodynamic treatment—for example, the awareness and identification of repressed memories and their impact on current feelings.

For social constructionist–oriented practitioners neither of these approaches is out-of-bounds. The assumptions and beliefs of each approach, and the language that constitutes them, render the ways problems are constructed and their treatment sensible and appropriate. Both problem and treatment reflect and generate each other.

Theoretical allegiances extend beyond problem definitions and practice techniques to how we value different forms of information or understanding. Behavioral practitioners, for example, will likely be proponents of evidence-based practice, believing that randomized clinical trials provide the most authoritative information for practice. They will also be interested in concepts like practice effectiveness and "what works." On the other hand, the relative value of learning the client's narrative will likely be low (the very idea may seem like fiction). In addition, the nature of the practitioner-client relationship and the importance or relevance of dialogue may be secondary to carrying out particular methods in a precise manner.

Social constructionist–informed practitioners tend to adopt a pragmatic position, looking at what seems to be most useful in a particular situation. Of course, determinations of "most useful" will be congruent with social constructionist ideas which will invite particular understandings and justify related ways of working with others. In this sense all belief systems are similar and social construction does not claim superiority. It too is a social construction, albeit one that its adherents believe leads to better ways of practicing. One notable difference from other approaches is the reluctance to prescribe particular techniques as constituting social constructionist practice. Rather, practitioners' actions emerge from the interaction with their clients. In other words, the ever evolving, co-constructed character of the relationship, not particular methods or techniques, guides practitioners' actions.

Not having a prespecified "toolbox" of techniques increases uncertainty and decreases professional authority. While practicing from such a position may generate anxiety, it also enables greater freedom to respond creatively to the nuances and particularities of the situation. The case examples in this book illustrate this theme—showing different ways that social constructionist ideas are taken up and expressed in practice. The aim of this approach is to be instructive without being formulaic or authoritative.

My Constructionist Journey

No one learns about social construction, or any other framework, in a vacuum. It therefore seemed relevant for the chapter authors to address how they encountered social construction and what ideas attracted them. In my own case, social interactions have always fascinated me. From my early undergraduate courses in social psychology in which I was captivated by symbolic interactionism, to my MSW studies where I specialized in group work, and then to my doctoral studies, which focused on marital relationships, the interdependencies, intricacies, and mysteries of social relations seemed central to understanding social life.

Despite these interests, my graduate work was primarily informed by conventional research, and my practice approach was behavioral. At the time (early- to mid-1970s), my allegiance to empirical methodology and behaviorism led me to overlook their limited capacity to address the dynamics of social processes. Ironically, it was through a behavioral psychologist, Michael Mahoney, that I was introduced to critiques of the dominant views of science that undergirded these approaches (e.g., Kuhn, 1962; Weimer, 1979). Mahoney's own book on the psychology of scientists (1976) shattered the mythology that many (including me) held about the characteristics of scientists and how they performed their work. I found this literature to be revelatory and attempted to integrate these ideas with my social work–based commitment to social justice and to apply this thinking to social work research and practice (e.g., Witkin, 1989; Witkin and Gottschalk, 1988). While engaged in this project, I came across Ken Gergen's article "The Social Constructionist Movement in Modern Psychology" (1985), in which he outlined salient assumptions and beliefs of social construction. These were exciting ideas! In particular, the notion of language as constituting rather than reflecting what we take as real and the idea of challenging taken-for-granted beliefs seemed supportive of my own beliefs and values. As often happens in such encounters, I experienced an articulation and crystallization of my own inchoate thoughts, like seeing an out-of-focus image suddenly achieve laser clarity. I also found many social constructionist ideas to be congruent with my vision of social work, a topic I discuss in the next chapter.

As I continue this intellectual journey into the present, my understanding of social construction changes and deepens. And its implications and applications keep expanding. The current work is one such manifestation of this ongoing development.

Organization of the Book

The primary aims of this book are to introduce students and practitioners to the salient ideas of social construction and to illustrate some of the ways these ideas influence and are expressed in practice. I hope these illustrations will address questions you may have about social construction's relevance and applicability to social work and encourage you to explore its potential expressions in your practice.

Given these aims, the book is written in a style intended to be reader accessible, particularly to those not versed in "postmodern speak" (more about this in chapter 2). Academic formats, while not ignored, were flexibly applied to allow more personal, essay-style narratives. A "telling" rather than a "showing" writing style was used (Taylor, 2008), in which authors are conspicuously present within the text. The practices they write about are embedded in their biographies. Ample use of case examples creates a bridge between concepts and their application, helping readers see the possibilities of practices inspired by social constructionist ideas. Although authors present their topics in different ways, each was guided by the following structure:

1. Tell readers something about you. Locate yourself—geographically, culturally, socially, and professionally. Describe the nature of your practice. Add anything else that will give readers relevant context to understand your ideas.
2. Briefly describe the history of your relationship with social construction, such as your initial or early exposure to ideas, what appealed to you, and their relevance to your area of interest.
3. Discuss your understanding of social construction and its most important ideas.
4. Discuss how your practice is informed by social constructionist ideas—for example, how your awareness of practice changed and how you translated social constructionist ideas into practice.
5. Describe your practice using illustrative case examples.
6. Discuss how you deal with issues and challenges to a social constructionist–informed practice—for example, demands for evaluation, institutional/organizational requirements (e.g., managerialism), or more directive political action.
7. Speculate briefly on future trends, possibilities, and needs in relation to social constructionist–informed practice.
8. Provide a summary and conclusions.

While these guidelines were intended to provide a common framework for the chapters and overall coherence for the book, they were flexible enough for authors to tell their social constructionist–themed stories. There was no attempt to have authors sound alike; rather, the intention was to provide adequate literary license to enable them to write in a way that made their descriptions interesting and their practice illustrations genuine. We do not take up, articulate, or express ideas in the same way, and I made no attempt to impose such uniformity on the chapters. This meant redefining the oft-identified "unevenness" critique of edited books as a strength rather than a weakness.

The diversity of the authors' backgrounds, their practice interests, and their understanding and use of social constructionist ideas demonstrate a range of interpretations and approaches. They illustrate the adaptability and applicability of social constructionist ideas to diverse international contexts, practice settings, and issues. Of course, this sampling is not exhaustive and social constructionist–oriented practitioners operate in other areas not specifically addressed here (for example, see Atwood and Dreher, 2010; Browne, 2004; McNamee, 2002). Of importance to social workers is the focus on different marginalized groups, such as children who suffer abuse and neglect, "resistant" adolescents, disadvantaged families, indigenous people, refugees, and men who have sexually abused children.

The Chapters

"An Introduction to Social Constructions" (chapter 2) invites you to reflect on what may be a new way of thinking about the world. I attempt to provide basic information about social construction to facilitate understanding of the following chapters that focus on how social construction can inform practice. A brief discussion of the historical context of social construction, particularly its postmodern connections, is followed by a discussion of variations and commonalities in how social construction is understood. Particular attention is paid to the central role of language and how it functions within micro and macro discursive contexts. The chapter concludes with a discussion of the similarities and differences between social construction and social work. In the case of differences, I try to show how social construction can enable social work to move closer to its claim to be "social" work.

In chapter 3, J. Christopher Hall compares traditional assessments in clinical practice to his use of constructionist-based assessment. The latter complicates the concept of "problem" by considering it culturally and relationally, and by allowing for multiple interpretations with no one interpretation singled out as "truth." Chris describes his pathway to social construction as beginning with his childhood participation in the well-known Louisville Twin Study. These early and ongoing experiences with research (he was in the study for sixteen years) were influential in his seeking alternative perspectives. He uses case examples to describe three styles of social constructionist–informed assessment: a polylingual, collaborative approach, which seeks an understanding of the client's theory of the problem and of change; a deconstructive practice approach, which explores the client's understanding of the construction of the problem and of the solution; and a nonpathology, strengths-based approach.

In chapter 4, Ruth Dean describes how she was introduced to social construction through her doctoral studies in the late-1980s. Having been educated in the psychodynamic tradition, social construction provided a way to address social context, so relevant to the oppression and economic disadvantages experienced by many of her clients. Her interest in social construction led her to study narrative therapy and then to practice and eventually teach it. Ruth elaborates on her integrative understanding of social construction and provides case examples that illustrate how she has used ideas such as practitioner transparency, collaboration, and respectful curiosity in her practice. She discusses how she teaches social constructionist ideas such as "multiple truths" to clients and connects them to social justice. She also shows how she has integrated narrative with contemporary psychodynamic theory and social construction.

The practice approach called critical reflection is the focus of chapter 5 by Fiona Gardner. According to Fiona, critical reflection is both a theory and a process enabling practitioners to examine taken-for-granted assumptions and values in the light of their social context. Using a critical reflection incident from her own social work practice, she illustrates how assumptions about another culture, in this case an indigenous Australian community, can inhibit an effective working relationship. A conversation with a member of that community—while sitting in a car in the rain—challenged her to move outside existing cultural and professional understandings and led to new and deeper levels of meaning and connection. Fiona also discusses reflexivity as an aspect of social construction and its use as an aid in deconstructing assumptions and extending possibilities.

Nigel Parton focuses on child protection work in chapter 6. He begins by recalling how the tragic death of a child in 1973 and the subsequent public inquiry inspired him to explore new perspectives for advancing policy and practice. Drawing upon the constructionist-oriented, U.S.-based social problems literature, Nigel describes his attempt to analyze the conceptual category of child abuse and how it had been constructed as a social problem requiring state intervention. He also discusses his more recent focus on deconstructing policy development for the purpose of trying to work out "what is going on" so that critical perspectives—at the level of policy—can be developed. Finally, Nigel discusses his development and use of an approach to practice he calls "constructive social work" (Parton and O'Byrne, 2000) and its current application in a child welfare agency. His overall aim is to consider how these approaches can make a difference in the way we think about both policy and practice and, crucially, inform what we do on a day-to-day basis.

Continuing the theme of child welfare, Deborah Major (chapter 7) suggests that the social constructionist emphasis on contextual meaning makes it particularly well suited for practice with families in the child welfare system. According to Deborah, this emphasis is critical since parents in these families are often judged as if they enjoyed the same opportunities available to middle-class families, but simply choose to turn them down because they prefer lives mired in chaos, violence, or addiction. She describes how her early practice experience led her to social construction, in particular, the demands on children in foster care to reconstruct their identities and to resist others' attempts to ascribe an identity to them. Using case examples, she describes how a social constructionist framework helped her to invite children and parents to explain how they viewed their worlds and to listen to the meanings of their relationships and how they saw those relationships operating in their lives. In addition, it enabled her to include herself and her role in these relationships as part of what was being evaluated. She examines a case involving serious injury where it nevertheless became possible to advocate with guardians and judges for returning the children to their parents.

A different aspect of child welfare work is taken up in Trish Walsh's chapter 8 exploration on being an expert witness. Drawing on a Foucaultian analysis of the relationships among power, knowledge, and discourse, she redefines the role of the "expert" witness in order to open up possibilities for creative practice. For Trish, adopting a social constructionist mindset means remaining wary of the tendency to label or essentialize others' experiences and to avoid being reductionist. In her role as an expert witness, social construction provides flexibility, allowing her. to set aside unanswerable or unhelpful questions; reframing concerns in ways that promote joint work rather than conflictual positions; and allowing her to search for new solutions before legal interventions restrict these options. Although social constructionist ideas do not in themselves address the complex economic, environmental, psychological, and interpersonal factors that contribute to problems of child maltreatment, they can provide a strategy for rendering less rigid the demands of expert-led child protection and legal systems.

Working within a family context, Sally St. George and Dan Wulff (chapter 9) discuss how to connect the problems encountered in clinical settings to broader social issues that contribute to those problems. Integrating social constructionist ideas with family therapy and social work, they demonstrate through case examples how their work addresses issues of gender imbalances and violence in society. Sally identifies discourses that allow her to converse with families in ways that help them solve/resolve/dissolve their presenting issues while simultaneously raising the issue of discrimination in gender relationships. Dan shows how he works with families to address their concerns while not reinscribing the use of violence (verbal and/or physical). In both of these initiatives, they demonstrate that social workers and family therapists can perform their therapeutic work and promote social justice. This blending of therapeutic work and activism presents a challenging and exciting re-visioning of therapeutic work.

In chapter 10, Marie Keenan discusses the contributions of a social constructionist perspective in her work with child sexual offenders. Drawing on her clinical and research experience with victims and perpetrators of sexual offenses and the relevant literature on the subject, she describes how social constructionist thought has enhanced her theoretical and practice endeavors in this area. Focusing on conversations with men who have committed such offenses, she discusses challenges to generating a space in which meaningful dialogue can take place and where hope can be maintained. She draws on an allegory from Celtic mythology, "The Fifth Province," to help create such a dialogical space. She also discusses the challenges of using a social constructionist perspective in this politicized and highly policed area of professional practice and the difficulties of adopting a research and practice position not premised on a notion of "scientific certainty."

Moving from work with a therapeutic population to a professional one, Wai-fong Ting (chapter 11) describes her work with teachers interested in better addressing the challenges arising from changing societal and educational factors—for example, declining birth rates and increased managerialism. She describes her early experience of researching teenage suicide and her puzzlement over the absence of the teens' own voices in the research literature. This led her to embark on a project in which youth served as collaborators in generating narratives about their own lives. Her experiences led to formal study of narrative, the approach she used in her work with the teachers in helping them view their "problem-saturated" story and how it affected their sense of agency and commitment. She worked with this group to develop an alternative story in which they were more reconnected with the values and ethics that undergirded their career choice. As these values and commitment were made more explicit and available to the teachers, they became more energized and empowered to re-embark on a more positive collaborative educational endeavor. Her chapter documents the journey of how this social constructionist–informed narrative supervision and professional development project helped teachers reauthor their narratives and bring them back in touch with their lost vocational mission.

Chapter 12, by Martha Kuwee Kumsa, is an autoethnographic tale of courage, passion, and struggle. She uses this writing format to share her exposure to and engagement with social constructionist ideas as they relate to the discursive practices of the nation-state, a topic infrequently explored even in this era of increased globalization. Addressing the dominant influence of the Western world, Martha attempts to increase readers' awareness of lives situated in different cultural contexts. Her chapter is divided into three parts. Part one includes stories of her encounters with the term "woman-at-risk," a label ascribed to her by international human rights organizations. In part two, she shares her sense of social construction, focusing on her personal and collective historical trajectory vis-à-vis the nation-state. Part three focuses on a case illustration of how her sense of social construction plays itself out in a social work encounter between a woman-at-risk and youth-at-risk. She discusses the difficult challenges and consequent creative possibilities of social construction that come out of such encounters. Martha concludes her chapter by speculating about where social construction leaves us as individuals and collectives.

So there you have it. Twelve chapters that I hope will interest you, intrigue you, and enrich your understanding of social construction and its applications to practice. The various cultural contexts of the contributors speak to social construction's adaptability and capacity to accommodate a range of beliefs, worldviews, and practice settings.

As you read this book, I encourage you to reflect on these ideas, to use them as entrées into dialogues, and to explore their possible expressions in your practice. Try to envision the ways in which the practices presented do not automatically accept or run counter to the prevailing orthodoxy about human behavior. A striking example is Marie Keenan's chapter on working with men who have sexually abused children. This population is often assumed to no longer be persons in the sense that personhood warrants certain kinds of treatment from others and from society. Marie does not accept this position as her starting point but insists on retaining these men's personhood. The result is a way of thinking and practicing that is decidedly different from typical intervention approaches.

This case also illustrates the courage it sometimes takes to practice from an atypical perspective. Dominant discourses are not only expressed in the language we use but in the institutions (e.g., legal, educational, medical) that organize our lives, including their material and regulatory structures, their assumptions, and their values. Working from a competing discourse can bring condemnation and criticism. However, I would submit that it is the willingness to explore such alternative spaces that is among social work's greatest contribution and, as I discuss in the next chapter, what makes social work and social construction such a complementary pairing.

References

Atwood, J. D. and L. J. Dreher (2010). A social constructionist approach to therapy with couples with a chronic illness. In J. D. Atwood and C. Gallo (Eds.), *Family therapy and chronic illness* (pp. 99–118). New Brunswick, NJ: Transaction.

Browne, B. W. (2004). Imagine Chicago: A methodology for cultivating community. *Journal of Community & Applied Social Psychology*, 14(5): 394–405.

Gergen, K. J. (1985). The social constructionist movement in modern psychology. *American Psychologist*, 40(3): 266–275.

Kuhn, T. S. (1962). *The structure of scientific revolutions*. Chicago: University of Chicago Press.

Mahoney, M. J. (1976). *Scientist as subject: The psychological imperative*. Cambridge, MA: Ballinger.

McNamee, S. (2002). Appreciative inquiry: Social construction in practice. In C. Dalsgaard, T. Meisner, and K. Voetmann (Eds.), *A symphony of appreciation: Development and renewal in organisations through working with appreciative inquiry* (pp. 110–129). Copenhagen, Denmark: Danish Psychology Press.

Parton, N. and P. O'Byrne (2000). *Constructive social work: Towards a new practice.* New York: St. Martin's Press.

Taylor, C. (2008). Trafficking in facts: Writing practices in social work. *Qualitative Social Work,* 7(1): 25–42.

Weimer, W. B. (1979). *Notes on the methodology of scientific research.* Hillsdale, NJ: Lawrence Earlbaum.

Witkin, S. (1989). Scientific ideology and women: Implications for marital research and therapy. *Journal of Family Psychology,* 2(4): 430–446.

Witkin, S. L. and S. Gottschalk (1988). Alternative criteria for theory evaluation. *Social Service Review,* 62(2): 211–224.

[2]

An Introduction to Social Constructions

STANLEY L. WITKIN

Few intellectual movements in social work have generated as much controversy as social construction.[1] Some see it as a perilous trend inimical to the development of a more scientifically based social work (e.g., Reid, 2001), while others consider it a promising alternative to ways of thinking that have contributed to suffering and oppression (e.g., Parton and O'Byrne, 2000). Between these positions are many other views that take up social construction in various ways (e.g., Payne, 1999). This chapter attempts to provide an overview of some ideas commonly associated with social construction and their relevance for social work. I will show that social construction has broad applicability to the beliefs, values, and practices that characterize social work. In some areas, there is a remarkable congruence between social work and social construction; in others, social construction invites us to rethink how we understand and practice social work. Since it will not be possible to cover these ideas in depth, I provide resources for further reading at the end of the chapter.

As I write this chapter, I hold certain assumptions about you, the reader, and why you are reading this book. First, I assume that you are most likely a social work student, educator, or practitioner.[2] Second, I assume that you are curious about social construction and wish to learn more, or that you already have an interest in social construction and want to learn about its applicability to social work or related fields, or (and not mutually exclusive with the other assumptions) that you have been assigned this book for a course you are taking. Although there are undoubtedly other readers and reasons, the above constitutes my imagined, primary audience, the group to whom I am writing. Thus, I will not presume prior knowledge of social construction, only curiosity, interest, or, in the case of a course requirement, a sense of obligation. Regardless of your reasons for reading, I hope my writing is accessible and interesting. I also invite you to actively engage with the material, treating it more like a conversation than a factual tome.

Like any theoretical or conceptual framework, social construction owes much to other intellectual and social developments. Broadly conceived, these developments could be considered part of the postmodernist movement as it developed in the period following the Second World War. While the complexity of postmodernism is beyond the scope of this chapter, it can be thought of as a cultural and intellectual movement whose orientation and beliefs contrast with those associated with the historical period known as the Enlightenment.[3] This period is also referred to as the start of the modern era, hence the term modernism. Of relevance here are modernist values of individualism and beliefs in reason and science as the avenues to universal knowledge and inevitable progress. In the early-eighteenth century, these beliefs provided a striking alternative to the widespread authority of religious dogma. Similar to the rejection of religious authority, postmodernists believe that modernity's promise to realize "the emancipation of humanity from poverty, ignorance, prejudice, and the absence of enjoyment" (Lyotard, 1988) is no longer viable. Rather, postmodernism eschews reliance on such "meta-narratives" (overarching, transcendental beliefs) in favor of historically, culturally, and socially contingent beliefs that are always changing.

Postmodernism itself is not an easy term to explain as it is subject to a "certain semantic instability" (Hassan, 1993: 276) and a lack of consensus among scholars. In a general sense, we may think of it as "a way of understanding the world" (Lemert, 1997). More specifically, different scholars have highlighted the ways in which this understanding differs from modernist thought. For example, Alvesson (2002) identifies five themes of postmodernism including:

> *The centrality of discourse,* in which language is viewed as a constitutive force and objects of the world are discursively produced;

Fragmented identities, which rejects the view of individuals as bounded, encapsulated beings having a particular essential nature in favor of fluid, multiple selves;

The critique of the idea of representation emphasizing the arbitrary links between words and what they are assumed to represent and the rejection of language as a "mirror of nature";

The loss of foundations and the power of grand narratives, in which there are no ultimate bases of knowledge claims, rather knowledge is considered local, temporal, and historically and culturally contingent, a position that invites multiple voices; and

The power-knowledge connection, which rejects the notion of neutral or value-free knowledge and considers different accounts to always favor particular understandings and actions over others.

These themes of postmodernism spawned several interrelated critiques focusing on the historical, social, ideological, philosophical, and linguistic dimensions of knowledge (see Gergen, 1994 for a more detailed exposition).[4] In large part, these critiques were aimed at how what we take to be knowledge is produced (primarily through science and its expression in research) and how it functions. Rather than accepting the dominant views of science and research (for example, that research knowledge gets us closer to "Reality"), these critiques proposed alternative accounts of knowledge generation that tended to unseat mainstream science from its sacrosanct position. Challenging such core beliefs enabled new alternatives, such as social construction, to develop. A few illustrative examples follow.[5]

A landmark work in the area of historical and social critique was Thomas Kuhn's *The Structure of Scientific Revolutions* (1970), which challenged the conventional view of science as a cumulative, knowledge-building activity. Kuhn's historical analysis portrayed science as a decidedly social enterprise in which knowledge progression, rather than following an ever-upwards linear trajectory, was characterized by periods of puzzle-solving and clashes between proponents of different "paradigms" (all-encompassing views of a science). According to Kuhn's historical analysis, victory in these competitions was not a function of the truth value of the paradigm, but of social and cultural factors operating within communities of scientists. As Kuhn concluded, "We may have to relinquish the notion, explicit or implicit, that changes of paradigm carry scientists and those who learn from them closer and closer to the truth" (171).

Kuhn's text and those of other philosophers who questioned the canonical authority of science (e.g., Feyerabend, 1975) generated space for other types of critiques. Among the most visible were those that questioned the neutrality of science and its claim to depict an objective world. Critics argued that science was ideological: it holds to a particular version of events and maintains its own authority through the control of knowledge in the service of powerful interests. Similar to Kuhn, these authors made visible the extra-scientific factors at play in the development of scientific theories and the construction and interpretation of research. Significant here—and probably most familiar to readers—were feminist critiques that challenged the notion of gender neutrality in science. For scientists like the physicist Evelyn Fox Keller, "Science is the name we give to a set of practices and a body of knowledge delineated by a community, not simply defined by the exigencies of logical proof and experimental verification. Similarly, masculine and feminine are categories defined by a culture, not by biological necessity. Women, men, and science are created, together, out of a complex dynamic of interwoven cognitive, emotional, and social forces" (1995: 4). Inspired by this understanding, studies demonstrated how the failure to question dominant societal assumptions (e.g., about gender) led scientists to reproduce and legitimize these beliefs in their research (see, for example, Martin, 1991).

Language is a central form of expression for all manner of intellectual endeavors. Another avenue of critique was generated by scholars interested in the structure and use of language and how literary conventions and rhetorical expressions shape knowledge production. Work about interpretation and meaning was particularly (and ironically) influential in generating reinterpretations and new meanings for scientific texts. These critiques have been associated with concepts such as deconstructionism, a term formulated by the French theorist Jacques Derrida. Although the meaning of deconstruction is elusive, Derrida (1983) suggested it be thought of as a "strategic device" (40). It is typically used, at least in social work contexts, as a term for "unpacking" the multiple meanings of texts. A related area of literary critique focuses on scientific writing as a literary genre, ". . . how the work of science is necessarily grammatical: naming, constructing, and positioning the social and natural worlds . . ." (Luke, 1993: xiv). For example, the reporting of science as expressed in research studies is always an attempt to persuade particular audiences of the merits of its argument.

This is the domain of rhetoric. Various persuasive strategies can influence the acceptance or rejection of a position (e.g., Lyne and Howe, 1986). Such studies show that it is not data alone that play a role in the credibility of scientific judgments.

An important contribution of social construction has been to integrate these critiques using them to decrease the impenetrability of scientific authority. This in turn, has generated new ways of thinking that I believe generate novel possibilities and opportunities for social workers. But critique is not an end in itself and social construction is also concerned with the development of new practices and models of understanding (as the following chapters in this book demonstrate).

Defining Social Construction

Social constructionists tend to be adverse to the limitations of precise definitions. They view the "is" of identity (i.e., social construction is . . .) as more restrictive than helpful. Thus, if you are asking yourself, "but what *is* social construction?" you may find my response elusive and frustrating. It might help to think of this task as similar to defining social work; specific definitions rarely seem to capture its nuances and complexities. This is not an argument for ambiguity; only that formal definition often functions as a way of generating an authoritative statement of what something is while excluding everything else. As discussed below, and in the title of this chapter, social construction is best considered in the plural. There is no one "official" version, although most share certain features. To provide you with a sense of social construction without closing off the many ways it can be construed, I share some statements from different authors followed by my own commentary.[6]

> The leading idea always has been that the world we live in and our place in it are not simply and evidently "there" for participants. Rather, participants actively construct the world of everyday life and its constituent elements (Holstein and Gubrium, 2008: 3).

Social constructionists do not assume a pre-existing world waiting to be discovered. Rather, it is through social interchange that what we take as the realities of the world come into being. This has important implications for social work and leads us to consider our own participation in "world making," the realities we and others experience.

> In a wider sense of "social construction," everything, including giraffes and molecules, is socially constructed, for no vocabulary (e.g., that of zoology or physics) cuts reality at the joints. Reality has no joints. It just has descriptions—some more socially useful than others (Rorty, 1998: 83).

This statement overlaps the previous one but adds the dimension of language. The ways in which we describe the world are mediated by language; no one linguistic representation is closer to reality than any other. Thus, social constructionists are more interested in the utility of descriptions than in their "Truth." Social workers, too, might benefit from focusing more on how language functions than on its veracity—for example, emphasizing the implications of psychosocial theories of development for how we understand and treat others than arguing about their ultimate truth.

> I will take constructionism to represent a range of dialogues centered on the social genesis of what we take to be knowledge, reason, and virtue on the one side, and the enormous range of social practices born and/or sustained by these discourses on the other. In its critical moment, social constructionism is a means of bracketing or suspending any pronouncement of the real, the reasonable, or the right. In its generative moment, constructionism offers an orientation toward creating new futures, an impetus to societal transformation (Gergen, 1999).

The centrality of language is extended in this statement. Social construction is considered as two kinds of dialogues: those concerning the social origins of what is regarded to be true, rational, and moral, and those about the practices that these dialogues generate and maintain. Gergen further distinguishes between two aspects of social construction that he terms its critical and generative moments, the former encouraging critical analyses, the latter, alternative ways of living.

Another way of understanding social construction is to consider it along two interrelated dimensions: product-process (Pearce, 1992)[7] and micro-macro. In the product-process dimension, the emphasis is on what and how, respectively. The *what* constitutes the socially constructed product—for example, mental illness, childhood, emotion, and their connections to historical, cultural, and social factors. In the process case, we examine *how* things become socially constructed—for example, how we construct factual accounts through dialogic processes.

The second dimension, micro-macro, is familiar to most social workers. Applied to social construction, a micro-orientation focuses on interpersonal contexts, such as dyads or families. Macro-oriented social constructionists emphasize broader historical, cultural, and social factors. An example here would be how our understandings of ideas like mental illness or family are connected to historical and cultural contingencies (this is taken up in the section on discourse).

These orientations are neither independent nor mutually exclusive and illustrate some of the ways social construction is used. Despite these variations, it is possible to glean some general commonalities among most descriptions of social construction.[8] These include:

- A view of knowledge as historically, culturally, and socially contingent. There is no ultimate, transcendent foundation, such as sense experience, that arbitrates between what is true or false.
- A concern with the social generation and maintenance of meanings, particularly through language use. For social constructionists, language is a constitutive force, not a transparent vehicle that reflects reality.
- A critical stance toward taken-for-granted knowledge—for example, the common dichotomous categories, such as male-female, heterosexual-homosexual, that shape our understanding of reality.
- A view of knowledge as a form of social action. Different constructions invite and justify different kinds of actions.
- A belief that knowledge is sustained by social processes (particularly language). What we know becomes instantiated in the way society is organized and inscribed in our social institutions.

Gergen and Gergen provide what is perhaps the most succinct statement of social construction's central idea: "We construct the world" (2004: 8), although as they caution, the simplicity of this idea is both profound in its implications ("The basic idea asks us to rethink virtually everything we have been taught about the world and ourselves") and complex in its expressions. Note, too, the word "we" in this statement. It is not "I" that constructs the world, but "we," that is, people in relation. This foregrounding of the social is another fundamental idea of social construction. In my experience, this is a crucial and radical shift (and not surprisingly, a difficult one to accept) as it runs counter to the strong currents of individualism embedded in Western cultures.

Writing Social Construction

Some of the ideas explored so far can be illustrated by examining a common challenge for those writing about social construction, or from a social constructionist perspective: how to make such writing accessible. As an expression of postmodern thought, the language of social construction can seem arcane and unfamiliar. Although in some cases, such language might be judged as unnecessary or as a misguided display of erudition, it often reflects a struggle not to reproduce the very assumptions and understandings that the writer hopes to dislodge—or, to put it affirmatively, to say something new. This struggle is based on the aforementioned idea that our beliefs about reality are largely constituted by language. In other words, the language that we use to represent the world, including ourselves and others, generates what we take as real. Things like aardvarks, bicycles, and depression "exist" because of the words that name them and render them visible and intelligible. Additionally, as linguists have argued for quite some time, the relationship between a symbol (e.g., a word) and the thing symbolized is arbitrary. Despite Shakespeare, a rose may not be a rose by any other name, or even a flower! That is, "it" is not any *particular* thing until we name it.

These beliefs represent a profound shift in thinking from the long-held view that language is a relatively transparent vehicle for representing reality, that it *reflects* what is "out there." This view, often termed correspondence theory (see Rorty, 1979), sees language as a way of conveying information about reality. But how can "the real" and the language used to represent it be disentangled? Any attempts to do so likely would require language, further complicating this conundrum.

As noted previously, understanding how language functions limits the ability of "old" language to express new ideas, perspectives, and analyses. Common usage patterns that have developed over time give words familiar meanings. These meanings help coordinate our actions and enable us to carry out our everyday activities. However, while such common

An Introduction to Social Constructions

understanding is essential, it also makes it difficult to create new meanings without introducing new words or using the common words in novel ways. This tension is expressed by R. H. Brown (1990: 60): "One must use a known language, with its inherent vantage point and presuppositions, to say anything intelligible. *But it is difficult to convey a new vision in an established discourse.* If the new perspective is too closely wedded to a new mode of representation, it will appear incomprehensible to users of the old. But if the new vision is encoded in the old language, this very language, although easily comprehended, may contradict the new message that the author is struggling to express" (emphasis added).

Something similar to this happens whenever neologisms—new words, new combinations of words, or new meanings of words—are incorporated into language. Think of words like blog, locavore, carbon footprint, or road rage. In part, these words were invented to express new ideas that the "old lexicon" could not capture. Although at first such words may seem unclear or strange, they soon become part of everyday discourse.

The arbitrariness of the relationship between word and thing (or signifier and signified to use linguistic terminology) and language as a constitutive force are further illustrated in the following example. Imagine that you observe two people interacting. How do you know what is happening? Typically, you interpret (give meaning to) their actions based on your knowledge of cultural and social norms and the immediate context. You may also draw upon your own relationship history (e.g., you may be reminded of something you've experienced) and your linguistic resources—the words available to you. Let's say, for instance, you observe an adult and a child.[9] The adult is moving his finger near the child's face, and the child has her head down. Based on your knowledge and experience, you might assume that you are observing an act of discipline. This interpretation might be different if the setting was a theatrical production or if the child and adult were laughing. Your interpretation might also change depending on your particular standpoint. For example, consider how the situation might be "read" differently if you were a child psychiatrist, a protective services social worker, a believer in the "spare the rod spoil the child" philosophy, a person from a non-Western culture, or a children's rights advocate. These factors will influence what is noticed (for example, gender, ethnicity, facial expressions, volume and intonation, posture, and presumed relationship) and their significance, which in turn influence interpretations. In other words, we attempt to make sense out of our observations using a variety of cues and signs, and multiple interpretations are always possible.[10]

Now let's go even further and consider what happens when you tell someone else (or even yourself) what you observed. Which words will you choose to describe the event: disciplining, scolding, explaining, teaching, criticizing? And what is the relationship between the words chosen and what actually happened (assuming there is an "actually")? Also, consider that once those words are spoken, to yourself or others, they in effect "become" the event.

For social constructionists, this example illustrates how language is central to our understandings. And language, being an historical-cultural expression, can vary across temporal, physical, and social contexts. One implication of this is that any description of an action, experience, or event could be otherwise. What we call something is not compelled by some natural or inevitable relationship between object and word, but by historical, cultural, and social factors that have led to certain associations. For example, there is nothing about the object we call a tree that compels us to use that word to signify what it is. We could just as easily call it a bush or *puu* (the Finnish word for tree), or even kangaroo. Now you might be saying to yourself, "Right, if I call a tree a kangaroo not only will no one know what I am talking about but they'll question my sanity." Such a reaction makes an important point. It matters what we call things, not because they have inherently correct names, but because language is the primary way that we coordinate our actions with others. We need general agreement about the symbols we use to signify things. If we persist in assigning idiosyncratic meanings to objects and events, others may begin to wonder how we are perceiving the world and whether they can relate to us in complementary ways.

Given this line of reasoning, it seems reasonable to ask how words get their meaning. A common response might be from dictionaries. Aren't they repositories of meaning? Yes, dictionaries do provide various accepted definitions for words; however, they do not address the issue that we have raised, that of the relationship between a word and whatever it stands for. Take the word "grab," for example. If I looked in a dictionary I might find the definition "to take or seize," that is, other words. But what do *these* words mean? If I look them up in the dictionary I find that they are defined by still other words. This could go on indefinitely, each definition subject to further definition. The French philosopher Jacques Derrida called this process deferral; that is, meaning is deferred to other words. He also noted that words gain their meaning by being differentiated from other words— what they are not. We know the meaning of "grab" by differentiating it from words like "caress" or "request." In fact, Derrida (1982) came up with a new word to express this idea—différance—which indicated a combining of the ideas of difference and deferral. (Of course, this word too is subject to difference and deferral.)

Another philosopher, Ludwig Wittgenstein, believed that the meaning of words depended on how they are used: "think of words as instruments characterized by their use" (1965: 67). For Wittgenstein, the meaning of a word was not its dictionary definition, but its use in social practices (what he called a "language game"). For example, if I ask "How old are you?" you likely would answer by stating a number, which in turn would signify a duration of time using a metric called "years" beginning with an event called "birth." We take this number to represent something called "age." If I pose the same question to a young child, she might also answer with a number (e.g., "two") because she learned from her parents what to say in response to such a question. For the child, the response does not have the meaning described above; she is playing a different language game. Most adults would understand, at least tacitly, that they are playing different language games when asking this question of a young child or an adult. We might consider the use of language games in practitioner-client interactions. Are we using the same sets of rules? Do we teach clients how to "play" a particular game?

Wittgenstein used the idea of "language game" to illustrate different ways people learn to use language. Particularly important is how words are used in particular contexts. Wittgenstein called these larger contexts "forms of life." An oft-quoted phrase of Wittgenstein is that "if a lion could speak, we could not understand him" because we would not understand his form of life, the context—the background assumptions and presuppositions—that give his words meaning.

As you think about this, you might be wondering: Do words ever connect to "real world" objects? This is an important question, but consider that the question already assumes the existence of something called "real world objects." Such objects may exist, but how would I know this without the words that designate them? For example, the word "flower" is used to designate some object. But what is the object—a flower! And what is a flower? If we could look it up in the dictionary we would find, as noted above, not objects, but other words.

For social constructionists, the question of whether or not there is a "real world" is moot. Whatever is, is; however, our understanding of the world and our ability to communicate about it requires language. So my answer to the original question is that words connect to real world objects whenever there is agreement that they connect and when "real world" is taken to be another designation. This is not to say that people do not *experience* things as real, or that certain things are real and others are merely social constructions. The point is that what we take as real can vary and change depending on historical contingencies, cultural traditions, and the vicissitudes of social interchange.

Okay, back to earth. What does all this have to do with social work practice? Let's imagine that we adopt the ideas we've explored: that language constitutes rather than reflects what we take as real, that the relationship between word and object is arbitrary, that meaning is related to use, and that understanding depends on knowledge of the larger context—the background assumptions and beliefs that are inextricably tied to interpretation. For starters, these ideas suggest that when we describe something, we are not simply reporting on something outside of ourselves and our language, but proposing a reality, one of many possible realities. Suppose a client tells you that he is depressed. He describes how no one likes him and how everything he does turns out bad. Your first inclination might be to ask, is this true? Is he *really* depressed? For the constructionist-informed practitioner such a question is not the most relevant. If language constitutes reality, then in one sense we might say that this person is reporting a truth; he is using certain words that, in our culture, provide an intelligible interpretation of his experience—for example, "no one likes me" and "depressed." In addition, the statement "I am depressed" (along with other actions) is part of that truth; it is how the person "performs" depression and gives it meaning. This "truth" is useful as information about how this person is making sense of his experience. As a practitioner, you might want to explore how this way of understanding functions in this person's life and what alternative meanings might be possible.[11] Note that the alternatives (e.g., the demands of my job have kept me from socializing with others) are no more or less true—in some ultimate sense—than the client's account; they are simply alternative ways of making sense out of the person's experience.

An Introduction to Social Constructions

Social Construction and Truth

As our discussion suggests, for social constructionists, truths tend to function as ways of justifying beliefs. In other words, when we say a belief is true we justify holding such a belief. The claim of truth provides rhetorical authority. It legitimates certain actions and dissuades others.

Social constructionists do not deny truth, but they are troubled by Truth (capital T intended). According to the philosopher Richard Rorty, "No description or interpretation is closer to reality than any other. Some are more useful for some purposes, but that's about all you can say" (Rorty, 2000). Still, human social life would be intolerably difficult and probably not possible without treating some beliefs as true. It is when we see our truths as universal and transcendent that they become problematic. For social constructionists, truth is multiple (truths), contextual, and communal; that is, truths rely on social processes for their intelligibility and sustainability. Within different "discourse communities," different beliefs will function as truths. These beliefs tend to be functional within the communities in which they operate. Conflict often arises when one community tries to impose its truths (e.g., scientific, religious, or cultural) on other communities. The imposition of Truth (even when its aim is to enlighten) is to privilege a particular understanding or way of knowing and to diminish others. Thus, a more useful approach would be to ask *whose* truth is being asserted and how does it function in this community? Such an orientation aligns social construction with social workers' professed belief in legitimizing marginalized voices.

Discourse

As discussed, multiple interpretations of things or events are always possible. However, some interpretations will be favored more than others. Is it because they are considered "closer to reality," or, as Rorty suggests, because they are "more useful"? This is where the notion of discourse is helpful.

Discourse is a word with many meanings. Most commonly, we think of discourse as a verb (as when we engage in discussion) or as a noun (as in a speech on some topic). In both cases, there is a sense of seriousness about the activity; that is, we do not call something discourse that is frivolous or comedic. If you look up the word "discourse" in a dictionary, you will find meanings like "serious conversation" and "serious speech or piece of writing" (*Encarta Dictionary*, 2009). So broadly speaking, we might say that in everyday usage, discourse refers to forms of communication that have a relatively serious tone.

Within a social constructionist framework, discourse has additional meanings. In fact, depending on your particular "take" on social construction and your interests, the meanings can range broadly. Burr (2003) uses the micro-macro distinction, discussed earlier in relation to social construction, as a way of differentiating two widely used applications of discourse.

MICRO CONTEXT

In the micro context, discourse is about how people use language to coordinate their actions and to accomplish things, how they co-construct understandings about values, aesthetics, truths, and realities. The emphasis is on interpersonal interaction. One might say that in the micro context the verb sense of discourse is emphasized with the focus on how things get done. Discourse is both constructed and constructive (Potter and Hepburn, 2008).[12] It is constructed in the sense that it is constituted by words, grammars, and elements of language; it is constructive in that it uses these symbolic resources to create ways of understanding.

Practitioners and researchers working from this framework are interested in the ways people interact to express different versions of reality. For example, Guendouzi (2005) showed how mothers of young children use talk to construct different versions of reality about themselves. The women in her study discursively presented themselves as "good mothers" by demonstrating, for instance, that they have attributes like caring and protectiveness. Similarly, a practitioner might be interested in how people go about describing their family, noting the words and rhetorical strategies members use to position themselves and justify particular actions.

Another constructionist-oriented approach to understanding discourse within an interactional context is that of positioning theory (Harré and van Langenhove, 1999). You may be familiar with the sociological concept of role: the expected attitudes and behavior of socially identified positions. People enact particular roles in relation to others who occupy complementary roles, for example, a teacher and a student. Positioning theory extends this concept with one that is more flexible and dynamic. Positions, from this perspective, are the discursive stances that people adopt, or are ascribed, in their interactions. Such positions can be relatively stable, like teacher, or they can be fluid, like that of an honest person. An important view of positioning theory is that positions are associated with rights and duties. For example, a parent has the right to speak to his or her child in certain ways that a non-parent does not. A parent also has certain duties toward that child. According to van Langenhove and Harré (1999), positioning is a consequence of three interdependent background conditions: illocutionary force, or the social significance of an utterance; storyline, or the cultural narratives that provide intelligibility to positions (e.g., the overburdened parent, the good Samaritan); and position, the rights and duties associated with various signs and utterances (Harré, 2004, 6).

Positioning theory provides a framework for interpreting how discursive acts function in ways that influence our understandings and actions. Harré (2004) gives the example of an interaction between a person with Alzheimer's disease and her caregiver in which the latter states that their charge is incapable of understanding. This type of "malignant positioning," as they call it, positions the other as outside the sphere of human interaction, thereby disqualifying their attempts at communication. Such positioning may be recognizable to social workers who work with people from marginalized groups—for example, people with schizophrenia. In contrast to malignant positioning, we can consider "strength positioning," which ascribes to someone the right to be heard and responded to in a way that acknowledges their personhood.

MACRO CONTEXT

Understandings of discourse at the macro level are substantially informed by the work of the French philosopher and historian, Michel Foucault (e.g., Foucault, 1972, 1980). Foucault viewed discourse as a system of representation that shapes beliefs, meanings, and their expression. He was interested in why certain beliefs and ways of understanding become dominant in different historical periods and how these characteristic ways of thinking (what he called episteme) are maintained. Although speech and writing are central aspects of discourse, Foucault expanded the concept to include how language is inscribed within organizations and institutions. His most famous example is the panopticon, a prison built in such a way that prisoners are always visible to their guards. Another example would be the hierarchical way a hospital is organized. One might say that this organization inscribes medical discourse such that different staff, for example, doctors, nurses, and orderlies, occupy particular niches that reflect beliefs about illness and how to best treat it.

Foucault wrote that discourses are "practices that systematically form the objects of which they speak" (Foucault, 1972: 49); that is, discourses do more than *represent* objects and people, they construct them. Through discourses, we come to recognize something as intelligible. For example, psychological discourse enables us to "see" various psychological conditions or syndromes within people. These conditions are further inscribed and maintained by such things as psychological tests. Thus, a condition such as "borderline personality disorder" is rendered visible and intelligible through psychological discourse.

This conception of discourse has important implications for social workers. Discourses are never neutral. As Fiske (1987) writes, "[the] meanings [of a discourse] serve the interests of that section of society within which the discourse originates and which works ideologically to naturalize those meanings into common sense. . . . Discourse is thus a social act which may promote or oppose the dominant ideology" (11). Therefore, discourses are intimately related to power.

Leslie Miller (2008) addresses this relationship: "A discourse asserts a preferred version of the world, one that disqualifies competing versions; in the hospital I am a patient (not a member of a church, let's say), and medical discourse stipulates *this* 'me' as the real and true one" (252). Different versions of events invite different practices. They justify certain ways of treating people and discourage other ways. Burr (2003, 68) argues,

> What it is possible for one person to do to another, under what rights and obligations, is given by the version of events currently taken as knowledge. Therefore, the power to act in particular ways, to claim resources, to control or be controlled depends upon the knowledge currently prevailing in a society. We can exercise power by drawing upon discourses, which allow our actions to be represented in an acceptable light.

Thus, how we comprehend things such as health and illness, difference, and families (themselves socially constructed entities) will allow certain actions to be sanctioned and others condemned, some to be encouraged and others thwarted, some viewed as sensible and others irrational. Examining such discourses can help social workers and others understand how discourses and our participation in them constitute clients and our relationships to them, as well as identify possible alternatives.

Social Work and Social Construction

As you read this brief introduction to social constructionist ideas, you may have noticed certain similarities or areas of congruence between social construction and social work. These connections also captured my attention when I first studied social construction. There seemed to be a natural fit between many social constructionist ideas and my understanding of social work. There also were differences that I believed could be beneficial to social work. I discuss some of these areas of congruence and difference later in this chapter.

THE HIGHLIGHTING OF ALTERNATIVE DISCOURSES

According to Foucault, discourses operate within "discursive fields" of multiple discourses. Typically, one discourse is dominant with others contesting its position and offering alternative ways of making meaning. Weedon (1997: 34–35) writes,

> Within a discursive field, for instance that of law or the family, not all discourses carry equal weight or power. Some will account for and justify the appropriateness of the status quo. Others will give rise to challenge existing practices from within or will contest the very basis of current organization and the selective interest that it represents. Such discourses are likely to be marginal to existing practice and dismissed by the hegemonic system of meanings and practices as irrelevant or bad.

These marginal discourses and the alternative visions they offer tend to be associated with categories of people who are disadvantaged by the "meanings and practices" justified by dominant discourses. Social workers are sensitive to and aware of these alternative discourses and try to bring legitimacy and awareness to them. Similarly, social constructionists question the authority of dominant discourses and propose alternatives. They are interested in alternative understandings and the social processes by which certain discourses "rise to the top" and what maintains them.

AN EMPHASIS ON CONTEXTUAL UNDERSTANDING

The long-standing social work notion of person-in-environment recognizes that people cannot be properly understood apart from the environments they inhabit (e.g., Gitterman and Germain, 2008). Similarly, social construction emphasizes the historical, cultural, and social contexts of beliefs. However, whereas the acontextual orientations of essentialism and individualism are incongruous with social construction, social work's stance, as evidenced in its writings and practices, is more ambiguous.[13] Also, for social constructionists the environment is as much a social construction as are people, and the relationship between them is not taken as a more veridical reading of reality, but as a more useful way of understanding.

A RECOGNITION AND SENSITIVITY TO THE INEVITABILITY AND IMPORTANCE OF VALUES

Values are integral to social work. They form the basis for its development and function as guides to its practices. Although not subscribing to specific values like social work, social construction holds that there are no value-free actions or beliefs. Our theories and practices always favor certain ways of perceiving, understanding, and doing. Explicating these values is important for understanding their implications and potential contributions. Although neither social workers nor social constructionists would argue for the imposition of one's values on others, social workers conducting mainstream research are more apt to emphasize eliminating or controlling values whereas social constructionists would favor value transparency and exploring how they function.

ENCOURAGEMENT OF MULTIVOCALITY

In a publication more than a decade ago, I wrote that ". . . social workers believe that it is important for those who are silenced—for whatever reason—to have a voice. We also tend to believe that those who are marginalized in society have a perspective that is valuable for the rest of us to hear" (Witkin, 1999, 7). Social constructionists similarly believe that we must be attentive to the various perspectives that may exist on a topic. Often, these voices reflect a different assumptive world, thereby exposing beliefs that have blended invisibly into the pervasive background of our social lives. Both social work and social construction recognize the importance of challenging dominant knowledge systems and providing avenues for silenced voices.

QUESTIONING THE ASSUMED AND TAKEN-FOR-GRANTED

Questioning the taken-for-granted and assumed is an important function of social construction. It is captured in Foucault's notion of "problematization," to not take for granted what is taken for granted, but to treat such beliefs and assumptions as ways of understanding that have gained a status that renders them relatively impervious or invisible to traditional analyses. To problematize means to view this status, not as a reflection of the ways things "really are," but of some social process such as a relation of power (Smith, 1987). Similarly, it is integral to social workers' view of the world that we do not uncritically accept commonly held explicit or implicit beliefs about our clients or the causes of social problems such as poverty and crime, or the ability of people to change, or the relationship between people and the social environment.

CONCERN WITH GENERATING A MORE HUMANE SOCIAL ORDER

Perhaps, more than any other area, this is where social construction and social work find common ground, albeit in different ways. Although not often explicitly stated, you can plausibly interpret social constructionist literature as generating the possibility of new futures in which people are tolerant and respectful of many views and traditions and in which the highest value is placed on civil discourse and coordinating actions toward compatible ends. For social workers, the idea of a more just social order is a central aim of the profession. While social work is more definitive and explicit about what this might mean (e.g., human rights), and social constructionists are more apt to leave the response to this question open, the vision and importance of acting in the service of generating a better world is a shared aim.

These commonalities suggest a strong congruence and complementarity between social construction and social work. There are other areas, however, where the differences are more pronounced.

USE AND MEANING OF THE WORD SOCIAL

Although both social construction and social work share the word "social," the significance and meaning of the word differs. Whereas the social is central to the meaning of social construction (for example, the idea of knowledge as socially constituted and sustained), social work, particularly in the Western world, seems uncertain about its social dimension. Much of (Western) social work language is individualistic—consider self-deter-mination and individual rights—as are its practices, most notably, in the field of individual therapy. Social construction's foregrounding of the social can help illuminate areas in which social work has adopted an individual-istic orientation and suggest alternative conceptualizations. For example, for social constructionists, persons are social not only because they are socially interactive but because they are socially constituted. Similarly, as noted previously, what is termed the environment can be considered a social construction, not a "thing" that exists unambiguously and independently. These expanded uses of "social" would bring social work's understanding of persons and environments more in line with its name.

A second example of differences in the use of the social can be seen in the social constructionist notion of relational responsibility, which reframes individual actions as relational ones (McNamee and Gergen, 1999). These authors write, "We are drawn to the possibility that there are no untoward events (crimes, injustices, inhumanity) to which we have not all made a contribution, whether by our language, actions, or physical existence" (17). While this position is embraced by some practitioners (see Gardner's chapter in this volume), a more individualistic orientation seems to guide programs aimed at particular marginalized classes of people (see Keenan's chapter in this volume).

ORIENTATION TOWARD SCIENCE AND ITS EXPRESSION IN RESEARCH

Whereas social construction maintains a critical stance toward science, par-ticularly towards claims of self-referential authority or incorrigible knowl-edge (e.g., Gergen, 2009), social work has an ambivalent standpoint. One expression of the latter is the "social work as science or art" arguments that appear periodically. Recently, the popularity of evidence-based practice and its association with traditional research (e.g., experimentation, measure-ment) seems to be moving social work away from a critical perspective. In this sense, social work, at least in the United States, seems intellectually conservative relative to its progressive social views. An explanation for this schism can be found in the history of the social work profession and its tenuous position in the academy. Acceptance as an academic discipline (i.e., a social science) is facilitated by the adoption of scientific canons. While social constructionists do not eschew research, they tend not to privilege its authority nor restrict its expressions.

An extension of the above difference is that social constructionists, relative to social workers, focus more on the function of beliefs than their veracity. That is, while the notion of truths (small t and plural) seem evident in many of social work's positions on diversity and marginalization, it seems to be put aside when considering science and research. In contrast, social constructionists see truth as local and historically and culturally embedded and reject the idea of establishing a universal truth through research.

Understandably, in many ways social work remains mired in its modernist roots, and, therefore, the differences with social construction reflect their relative modernist and postmodernist orientations, respectively. For example, the shift from language as representative to constitutive and the de-privileging of science do not have the same currency within social work as they do within social construction. On the other hand, the integration of social constructionist ideas has shown potential for changing how social work is understood and practiced. One illustration is Parton's and O'Byrne's (2000) constructive approach that "emphasizes process, plurality of both knowledge and voice, possibility and the relational quality of knowledge. It is affirmative and reflexive and focuses on dialogue, listening to and talking with the other" (184). Other less formally articulated but no less innovative applications have been taken up by practitioners in a variety of ways. The chapters in this book illustrate many of these applications and the possibilities for new ways of doing social work.

Notes

1. See Atherton (1993) for a discussion of the controversy in social work.
2. These groups constitute my imagined primary audience; however, I believe this material will also be relevant to those in allied fields.
3. The Enlightenment took place in Europe beginning in the early-eighteenth century, although some scholars date its start to the seventeenth century.
4. It is important to distinguish between critique and criticism. The latter functions primarily in a negative way, identifying what is wrong with something. In contrast, critique is used here as a way of opening new avenues of exploration.

5. The following discussion highlights just a few of the many scholars whose work has contributed to the development of contemporary social constructionist thought. Interested readers should consult the reading list at the end of the chapter.
6. My aim in commenting on these quotations is to help readers gain a general understanding of some of the ways the concept of social construction has been understood, particularly in the context of this chapter. It is not to argue for the true meaning of the author's statement.
7. Pearce also includes another dimension (he uses the word "distinction") based on "say[ing] something about the products or processes of construction . . . [and] join[ing] with the processes that they study" (156).
8. Based on the writings of Kenneth Gergen (1985) and Vivian Burr (2003), two prominent social constructionist scholars.
9. Note that this observation is itself an interpretation; that is, we see interpreted reality.
10. Even what is "there" to observe has already been interpreted. Consider in the example "observations" like "adult," "child," "fingers," and "near."
11. There are other issues involved here, such as how does a person know what s/he is feeling. For the constructionist, such reports of feelings are social expressions rather than reflections of inner states. This is not to deny someone's experience; rather it is to see it as one of many ways to describe it.
12. Potter and Hepburn (2008) call this "discoursive constructionism."
13. For an interesting discussion of one social worker's attempt to reconcile a belief in environmental essentialism and social construction, see Besthorn (2007).

Recommended Readings for Further Study

This is just a small sample of books that might be of interest to readers wishing to delve deeper into social construction. There are numerous other books and articles, including those that apply social constructionist thinking to particular topics.

Berger, P. L. and T. Luckmann (1966). *The social construction of reality: A treatise in the sociology of knowledge.* New York: Doubleday.
    The book most responsible for introducing the term "social construction" into the social sciences. Discusses how social reality is constructed, internalized, and legitimated.
Burr, V. (2003). *Social constructionism* (2nd ed.). London: Routledge.
    An introductory text on social construction. Interesting chapters on discourse and its role in social life.

Gergen, K. J. (2009). *An invitation to social construction* (2nd ed.). Thousand Oaks, CA: Sage.

A reader-friendly introduction to ideas, applications, and implications of social construction by one of its leading contributors.

Gergen, K. J. (2009). *Relational being: Beyond self and community.* New York: Oxford University Press.

An argument for replacing the dominant view of the bounded, autonomous self with one of relational being that emerges from social interaction. Both erudite and accessible, Gergen applies his views to everyday life and professional practice.

Hacking, I. (1999). *The social construction of what?* Cambridge, MA: Harvard University Press.

A more philosophical take on social construction, its forms, meanings, and uses.

Holstein, J. A. and J. F. Gubrium (Eds.) (2008). *Handbook of constructionist research.* Thousand Oaks, CA: Sage.

An edited collection of how varieties of social construction are used in the process of inquiry to explore a range of topics.

References

Alvesson, M. (2002). *Postmodernism and social research.* Buckingham, UK: Open University Press.

Atherton, C. R. (1993). Empiricists versus social constructionists: Time for a cease fire. *Families in Society,* 74: 617–624.

Besthorn, F. (2007). En-voicing the world: Social constructionism and essentialism in natural discourse—how social work fits in. In S. L. Witkin and D. Saleebey (Eds.), *Social work dialogues* (pp. 167–202). Alexandria, VA: CSWE Press.

Brown, R. H. (1990). Social science and the poetics of public truth. *Sociological Forum,* 5(1): 55–74.

Burr, V. (2003). *Introduction to social constructionism* (2nd ed.). London: Taylor & Francis.

Derrida, J. (1982). *Margins of philosophy* (trans. Alan Bass). Chicago: University of Chicago Press.

——. (1983). The time of a thesis: Punctuations. In A. Montefiore (Ed.), *Philosophy in France today* (pp. 34–51). Cambridge, UK: Cambridge University Press.

Discourse (2009). In Microsoft Encarta world English dictionary [software]. Redmond, WA: Microsoft Corporation.

Feyerabend, P. (1975). *Against method.* London: New Left.

Fiske, J. (1987). *Television culture.* London: Methuen.

Foucault, M. (1972). *The archaeology of knowledge.* London: Tavistock.

——. (1980). *Power/Knowledge.* Brighton, UK: Harvester.

Gergen, K. J. (1994). *Realities and relationships: Soundings in social construction.* Cambridge, MA: Harvard University Press.

——. (1999). Social construction and the transformation of identity politics. http://www.swarthmore.edu/Documents/faculty/gergen/Social%20Construction_and_the_Transformation.pdf (accessed on July 5, 2011).

——. (2009). *An invitation to social construction* (2nd ed.). London: Sage.

Gergen, K. J. and M. Gergen (2004). *Social construction: Entering the dialogue.* Chagrin Falls, OH: Taos Institute Publications.

Gitterman, A. and C. B. Germain (2008). *The life model of social work practice: Advances in theory and practice* (3rd ed.), New York: Columbia University Press.

Guendouzi, J. (2005). "I feel quite organized this morning": How mothering is achieved through talk. *Sexualities, Evolution, and Gender,* 7(1): 17–35.

Harré, R. (2004). Positioning theory. http://www.massey.ac.nz/~alock/virtual/positioning.doc (accessed on, March 9, 2010).

Harré, R. and L. van Langenhove (Eds.). (1999). *Positioning theory.* Oxford, UK: Blackwell.

Hassan, I. (1993). Toward a concept of the postmodern. In J. Natoli and L. Hutcheon (Eds.), *A postmodern reader* (pp. 273–286). Albany, NY: State University of New York Press.

Holstein, J. A. and J. F. Gubrium (Eds.). (2008). *2008 Handbook of constructionist research.* New York: Guilford Press.

Keller, E. F. (1995). *Reflections on gender* (10th anniversary ed). New Haven, CT: Yale University Press.

Kuhn, T. S. (1970). *The structure of scientific revolutions* (2nd ed.). Chicago: University of Chicago Press.

Lemert, C. (1997). *Postmodernism is not what you think.* New York: Blackwell.

Luke, A. (1993). Introduction. In M. A. K. Halliday and J. R. Martin (Eds.), *Writing science: Literacy and discursive power* (pp. xi–xiv). London: Falmer Press.

Lyne, J. and H. F. Howe. (1986). "Punctuated equilibria": Rhetorical dynamics of a scientific controversy. *Quarterly Journal of Speech,* 72: 132–147.

Lyotard, J.-F. (1988). Interview. *Theory, Culture, and Society,* 5(2/3): 277–309.

Martin, E. (1991). The egg and the sperm: How science has constructed a romance based on stereotypical male-female roles. *Signs,* 16(3): 485–501.

McNamee, S. and K. J. Gergen (1999). *Relational responsibility.* Thousand Oaks, CA: Sage.

Miller, L. (2008). Foucauldian constructionism. In J. A. Holstein and J. F. Gubrium (Eds.), *Handbook of constructionist research* (pp. 251–274). New York: Guilford Press.

Parton, N. and P. O'Byrne (2000). *Constructive social work: Towards a new practice*. New York: St. Martin's Press.

Payne, M. (1999). Social construction in social work and social action. In A. Jokinen, K. Juhila, and T. Pösö (Eds.), *Constructing social work practices* (pp. 25–65). London: Ashgate.

Pearce, W. B. (1992). A "camper's guide" to constructionisms. *Human Systems: The Journal of Systemic Consultation and Management*, 3: 139–161.

Potter, J. and A. Hepburn (2008). Discursive constructionism. In J. A. Holstein and J. F. Gubrium (Eds.), *Handbook of constructionist research* (pp. 275–294). New York: Guilford Press.

Reid, W. J. (2001). The role of science in social work. *Journal of Social Work*, 1(3): 273–293.

Rorty, R. (1979). *Philosophy and the mirror of nature*. Princeton, NJ: Princeton University Press.

——. (1998). *Truth and progress*. Cambridge, UK: Cambridge University Press.

——. (2000). "Rorty on Truth." Accessed April 18, 2010, from you.tube.com/watch?v=CzynRPP9XkY.

Smith, D. E. (1987). *The everyday world as problematic: A feminist sociology*. Boston: Northeastern University Press.

van Langenhove, L. and R. Harré (1999). Introducing positioning theory. In R. Harré and L. van Langenhove (Eds.) *Positioning theory* (pp. 14–31). Oxford, UK: Blackwell.

Weedon, C. (1997). *Feminist practice and poststructuralist theory* (2nd ed.). Malden, MA: Blackwell.

Witkin, S. L. (1999). Constructing our future. *Social Work*, 44(1): 5–8.

Wittgenstein, L. (1965). *The blue and brown books*. New York: Harper Perennial.

3

Honoring Client Perspectives Through Collaborative Practice

Shifting from Assessment to Collaborative Exploration

J. CHRISTOPHER HALL

I begin this chapter with a confession: When I was a graduate student I disliked clinical theory. In fact, dislike may be too weak a word—I loathed clinical theory. I disagreed with clinical professors; I wrote papers counter to traditional clinical ideas; I found clinical theories objectionable in much the same gut-wrenching way that it is possible to dislike Brussels sprouts or liver (apologies to all those liver and Brussels sprouts lovers out there). I don't mean gut-wrenching in the nervous way. I was never afraid of clinical theory—I mean gut-wrenching in the marginalized and discounted way. Whenever clinical theory was presented, I felt *my* perspectives of the world and *my* ideas of self were somehow co-opted and diminished. Clinical theories seem to have a totality about them, a cementing kind of logic that traps dynamic and flexible understanding as they solidify into "correctness" or "truth." As a result, I was on guard against the limiting definitions of whatever clinical theory was to be discussed, and I tried as much as possible to protect my own understandings and perceptions.

The beliefs I held as a student about clinical theory and my defensive posture regarding my own perspectives were most influenced by my experience of being an identical twin and my sixteen-year participation as a subject in the Louisville Twin Study. Now, many years later, as a practitioner and associate professor, I imagine that my clients, as well as my students, may sometimes feel marginalized in the same way that I did when totalizing clinical theories[1] are used in practice or are taught as ultimate "truth" in the classroom. These experiences and beliefs led to my interest in social constructionism as a kind of meta-theory for practice. For me, social construction invites a way of being that maintains that there are multiple ways of understanding, and that all theories have merit within the parameters of their own construction. Most importantly, social construction places client understandings alongside traditional clinical theories in a nonhierarchical manner so I can practice with others without having to name one way of understanding as the absolute. My clients and I do not have to *inject* a clinical theory of understanding into our relationship that supersedes the understanding that is constructed *within* our relationship.

Most often in modern social work practice, the imposition of a totalizing clinical theory upon a client begins during the assessment. In this chapter I explain and demonstrate how I change the modern notion of an assessment in my practice in such a way that it does not encase my clients in rigid outside clinical definitions that may marginalize the meanings and understandings that are constructed in our discussions together in the space that we call practice. To me, making this shift very much depends upon understanding social constructionism and recognizing that constructionist-informed practice is a mindset, a way-of-being in relationships, rather than an application of techniques.

The chapter begins with a transparent discussion of what drew me to the constructionist position I hold, emphasizing my sixteen-year participation as a subject in the Louisville Twin Study. Next, I offer a brief explanation of social constructionism as it informs the mindset of my practice. I then discuss three specific ways in which I use social constructionism to inform my practice as an alternative to a traditional assessment and share real-case examples of each: (1) a polylingual collaborative approach, in which the client and I seek to match the client's theory of the problem, and solution to the problem, to compatible clinical approaches; (2) a strengths-based, nonpathologizing approach in which the client and I explore strengths rather than assess deficits; and (3) a deconstructive approach, in which the client and I explore the client's understanding of the construction of the problem and jointly decide whether the problem construction is in the client's best interest. While comparably constructionist, these exploratory approaches are unique, each challenging the notion of the static traditional clinical assessment and advancing social work practice in an ethical and collaborative way.

The Louisville Twin Study: Objectification, Imposition, and My Unknowing
Exploration of Social Constructionism

My history with social constructionist ideas is rooted in my experience as
an identical twin. Growing up as a twin gave my brother, Tony, and me a
keen awareness of ourselves in relation to one another. We were always
being judged concerning such things as who was taller, heavier, smarter,
and so forth. This was a constant occurrence and a ritual that is expected,
even to this day. The ongoing comparison had the effect of emphasizing
that we were defined by outside interpretations. We often felt as though
we were objects because we were in a constant state of being *objectified* by
others and almost always viewed as twins first and as individuals second.
In current discussions with Tony, we both recall that as children we felt that
we were never truly seen as whole individuals, rather we felt like a collection of variables in comparison to another collection of variables and were
in essence, growing up as objects of comparison. This had a very limiting
effect on how we understood ourselves. Nowhere was this more evident
than in our sixteen-year participation in the Louisville Twin Study, where
we were compared to each other by being quantitatively measured and
"objectively" defined via batteries of tests beginning at three months of age.

The Louisville Twin Study was initiated in the mid-1950s in Louisville,
Kentucky. According to Deborah Davis (2010), director of the Louisville
Twin Study, approximately 1700 twins participated over the study's forty-
year period. The study concluded in the late 1990s, but in 2005 efforts
were made to contact previous participants to extend the study; as of mid-
2008, the focus is to expand the study into new areas of adult health.

The study has had widespread influence on the social sciences, and I
estimate that results have been discussed or cited in over 100 juried papers
and books around the globe. The following description is from the official
Louisville Twin Study Web site (2010):

> The Louisville Twin Study was internationally recognized as one of
> the oldest, largest, and most comprehensive studies of child development
> related to multiple birth status and is unique because of the extensive,
> longitudinal assessments and . . . the relatively low rate of mobility out of
> the Louisville area . . . data consists of extensive longitudinal evaluations
> of child factors such as temperament, personality, cognitive abilities,
> physical growth, health status, accidental injuries, and school achievement

from birth through adolescence. Genetic data were collected on a sub-sample of the twins and their families. . . . Participants contributed significantly to our understanding of the complex interactions between genes and the environment. Twin and family studies provide a unique method to examine the many factors that contribute to developmental and health outcomes of children and to understand the underlying processes responsible for individual differences in those outcomes.

My first experience as a subject was in 1969, and my last testing was in 2005, at the age of thirty six. Tony and I were tested every three months during our first year, every six months until age three, annually until age nine, a follow-up test at fifteen years, and finally, in our case, testing at thirty-six years of age. During these tests the following protocol was utilized: "The Bayley Mental Scale was administered at three, six, nine, twelve, eighteen, and twenty-four months of age; the Stanford-Binet at thirty and thirty-six months; the WIPPSI at four, five, and six years; and the WISC or WISC-R at seven, eight, nine and fifteen years. Recently, (1980s) the McCarthy test has been substituted for the WPPSI at four years because it gives a broader sample of the child's behavior at this age. . . . Zygosity was established for same-sex pairs by blood typing on twenty-two or more red cell antigens" (Wilson, 1983: 300).

In addition to these tests, there were also interactive play observations, parent-child observations, height and weight measurements, discussions about diet and general physical information, and home visits to observe us in our natural environment and assess for environmental variables. The "naturalness" of this environment is a topic discussed later in the chapter.

The effect of these tests amplified the comparison by others and placed my brother and me in what became a definitional competitive position. The hour-long drive from our small Kentucky town to the tall building in downtown Louisville filled with doctors in white coats was quite intimidating for a child. To us, this was a mysterious and dangerous place. The entrance was always locked to protect against homeless people wandering in; inside were busy scientists and doctors with hard looks on their faces or pasted-on smiles as they passed in the halls. They were conducting important business, and we were their subjects. We felt that as scientists they had the power to unquestionably define us via an intricate, mysterious, and veiled process, which was amplified by a policy that did not allow us to know our scores. "How did I do Mom? Did I pass? How did I do compared to Tony, to everyone else?" She would reply, "It doesn't make any difference, you did fine." "Then why are we doing this Mom?"

The mystery of this veiled scientific process gave the data greater significance and evoked troubling questions. Why couldn't we know? Were these findings something we couldn't handle? What do these numbers say that I am? What do they say Tony is? Am I being protected from something that I am, should be, or won't ever become? Am I that much dumber than Tony that they would want to protect me, or vice versa? Am I normal? Is Tony normal? Is there some larger truth about me? Am I blind to myself?

The Relational Game of Objectivity and Its Effects

Researchers sometimes forget that they exact a toll on their subjects. Even though attempts at reducing harm are always paramount, the influence of the "objective" relationship and scientific data, which is culturally privileged over other ways of knowing, sometimes goes unnoticed. Questioning the process, even when it is uncomfortable, may be difficult, especially with children or those intimidated by the "experts."

It is the following paragraph from the study protocol that brings a smile to my face and is perhaps the basis of my present views on the scientific method in social sciences. It was certainly what my brother and I were most intimidated by, resisted, and later had the most fun with, when taking these "objective" tests. "At each visit, the twins were tested by separate examiners, who also alternated between the twins over successive visits. The test procedures were rehearsed intensively to assure comparability among examiners" (Wilson, 1983: 300). This sounds quite official, or perhaps inane, but in application, it was chilling. I remember the researchers' stone-like faces, specifically the tension in their eyes, as they strained to remain silent and to be coordinately objective so as to not contaminate the findings by latent variables. I am reminded of the way ornamental guards stand quietly and stare blankly when guarding the capital of wherever. Their facial expressions and overall tone was very strange for us, and I distinctly recall wanting to speak with my testers. It took years before I gained the nerve to do so. I would ask, "Why are you acting so weird?" "Who is behind the mirror, and why are they watching?" "Why won't you talk to me?" and as I got older, "How can you define me if you don't speak with me?"

The neutrality associated with objectivity breaks down when considered relationally. If one party takes an objective position, the other must take the position of being the object. It is in this way that objectivity can be seen to inflict certain *relational consequences* on subjects. Objectivity demands that subjects acquiesce to the position of being an object. Accepting a position as an object involves placing certain restrictions on oneself. In my situation it was expected that I behave by being quiet; not asking questions; not moving around, focusing, doing my best, and not thinking about Tony, what I should or shouldn't be doing, whether I missed a question or not, how the results may affect me or my future, who the person was sitting in front of me, who was behind the mirror, if my mom was behind the mirror, what my mom thought, if I was letting her down, and so on—and all the while, I was supposed to "just act naturally." How it is thought that data gathered from this relational objectivity game reflects anything other than the context from which it was gathered escaped me then and does so to this day. None of these data were "objective" and context-free; they reflected my brother and me reacting to very odd, unnatural situations with very strangely mannered people in white coats.

Thus, objectivity is not simply controlling variables in an attempt to determine definitional truth or to gain a valid assessment; it is a relational game that *both* parties must play. I was being invited to forget myself in context. The pressure of sitting in a room with an "expert" who was trained to define me by the parameters of some paradigm that would take precedence over anything that I said was quite intimidating. After sixteen years as a testing subject, I can confidently state that the social sciences are remiss, or perhaps arrogant, in not recognizing that objectivity changes the context, the relationship, and the thoughts, feelings, and behaviors of the human being invited, or forced, to self-subjugate into the relational position of "object." For this reason, I strongly maintain that acts of "objectivity" are acts of relational oppression (Hall, 2008).

The segmenting of our identities could only be tolerated for so long. The tension and sibling conflict generated from going to the clinic to be compared by imposing experts became too much, until around age nine when we rebelled against outside totalizing attempts at defining who we were. In retrospect, Tony and I wanted to be subjectively understood rather than objectively defined. The testers' silence, that so intimidated us in the clinic, lost its effect as we resisted the invitation to "behave" and to ignore the researcher–subject relationship in these testing situations. Our resistance took many forms. We finally began asking the examiners why they were acting so weird. "Just answer the questions" was the reply, and the test resumed. A card would be held up, and the tester would ask, "What do you see?" "I see a guy holding a card." "No, what do you see on the card?" "I see a guy's fingers over part of the picture on the card." "No, what's on the card?" "What did my brother see?" "I am going to ask you again, what do you see?" "A guy getting angry holding a card."

In retrospect, by rejecting objectification we chose to honor our voices in the relational negotiation of self through challenging these outside definitions of who others thought we were or of what we were supposed to become. We ran up to the one-way mirrors and peeked in. We talked to each other during testing by going to the bathroom at the same time. We asked questions about the examiners' height and weight, if they had gained or lost pounds, how smart they were, if they had kids. The climactic event was when a tester broke under Tony's persistent questioning about why he was acting so strangely. The examiner got up from the desk and yelled, "I quit, I am not doing this anymore. You're screwing with these kids' heads. I will not be a part of this. I can't take it." Tony and I glanced nervously at one another in the clinic, but the hour ride home was filled with an excitement that we didn't understand. Today, we feel that perhaps it was the excitement of expanded possibilities for an equal negotiation of self in our relationships with others.

With hindsight, Tony and I now recognize that we were playing with social constructionist concepts of identity in context, the negotiation of self, and the multiplicity of identity. We were making attempts to re-contextualize the experience. Nowhere was this more evident than during home visits. The official home visit protocol was described in this way:

> The home visit protocol was constructed of 200 items based partly on answers to interview questions and partly on direct observations. . . . Four factor scores were obtained from a factor analysis of the home interview items. The first factor was labeled "adequacy of the home environment," and items loading on this factor represented global judgments about the adequacy of the interpersonal and physical environment for promoting intellectual and social development, plus more specific judgments of play space and qualitative features of the home and furnishings. Characteristics of the mother were defined by three factors. The first factor was drawn from ratings of the mother's emotional reactivity (e.g., tension,

tolerance for frustration, mood, and activity level) and was labeled "maternal temperament." The second factor was represented by ratings of the mother's intellectual and verbal facility and home management skills and was termed "maternal cognitive." The third factor, termed "maternal social affect," was represented by ratings of the mother's sociability, talkativeness, and interpersonal warmth. These three factors, plus the "adequacy" factor, represented the bulk of the ratings made during the home visit. The four factor scores were combined with the measures of parental education and socioeconomic status as the composite profile of the home/family environment. These scores were subsequently analyzed for their relationship to offspring mental development during childhood (Wilson, 1983: 308).

Did you read the entire description above? If you skipped it or if it was tedious for you then you just had a brief experience of what it was like to interact with the testers who followed this protocol. Now consider what it was like for a child. I remember how strange it was to see these robotic-like people with clipboards and checklists come into our house and interact with us in ways that I imagined, at the time, that aliens might interact with strange Earth children. Tony and I were initially a little shy, but this was our home turf and as any young children might do with strange invading aliens, after some attempt at human-alien contact, we reverted to the game of, "Let's see how many ways we can bother the aliens and upset Mom." This took many forms, all of which you can guess children of our age would do (and perhaps you did as well). I do recall how *nothing* was like it normally was at our home during home visits. Mom always had a general idea of when they were to arrive, and she made sure everything was clean, our toys were picked up, and the television was off. We also were instructed to be "well behaved." If these visiting scientist thought they got the real story of our home life, they were blinded by their own theories of who they thought we were and the fancy language in their four factors of measurement protocol. Of note is that our father was left out of the home visit protocol, another indication of the culturally constructed nature of research.

Over time, Tony and I recognized that we were perceived differently by different individuals in different contexts and that outside definitions of us were never static. We also realized that these different perceptions pulled us to become different persons; our sense of self was dependent upon the relationships that we were in. We began to see that our identities were not static, but dynamic. We were perceived in different ways depending on the observer, our context, our moods, whether we were together or separate, and whether our identities were confused (if someone thought I was Tony or vice versa).

How My Sixteen-Year Experience As a Test Subject Has Shaped My Practice with Others

My experience as a test subject has directly influenced my views in practice and how I interact with my clients. While my clients generally do not have a twin to which they are compared, they are judged by some standard of cultural normality. This cultural normality, when applied to an understanding of the self, can be understood to create a *normalized comparative twin*, a normalized parallel-self representing the expectations of what we believe we should be, or how we should think, act, or score, to be considered *normal*. The construction of the normalized twin cannot occur without some form of judgment based upon a totalizing theory of normality.[2] This theory of normality is culturally created. As a result of being measured and quantified by this yardstick of normality, individuals may find themselves overcome by the pressure to compete with the constructed idea of a normal self. As a result, individuals may begin to define themselves as something other than normal, perhaps as failures, or as gradients of failure. This self-judgment has implications. They may find themselves giving up on their ability to live up to the cultural ideal of what they and others feel they "should" be. They may feel like failures in their inability to compete with the idea of the normalized twin and all it represents for them. Perhaps clients, like Tony and me, wish to be subjectively understood as unique, dynamic individuals in contexts rather than objectified and compared through assessment to an expert-oriented, culturally biased idea of a normalized self.

With this in mind, the most important lessons I have taken away from my experiences as a subject in the Louisville Twin Study are to not place my clients in a subordinate position that keeps me from hearing their ideas about problems and themselves, nor should I impose a definitional theory on them through a veil of objectivity. I will discuss the steps I take to avoid these kinds of objectifying practices later in the chapter. Additionally, I have come to have little faith in the notion of objectivity and the idea of the static, uncontextualized self. I question the culture of research in its construction of individuals as a collection of psychological and environmental predictor variables. This has resulted in my choice as a clinical practitioner and associate professor to not dissect myself into the two constructed halves of subjective and objective, as much empirical research and traditional practice requires. I instead transparently choose to keep together the passionate, caring, sensitive, so-called irrational parts of me with the intellectual, cognitive, logical parts of me. More directly, I have chosen not to break myself up into parts-of-me. While I am still becoming comfortable with the uncertainties and multiple perspectives of life that social constructionist thought invites, I am drawn to the dynamic light of possibility that is exposed in the absence of the shadow of mono-truth, that is, the totalizing view of one theory, of one way of understanding. I accept and respect the opinions of others and the ambiguity of life that is understood in social constructionist ways of thinking. The final result of these personal experiences is that I appreciate multiple possible interpretations of life. I nourish the ongoing awareness of, and respect for, diverse understandings in the ways that people come to understand themselves and the world around them.

My Practice As a Way-of-Being: Social Constructionism and Clinical Language Cultures

As an introduction to my way-of-being in practice, I wish to share a brief overview of how I conceptualize social constructionism and how it informs my practice. From my perspective, social constructionism is a philosophical approach maintaining that reality is uniquely experienced, interpreted, and created in relationships. Truth, from this perspective, is not something that is located outside of the observer discoverable through techniques of variable control but is uniquely constructed based on current and past relational understandings, education, socialization, and internalization of ideas about the world. This premise affords an understanding of reality as a multiverse rather than a universe because everyone may interpret an event, or series of events, in a unique and equally correct manner. Free from the notion of mono-interpretation, I do not focus on facts per se, but the construction of facts; not on normality, but the construction of normality. The exploration of multiple truths, theories, and understandings that are viewed as contextually and culturally created, and the implications of these accepted truths, form the central components of my practice.

You may recall that as a student I disliked clinical theories because many closed off possibilities. In contrast, constructionist ideas expand the range of possibilities that I can explore in my practice and elsewhere. I have found it helpful to break constructionism down into four general tenets which I will list followed by a brief discussion of each: (1) meaning is not inherent in an object, event, or relationship, (2) we bring meaning to events, objects, and relationships, (3) meaning is controlled by language, and (4) language and meaning are negotiated.

Meaning Is Not Inherent in an Object, Event, or Relationship

I am going to assume that you may be sitting when reading, so let's consider your chair for a moment. It is solid beneath you, it exists separate from you, it is real, but there is no inherent meaning to be discovered in it, just as there is no inherent meaning to be discovered from a tree, a table, a car, a computer, and so forth. These objects exist in the world, but the meaning of them does not emanate *from* them; instead meaning is *placed on* them via our interpretation of them. This seems simple enough and will be discussed again shortly. The same tenet (meaning is not inherent in an object) can be applied to events and relationships as well. While we are active participants in events and relationships, there is no inherent meaning that exists *within* them, rather the meaning in the event or relationship is applied *to* them via interpretation.

We Bring Meaning to Objects, Events, and Relationships

While the chair beneath you has no meaning existing inside of it to be discovered, meaning can be applied to it via our *interpretation*. The chair could be your favorite chair, or it could be the chair your grandfather gave you when he passed away and so forth, in each case the meaning is applied *to* the chair rather than being discovered *in* the chair. Likewise, just as with the chair, there is no meaning that can be discovered as existing inherently within an event. Rather, meaning is placed on an event via interpretation, and an event can have multiple, equally true interpretations. For example, an event can be constructed simultaneously as tragic, heroic, unsuccessful, and successful, depending on perspective. When your favorite basketball team loses, this is a disappointment, but this is simultaneously exciting for the team that won. This is an example of multiple truths.

Meaning Is Controlled by Language

So far we have established that meaning is not inherent in events, relationships, or objects but that we instead construct and apply meaning; also there can be mutually true meaning constructions. Taking these ideas and applying them to my practice affords me the ability to consider all clinical theories as equally true from within their constructed contexts. I am also free to consider my understandings, my client's understandings, as well as those meanings that are generated in our relationship, alongside these more traditional clinical constructions as equal. This acceptance of multiple ways of understanding is the key to my clinical mindset.

In my practice and teaching, I recognize that every clinical theory can be seen as a type of *clinical language culture,* each with its own way of interpretation, with unique constructed terminology (e.g., id, boundary, automatic thought), and each "true" from within the context of its own system of meaning. In this way, clinical theories can be revealed as constructed applied theories, such that all modern ways of working (psychodynamic, cognitive, behavioral, structural, etc.) are constructions—systematically constructed interpretations of how life events could be understood and how problems could be defined and solved. A visual example of how prominent, traditional clinical language cultures, developed up to the early 1980s, define client problems can be found in Figure 3.1.

What we see in the figure is that each clinical language culture interprets the problem and solution in a different way. For example, Jane Addams (1925) held that problems were a result of a disconnect between people caused by the breakdown of community during the Industrial Revolution as immigrants came to larger cities and as mass migration occurred from the farms to the cities. Problems, from Addams's perspective, were constructed as a disconnect between people. Her constructed solution was to establish settlement houses, such as the Hull House, where connections could be made between people and where communities could be developed. Freud (1900), on the other hand, constructed problems in a completely different manner, creating a new language to assist in his interpretation of events. The biophysical perspective is one that constructs the problem as

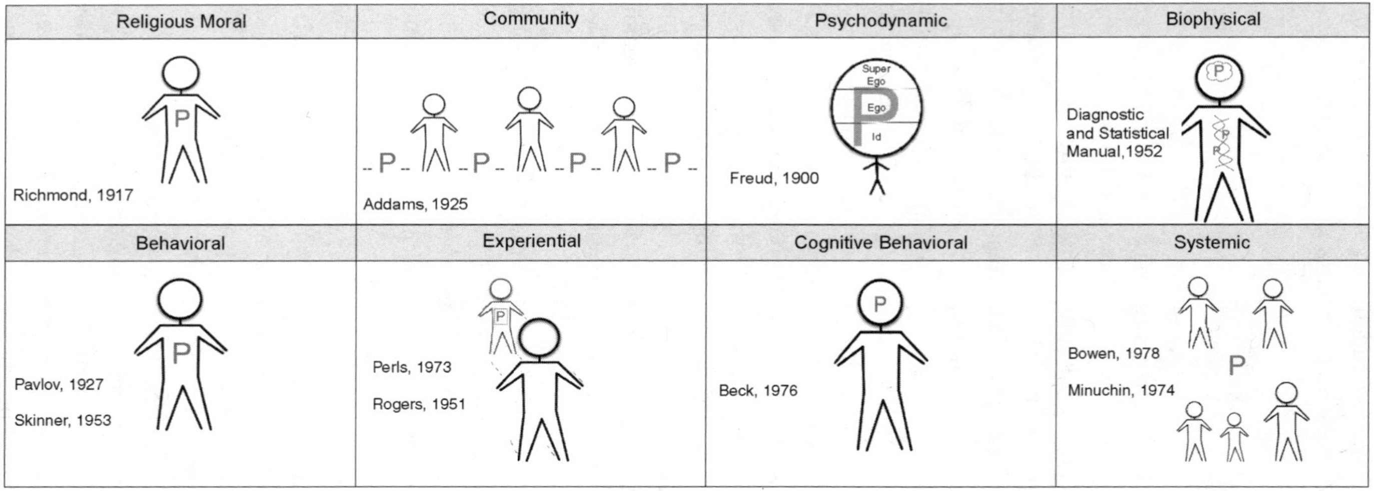

Figure 3.1 The shifting construction of the problem: prominent traditional language cultures of mental health through the early 1980s (P = problem)

faulty brain chemistry and faulty genes, with the creation of a language illustrated in the *Diagnostic and Statistical Manual of Mental Disorders* (DSM) beginning with the first edition (American Psychiatric Association, 1952).

The point is that all modern clinical approaches are elaborately constructed interpretations of "problems" and of "solutions," each with its own unique constructed language of interpretation and explanation. Recall that there is no inherent meaning to be discovered in an event, object, or relationship. With this understanding, any interpretation of an event from within the confines of a clinical language culture is constructed through that particular theoretical lens and is thus limited by the language of interpretation that coincides with that clinical theory. This is not to say that any of these ways of seeing are incorrect. Quite the contrary, each of these clinical language cultures has equal truth within the confines of its own paradigm but is simultaneously considered incorrect from another point of view. What is important here is that when I practice I acknowledge that each of these clinical approaches is a construction, not ultimate truth. I do not impose a way of understanding on clients but seek their own beliefs, and we decide together which interpretations are most meaningful for them.

Language and Meaning Are Negotiated

If there is no inherent meaning to be discovered in an event, object, or relationship, but instead we acknowledge that we place meaning upon events, objects, and relationships, and have multiple true interpretations of events, objects, and relationships, including those things that are constructed as problems, then it becomes clear that the meaning that will be accepted as "truth" is accepted through a process of negotiation. Given this idea, the first question that my clients and I sort out becomes: *Whose interpretation (construction) of the event/problem will be accepted as most helpful?* This is an essential question and can be understood from a constructionist perspective as a *negotiation* for meaning. What is important to note is that even though this conversation occurs in the confines of the office, the negotiation is entrenched in the cultural system of which we are all a part. To provide a visual example of this, refer back to Figure 3.1, where you will see the major approaches to practice and the changing construction of the problem across the history of mental health up to the mid-1980s. As each clinical language culture gained and lost prominence with practitioners, the

Figure 3.2 Hampton Institute pre-test showing First National subject/clients upon arrival

dominant construction of the problem changed. What is key to recognize for my practice is that my clients and I are not outside the cultural ideas of how problems are to be understood in the present time. With this understanding, I consider the construction of the problem and solution in our therapeutic relationship an issue of social justice and a political act (Hall, 2008). As a visual example of the cultural negotiation of normality and abnormality and how the selection of the problem construction is always political, refer to Figures 3.2 to 3.4 by Carrie Mae Weems (2000) entitled "The Armstrong Triptych."

The triptych is a compilation of three images. The first panel was taken in 1878, and it shows a group of First Nation men upon arrival at the Hampton Institute, a Western cultural training center established in 1868. In the first panel, the men are wearing their native clothing with traditional hairstyles, as they would exist in their culture. From a social constructionist perspective, the first panel represents the First People's negotiated normality in their cultural context. As Western settlers gained more power, First People lost their ability to construct typicality in ways that were traditional to them, therefore they found that their attire, language, and history were

Figure 3.3 Hampton Institute model for cultural normality: Brigadier General Armstrong and his family

Figure 3.4 The Hampton Institute post-test providing evidence of the transformation of the First Nation subject/clients into the cultural norm

constructed by the larger society, of which they were now a part, as problematic, abnormal, and something that needed to be solved. The middle photo is of Brigadier General Armstrong who was the creator and director of the Hampton Institute and representative of the group that had more negotiating power to construct normalcy and, in turn, to define abnormality. As a result of the changing construction of normality, First People cultures and their ideas were marginalized and considered a primitive and potentially dangerous way of being.

The natural linear progression from the construction of a problem is the development of interventions that will most efficiently solve the constructed problem. In this situation, the intervention was constructed in the form of Western cultural training institutions such as the Hampton Institute. The successful treatment can be seen in the third panel. The three panels taken together form a kind of evidence-based treatment where the problem was constructed as deviance from the negotiated cultural norm in which the West had dominance, the cultural norm was operationalized, a training and enculturation intervention developed, and the "positive" constructed result measured via a pre-photograph and post-photograph where the former deviant culture has successfully been enculturated into the dominant constructed normality as represented by the middle photograph. The evidence may support the effectiveness of the intervention but the outcome is oppression.

What is most important to understand through these historic photographs for my practice is that I maintain a mindset that there is no inherent meaning in normality or abnormality, rather that normality and abnormality are negotiated constructions based on culture and who has more negotiating power within that culture. As such, I seek my clients' understanding of how the problem and solution are to be understood, including making visible the current dominant cultural construction of the problem. It is absolutely paramount in my practice that I recognize that I am in a unique relationship with clients to either explore their range of understandings of the problems in their lives and potential solutions, or to reify the dominant clinical language culture of the day through the imposition of its construction of the problem *on* clients. In my opinion, an imposition of totalizing clinical theory is the definition of oppressive practice—the indoctrination of clients into a way of being in which they have no voice. The choice of indoctrination or collaborative exploration is not just a clinical decision but also a political decision. Deciding how problems and solutions are to be understood is an issue of social justice, and this choice is most clearly made during the assessment phase of the therapeutic relationship.

Limitations of the Traditional Assessment

The assessment in clinical practice has traditionally been the starting point of all interactions with clients. The guiding mantra has been to assess the problem via "expert and objective" analysis utilizing the dominant clinical language culture of the day and then to treat the problem based on that clinical language culture. Recall that each clinical language culture constructs the problem, intervention, and solution in a different manner, with different terminology. What practitioners and clients should be aware of regarding the traditional assessment is that when practitioners assess from *within* a modernist clinical language culture, they have already chosen how the problem will be understood by imposing a preconstructed theory of normality and by determining how the client may deviate from this normality via the specific language representative of that approach's assessment. As an example, recall the Armstrong Triptych and consider what an assessment would look like from the Hampton Institute. Would you view this assessment as "objective" or as culturally constructed? The Hampton assessment would apply the theory of normality already preconstructed as Western individualism and screen for forms of deviance from this constructed norm. Deviance from the norm would then be constructed as the problem to be treated. Thus, any time a model of practice is used which applies a theory of normality to a client, in order to assess by this construction of normality (e.g., psychodynamic—id, ego, super ego balance; structural—family system functionality; cognitive—functional thoughts; DSM—biophysical normality), the clinical theory has already preconstructed the problem *before* the assessment. Further, in the assessment process, no attention is paid to political, historical, and social influences that may influence the practitioners' and clients' ways of *seeing* the problem. Given the social constructionist premises discussed, it may be worth asking the following question of practitioners in social work and related fields: *If at the Hampton Institute First People had been afforded equal voice in the negotiation of what would constitute the problem and the solution to that problem, would the problem, intervention, and solution have looked different?* It is crucial to note that if First People had been afforded an equal voice in the problem negotiation it may have been constructed very differently, perhaps as a cultural issue of oppression.

The core of my practice is built from a version of this question. I continuously ask myself: *Is my client's voice afforded equal power in the construction of the problem and the solution to that problem, and if so, what are the ways that the intervention and solution can be collaboratively constructed to best assist my client in ways that he or she would like to be assisted?* This question is at the heart of everything that I do.

Shifting from Assessment to Collaborative Exploration

At this point we should have an understanding that my social constructionist informed practice invites challenging clinical language cultures that restrict the realm of my clients' possibilities and understandings of self—that I apply no theory of normality to my clients but instead collaboratively explore and expand upon their ideas of problems and of solutions. The intent of this effort is to assist my clients to better understand their lives in ways that are preferable to them. By providing my clients a voice in the negotiation of how problems and solutions are to be understood, I hope that my clients' voices are amplified and that as a result they have stronger opportunities to negotiate preferable meaning of life events and relationships. Finally, I do not reject traditional clinical theories, rather I do not use them to guide the understanding of the problem, nor do I impose them onto my clients.

The idea of therapy as collaborative exploration rather than as client indoctrination into predetermined clinical language culture shifts the notion of assessment dramatically from being a singular objective act of the practitioner to a shared responsibility of practitioner and client. The modern concept of assessment is no longer useful if it is accepted that there are multiple ways to understand problems and solutions and that the client has equal voice in the exploration of those possibilities. The assessment then shifts from being a standardized event that occurs at the beginning of counseling and that defines the client by a specific clinical language culture to a continuous reflection between me and my clients about ways to move together, ways to understand problems and solutions, and most importantly, the decision of whether this movement is helpful. With this understanding, I continuously strive to create a relational space where my practice with others can be as collaborative and reflective as possible.

In thinking through the ways that I do this, I have arrived at three approaches. I must admit that it feels a bit alien to me to break my practice down in this way, but I am not sure how else I can explain what I do clinically without doing so. These approaches are all similar in that they help me enhance client interpretations without being oppressive with outside clinical language culture. In my practice, client understanding takes precedence over theoretical understanding, and I am most interested in providing a place where they can be heard and understood in ways that matter to them.

I recognize that these approaches are constructions themselves and are by no means the only ways to equalize my clients' voices in practice. Visual examples of common social constructionist informed practices can be found in Figure 3.5.

Social constructionist informed practices began to be developed in the mid-to-late 1980s and the common thread between them is that the problem construction is not defined as something that is within clients, but is instead found either outside of clients to be explored, as with a narrative approach, or as a solution that is to be explored with clients, as in solution-focused, solution-oriented, collaborative language systems and open dialogue approaches. Further, in my work with clients, I try as much as possible to not use theoretical jargon but to instead use the words that clients bring to the session. My hope is that this privileges, or at minimum puts on par, the clients' language with that of the traditional "expert."

My Constructionist-Informed Practice Is a Way-of-Being

It is important to recognize that my practice is very much a way-of-being rather than a set of techniques. Every session is different and I have no manual or step-by-step procedure. Instead, I rely on an overall belief that I very much want to understand how the person sitting in front of me understands the problem and the solution to this problem. The approach I take depends on the kind of relationship that my client has with the problem when they come in to see me. Sometimes clients may come in and they have no real concrete idea of what the problem may be. They know that something is wrong, but they are unsure of what they are experiencing. In these situations, instead of answering the question for them, or imposing a clinical language culture via an assessment, we will explore the possibilities

Narrative Approach	Solution Focused & Solution Oriented	Collaborative Language Systems	Open Dialogue Treatment
White & Epston, 1990	O'Hanlon, 1993 De Shazer, 1985 Berg, 1994	Anderson, 1995	Seikkula & Olson, 2003

Figure 3.5 A sample of prominent social constructionist–informed language cultures developed from the mid-1980s to the present (P = problem; S = solution)

of understanding the problem and solution using a polylingual collabora-tive approach, which I will explain shortly.

When I work with clients who come in with strong beliefs against the definition of the problem that has been applied to them by outside sources, I use a strength-based approach to explore their construction of self, the problem, and the solution. This often happens with mandated clients who do not agree with the interpretation of the problem.

Finally, when I have a client who has firm ideas of the problem, but the problem definition may have been adopted from a source outside of them, I use a deconstructive approach so that we can collaboratively determine whether the problem definition adopted is in the best interest of the client. For example, I very often have clients who come in with the belief that they are problematic, or that they have a certain disorder. In situations in which problem constructions have had totalizing effects in their lives, we dis-mantle and question the construction of the problem using a deconstruc-tive approach to determine if the current understanding of the problem is in their best interest. The purpose is not necessarily to change their beliefs about the problem but to explore the range of possible interpretations of what they are experiencing so that alternative perspectives can be recog-nized and considered.

With all of these approaches, I seek to question and explore the problem construction with the client. Another way to put this is that the problem, rather than the client, is *problematized* and explored. Likewise, a good way to differentiate these approaches is that even though all three approaches seek to enhance the client voice in the negotiation of the problem and solution, they have a different focus. For example, the strength approach seeks to explore "What has gone well in your life, what do you have control over, and what don't others see in you that you would like them to see?" A deconstructive approach seeks to deconstruct the problem definition that the client has been recruited into and to help the client to determine if it is in his or her best interest by asking, "Where did this idea of the problem come from? Who benefits from this idea of the problem? Who does not benefit? Is this idea of the problem in your best interest?" Finally, a polylin-gual collaborative approach asks the question, "Which problem construc-tions and clinical language cultures will best fit with your interpretation of the problem and of the ideal solution?"

I will now discuss each of these approaches in more detail with examples from my practice. I wish to note the difficulty of providing comprehensive examples as clinical relationships are complex and I rely on a construction-ist mindset rather than a series of techniques. Nevertheless, what follows are real-life examples from my practice that accurately reflect my conversations with clients as I remember them. Names have been changed to ensure confidentiality.

POLYLINGUAL COLLABORATION

A polylingual collaborative approach is based on the idea that clinical approaches are constructed clinical language cultures and that the use of these approaches in practice is governed by a collaborative decision between me and the client. Because practice approaches are understood as different language cultures, it is important that I be clinically multilingual and polyvocal in my relationships with clients—multilingual in the sense that I am able to understand a wide range of clinical language cultures, and polyvocal in that I can utilize these languages separately or blended with the client in collaborative ways. My relationship with my clients takes precedence over any clinical approach, and our use of approaches is informed by collaborative decisions made between my client and myself. An assessment in this regard is understood to be a collaborative decision on how the relationship will proceed and which clinical approaches, or blends of approaches, will be used to meet the client's goals. This exploration is guided by how well a given approach makes sense to the client, and modifying, or blending, approaches is determined collaboratively. I generally use polylingual collaboration when the client is confused about what the problem is and wants to explore different ideas about the problem and possible solutions as illustrated in the following exchange from a first session.

Dawn came to see me about a difficult situation with her marriage. After initial small talk and getting to know one another, we had the following polylingual collaborative conversation about how to proceed:

DAWN: I am here to talk to you about a problem that I am having in my marriage.

CHRIS: Okay, we can certainly do that. What is your understanding of the problem?

DAWN: What do you mean? I am not sure what you mean.

CHRIS: I mean how do you understand what is going on? Do you see this problem as something that is within you? Is it in the relationship?

Is it stress from other places? I am wondering how you understand the problem?

DAWN: It is kind of a combination. I know there is stress outside of the marriage that is affecting me and him, and you know the two of us as a whole, but I just feel like we should be handling this better, it seems like most people handle stuff like this better than we do.

CHRIS: Okay, so it sounds like we have a couple of things in your understanding, and I want to make sure I am hearing you correctly. You see stress as affecting the marriage, and you think that there is a general lack of ability to cope with this stress? There also may be an idea of how your marriage relates to the "normal" or "common" marriage—like you have an ideal marriage in your mind, but your marriage may not measure-up in some way to that ideal.

DAWN: Yeah, that's it. You know I really don't know if our marriage is the way that marriages are supposed to be. I mean are we supposed to be happy all the time? And then if not, how much are we supposed to allow to happen? And then the whole coping thing. I really would like, I mean, it would be good for both of us I think, if we could just learn to cope with stress. It's a really bad time, with jobs and the economy and all that.

CHRIS: Okay, then in our time together would it be helpful if we focused on the idea of marriage and what your ideas are about whether your relationship is what it "should" be in your eyes, and then also learn some general coping techniques to assist with stress?

DAWN: Yeah, that sounds good.

CHRIS: Now would you like at any point to bring your husband in to meet with us? Do you think that would be helpful?

DAWN: Yeah I do, but I'm not sure when.

CHRIS: Okay, how about we talk about that in the future as we get comfortable with one another? Is that okay?

DAWN: Okay, that sounds good.

In our first meeting the focus was to find out how Dawn understood the problem, then to determine what clinical language cultures may be helpful for her, and to match these clinical cultures to her situation. In this case, we decided that a narrative approach may be helpful as a way to collaboratively explore with her the discourse of marriage, and whether the idea of a "normal" marriage is beneficial as a comparative yardstick, or if she would like to redefine her idea of what a normal marriage is. We discussed whether it would be helpful to invite her husband in to discuss the idea of marriage as well. We also decided that an ecological approach may assist her and possibly her husband to develop coping and adapting skills to deal with stress coming from outside the marriage. These approaches were discussed openly and in later weeks blended with a solution-focused approach. All approaches were used in a polyvocal, collaborative manner, meaning that I did not impose these on her, nor did I use a manualized version of any approach. Instead, we made the choice about what to do collaboratively through a continuous exploration of whether what we were doing together was working. Questions were asked during every session such as, "How is this working for you? Does this make sense to you? Are you feeling like we are moving in the right direction? Are we talking about those things that you find helpful? Do you feel heard?" Based on responses to these questions we made collaborative decisions in session regarding what we would do next that would be most helpful.

STRENGTH-BASED, NONPATHOLOGIZING APPROACH

With a strength-based approach to practice we focus on my clients' ideas of solutions and ways in which they can utilize those skills and resiliencies within themselves and their relationships to reach the goals that they would like in their lives. The focus is much more on the desired outcome of the therapeutic relationship than on the problem itself.

In my practice, I most often use this approach when there is a clear difference between what the client views as the problem and what others view as the problem. Court-mandated clients are one example of this. Because mandated clients often have a clear understanding that they do not wish to acquiesce to the dominant construction of the problem, we focus on the positive outcomes that they would like from our time together. In many cases, even though the problem definition may vary between client and court, the solution is extremely similar. Focusing on the solution keeps us from getting caught in binary problem discussions of who is right and who is wrong. When using this approach I try to work as much as possible to amplify my clients' own natural strengths, values, and skills.

In this case example, I was working with a couple, Franklin and Mary, who had recently had their children taken away for negligent parenting, and were sent by the court for mandatory therapy. After initial greetings and some relatively uncomfortable small talk, the first session continued in the following manner:

> FRANKLIN: We don't want to be here, we've done nothing wrong. The court and investigators have said all these things about us; how we're bad parents, how we don't deserve our kids, and we don't agree! We don't think we're that bad!
>
> CHRIS: What don't they see in you that you would like them to see?
>
> FRANKLIN: What do you mean?
>
> CHRIS: It seems as though they have a picture of you as bad parents, but this idea of you is different from what you think that you are. What did they miss in your parenting, for example, what are you most proud of that maybe they didn't see?

Some discussion followed about the general surprise of this question and why I was being so "nice." After I assured them that they were in the right place, we continued.

> CHRIS: So what doesn't the Child Protective Service see about you that you would like them to see?
>
> MARY: Well, it's not like the kids are dirty, and they are happy. Yeah, I'll admit the house needs cleaning, but the kids don't; they're always clean.
>
> CHRIS: So you do a great job of keeping the kids clean, how are you able to do that?
>
> FRANKLIN: They have to take a bath when they get up every morning. I am on the late shift so when I come in around seven A.M. I get them up before I go to bed. I'll sit with them 'cause it is one of the only times during the day that I get to see them.
>
> CHRIS: You have a schedule that you keep to? And you are able to get the kids up. You have a plan. Have you always been this organized in this area of your life? Is this scheduling a skill? Not everybody has that kind of skill; I wish I had better scheduling skills myself actually. I think I could learn some things from you.
>
> MARY: Yeah, he has his faults, but he does get them kids in the bath each morning.
>
> CHRIS: Does this skill of scheduling that you all have, work in other parts of your parenting, too?

Here, by focusing on the strengths of the family and their understanding of themselves, I am assisting them to recognize that they do have parenting skills and that these parenting skills are worth noting. As the conversation continued I asked the following explorative questions.

CHRIS: How is this going for you all so far? Do you think we are making headway toward your goals of getting your kids returned?

FRANKLIN: Yeah, this isn't what I thought it was going to be. Look, we just want our kids back; I'm willing to do whatever it takes.

CHRIS: Well, perhaps we could use the strengths that you all already have as parents and expand those into areas that might need some help. One of the areas was keeping the house clean, I wonder how you could build on the skills you all have in scheduling to make that happen?

With this family I was attempting to collaboratively explore their understandings of what they were doing well and to support their definition that they were good parents. Their belief that they were good parents, and the court mandate that they become good parents, were aligned, so this was the focus of our work together. Later we spoke about more ways that they could build on the strengths that they already had in order to become even better parents, and then how we could work together so that the investigators could gain a more accurate and new picture of them as good parents. Thus, the goal of the parents, and of the court, was the same, and was eventually met without the use of problem-centered dialogue.

DECONSTRUCTION APPROACH

My focus using a deconstructive approach is to collaboratively separate my clients' perspectives of the problem from the dominant construction of the problem into which my clients may have been recruited. Most times in my practice when I work with clients who have strong views about the problem, but these views have come from outside sources besides themselves, we will use a deconstructive approach to separate how the problem is currently understood from how they would like to understand it. This often happens with clients who are in marginalized positions in the negotiation for meaning in their lives—for example, when a parent brings in a teenager and the parent tells me that he or she is a bad kid or has some kind of disorder. It is imperative that I work collaboratively with the teen to determine whether these views are in the teen's best interest. This is also important when working with minority members of a culture and those in positions of less power than others. Interestingly, I have also used deconstructive approaches with those who traditionally hold more power than others. White males in Western culture, for example, who may have been recruited into beliefs that they must be strong and domineering, when, in fact, these ideas may be causing great harm in their lives and in the lives of others (Hall, 2011).

Ultimately, when my clients and I take a deconstructive approach in practice, I seek to assist them to explore whether the present interpretation of the problem is in their best interest, and if other perspectives of the problem may be more aligned with their sense of self. The approach seeks to assist clients in having a stronger voice in the negotiation of how the problem, and subsequently the solution, will be understood. When I utilize this perspective, the client and I place how the problem will be understood as the central focus of the conversation, and questions are asked that deconstruct this current dominant construction. Frequent questions include: "Does the current understanding of the problem serve you in reaching life goals, or could we see this problem in a different way? Is this problem construction in your best interest? Are there other ways we could view the problem that would be more helpful?" Through these kinds of questions I hope that my clients are afforded a stronger voice in the construction of the problem and solution. The following is an example from my practice with others.

Jessie is an African American male, age sixteen, who has been brought to me by his mother who is worried about him. The mother explained to me on the phone that she "fears" he is gay. Jessie and I meet together for the first time, and after initial small talk and rapport building the conversation progresses.

CHRIS: Hi, could you help me understand what you have come in for?

JESSIE: You already know, my mom said everything, and it is all there in my file, too.

CHRIS: Jessie, is it okay if I call you Jessie? (*Head nod.*) I sometimes don't pay attention to files. Files represent views of you that may or may not make sense to you. What I am most interested in is what makes sense to you. The same with your mom. She has ideas about what is going on but those ideas belong to her. Your ideas are important, and I want to hear your voice and your ideas about what you want for your life; then we can talk a little bit about how we may be able to work together to get you where you would like to be.

JESSIE: Well, you know, what they all said. I am a problem, I have this depression disorder, and I ain't no good.

CHRIS: Jessie, could I ask you some questions about this picture of you that you just shared with me? What I am interested in is where this idea came from that you are a problem.

JESSIE. Well, from all of you all doctors, and from my family. I been in and out of hospitals since I was thirteen, and I always been told that there's something not right with me. That I can't control myself.

CHRIS. Who benefits from this idea?

JESSIE: What?

CHRIS: Who benefits from the idea that you are a problem and that you can't control yourself?

JESSIE: I guess nobody, I mean, I don't know. I don't understand.

CHRIS: Sorry about confusing you, and thanks for letting me know. I appreciate your openness. I am interested in where the idea came from that you are a problem, and who benefits from the idea of you being a problem? It seems like there are many times in your life, more times than not actually, that you are able to control your moods, that you have been successful at those things that you put your mind to. Right now, for example, we are talking together very well, yet for some reason you have been defined as being a problem. I am wondering who that view benefits? Let me ask in a different way. Does the idea that you are a problem benefit you?

JESSIE: Not really. This is weird.

CHRIS: What is weird about this?

JESSIE: I just never had anybody talk to me like this before.

CHRIS: I know this can seem weird, especially if you are used to people like me telling you what you are and diagnosing you. Instead of diagnosing, I am really interested in who you think you are, and how you may have gotten to this point where you have been called a problem. It seems like you have done some very successful things in your life. I am interested in why you have not been called a success, for example, why you have been called a problem, and if this is what you want? Do you see yourself as a problem?

JESSIE: Sometimes I do, and sometimes I don't.

CHRIS: Tell me about some of those times that you don't.

As the conversation progressed Jessie shared with me times when he did not feel like a problem. These were times like, "when I'm around other people like me, when I am not seen as a loser, when I can just be me." The intent in questioning the problem was to determine the extent to which the problem had gained control over his sense of self and how he had resisted its influence in his life. Through a deconstruction of the dominant problem construction, Jessie decided that his "problem" with being depressed was not a biophysical problem but a natural reaction to being marginalized in two ways, first as an African American male, and second as a gay male. His identity had been problematized by his family and by the dominant culture. He had internalized these beliefs about himself, and as a result, was very down and sad as his voice was marginalized in the negotiation of his own identity. Eventually we were able to create definitional space for him, a space where he could have more negotiating power in his life. As a result, he was able to move out of the definitional shadow of his mother's ideas about who he was supposed to be, as well as the dominant cultural ideas of what normal is and how he was supposed to be to fit in as both an African American and a gay male. With a stronger voice in the negotiation of the meaning in his life, he had a better chance to define it in ways that were congruent with how he would like to be. In our work together it turned out that it was the totalizing definition of Jessie as a problem that was, in fact, the problem. His sadness was a natural consequence of not having an equal voice to negotiate and construct his identity in ways that he wished, but instead, having to co-opt and subjugate himself to live up to the expectations of others.

Final Reflections: The Peril of Objectivity for Clients, Practitioners, and Researchers

As noted previously, social constructionist informed practice for me is a mindset, not a set of techniques. This mindset encourages a shift from the traditional assessment to collaborative exploration based on multiple ways of understanding problems and solutions and recognizing clients' views as equal, if not more important, than those of traditional clinical language cultures. This mindset does not negate other traditional clinical theories, rather it allows clients to direct what is most helpful to them.

As my chapter comes to an end, I would ask you to reflect back on the Armstrong Triptych (Figures 3.2 to 3.4) discussed earlier. The triptych is one image of many in an exhibit that shows the impact of the Hampton Institute in the late 1800s. The final photo of the exhibit is the same Armstrong family portrait that we have seen in the middle panel of the triptych, with the following words overlaying the image: "With your missionary might you extended the hand of grace, reaching down and snatching me up and out of myself" (Weems, 2000: 83).

With the modern imposition of totalizing clinical theory on clients, we as practitioners risk becoming identity and culture snatchers, whereby we define people as abnormal by a culturally constructed theory and then label and treat them into this constructed normality. The notion of objectivity becomes one of a sterile veil that allows us to pretend that we are somehow not part of this non-collaborative system of totalizing clinical theory stamping. For me, a social constructionist informed practice reduces the possibility that as a practitioner I am acting as a social control agent by using my services to impose ideas of constructed normality to which my clients must measure.

It is also important to note that the potential snatching of others via the imposition of totalizing clinical theory may have effects on practitioners, as well. Recall that objectivity is a game that both researcher and subject must play, and just as taking the position of the object had effects for me in the Louisville Twin Study, so too does taking the position of the observer. The effect of the segmentation of self into variables has ramifications. At six years old, I first saw the strain that empirical researchers were under in their relationships with me as an object, and when the tester broke ranks and stated that he could not hurt people anymore, I experienced what I now see as a beautiful crack in objectivity. Many years later, I recognize that the testers' strain was a potential consequence of the objectification of self in our constructed relationship as subject and tester.

As a memory of that moment, on my office wall I keep a quote from the biography of arguably one of the most influential scientists in history to remind me to learn from the wisdom and mistakes of others. In 1887 he offered a warning about the possible long-term effects of the self-dissection involved in the relational game of objectivity. I understand his voice from the past as a challenge to our field to save not just our clients from practices that restrict possibilities, but ourselves as well, from the consequences of self-imposed restrictions of objectivity.

> I have said that in one respect my mind has changed during the last twenty or thirty years. Up to the age of thirty, or beyond it, poetry of many kinds . . . gave me great pleasure, and even as a schoolboy I took

intense delight in Shakespeare, especially in the historical plays. I have also said that formerly pictures gave me considerable, and music very great, delight. But now for many years I cannot endure to read a line of poetry: I have tried lately to read Shakespeare, and found it so intolerably dull that it nauseated me. I have also lost almost any taste for pictures or music. . . . My mind seems to have become a kind of machine for grinding general laws out of large collections of facts, but why this should have caused the atrophy of that part of the brain alone, on which the higher tastes depend, I cannot conceive. . . . if I had to live my life again, I would have made a rule to read some poetry and listen to some music at least once every week; for perhaps the parts of my brain now atrophied would thus have been kept active through use. The loss of these tastes is a loss of happiness, and may possibly be injurious to the intellect, and more probably to the moral character, by enfeebling the emotional part of our nature (Darwin, 1887: 100–101).

It is important for us to recognize that we exist not in isolation, separation, or objectification, but in interconnected, co-constructed relationships with one another, and during those times when we construct one another as practitioner and client, or subject and tester, that we not forget that we are in a shared space of co-construction and reciprocal influence. It is my hope to work together in this space we call practice and research in a manner that equalizes power and opens possibilities for the exploration of preferred ways of being for all.

NOTES

1. A totalizing clinical theory is a theory of explanation that leaves no room for other ways of understanding. It is an authoritative, definitional gaze that applies a rigid theoretical framework of explanation upon a person without the other being able to share in the conversation of definition. It is a description of a relationship of power. In practice, I use the phrase totalizing clinical theory to denote the use of any theory which supersedes the understandings of the client and/or does not place the client's views of the problem(s) and solution(s) in equal status to the clinical theory being applied.
2. A totalizing theory of normality is the dominant discourse of "normality" constructed by a culture into which a person may have been recruited into accepting (knowingly or unknowingly), internalizing, and consequently

self-subjugating around ideas of what he or she is supposed to be and do in order to be considered "normal." This is a description of a relationship of power between dominant cultural discourse and an individual of that culture.

References

Addams, J. (1925). *Twenty years at Hull House*. New York: Macmillan.

American Psychiatric Association (1952). *Diagnostic and statistical manual of mental disorders*. Washington, DC: Author.

Anderson, H. (1995). Collaborative language systems: Toward a postmodern therapy. In R. H. Mikesell, D. D. Lusterman, and S. H. McDaniels (Eds.), *Integrating family therapy: Handbook of family psychology and systems theory* (pp. 27–44). Washington, DC: APA.

Beck, A. (1976). *Cognitive therapy and the emotional disorders.* New York: International Universities Press.

Berg, I. (1994). *Family based services: A solution-based approach*. New York: Norton.

Bowen, M. (1978). *Family therapy in clinical practice*. New York: Aronson.

Darwin, F. (1887). *The life and letters of Charles Darwin*. Vol. 1. London: John Murray.

Davis, D. (January 14, 2010). Personal communication.

De Shazer, S. (1985). *Keys to solution in brief therapy*. New York: Norton.

Freud, S. (1900). *The interpretation of dreams, "die traumdeutung."* Leipzig, Germany: Franz Deutike.

Hall, J. C. (2008). A practitioner's application and deconstruction of evidence-based practice. *Families in Society,* 89(3): 385–393.

——. (2011). A narrative approach to group work with men who batter. *Social Work with Groups,* 34(2): 1–15.

Louisville Twin Study Web site. https://louisville.edu/medschool/pediatrics/research/child-development-unit/louisville-twin-study.html (accessed on February 21, 2010).

Minuchin, S. (1974). *Families and family therapy*. Cambridge, MA: Harvard University Press.

O'Hanlon, W. (1993). Possibility therapy: From iatrogenic injury to iatrogenic healing. In S. Gilligan and R. Price (Eds.), *Therapeutic conversations* (pp. 3–17). New York: Norton.

Pavlov, I. P. (1927). *Conditioned reflexes*. London: Oxford University Press.

Perls, F. (1973). *The gestalt approach and eye witness to therapy*. Palo Alto, CA: Science and Behavioral Books.

Richmond, M. (1917). *Social diagnosis*. New York: Russell Sage.

Rogers, C. (1951). *Client-centered therapy*. Boston: Houghton Mifflin.

Seikkula, J. and M. Olson (2003). The Open Dialogue approach to acute psychosis: Its poetics and micropolitics. *Family Process*, 42(3): 403–418.

Skinner, B. F. (1953). *Science and human behavior*. New York: Macmillan.

Weems, C. M. (2000). *The Hampton project*. New York: Aperture.

White, M. and D. Epston (1990). *Narrative means to therapeutic ends*. New York: Norton.

Wilson, R. (1983). The Louisville Twin Study: Developmental synchronies in behavior. *Child Development*, 54(2): 298–316.

4

Becoming a Social Constructionist

From Freudian Beginnings to Narrative Ends

RUTH G. DEAN

Little did I know when I chose "pre-social work" as an undergraduate major in college, that it would lead to my becoming a social constructionist and a teacher of narrative therapy. As a seventeen year old heading off to college from a city in the mid-western United States in 1955, the idea of a career of any kind was far from my mind. My friends and I, all from middle-class families, subscribed to the view that college was a place to find a husband. True to our cultural surround, we were not particularly concerned with discovering our life's work. A career was only something to "fall back on" if your husband died or, even worse, divorced you. Most of my friends majored in education because becoming a teacher was one of the few "acceptable" choices available to women at that time. But my mother had been a social worker, and so, unlike my friends, I knew that social work was an option.

While in college, my first efforts at social work practice involved leading groups at a settlement house that served economically disadvantaged families. I saw the ways that poverty, racism, and other forms of injustice restricted the lives of the exuberant African American girls in my groups. They had so much energy to invest in group activities but so few other

This title is intended to respectfully reference the book, *Narrative Means to Therapeutic Ends* co-authored by Michael White and David Epston. This book introduced me to their work and started me on the journey described in this chapter.

opportunities for channeling their interests and excitement. Feeling un-prepared to help them, I hoped that furthering my education by obtaining a masters degree in social work would equip me to better serve their needs and the needs of others like them.

Theoretical and Clinical Beginnings

When I entered social work school in the late fifties, interest in the social context of people's lives and in social action had receded in social work education in the United States as the profession's infatuation with psycho-analytic theory took hold. An objectivist orientation to knowledge dominated the curriculum as the profession strove to become more scientific. Postmodern thought had not yet made an appearance. It would arrive soon in sociology with the seminal work of Berger and Luckmann, *The Social Construction of Reality* published in 1966, and in psychology with the writings of social psychologists Ken and Mary Gergen in the 1970s and 1980s. But these ideas came much later to social work.

As a young MSW student, I zealously studied psychoanalytic theory. I learned how to construct psychodynamic formulations that defined my clients' problems along psychological lines. I was deeply troubled by the abject poverty I observed through home visits, and I was impressed with the courage with which people dealt with these unjust conditions—but I did not know what to do with these concerns. I was taught to look for symbolic meaning and provide insight and corrective emotional experi-ences to clients. Attention to the social contexts of people's lives was not totally missing, but it held less sway than psychological understandings. I was taught Freudian theory as if it was the "truth," and I was a devout believer. These beliefs took me away from the social insights I derived from the girls' group and in the direction of intrapsychic change through counseling.

Considerable time passed before I was able to move beyond this view of the "truth" of psychoanalytic theories and discover social constructionism. This occurred during my doctoral studies in the late eighties. But I am get-ting ahead of my story.

After I graduated from social work school, my adherence to a Freudian, psychoanalytic theoretical perspective continued in my work at Beth Israel, a large, urban, Harvard University teaching hospital in Boston. The social service department was closely aligned with the psychiatry clinic, which was directed and staffed by some of Freud's disciples who migrated to this country from Europe at the time of World War II. Gradually object relations and self-psychological theories were added to the traditional Freudian and ego psychology orientations that informed teaching and practice in the clinic. I learned these newer psychodynamic perspectives from psychiatric and social work supervisors, and my idea of the meaning of "psychodynamic" expanded. This would happen again in the nineties as I learned about attachment theory and neuropsychology. I conceptualized my work on the medical and surgical floors and in the out-patient psychiatry clinic according to psychodynamic principles. I began to teach these theories to social work staff through seminars and supervision. The atmosphere was collaborative, nurturing, and exciting.

In the seventies and eighties, the relative affluence of the health care system and the support of teaching institutions (Sabo, 2000) produced a climate in the hospital that supported long-term, open-ended psychotherapy for all clients regardless of their ability to pay. My practice gradually became centered in the psychiatry clinic where I saw young college students and adults in treatments that typically lasted for several years. It was a superb learning experience, albeit limited in terms of models of change and sociocultural awareness.

Changes in Mental Health Care

Family therapy models were introduced at Beth Israel in the in-patient psychiatric service in the seventies. With this model, families became a locus for change and not just sources of information or resources in discharge planning. In a setting so dedicated to intrapsychic change and psychodynamic theory, there was considerable resistance to this approach. While these early models shifted the focus to a systemic perspective and the relational context of people's lives, they were based in a modernist orientation. The view of the therapeutic relationship was hierarchical, with the family therapist perceived as the expert who could disrupt family patterns and change them for the family therapist's idea of what was best.

In addition to the advent of family therapy in the sixties, several other interrelated occurrences in the next decade drastically changed mental health practice and my experience as a therapist in a hospital mental health clinic. First, advances in science regarding the biological and biochemical aspects of mental illness led to more effective psychotropic medications and a much heavier reliance on them in the treatment of mental illness (Lightburn and Sessions, 2006). The second major change was the development of the community mental health movement in the late sixties and the effort to make health and mental health care local and accessible to all. This change, along with the growing effectiveness of psychotropic medication, made the third change, deinstitutionalization, possible. Many in-patient mental hospital facilities closed, and patients were relocated to group homes in the community. They were treated with a combination of group programs and brief hospitalizations in hospital-based units serviced by interdisciplinary teams.

The fourth change was the advent of managed care, which put insurance companies in charge of decisions regarding choice and length of treatment for which providers would be reimbursed. Managed care required that insurance forms be filled out with appropriate diagnoses and in some cases treatment plans. Short-term therapy became the rule for those dependent on third-party payers. Cognitive-behavioral therapy fit well with these short-term models. It had a research base and offered practical, step-by-step solutions for treating certain conditions, and so its use was encouraged.

With these changes, lines between the disciplines of medicine, psychiatry, psychology, social work, and nursing were more tightly drawn. Many psychiatrists specialized in psychopharmacology, as well as psychotherapy. But now, psychotherapy was increasingly conducted by social workers, psychologists, and clinical nurses in clinic setting and private practice (Sabo, 2000). While interdisciplinary work continued, teams became hierarchical with doctors in charge. There was more rigidity over designated professional roles and functions. Questions were raised as to whether or not social workers could write psychiatric diagnoses without medical training. Instead of functioning as independent practitioners, social workers were required to work with psychiatrists, who would be responsible for making diagnostic and treatment decisions and signing insurance forms. The social work profession responded to the pressures of these competitive forces by obtaining licensure in states across the country. From a theoretical perspective, the overarching paradigm that prevailed in institutional practice still placed a heavy emphasis on an objectivist orientation to knowledge.

Becoming a Social Constructionist

Changes in My Career

In addition to the major changes at the hospital, several changes in my life brought me closer to learning about social constructionism and narrative therapy. I left the hospital in 1979 after joining the faculty at Simmons School of Social Work in 1978. While my expertise in teaching clinical practice from a psychodynamic perspective was valued at Simmons, psychodynamic theory was only one part of the curriculum. I needed to learn practice models more closely aligned with social work values and interests.[1] To that end, I began my doctoral studies in social work and was introduced to social constructionism in a philosophy of knowledge course. This orientation was enormously appealing—I felt like I had found my theoretical home.

Although psychodynamic theory had evolved considerably since my graduate days and still seemed relevant to my practice, it also felt narrow and confining. Its lack of attention to social context had always concerned me as I watched some of my hospital clients deal with racism, poverty, illness, and other harsh realities of their lives. With its emphasis on the ways that problems were socially constructed, constructionism brought to the forefront the social context of people's problems. It also aroused my interest in the operation of power dynamics in society and the ways that dominant groups controlled public and professional discourse.[2]

Introduction to Narrative Therapy

Concurrent with my doctoral work, I discovered that narrative therapy, based on a postmodern, social constructionist perspective, was being taught in Boston, and so I studied it at the Cambridge Family Institute.[3] I also attended conferences in Australia and the United States sponsored by Michael White, the founder of narrative therapy, and his colleagues at the Dulwich Centre in Adelaide, Australia. These conferences drew people from many parts of the world—each with a unique story that showed the adaptation of narrative approaches to various local contexts. The conferences honored this diversity of perspectives and particularly acknowledged the indigenous populations of the areas where they were held.

It was a heady time. I appreciated the way that narrative therapy was rooted in social constructionism, and this perspective allowed me to more fully honor context, respect diversity, and consider the effects of social injustices. I found its methods to be extremely respectful of clients' prerogatives. I also enjoyed its playfulness. I began to teach narrative approaches to therapy at Simmons and to use narrative techniques in work with children, adults, couples, and families. I also began to write about its use with individuals and groups, its influence on teaching, and the way it informed ethical analysis (Dean, 1998, 1995, 1993a, 1993b; Dean and Fleck-Henderson 1992; Dean and Rhodes, 1998).

Understanding Social Constructionism

DEFINITION

My understanding of social constructionism gradually evolved as I taught and wrote about it. I learned that social constructionism was part of postmodernism, a philosophical movement, that began in the 1960s and challenged the objectivist roots of science and the post-enlightenment belief in a knowable world. Post-structuralism and constructivism are other strands of this movement (Burr, 1995).

Social constructionists believe that knowledge is a product of social interchanges and agreements that occur in particular historical, political, social and institutional contexts (Berger and Luckmann, 1966; Gergen, 1985; Gergen and Gergen, 1983). In other words, the ways we understand the world are products of the communities, cultures, and historical moments of which we are a part (Burr, 1995). This orientation to knowledge leads to a critical stance toward meta-theories and taken-for-granted assumptions. It recognizes that power and knowledge are intimately intertwined and that dominant power groups are able to influence the way reality is rendered (Foucault, 1982, 1994).[4] It asserts that we can never fully separate our interests and values from our observations and, therefore, there can be no "objective truth." Instead, multiple understandings are possible.

Implications of a Social Constructionist Perspective

The implications of a social constructionist perspective are as follows:

First, it challenges the idea that there are given, predetermined structures or essences (Burr, 1995).

Second, it declares that language shapes meaning and experience; it is not a mirror that reveals nature (Hartman, 1991; Stern, 1997).[5]

Third, in a social constructionist perspective, meaning is interpersonally constructed in conversation. The ambiguity of language and its idiosyncratic uses adds to the complexity of this process. Narrative therapists cannot be experts at "knowing" another's meaning but only increasingly skilled at facilitating a conversation in which it will emerge.

Connections Between Social Constructionism and Narrative Therapy

My immersion in social constructionism led quite naturally to narrative therapy, an approach located within this orientation to knowledge. The narrative analogy was a natural for social constructionists who understood that we cannot know the world directly but only through lived experiences, organized through stories (White and Epston, 1990). Stories that people believe about themselves become the templates through which they live and perform their lives. Because each performance is different, it has the potential for rewriting and expanding (or contracting) a story. The constructionist understanding that words shape meaning is consistent with a narrative model of therapy that privileges clients' stories.

Social constructionist ideas are key to narrative approaches to therapy. If stories organize the ways people make sense of their lives, then changing a story might offer a new meaning and way of living. In a narrative model, people seek therapy when the stories they have about their lives no longer work. Narrative therapy offers the possibility of alternative stories that can be more fulfilling and satisfying (White and Epston, 1990). Multiple perspectives are emphasized instead of single truths. Expertise is located in the client as well as the therapist, and it is shared. The aim of a narrative therapy is to help clients change their stories to ones that are more consistent with their values and beliefs, which become more apparent in the process of change.

Comparisons Between Narrative Therapy and a Psychodynamic Perspective

Conflicts with Psychodynamic Learning

As indicated earlier, psychodynamic theory was my initial orientation to clinical practice. As my social constructionist leanings pushed me in the direction of narrative therapy, I was caught in a difficult intellectual dilemma. Psychoanalytic theory was such an integral part of my development as a clinician that it was basic to my thinking. Yet, I found narrative therapy to be intriguing. Its premises resonated with my growing interest in more collaborative ways of working that privileged clients' knowledge and contributions. I also found certain narrative techniques to be very helpful in opening up stuck conversations. Both approaches were very useful despite being diametrically opposed in terms of their basic orientations to knowledge and practice.

Psychodynamic theory presumed underlying, symbolic meaning in people's conversation and behavior. These meanings could best be interpreted by the therapist, an expert in the use of complex theories of psychic structure and relational development. In a psychodynamic perspective, behavior can be unconsciously motivated and individuals may need help in uncovering hidden thoughts and understanding them. Early history is important and is reconstructed as an aid in understanding. In traditional psychodynamic models, there was often only one meaning to behavior—best interpreted by the analyst or therapist based on theoretical understanding. Each person had a core set of dynamics: conflicts, defenses, and ways of relating that were revealed in therapeutic conversations.

I enjoyed the richness and complexity in psychodynamic theories, and they helped me understand a client's behavior or my own reactions in a session. I did come to see the different psychoanalytic schools of thought as "stories" or myths and not the "truths" I thought them to be earlier in my training (Schaefer, 1979). I also, with a certain lack of ease, accepted my role as "expert" in the therapy duo because my early psychodynamic training encouraged me to do so.[6] I had learned that the therapist was the one best able to determine what was going on in a client's life, what various statements or behaviors meant, and how to use this understanding to promote change. This amount of power was daunting at first, but I assumed that it went with the responsibility of being a therapist.

But this orientation was in total contrast to a narrative approach that focused on the meanings developed in conversations between a client and therapist. There was no interest in underlying meaning or early history, but instead, with developing a more detailed narrative through exploration. White (2007) rejected the idea of a "core self" and instead spoke of "association of life" which included all who were influential in positive ways in one's life. The therapist focused on these people and encouraged clients to think about them, consider their import, and imagine which aspects of one's identity they would support and cherish. Whereas psychodynamic theory would help the client become aware of aspects of earlier relationships that had been *internalized* and were now influencing behavior in conscious and unconscious ways, narrative therapists would explore the stories of the actual relationships. White refers to this technique as "remembering." Consider the following example to illustrate the differences between these approaches.

CASE EXAMPLE

A middle-aged, upper-class, WASP, recently divorced woman expressed concern in a therapy session about a new relationship with a Jewish man whose cultural background was very different from hers. She enjoyed breaking out of the mold of meeting only "upper-class WASPs" with whom she was "supposed" to connect. She found this new man to be a good match for her intellectually. He was interesting and fun to be with, and she was having the best physical relationship she had ever experienced. But she was uneasy about their social and cultural differences.

Instead of using a psychodynamic approach and focusing on the internalized relational sources of her attitudes, I took a narrative tack and asked if there was anyone in her family who might have appreciated her boyfriend. After some exploration, she remembered a seemingly critical comment of her father's about her tendency to make "safe choices" at the time of her marriage to a man from a WASP background similar to her own. I wondered what her father (a man whom she described as artistic, eccentric, and much beloved by her) would think of the man she was now dating. "He would find him interesting and enjoy him," she replied. We considered what her father thought of making "safe choices" and how he might appreciate her newly found ability to move beyond the safety of the community she knew so well and the behavior it required. While her father was interested in many different kinds of people, she also knew that he would want to make sure that this man treated her well. As she recalled her father's capacity to expand his social circles, she felt more confident in exploring this new relationship. Through reconnecting with her father (a member of her "association of life") and considering his beliefs, she began to reconsider the values and preferences that aligned her with her father and resist those that came from the social pressures in her community.

In this instance, I turned to a narrative technique because it offered an *in vivo* experience that captured the client's interest. She enjoyed reconnecting with her memories of her father and his unconventional attitudes, and this seemed to open up possibilities for her. But if she had seemed unable to reflect on her concerns and shift her behavior, I might have moved to a psychodynamic approach to uncover the unconscious, constricting internalized messages and conflicts that the new relationship was stirring up.

Integrating Psychodynamic and Narrative Ways of Working with Clients

There was much that appealed in narrative therapy. Despite my psychodynamic understanding that problems developed from *internalized* conflicted and destructive relationships, I could see that the narrative techniques of *re-membering*, as discussed in the above example, could be very effective. I also found that *externalizing problems*, another narrative technique, was very helpful to clients. In order to externalize a problem such as depression, I might ask "What are the ways that depression tends to invade your life?" Once a problem was named and externalized, clients could be helped to find exceptions to times when the problem took over. Then, by analyzing these "counterplots" or "unique outcomes," an alternative story that was not dominated by the problem would begin to emerge (White, 2007).

The narrative emphasis on therapy as a conversation in which the therapist is a collaborator and not an expert resonated with my growing appreciation for clients' understandings of their situations. However, from a narrative orientation, the psychodynamic focus on underlying meaning and repetitious patterns was seen as the therapist responding from a position of "expert." By helping clients see repetitious patterns that were pathological or uncovering underlying longings deemed self-destructive, the therapist was operating on the basis of normative ideas of what comprised healthy behavior and how people were supposed to be. And from a psychodynamic perspective, the narrative focus on clients' perceptions and behavior could seem simplistic and limited.

While the contradictions in these frameworks were troubling, my concerns were reduced when some members of the psychoanalytic community took up the postmodern, social constructionist perspective views. Roy Schaefer (1979) described theories as "myths." Donald Spence (1982) spoke of the difference between narrative and "historical truth." He questioned the way that psychodynamic psychotherapy was considered to be a process through which the therapist could discover the truth of clients' experiences and showed that the view of the client's history was inevitably a reconstruction. Irwin Hoffman (1991) declared that therapists' participation affects what they see and understand in the therapeutic process. He wrote that therapists' awareness is inevitably partial and clients' understandings offer important additional information. Hoffman named this a social-constructivist paradigm to emphasize the socially constructed nature of the therapeutic interaction (1991). He recommended that therapists adapt a position of uncertainty regarding the meaning of any therapeutic interaction. Because therapists' subjectivity was always implicated, they could not claim to be objective observers (Aron, 1991; Renik, 1993). Donnel Stern (1997) focused on the ways that a therapist's contribution to the process was one of many possible choices arising from the therapist's "unformulated experience." The emphasis was on increased authenticity and transparency in the therapeutic relationship and not "objectivity." This writing, which gradually became more influential in psychoanalytic circles, validated my efforts to combine these seemingly antithetical perspectives.

Even with these advances in psychodynamic theory, major differences remained between these perspectives. First, psychodynamic theory concerned itself with internal psychological life and explanations of behavior that referenced this while narrative therapy stayed aligned with clients' actual current experiences and not with internalized relationships or symbolic meaning. Narrative therapy resisted diagnoses and understandings of behavior based on ideas of the ways people are "supposed to be" (White, March 2006, personal communication). It sought affirming experiences and recollections as avenues to change.

In narrative approaches, the therapist's role is de-centered; the therapist is not an expert but operates from a position of "not-knowing" (Anderson and Goolishian, 1988). While psychodynamic therapy has also moved away from the view of therapist as expert, it still acknowledges the inevitable, unequal power dynamics and their emotional sequelae (Hoffman, 1998, 1992). In psychotherapy, examining the therapeutic relationship is considered an important avenue for understanding the client. In newer, intersubjective psychodynamic models, the impact that client and therapist have on one another becomes a source of information and focus of discussion. On the whole, the overlap between these orientations was expanding. For me, the range that they offered combined was essential.

A Narrative Approach to Therapy

Hallmarks of a Narrative Approach

What were the hallmarks of a narrative approach to therapy that derived from a social constructionist perspective? First, the belief in multiple realities promoted the use of multiple theoretical understandings with each making a contribution. No single meta-theory or explanation was regarded as "truth." This belief helped in therapy with couples or families when it was important to elicit and consider the perspectives of each family member.

Second, the belief that meanings were socially constructed had important implications for the use of diagnoses. The process of making a diagnosis was grounded in an objectivist orientation. Recognizing that clinical labels, while social constructions, were given a "truth status" and used as norms through which people's lives were assessed (Foucault, 1980 in White and Epston, 1990: 19), I learned to be very sensitive when required to use them. Diagnoses created meaning and had the power to affect how a person was seen over long periods of time. In a system that utilized diagnoses, the therapist was the expert who defined the client. A constructionist approach might result in therapists developing diagnoses in collaboration with clients when they were required to do so by institutions or insurance practices. Constructionists saw assessments as fluid and subject to change over time (Anderson and Goolishian, 1988).

Social constructionists maintain that language generates what we experience as realities. For narrative therapists, if words created rather than revealed meaning and if problems were embedded in the stories that people held about their lives, then change occurred when people were enabled to move from stories that were "problem-saturated" to alternative narratives that were preferred (White, 2007; White and Epston, 1990). Life was multistoried, and often narratives of strengths and abilities that existed at the margins of people's awareness could become more dominant (White and Epston, 1990). Problems were externalized. It was not the person but the problem that was the problem. "Unique outcomes" when the problem had been challenged or overcome were used to create a different narrative (White, 2007; White and Epston, 1990). In becoming aware of this new narrative, clients were helped to notice values and beliefs that were intrinsic to their identities but not heretofore as apparent. These were the central practices in a narrative approach.

Finally, the therapeutic relationship was importantly changed in the context of a social constructionist orientation to therapy. If the therapist was no longer considered an all-knowing expert, then therapy became a collaborative conversation in which the client's expertise was sought and equally valued. It was understood that therapists as well as clients had blind spots and gaps in awareness. At times, clients' observations of therapists were important contributions to the process (Hoffman, 1991, 1992). The therapist aspired to a stance of "not knowing" in order to honor the client's knowledge and expertise and learn as much as possible about the client's situation (Anderson and Goolishian, 1988). This collaborative effort at understanding allowed for more openness and freedom for the therapist and more spontaneity within the relationship.

An Idiosyncratic Approach to Narrative Therapy

My use of narrative approaches was not what I thought of as narrative in its "pure form" as defined by White and others (White, 2007; White and Epston, 1990). Since I found both psychodynamic and narrative perspectives helpful, my work involved an amalgam of both. Because of my social work background, issues of diversity, culture, oppression, and social justice were also important influences in my teaching and practice. The following examples, strongly derivative of the work of White, David Epston, and other narrative therapists, show how these influences appeared in my work.

Narrative Practices: Externalizing the Problem and Re-authoring[7]

"Externalizing the problem" was one of the earliest techniques described by White and Epston (1990). Problems were named and objectified and placed outside of the persons who complained of them. Once problems were externalized, clients could work on their relationship to the problem. They could be helped to find exceptions that were not consistent with dominant, problem-saturated stories of their lives. These discoveries led to re-authoring conversations that stressed preferred aspects of people's identities (White, 2007). Here is an example of one of my earliest uses of this technique that also shows the introduction of some psychodynamic thinking.

The client, a twenty-eight-year-old man who was a successful software designer, entered a session expressing considerable shame at his tendencies to be a "loner." He had just come back from a work conference in San Francisco and had been severely criticized by a co-worker for going off on his own during the meetings and not sticking with the group from work. He was puzzled by this reaction. It had never occurred to him to hang out with the people from his workplace—he was more interested in exploring San Francisco.

Concerns about his relationships brought him into therapy a year earlier. In the beginning, using a psychodynamic emphasis on history and early relationships, we spent considerable time trying to understand the origins of his discomfort with people and the source of his extremely negative views of himself. We thought it might be because he was an only child born to older parents who were critical and distant and left him alone a great deal of the time when he was young. We had discussed in some detail how painfully shy and uncomfortable he had been when he was growing up. Despite his continued shyness, he had a few friends who seemed to like him a lot. Nonetheless, he was very unsure of himself in all his relationships.

In this session, I first tried to engage him in a discussion that linked his behavior in San Francisco to our previous discussions of the impact of the isolation of his childhood on his adult life. I was operating from a psychodynamic perspective and thinking that this exploration would help him understand his reaction and reduce his self-criticism. Instead, focusing on these early life experiences only seemed to make him feel more despair about himself.

Unsure of how to help him and concerned about the level of self-hatred that he was expressing, I tried a narrative strategy. I wondered aloud if there might be another story about "aloneness" that carried a different meaning. I said that I had the feeling that he was a person who "coveted aloneness"; sometimes, he really "relished" it. He agreed but said he thought this was a terrible way to be. Without challenging this judgment, I asked if he could think of other qualities he had that went with "coveting aloneness."

Returning to his experience at the conference, he explained that he enjoyed being independent. He had an agenda of sights he wanted to see in San Francisco. He wouldn't have minded if someone had accompanied him while he followed his agenda but he didn't want to give it up to be part of the group. I repeated these ideas, suggesting that his experience in San Francisco seemed to be telling us that he was a person who valued independence and having his own agenda. Together we elaborated on the importance of these qualities and their effects on his life. I pointed out that not everyone had the capacity to be alone. We decided that his independence and his ability to develop his own agenda were important things to know about himself. He began to consider that he might even value these abilities. (This is a variation on the narrative strategy of externalization. We had named the problem and slightly changed its meaning by describing aloneness as something that could be "coveted" or "relished." Then we elaborated on the new, preferred story and what it told him about his interests and values.)

Feeling better about his inclination to be alone and follow his own agenda, he was able to acknowledge conflicting wishes; sometimes he sought aloneness, and sometimes he wanted to be with people. At times it was hard for him to sort out which he preferred. At this point in the session, I reverted to a psychodynamic understanding of his behavior. Our narrative work had helped him to be less defensive about his "loner" tendencies and able to acknowledge an internal conflict about being with people to be explored at a later time.

At the end of the meeting, he told me, "You said something that really helped me tonight." When I asked what that had been he became playful and teasing, in contrast to his earlier, depressed mood, and said, "I'm not going to tell you." Then he relented and explained, "It had never before occurred to me that coveting aloneness could have its good side." He seemed genuinely pleased when he left and told me later that this conversation marked a turning point in the treatment as he began to feel better about himself.

In constructionist terms, we had co-created a new story. It wasn't that he necessarily became less desirous of being alone, but his relationship to that aspect of himself had changed. I asked questions that allowed him to generate a different story about being a person who chose to be alone. Together we named the attributes we were discussing in ways that allowed him to appreciate them more. He then was able to elaborate on the new story and incorporate it into a more positive view of himself. I was active, and I was not neutral. This was in keeping with the post-positivist belief that there are always values implicit in the questions therapists ask and the ones they don't ask and in the ways they name and call attention to some things and ignore others.

I moved from an initial psychodynamic approach to a narrative one and then back to a psychodynamic way of thinking. The narrative approach of externalization offered a technique that helped move the interview along when a psychodynamic approach to underlying meaning had been ineffective. Then, after the narrative technique helped him find a more positive way of thinking about himself, psychodynamic theory allowed us to see that he was conflicted about being a loner and that it might be helpful if he more fully understood this conflict. Finally, in keeping with narrative beliefs in collaboration and transparency, I sought his idea of what was and wasn't helpful in the treatment.

This example illustrates how I began to incorporate narrative approaches within my usual way of working with clients. I had not replaced psychodynamic theories with narrative therapy but instead was using these ideas in combination and enjoying greater flexibility.

The Narrative Strategy of Letter Writing: Two Examples

Social constructionism and narrative approaches generate space for alternative forms of expression. One way this is accomplished is through letter writing (Penn and Frankfurt, 1994, White and Epston, 1990). This narrative strategy was particularly useful in my work with Jasmine, an eleven-year-old, African American girl brought to the clinic by her mother, Vera, who was worried about her misbehavior at home and at school. An older sister had become rebellious as a teenager, eventually running away from home and turning to drugs. Now her mother was worried that Jasmine was heading in the same direction. Vera was just recovering from an addiction to heroin and had little patience for the antics of a precocious eleven-year-old. Despite her interest in getting treatment for her daughter, Vera's job prevented her from participating in the treatment and interfered with Jasmine's steady attendance. The treatment was short—four sessions—and fragmented. I used letters to create some continuity for them and myself and to provide Jasmine and Vera with something in writing that could represent the work we had started. In this series of letters, you can also find examples of externalizing the problem and re-authoring. The first letter was written after our second visit: when Jasmine reported progress in "STAYING OUT OF TROUBLE."[8]

March 30

Dear Jasmine,

I was very happy to see you yesterday and it was so nice when you smiled and told me that you were doing so well at school. I told you during our meeting that I would write down the things we figured out were helping you and send you a list so you could read it and use it to help you with your project in school.

You told me that you were "STRAIGHTENING UP" and we decided that you were getting much better at TAMING YOUR TEMPER. You did think that you have a very quick temper but lately you have become much better at slowing it down. Here are the things that you thought were helping you:

IN SCHOOL

1. *When TROUBLE comes your way you KEEP ON WORKING.*
2. *You don't pay any attention to TROUBLE MAKERS when they come near you.*
3. *You are getting better at STAYING AWAY from TROUBLE MAKERS.*
4. *When TROUBLE or TROUBLE MAKERS come your way, you think about not getting any more of those bad marks that disqualify you from special trips and other treats. I think you call them P.S.'s.*
5. *When you wanted to run out of class to talk to your friend Candace, you remembered about trying not to get any more P. S.'s.*
6. *In Mr. Green's class you stayed busy and wrote problems on the board.*

AT HOME

1. *When you think you are going to lose your temper it helps to walk away.*
2. *When TROUBLE comes your way, you try not to say the worst things you think of.*
3. *You try not to react to some of the things people say that upset you.*

These are some of the things that you have been doing that helped you have three good days at school so far. Staying away from TROUBLE has made it possible for you to go on a field trip and to eat with the "regular kids" and help out in the school office. There have also been fewer fights between you and your mother. I was very impressed with all the things you have been doing and the good results you have been getting. I hope this list helps.

Your ally in TEMPER TAMING, STAYING OUT OF TROUBLE, AND "STRAIGHTENING UP,"

Ruth Dean

On the next visit, Jasmine reported a mixed record. She showed considerable insight into the ways that overenthusiastic faculty and staff were complicating the process of "STRAIGHTENING UP." She said she liked receiving letters from me in between appointments and so I wrote again.

April 9

Dear Jasmine,

I really was glad you were able to come this week. You helped me understand the reasons that it is hard to stay in CONTROL OF YOUR TEMPER. It seems that after some time of "straightening out" and BEING IN CONTROL everyone was praising you and the pressure was really building up. You decided that it was too hard DEALING WITH PRESSURE and the only way to get rid of the pressure was to go back to the old ways that get you in TROUBLE.

You said it would be easier to keep away from TROUBLE if people at school would give you a little room and not comment on your clothes, touch you, or follow you. We also understood that some of the ways you have been trying to say this to teachers might get people angry at you.

You said that you don't want special deals that feel like bribes but you do want the usual privileges that go with good behavior when you earn them. You do like getting grapefruit because you can share it with your friends. You also want your old deal back with Mr. Green. If you have four good days then you get to have Friday off.

You asked me to explain to your teachers about the pressure you feel when they praise you a lot. You said, "It's okay to tell me I'm doing good once in a while but they shouldn't overdo it. They can put it in my weekly report." You said it would be good for me to pass this information on to your teachers so I will send a copy of this letter to the school social worker so that she can share our ideas with them.

I'm glad we tried the Talking, Feeling, and Doing Game—that was fun. I'm looking forward to seeing you next week and to our secret plan.

Your friend in DEALING WITH PRESSURE,

Ruth Dean

Jasmine came for her next appointment and we followed through on our secret plan to go out to lunch together and celebrate the progress she was making. But then she stopped coming and I could not get in touch with her or her mother because their phone was out of service. I called the school in an effort to find out how she was doing. Jasmine happened to be working in the office answering phones that day and so I was greeted by an enthusiastic voice exclaiming "Ruth Dean!" "Is that you Jasmine?" I asked, and then inquired as to how things were going. The following letter summarizes what transpired.

May 14

Dear Jasmine,

I was so happy to get to speak with you when I called your school. I'm glad you could tell me about the new plan for you to go to Dimmock which is closer to home. I think that's a good idea—especially if it means your mother can come for some meetings with you. It is nice that we had a chance to have our lunch together the last time we met—sort of like a good-bye lunch.

Do you remember when we were playing the Talking, Feeling, and Doing Game? We had to answer a question about what the title would be of a book written about each of us. You said the title of the book about you would be, "A KID WITH AN ATTITUDE."

I have been thinking about that title. It made me think that your ATTITUDE is important and helps you feel strong and special even though it gets you in trouble sometimes. It might help to talk to your new counselor about that and see if you can figure out how to have a strong attitude that doesn't cause TROUBLE.

I think you are a strong and very nice person and I think that your strength will help you TAME YOUR TEMPER and keep in CONTROL if you work on those things.

I enjoyed knowing you and working with you Jasmine.

Your friend in STAYING OUT OF TROUBLE,

Ruth Dean

I decided it might be helpful to write to her mother as well, even though we had not had contact since the initial visit and she had not told me of the decision to change clinics.

May 14

Dear Vera,

I spoke with Jasmine at school and she told me about the new plan to go to the clinic at Dimmock Street. She said that because Dimmock is closer, you thought it would work better and that maybe you could go there with her sometimes after your work. That sounds like a good plan to me.

I think that these troubles with Jasmine must be very hard—especially when they remind you of the problems with your older daughter. I hope you can hang in there with Jasmine because I know you have a lot to teach her about getting life under control since you have accomplished that yourself in some important ways. And I think she wants that help from you even though she can't show it easily and she pushes your buttons a lot.

Good luck Vera; if I can be of help in the future, please call.

Sincerely,

Ruth Dean

I did not know how these last letters were received by Jasmine and her mother. From her earlier comments, I thought Jasmine would like them. They created a sense of continuity and provided some closure for me and I hope for Jasmine and Vera. In the last letter, I tried to honor the cultural discourse that could allow Jasmine to see her "attitude" as a strength and not just a problem. I considered her "attitude" a way of resisting pressures that threatened her exuberance and spontaneity, and I wanted to support it. At the same time, I wanted to encourage her to find constructive ways to express it. I was also aware that possible *social injustices* in Vera's life, such as the lack of power to change a rigid work schedule, might have made keeping appointments difficult.

EXAMPLE TWO

Having found letter writing to be helpful with Jasmine, I began to use it more often. In a couple therapy, the following letter was used to promote the processes of externalizing and re-authoring.

March 10

Dear Lois and Al,

At our last meeting you reported that there have been some new developments in relation to the BICKERING that has taken over your family. Since

I am very interested in your progress in these matters, we discussed these new developments in some detail. I asked if you would find it helpful if I wrote up our discussion and sent it to you and you said you thought it might.

Here are some of the things that you thought seemed to be helping you diminish BICKERING and increase pleasant time together as a couple and family.

1. *Al has been working on noticing himself.*
2. *During a recent argument Al realized that it is better to stop fighting and not have it ruin the day, and so he said, "I'm wrong and let's stop fighting."*
3. *Lois appreciated hearing Al say he was wrong, and this allowed her to stop her side of the argument and take time out. She thinks that Al's saying "I'm wrong" was a crucial part of what allowed her to stop.*
4. *Lois was able to stop feeling angry when this happened and think of other things.*

Then we talked a little about the ways that your son Bob is responding to BICKERING. He is questioning unpleasant ways that you talk to one another, but he is also adopting some of the ways of BICKERING. I wondered if you could enlist Bob in your efforts to end BICKERING and have more pleasant times together as a family. Since he seems to be objecting to bickering, we talked about how he might get involved in thinking of some things he could do that would take some of the pressure off you two, like getting his own breakfast or doing his school homework. It seems like you have already got him started on some of these projects.

Have you noticed how BICKERING seems to thrive on pressure and tension?

Your ally in diminishing BICKERING,

Ruth Dean

My use of letter writing enabled me to embrace a more whimsical approach to therapy. The letters were always written with the client's permission. While most clients found them helpful I did experience one important exception. A fearful client finally confessed, after several weeks of receiving letters from me, that she never opened a letter until right before her next session. She explained that if there was something in the letter that was upsetting, she did not want to have to wait to see me and talk about it. After discussing her concerns, it became clear that for this particular client, written words were dangerous. In her mind, the letters had the power to take over her thoughts and derail her progress. She needed the freedom to come to each session without having my meaning inscribed on what had occurred in our previous meeting. I stopped writing.

The Therapeutic Relationship

This last example points to characteristics of the therapeutic relationship and the therapist's stance in a narrative model. The therapist is active in the therapy in order to open up new possibilities for engagement. Most often this activity takes the form of asking questions and developing more detailed or "thicker" descriptions of preferred aspects of the client's life (White, 2007; White and Epston, 1990). The therapist's expertise is used to facilitate conversations that will enable clients to learn more about their interests and values and the people in their lives who support new positive developments. The therapist does not impose meaning but rather facilitates the expression of the client's meaning and intent. Whereas the therapeutic relationship is a subject of interest and a focus for discussion in psychodynamic psychotherapy, in a narrative model, the therapist is de-centered and the relationship, although facilitative, is not discussed.

The Use of Documents

Another way that writing could be incorporated in narrative therapy is through the use of documents (White and Epston, 1990). I used this technique in a situation with a client who was in the process of divorcing her husband, a decision about which she was pleased. In a session that occurred right before she went on vacation, she paused as she got ready to leave my office and commented that another person she really needed to divorce was her mother. She was referencing the extent to which she had internalized and was dominated by her mother's very critical attitude toward her and other people. I told her a little about the documents designed by White and Epston and their clients (my client was a therapist) and suggested that she might write a document that initiated a divorce from her mother. She returned from vacation with the following declaration of independence:

Divorce Decree from Alice Smith by her daughter or . . . Declaration of Freedom from insidious, internal negative messages instilled by my mother in which a born-again cynic tries to eradicate that part of her self, but is there anything else there?"

She went on to itemize the ways in which these messages had been destructive—for example,

"Whereas the above mentioned messages have . . . paralyzed me to the point that any other strengths I might possess are incapacitated, further fueling my sense of inadequacy, etc."

The document concluded with the following declaration:

"I vow not to subject myself to my family's tyranny anymore . . . (and to) think of my life in narrative rather than argumentative ways . . . and to take more risks in relationships—(ugh)—well anyway, send my therapist this letter and let her not read it if she doesn't feel like it."

The document represented an important step forward in the therapy and continued to be a reference point as we addressed the intensity of her self-criticism throughout the course of our work. It allowed the client to let go of the negative aspects of her past relationship with her mother and to enjoy the adult relationship that was possible in the present.

The kinds of documents recommended by White and Epston were considered "counter" to the usual social service agency files in that they did not specify problems, spoil identities, or aid in marginalizing the people they described (1990: 190). Instead, "counter-documents" emphasized clients' competencies and signaled the achievement of a new, preferred status. Both letter writing and "counter-documents" were part of a literary approach to therapy in which writing is used to create new meanings and possibilities, and stories that are preferred replace problem-saturated narratives.

Teaching a Constructionist Orientation to Clients

An additional way that I have used social constructionism in my practice involves teaching this orientation to clients. It has been especially useful in work with couples or families when people were arguing about who is "right" or about the "right" way of thinking about something.

I began by introducing clients to the idea that they were operating out of an orientation to knowledge that is known as "objectivism," a perspective that posits that there is a single "truth" and it can be known. I explained that while some people saw the world in these "objectivist" terms, others held a different orientation to knowledge called social constructionism that declared that there were multiple possible truths or perspectives, and that all views were partial and contextual. We then considered the difference between these positions and the effect it would have on their ways of being in relationships if they held one orientation or another. If they were to adopt a constructionist orientation, would they continue to fight as much? What if they believed that there could be more than one way to approach an issue? What if they got interested in understanding each other's perspectives and the contexts in which they arose?

Consider a few examples: A couple, Joe and Tom, argued about many aspects of their lives. Joe made a decision concerning tickets for a trip. Then Tom wondered if Joe made the best arrangements. Joe found this very annoying, but Tom protested that he was only interested in finding the most efficient or effective way of doing something; he wanted to make the "best" decision. Each had a different idea of the "right" way to book their trip. When they recounted this fight, I first spoke about the difference between objectivist and social constructionist orientations. I suggested that if they took a constructionist perspective that allowed for multiple possibilities, we might say that each way had some merit—and neither was necessarily "right." Considering this possibility they stopped fighting about the arrangements and began to wonder why the fight had become so heated.

In a therapy session with another family, Sam, a very bright seventeen-year-old, complained that he couldn't talk to his family. At the dinner table, he wanted to have objective, clear discussions of issues, based on facts, and he wanted to arrive at truths. He complained that his parents and brother were unable to prove their points, back up their arguments, and cite their sources. He said it was useless to talk with them—why bother? They protested that he turned their dinner table discussions into very unpleasant arguments that he dominated. They were not so interested in arriving at "truths" but preferred to hear each other's perspectives. I introduced the idea of two very different orientations to knowledge. I asked Sam if he was aware that he was representing an objectivist approach to knowledge while his family seemed to be committed to a social constructionist approach. Once we defined these differences and acknowledged that Sam was representing a legitimate orientation to knowledge but not the only one, it became more possible for them to consider ways of improving their dinner table conversations.

In yet another situation, a teenager loudly proclaimed that his mother was "wrong" when she told him it was unsafe for him to go to a rock concert. He shouted that all his friends were going and that "it was a fact that it was safe." His mother was equally vociferous in proclaiming the "rightness" of her position that this was a dangerous event. She said, "That's the fact. Everyone knows that rock concerts are dangerous." I asked if they would be willing to consider that they were expressing different beliefs and not necessarily "facts" about the event in question. Could each explain the reason for his or her perspective? Could each understand the other's position? Once this discussion was about perspectives, it became possible to increase understanding and reach an outcome that satisfied the need of each.

These discussions were intellectual and abstract. They didn't address all that was going on in the arguments. They did provide a framework that allowed people to move away from an objectivist orientation. The conversations opened up and created room for accommodation. Although I stepped into the position of "expert" by providing the framework of different orientations to knowledge, I did this in order to facilitate a conversation through which clients could define their own positions. I did not claim expertise about their lives.

These examples demonstrate my use of the narrative practices of externalization, re-authoring, re-membering, letter writing, documents, and teaching about constructionism. Inspired by the work of Michael White, David Epston, and others, I have tried to use narrative approaches in ways that were true to my belief in the possibility of combining multiple approaches in a single therapy.

Challenges and Future Directions

CHALLENGES

Today, narrative therapy is an accepted part of social work curriculum, often taught as a practice elective. Social work students find it especially compatible with the values and orientation they are learning. By its very nature, it respects and appreciates diverse ways of living.

On the other hand, empiricist methods in general and evidence-based practice, in particular, have been making a "comeback" in schools of social work and have challenged the teaching of narrative approaches and social constructionism. White and Epston have discussed their opposition to applying a "logico-scientific mode of thought" to clinical work (1990). They explained that the formal logic of an empiricist approach looks for universal truths while a narrative mode of thought values particular experiences of individuals at specific points in time. In the "logico-scientific" method, individuals are seen as responding to "impersonal forces" internal or external to themselves, whereas in the narrative approach, individuals are considered the protagonists in their stories. In narrative work, stories are co-constructed by therapist and client; in the logico-scientific model the therapist is considered a neutral observer who stands apart and is able to make objective determinations about the client.

For many narrative practitioners, the "proof" of effectiveness of narrative practices has been found in the responses of clients who found it helpful. In a paradigm that prizes subjective reality, this form of validation is preferred to approaches that objectified clients and quantified and generalized results.

In my experience, once students have been taught the difference in these orientations to knowledge and the research approaches embedded in each, they quickly began to develop "evidence" regarding effectiveness from individual client reports. This was done by working with clients at the start of a therapy to determine what the signs of success of their work would be. Then, ongoing discussions of what was helpful and evaluations of progress were used to determine "evidence" of effectiveness. Despite the current emphasis on empirical, evidence-based practice in social work curricula, my students remain enthusiastic about narrative therapy and interested in finding ways to use it and reveal its effectiveness.

FUTURE DIRECTIONS

With the death of Michael White in 2008, many teachers and narrative therapists became concerned as to who would provide future leadership in the field of narrative therapy. Fortunately there are many centers around the world where narrative therapy is taught and practiced. These include The Evanston Family Therapy Center of Chicago run by Jill Freedman and Gene Coombs; two groups in Adelaide, the Dulwich Centre and Narrative Practices Adelaide; the Family Center in Auckland, New Zealand, with Johnella

Bird; the Calgary Family Therapy Centre with Karl Tomm; and the Narrative Therapy Centre in Toronto—just to mention a few. A look at the Web
sites of these different groups indicates that there are many vibrant centers
of activity with multiple opportunities for learning narrative practice and
evolving as a narrative therapist.

But it is clear that financial pressures on social service agencies and
teaching institutes caused by the current economic recession have resulted
in diminished service and teaching possibilities. While these financial pressures could be threats to the future success of narrative therapy they could
also encourage its use. The short-term nature of narrative therapy, may
make it appealing at a time when therapeutic resources are being stretched.

Several excellent new books on social constructionism and narrative
therapy comprise other hopeful signs for the future of this orientation. Fortunately for his followers, Michael White's *Maps of Narrative Practice* published in 2007 offers an elegant summary of his therapeutic approaches.
His whimsy and creativity are richly documented in the many detailed
transcripts of his work that are included. Gary Paquin's book, *Clinical Social Work: A Narrative Approach* (which I was privileged to review) is a useful new resource written especially for social workers showing how foundational social work beliefs in social justice, empowerment, community,
and sensitivity to diverse ways of life are intrinsic to narrative work. The
pedagogy of narrative practice has been richly served by Peggy Sax, in her
recent book, *Re-authoring Teaching: Creating a Collaboratory,* which shows
how narrative methods can be implemented to re-author teaching. Most
recently, some of Michael White's colleagues have published a new volume
containing his "never-before-published papers, interviews and paragraphs
of 'thoughts," entitled *Narrative Practice: Continuing the Conversations,* a
most welcome addition to the narrative literature.

Conclusion

As I review my chapter, I see that although my beginnings as a social worker
had little to do with being a narrative therapist and a social constructionist,
I did appreciate the ways people's problems were, in part, constructed by
the social circumstances of their lives at the start of my career. But these
interests, stimulated by the girls' groups I led, did not come to the surface
again until I discovered postmodern writing and social constructionism as

a doctoral student. Utilizing a narrative approach to therapy was a natural outgrowth of these developments.

The understanding that knowledge is constructed, contextual, and political, and that multiple perspectives are to be honored, has enriched my development as a teacher, a clinician, and a person. It has enabled me to practice with more spontaneity, transparency, and authenticity. It has encouraged me to teach from a critical perspective and to honor students' personal narratives and individual ways of approaching their work. And it has brought me back to the social and political concerns that were part of my early interest in social work.

These concerns echo my mother's career that began as a supervisor in the first federally funded public welfare agency created at the time of the Great Depression. Her involvement with the birth of the social welfare system in the United States has become more meaningful to me as I have watched government efforts to dismantle the safety net during the Bush administration and seen resistance to health care reform initiated by President Obama. The programs that President Roosevelt introduced in the 1930s and 1940s showed that a different reality could be socially constructed out of the chaos of the Depression.

My participation in social activism has increased as I have aged and watched the United States reject the ideal of providing supports for those in need. To my way of thinking, social constructionism offers a framework that supports efforts to create a better order. If our understandings (and actions based on these understandings) are socially constructed, then they can be reconstructed. While we acknowledge and embrace multiple ways of defining social justice, we need not abandon our efforts to achieve these goals. Our global connections make social justice achievable to an extent never before thought possible. They also make it an "absolute" necessity.

Notes

1. Social work values placed heavy emphasis on social justice and approaches suited to diverse population. In many social work programs, psychoanalytic theory and the highly hierarchical model of therapy associated with its beginnings were criticized and considered less relevant to social work. Instead, collaborative models were sought that acknowledged clients' unique perspectives and strengths, such as narrative therapy or the strengths perspective.

2. My early professional experiences at Beth Israel had taught me much about the politics of care and the arbitrary ways in which power operated. I saw

how expertise could be conferred or taken away by those at the top of the hospital hierarchy—doctors.

3. While not a part of the academic curriculum, narrative therapy was being taught at various family therapy institutes around the world with the Dulwich Centre in Adelaide, Australia, where it originated, as the epicenter. I was fortunate to study narrative therapy at the Cambridge Family Institute in Watertown, Massachusetts, with two talented teachers, Sally Ann Roth and Kaethe Weingarten.

4. This occurred at the hospital where patients' social problems were the focus of social workers and of limited interest to medical staff despite the known interaction of biological, social, and psychological factors in health. As a result, the idea of what was "wrong" with the patient might have been extremely limited if not for the social workers' efforts to create a more complete picture that included social factors.

5. I found a way to teach this idea to a social work practice class when a student declared that she was working with "broken families," in her field placement agency. I asked the class to consider the implications of the term, "broken families." If there are "broken" families are there also "unbroken" families? What standard determines these categories? What would it be like to be told that you are from a "broken" family? What subtle impact might this expression have on the worker who uses it? The class soon saw that words shape understanding and uphold certain values and demote others. They also recognized that language is political and a form of social action. What if the definition of "unbroken" families left out single-parent families or families with same-sex parents?

6. The idea of therapist as expert has been questioned by contemporary psychoanalysts such as Aron (1991), Hoffman (1991), and Renick (1993), who take a social constructionist perspective and describe a more collaborative approach with clients.

7. A slightly different version of this case appeared in "Making the professional personal and personal professional," in J. J. Shay and J. Wheelis (Eds.), *Odysseys in Psychotherapy*, New York: Ardent Media Inc, (2000), 67–95.

8. I used capitals and bolding for emphasis and to set apart and externalize a problem or attempted solution.

References

Anderson, H. and H. A. Goolishian (1988). Human systems as linguistic systems: Preliminary and evolving ideas about the implications for clinical theory." *Family Process*, 27(4): 371–393.

Aron, L. (1991). The patient's experience of the analyst's subjectivity. *Psychoanalytic Dialogues,* 1(1): 29–51.

Berger, P. and T. Luckmann (1966). *The social construction of reality.* New York: Anchor.

Burr, V. (1995). *An introduction to social constructionism.* New York: Routledge.

Dean, R. G. (1993a). Constructivism: An approach to clinical practice. *Smith College Studies in Social Work,* 63(2): 127–146.

———. (1993b). Teaching a constructivist approach to clinical practice. Published simultaneously in *Journal of Teaching in Social Work,* 8(1/2): 55–75 and J. Laird, (Ed.), *Revisioning social work education: A social constructionist approach* (pp. 55–75). Binghamton, NY: Haworth Press.

———. (1995). Stories of AIDS: The use of narrative as an approach to understanding in an AIDS support group. *Clinical Social Work Journal,* 23(3): 287–304.

———. (1998). A narrative approach to groups. *Clinical Social Work Journal,* 26(1): 23–37.

Dean, R. G. and Fleck-Henderson, A. (1992). Teaching clinical theory and practice through a constructivist lens. *Journal of Teaching in Social Work,* 6(1): 3–20.

Dean, R. G. and Rhodes, M. (1998). Social constructionism and ethics: What makes a "better" story? *Families in Society,* 79(3): 245–261.

Foucault, M. (1980). *Power/knowledge: Selected interviews and other writings.* New York: Pantheon.

———. (1982). The subject and power. In H. L. Dreyfus and P. Rabinow, (Eds.), *Michel Foucault: Beyond structuralism and hermeneutics.* Chicago: University of Chicago Press.

———. (1994). *Power.* Vol. III, James D. Faubion (Ed.). New York: New Press.

Gergen, K. (1985). The social constructionist movement in modern psychology. *American Psychologist,* 40(3): 266–275.

Gergen, K. J. and M. M. Gergen (1983). Narratives of the self. In T. R. Sarbin and K. E. Scheibe (Eds.), *Studies in social identity.* New York: Praeger.

Hartman, A. (1991). Words create worlds. *Social Work* 26(4): 275.

Hoffman, I. Z. (1991). Discussion: Toward a social-constructivist view of the psychoanalytic situation. *Psychoanalytic Dialogues,* 1(1): 74–105.

———. (1992). Some practical implications of a social-constructivist view of the psychoanalytic situation. *Psychoanalytic Dialogues,* 2(3): 287–303.

———. (1998). *Ritual and spontaneity in the psychoanalytic process: A dialectical constructivist view.* Hillsdale, NJ: Analytic Press.

Lightburn, A. and P. Sessions (2006). *Community-based clinical practice.* New York: Oxford University Press.

Paquin, G. W. (2009). *Clinical social work: A narrative approach.* Alexandria, VA: CSWE Press.

Penn, P. and M. Frankfurt (1994). Creating a participant text: Writing, multiple voices, narrative multiplicity. *Family Process*, 33(3): 217–231.

Renik, O. (1993). Analytic interaction: Conceptualizing technique in light of the analyst's irreducible subjectivity. *Psychoanalytic Quarterly*, 62 (4): 553–571.

Sabo, A. (2000). Introduction: Psychotherapy at the start of a new century. In A. N. Sabo and L. Havens (Eds.), *The real world guide to psychotherapy practice* (pp. 1–13). Cambridge, MA: Harvard University Press.

Sax, P. (2008). *Reauthoring teaching: Creating a collaboratory*. Rotterdam: Sense.

Schaefer, R. (1979). On becoming an analyst of one persuasion or another. *Psychoanalytic Journal for the Study of Interpersonal Processes*, 3: 345–360.

Sessions, P. and A. Lightburn (2005). What is community-based clinical practice? Traditions and transformations. In A. Lightburn and P. Sessions (Eds.), *Handbook of community-based clinical practice* (pp. 3–18). New York: Oxford University Press.

Spence, D. (1982). *Narrative truth and historical truth: Meaning and interpretation in psychoanalysis*. New York: Norton.

Stern, D. B. (1997). *Unformulated experience*. Hillsdale, NJ: Analytic Press.

White, M. (2007). *Maps of narrative practice*. New York: Norton.

———. (2011). *Narrative Practice: Continuing the Conversations*. New York: Norton.

White, M. and D. Epston (1990). *Narrative means to therapeutic ends*. Adelaide, Australia: Dulwich Centre Press.

5

The Car, the Rain, and Meaningful Conversation

Reflexivity and Practice

FIONA GARDNER

My introduction to social constructionism came early. I was born in Scotland and emigrated with my family to Australia when I was nine. Being transplanted in another country provided an early demonstration of how differently people perceived me and my culture—a beginning and, of course, unarticulated understanding of social construction. At school, for example, I was teased initially for being a "POM." When I asked what this meant I was told "prisoner of mother England"; when I answered "I'm not English, I'm Scottish," the teasing stopped immediately. For a nine-year-old this was primarily a relief, but it demonstrated to me that "problems are socially constructed . . . they can be defined in different ways" (Wood and Tully, 2006: 19), and therefore a variety of responses are possible. Stating that I was Scottish clearly meant for those teasing me that the issue of my "otherness" had shifted somehow, which changed their reactions and left me wondering what it all meant.

My social work training provided language for this experience, impressing upon me the importance of context, culture, structure, processes, and the need to ask how else might things be seen. This approach was reinforced by practice with a wide range of communities and issues, mainly in rural Victoria, and also in Bristol, United Kingdom. Much of my practice involved working with those on statutory orders: prisoners and ex-prisoners, young people on some kind of court order, families where children were considered to be at risk. For many of these individuals and families the social perception, often internalized by them, was that they were somehow lacking, or more judgmentally, disadvantaged, inadequate, or delinquent. Prison officers tended to label all prisoners as hopeless, for example; the police had a dismal view of the possibilities of people changing from "bad" to "good." I was conscious that in building relationships with them, I saw that other social constructions were possible of abilities and resources, as well as of the structural issues that influenced their position. A more complex picture of the world and the place of individuals in it always emerged. Sometimes it was possible to work in a way that enabled people also to see that other perceptions were possible. Having a local football team come and play football with a group of prisoners, for example, changed some views, for football team members of prisoners and for some prisoners of themselves.

When, by chance, I started teaching social work in the mid- to late-1990s at La Trobe University in Victoria, Australia, I finally came to grips with reading about postmodernism and social constructionist informed practice and recognized this as further naming and illuminating what I thought social work practice was about. It also reinforced some of my previous practice understandings, the sense, for example, that there are many ways to look at anything. Parton and O'Byrne's (2000) view that "Constructionism cautions us to be ever suspicious of our assumptions about how the world appears and the categories that we use to divide and interpret it" (25) fitted with my experience, as did their comments about the continuing and complex influence of history and culture. Clearly, there are many variations in writing about social constructionism with different emphases, although there is also general agreement that social constructionism affirms that each person is an active agent in creating their own world of meaning (Kondrat, 2002). I found this helpful but also noticed that there seemed to be tension in such writing between those who saw social constructionism as more focused on the micro-level and those articulating what I saw as a key link between social work advocating for a socially just society and the requirement to "encourage, facilitate and legitimate diverse knowledge traditions and forms of expression" (Witkin, 1999: 7). Related to this was the criticism of too extreme a position on postmodernism and social constructionism by those like Ife (1999), who argued that there needs to be some agreed principles in relation to social justice, for example, rather than accepting that everything can be seen as socially determined. Others expressed the concern that Bowers (2005) identifies that a social constructionist approach can foster thinking individually at the cost of a community perspective. Along with social workers and students, I continued to wrestle with exploring and grounding these ideas in social work practice.

This was furthered by working with Jan Fook at the Centre for Professional Development at Latrobe University for four years in the 2000s, running workshops using critical reflection for professionals, mainly in the health and social welfare fields. Critical reflection, as we used it, provided both the necessary background theory, as well as a process enabling workers and/or students to put these and related theories in practice through examining their taken-for-granted assumptions and values in the light of their social context. It was clear that critical reflection is particularly powerful in enabling workers to make links between the individual and society and in connecting changed awareness with changed action underpinned by a social justice perspective (Fook and Gardner, 2007). Critical reflection enabled me to put the ideas of social construction into practice, to unearth the different meanings, assumptions, and values that could be implicit in a practice experience. Critical reflection was also explicit about the need to work from a social justice perspective—while acknowledging that what this might mean would need to be determined in any particular context.

In my current role, I coordinate a social work course at a rural campus of LaTrobe University which has a large urban campus and four rural campuses. I am based in a large provincial city, and continue to run workshops for professionals using critical reflection, both here and elsewhere, and run ongoing supervision groups and also use critical reflection in teaching. Living and working in a rural environment in itself prompts a social constructionist understanding, given that there is a constant interaction between what are perceived as more rural and urban issues and perspectives. My teaching has been primarily in the areas of community work, working with social diversity, and working with individuals, families, and groups. This combination in itself often confronts expectations: the combination of working with individuals as well as communities is a constant reminder to me and to students that it is important to view the world through more than one lens. The subject "social work and social diversity" is also an opportunity for exploring a social constructionist view of the world. In all of these subjects, I encourage students to reflect critically, to endeavor, as much as possible, to move from their own shoes to see the world and the experience of others from different perspectives. Some students engage enthusiastically with this and are also able to imagine how others might perceive them in a variety of ways. Others struggle with it, particularly in naming how the social constructions that other people have might affect how they themselves are perceived—that a Muslim man might not see them as trustworthy, for example, simply because of their gender and culture or that an older woman might feel judged by the assumptions and values of a younger worker. One of the approaches that has been useful in enabling students to practice social constructionism is *reflexivity*.

Reflexivity is one of the underlying theoretical approaches in critical reflection and provides a tool that enhances understanding of how we both construct our own social understandings and are impacted by the social understandings of others. Iversen, Gergen, and Fairbanks (2005) suggest that a "constructionist critique calls upon us to recognize that we live in conflicting communities of the real and the good, and if we are to go on together, reflexive dialogue is essential" (697). This chapter uses a specific practice experience—a meaningful conversation in the rain—to explore the use of reflexivity in social work. In deconstructing and reconstructing this experience, I am using both the theory and process of critical reflection. This approach to critical reflection is underpinned by several theoretical approaches and conceptual frameworks: reflexivity, as well as postmodernism, reflective practice, and critical social theory. The process involves unearthing implicit assumptions and values in a way that encourages understanding of the connection between the individual's experience and the social context and is expected to lead to change (Fook and Gardner, 2007). It provides a means to link the social constructionist understanding of individual and social experience with the ability to act as a practitioner.

This particular example illustrates how we make assumptions in our perceptions of individuals and communities and also about how we are perceived. Using reflexivity as a tool can sharpen a social constructionist approach by furthering the articulation of such assumptions, unearthing their personal, professional, and social influences. Parton (2007) suggests that reflexivity is at the core of social constructionism, validating focus on feelings and how these connect to judgments we make. Reflexivity is used in both research and practice as a way of exploring the connection between individuals' perceptions of themselves and the influence of their social context (Freshwater, 2002). As White (2006) suggests, reflexivity, like social construction, invites social workers to see the world from many perspectives, rather than one dominant narrative, and to be conscious of how language can be used to limit or extend possibilities. For this practice example, reflexivity as a tool was particularly useful in deconstructing differences in perceptions and in reconstructing them to perceive differently.[1]

Use of Critical Reflection

How critical reflection is understood and articulated varies considerably (White, Fook, and Gardner, 2006), with some writers and practitioners talking about reflective practice, critical thinking, or critical reflection as the same and others seeing these as different. I use a definition related to workshops run by Jan Fook and me, in which critical reflection is defined as both a theory and a process involving "the unsettling and examination of fundamental (socially dominant, and often hidden) individually held assumptions about the social world, in order to enable a reworking of these, and associated actions, for changed professional practice" (Fook and Gardner, 2007: 21). These workshops, with participants primarily from health and social care fields, began with the facilitator presenting the underlying theory of critical reflection, then modeling the process using an incident from her own experience including identifying the background or context of the incident, the specific incident, and some beginning thoughts about why it was significant. This modeling process is important partly to indicate how the critical reflection can work, and also to demonstrate that the facilitator is also prepared to be open to the process.

Each participant was then asked to share an experience or incident, generally from their own practice. "Critical" or significant incidents are often used in critical reflection training, both for students and workers in social work and other disciplines (Francis, 1997; Fook and Gardner, 2007). In the process used at the Centre, participants are asked to bring an experience that they see as significant to them, not critical in the sense of traumatic, but rather an experience that they would like to learn from. Overall the aim of working with this incident is to ensure and promote effective practice with workers feeling a greater sense of agency, that is, the ability to act in ways that are congruent with their preferred values and assumptions. The process involves two stages. Stage one involves deconstructing the incident, seeking to understand their own and others' feelings, thoughts, underlying assumptions and values, and the influence of social context. Generally, this includes understanding that there are more ways that this incident can be perceived: that, in a sense, the person with the incident had a particular social construction of what happened and how that was perceived, but there are other ways of perceiving this. Sometimes the group will brainstorm possibilities to free the person from one set of perceptions. The second stage engages with the new understanding, including possible new assumptions and/or affirmed past assumptions and exploring what this might mean for changed practice.

The underlying theory of critical reflection provides important prompts in exploring an incident. As well as reflexivity, the theory underlying or influencing critical reflection includes reflective practice, postmodernism, and critical social theory. These are not completely independent, but each has a particular contribution to a critically reflective approach. Briefly, reflective practice encourages awareness of the practitioner's own theory base: the ideas they have generated about their practice, the assumptions made about what works and what doesn't. Compared to critical reflection, there is not necessarily a focus on the influence of the social context related to critical social theory. A reflective practitioner also seeks to understand where their "espoused theory" is not congruent with their "theory in practice," that is, what they say or think they believe is not the same as how they act (Schon, 1983). Postmodern thinking prompts awareness of dichotomous thinking, that is, seeing the world in pairs of opposites: worker/client, able/not able, white/non-white. This type of thinking creates an artificial and simplistic division that implies that one is better than the other, and fosters seeing a particular person as part of a group that is "other" than the worker (Fook, 2002). Connected to this is the understanding of how social constructs are created: the need to see that each person has a multiplicity of roles and perspectives, is complex rather than one-dimensional, and that any situation can be seen in a variety of ways. Rolfe, Freshwater, and Jasper (2001) call this "reflective skepticism" which "protects us from accepting 'universal truths' or that there is only ever one explanation for an event or one way of looking at it" (73). Social constructionists (and postmodernists) would be more likely to talk about the influence of dominant discourses: the main ways of thinking in the mainstream culture.

These ways of thinking also connect to the use of critical social theory, which often (though not always) differentiates between what writers mean by reflective practice and critical reflection: Critical reflection includes the centrality of understanding how social structures influence people's lives, partly through them "taking on board" or internalizing the norms of the society they live in (Allan, Pease, and Briskman, 2003). A man who is laid-off at 50, for example, may internalize the view expressed in his society that middle-aged men are no longer useful. Some current social constructionist writing articulates a similar view, suggesting the worker's role is "to help the client deconstruct oppressive cultural discourses and reinterpret experience from alternative perspectives" (Wood and Tully, 2006: 44). Critical social theory also advocates a social justice approach (Brookfield, 2005), which may not be as clear in some definitions of social constructionism (White, 2008), though others make this connection clear in talking about critical social constructionism (Roche, 2007); for example, the expectation that common principles relating to social justice and human rights should underlie practice and guide decision making about abusive behavior.

In this chapter, I explore my experience of using reflexivity to deconstruct a practice experience with a small group at a Transforming Social Work Conference.[2] I am partly doing this as an example of how I practice with reflexivity, which encourages awareness of the influence of personal experience within particular relationships and how this might influence perceptions of self and others (Taylor and White, 2000). Social work practitioners, like researchers, "do not simply observe in a neutral fashion. . . they construct versions of cases, and, in this sense, make knowledge about patients and service users" (Taylor, 2006: 75). Understanding reflexivity means that we can't say that we separate out the personal and professional, but rather that we understand how our personal selves affect us as professionals. While there are varying definitions of reflexivity, Freshwater (2002) suggests "one cannot avoid the fact that it essentially involves the subjective self, and the ability of the self to turn back on itself" (229) which Johns (2002) talks about as the "reflexive spiral of being and becoming" (51). It is important to see that reflexivity is "the ability to recognize that *all* aspects of ourselves and our contexts influence the way we research (or create knowledge)" (Fook and Gardner, 2007: 31). We can think about our ideas or awareness about what is happening being influenced by what is embodied or physical, social, emotional, and intellectual, and by our reactions. These will be explored in relation to the following incident.

The Car, the Rain, and Meaningful Conversation

Background to the Incident

I was working as a social worker in the regional office of a large government department with responsibility for family, youth, and children's services. While the language of the time was different, this included responsibility for "child protection," working with families where children were perceived to be at risk. The town in which the regional office was based had a significant indigenous Aboriginal population with their own Cooperative Health Service. The department managed two indigenous family group homes, employed an indigenous welfare officer, and had formed a "welfare committee" to act as a forum for liaison and service development with the indigenous community. When I started work with the department, the previous liaison person had left and the committee hadn't met for months. The indigenous community requested that a new liaison worker be appointed and the committee started up again. I volunteered, based on a commitment to working with what was clearly the least privileged group in town and valuing the place of the indigenous community. However, it seemed that the committee's initial interest soon died—people were inconsistent about coming to meetings and seemed to be reluctant to agree to "do" anything.

The Specific Incident

I had gone to a committee meeting on a rainy afternoon. We were to meet at a different place from usual, and when I got there, the building was locked and there was no one around. I went back to my car, and for some reason, decided just to wait. After a while, a woman from the indigenous community (who I will call Felicity), who was part of the group, arrived. We checked again on the building, and still no one was there. Since it was still raining, drizzling gently, she suggested that we wait in my car and see what happened. As we sat, Felicity told me the story of her family.[3] Her mother, Rose, was one of the "Stolen Generation,"[4] taken from her family who lived in an isolated rural community, when she was eight, initially to be educated in an orphanage, then later sent to Sydney, a major city, to work as a maid. Her family didn't know where she had been taken and weren't able to find out. Rose had little money and didn't try to find her family for many years partly from a feeling of shame about what had happened. She married at eighteen to a non-indigenous man with whom she had two children. He was abusive to her and she left him, taking the children, when she was twenty-three. She was thirty when she reconnected with her family. By then, her own mother, Felicity's grandmother, had died, from Felicity's perspective, at least partly from grief. The impact of both the separation from her family and the death of her mother continued to affect Felicity's mother and so the family. Her mother had periods of severe depression, although being reunited with her family had been and continued to be a healing experience.

I felt profoundly moved and humbled by the story and by Felicity's openness in sharing it with me. Although she was calm, she too was obviously moved by the retelling of her story. We both ended up with tears in our eyes.

Reflecting on the Incident

The critical reflection process encourages the person with the incident to explore the significance of what it means for them. What are the feelings, the emotions, and what is influencing them? What are the underlying assumptions and values expressed here? Where were Felicity and I each coming from? What brought about this experience? What was the influence of our social context for each of us? And what did I learn from it? What would I want to change in my practice as a result?

Reflexivity is central to understanding the dynamic between Felicity and I and in understanding how my perceptions of myself and the indigenous community were blocking our working together. Reflexivity encourages awareness of how persons perceive themselves, as well as how they perceive others. In this example, I had initially perceived myself as an aware and enthusiastic worker—a social worker with understanding of indigenous issues and the conflicts, partly related to the history of colonization in Australia, that existed between indigenous and non-indigenous cultures. As an immigrant, I had experienced what it felt like to be considered "other"—such as the example used at the beginning of this chapter. As an adolescent, I observed the way that overseas students were seen in my school and how easy it was to be labeled different in a way that made it very hard to move beyond certain expectations. I had worked in a different community in Victoria with indigenous families and experienced some of the damage of indigenous children being placed with non-indigenous foster families and being adopted by non-indigenous families.

I thought my energy and passion for this work would be an advantage. My perception was that the indigenous community would be interested in working with the department—partly because they had requested the committee start again—and my related assumption was that we would be able to "get on with things" quickly.

The next step in reflexivity is to be conscious of how you may be being perceived and how different this may be from your perceptions of yourself. This requires moving out of your own shoes into the shoes of the other and a willingness to look at yourself through another's eyes—as much as you are able. It is important to recognize that how you look, what you physically embody to others, can be significant. Doing this in retrospect, it was immediately clear that I epitomized a number of challenges in terms of acceptance by the community. For a start, I was relatively young—early thirties, female, clearly white, also social work–trained and so of the profession and from the department currently and historically responsible for removing children. I was the embodiment of "the people who take your kids away" both physically and socially.

Initially I distanced myself emotionally from these connections. As a social worker, I hadn't ever removed indigenous children except when requested by their families. I didn't identify myself with the white patriarchal and racist attitudes of the Stolen Generations. What Felicity's telling of her story did, though, was to enable me to see that in the eyes of the indigenous community, I am connected and that they are right to make that connection. Felicity told this story in a calm, matter-of-fact way; she didn't, it seemed, have an agenda of engendering guilt. Nevertheless, I felt ashamed; I understood from her story that I needed to make both connections and comparisons. I needed to come to grips with the connection between my current work for the department and my privileged and more powerful existence in Australian society, which continued to have, in many ways, the attitudes and circumstances that made it possible for the Stolen Generations to happen. I also needed to compare the possibilities for a white person in Australia with those of indigenous people both in the past and the present—that is, to recognize how the system continues to perpetuate the inequities and injustices of the past.

Understanding the interactional aspects of reflexivity would have helped me understand that our perceptions are inevitably influenced by history, as well as the current social context. Felicity's knowledge of the Stolen Generations and the history and social values that allowed that to happen were critical factors in her attitude toward me. I needed to recognize that "knowledge is also interactional—it is shaped by historical and structural contexts, and is made in a dynamic and political process. In this sense, what counts as knowledge is not a purely objective phenomenon, but is a result of a number of factors. It is normally forged through the broader social processes at play" (Fook and Gardner, 2007, 30). In a sense, what Felicity may have been doing was assessing how much *I* had internalized the prevailing social attitudes and how open I was to different perspectives.

Reflexivity prompts looking again at perceptions in the light of new perspectives or understandings. My perceptions were shifted by the conversation: I experienced Felicity's telling of her story as new knowledge that changed my awareness. Another way of putting this would be to say that my *subjective* understanding shifted from my previous cultural and personal history to taking on board a new experience; I perceived both Felicity and myself differently. This reinforces the social constructionist view that we can't understand a person in the abstract, but need to learn from the person's own perspective (Johnson and Munch, 2009). A social situation is best understood by eliciting the unique experiences of the people who are in that situation. Given the interactive nature of subjectivity, the Transforming Social Work group asked: What might Felicity's sense have been of this conversation? What did she hope for? Or did she have an intuitive sense of timing?[5]

Reflective practice prompts asking what your own particular assumptions are, as well as exploring what the assumptions of others might be. Others will have their own reactions and assumptions that provide another window of reflexivity. For example, in discussing this incident in the group, participants interpreted the car and its potential symbolism very differently, one seeing it as becoming a "sacred space" and another as a symbol of power. From a postmodern point of view, both are possible. From my perspective, the car did become like a sacred space—a place for telling a story that was both personal and emblematic of cultural experience. The feeling of it being profound was that I felt connected at a deep level to an excruciating part of Felicity's own as well as her family's and her community's experience. Making such deep connections is part of what both Felicity and I would have called a spiritual experience, a sense of relatedness at a level beyond the usual, and a transcendence of our individual selves to connection across boundaries.

The loss of children would be painful in any culture, but this kind of loss was also significant at other levels. What was made explicit was that indigenous culture was not acceptable, that children would be "better" if they were educated in different ways. The strength of this message and its implications are hard to leave behind, especially when implicit and explicit in Australian culture. At this time, too, in the 1980s, the implications were more consequential than currently, implicit in the policy and procedures of the department. The understanding of what is meant by family, for example, continued to be narrowly defined and to miss the different meaning for indigenous communities.

Again this connects to another aspect of reflexivity: "understanding that the knowledge or information we obtain or take in about a particular situation is at least partly determined by the kinds of tools and process we use to determine it" (Fook and Gardner, 2007, 29). Part of what I needed to recognize was that my perception of what was happening was influenced by what I and my department saw as legitimate knowledge. It wasn't possible, for example, to understand a different view of family because the language of family and the processes, questions, and tools of assessment all assumed a particular definition. This could also be extended to how progress was seen in working with the community. What was defined socially in the department and the broader community as success would be something like working on defined goals with clear outcomes: meetings held, minutes, activities. There was no room for seeing progress as improved relationships or understandings. I also needed to see that my behavior—my desire for meetings that worked according to a more conventional model—was also influenced by social and organizational expectations and didn't fit with indigenous culture. Once I became clear about this, I let go of such expectations relatively easily and simply prepared to work in ways that suited this particular community culture.

Working with reflexivity also means acknowledging the place of emotion and emotional reactions. I was clearly moved by Felicity's story, and my emotional reaction was important to her. My reaction to her story—the emotional impact of it being clear in my tears, as well as my expression, my responses, maybe simply my willingness to listen and to "be" with her, also changed her perception. It seemed that I became more worthy of trust and gained legitimacy because I was moved; I took her story on board and was impacted by it. It is impossible to know, of course, how much this was influenced by the circumstances; if we hadn't met in this way, would Felicity have created another way for this to happen? Was there some change in attitude in me implicit in my willingness just to wait, rather than saying if no one is coming, I'd better return to work?

An important connection in critical reflection is between reflexivity and critical social theory. This connection is an important part of the learning and movement from understanding to changed attitudes and actions. Recognizing the shame involved for me in the incident could have been disabling, although that was not, I believe, Felicity's intention. However, the critical in critical reflection prompts making links to a broader social understanding. It also encourages movement from insight to action—stage two of the critical reflection process. In this example, Felicity's perception of me may have already been changing; perhaps that is why she was prepared to tell her story. What then were the implications for change? Clearly nothing had changed at an intellectual level—I didn't have new knowledge. Subjectively, a significant change occurred: I understood the experience of the Aboriginal community differently, from a cognitive level, but more importantly from a deeper and more emotional level. This, in turn, led to a new way of working, based on deeper respect for the community's culture and approach to change. This meant more willingness to sit with people, simply to be rather than do, to wait until relationships were established in a way that meant it was possible to start to act on agreed projects. Significantly, once we had established a relationship of mutual understanding, change beyond what I had imagined was achieved.

What Does This Experience Say About the Value of Reflexivity?

First, it suggests that we need to recognize that how we perceive ourselves as workers is not necessarily how others perceive us. We may embody a series of assumptions for others by the way we look or through the organization we represent. This is not necessarily something we can or should do anything about; what is important is to recognize what that means about the work needing to be done to understand the resulting reactions. I couldn't do anything about how I looked; I was there because I was a social worker working for the department. But I could have better imagined what these might represent for others and accepted that it was going to take time to be seen as more of a whole person. I could also have made explicit this tension, which might also have shifted perceptions and changed the subjective interactions between us—though this might have had the risk of being too confronting. This is often a challenge for workers: How do we move beyond what our organization or profession is seen to represent? Being aware of this at least means that as a worker you are prepared to allow time for a more positive relationship to develop, less likely to react to a negative projection.

Second, and perhaps more difficult to accept, is that the other person may be right that we represent a particular perspective more than we have been able to acknowledge. We need to be aware of the assumptions we are making in our perceptions of others, to understand the extent of our own "conditioning" or internalizing of social norms and values, and to be constantly watchful in order to have some degree of confidence that we don't continue to express them unwittingly. In using reflexivity, we are reminded to acknowledge the influence of history, as well as culture, in forming our assumptions and values about how things are and "should be." This applied to me not only in thinking about the influence of history but also in wanting to impose my usual "doing" style on the community. It can also apply to how much we have absorbed the norms or expectations of the organization. New staff often usefully shock those who have come to take much of the organization's ways for granted by questioning "how things are done around here."

Third, we need to give ourselves over to the experience of the other as much as we are able to. This means being able to loosen the assumptions and values, our own history, so that we can as much as possible see through another lens. We also need to recognize the assumptions we are making individually and collectively and how these may or may not be relevant. For example, in the group, I was asked about whose car we sat in, the assumption being that if it was my car, I would have more power and if it was Felicity's she would have more power. In fact she suggested we get into my car, so in a sense she had the power of suggesting what we did, rather than whose car being the determinant of greater power.

Fourth, we need to acknowledge the complexities of power. In many ways, I was perceived as being more powerful in this situation. I was from the agency that had power over the community in terms of control over relevant resources and decisions that impacted the lives of many in the community. I also had the implicit power of being white and so part of the dominating culture, and of being a professional seeking to work in what was seen by my organization as a professional way. However, clearly the community could also exert power by simply not being prepared to "work with me." Exploring reflexively encouraged me to think about how power was operating in this situation and how to seek to relinquish power in seeking ways to work together, such as by waiting to hear the community's alternative ideas about how things could be done and by working from their priorities rather than mine.

Finally, reflexivity prompts recognizing the place of emotion. Accepting the feeling of shame meant recognizing how the current community and the department I worked for perpetuated the experience of the Stolen Generations. This created a preparedness to listen to the experience and wisdom of the indigenous community and over time see that their way had much more to offer, to be learned from—for ways of working with not only the indigenous community but also the non-indigenous community.

Implications for Using Reflexivity in Practice

One of the key implications of using reflexivity for me is the value of actively learning from experience and applying this learning to practice. In this example, the learning is from three angles: my learning about my own social constructs, my perspectives, and reactions about my own experience; learning from Felicity and her family's experience, their different constructs and perceptions; and learning from the experience in the car. My practice of critical reflection for myself and with other people has suggested that using a *particular* experience for learning is powerful. Writers who explore learning from experience and using reflection for practice vary in advocating learning from your own experience compared to learning from other people's experience.

Part of what worked for me here was being able to explore an experience in depth, rather than looking at experience in general. For example, I could have raised here the difficulties of engaging with the indigenous community, which would probably have led to a wider discussion and most likely a theoretical discussion about such issues in general. Because I raised this scenario as a particular example of a general issue, it was possible to explore it in greater depth, seeking to understand the specific assumptions and values underlying what was happening. We could look at the specific social constructions that each person in the incident had projected onto the others. Connected to this, and again part of learning from experience, is the emotional content of the example. I chose it or it had come to mind because it had left me feeling moved and humbled and also puzzled about why this had felt like such a pivotal moment. Ideally, I would move to a position where "To be reflexive is to have an ongoing conversation about experience while simultaneously living in the moment" (Hertz, 1997: viii).

The value of practicing critical reflection in a group is also illustrated here. In this example, the group I presented to was able to take me to a new level of understanding through their questions and responses. They asked reflective and reflexive questions, helped identify feelings, thoughts, and perceptions, helped deconstruct and reconstruct, and made links to the social context. It can be hard to do this on your own given that our assumptions and perceptions can be so deeply submerged. Bolton (2001) advocates the use of "a critical group (or co-mentor) to encourage the searching out of material (professional, political, and social texts) from as wide a sphere as possible" (55). However, the group demonstrated the complexity of the participants' own perceptions—the need for all group members to be aware of their own assumptions and constructs. When I talked about being in the car with Felicity, others had strong responses of their own: one expected that I would feel "trapped," another that the car would be a "contemplative space with cleansing rain." The latter was closer to my sense of it as a safe, open space. While both were helpful to react to, this demonstrated the complexity of working in a group and managing everyone's reflexivity.

Using reflexivity also highlighted where my assumptions about practice were inappropriate. Clearly at an interpersonal and group level, my behavior needed to change. I needed to recognize the importance of being with as well as doing with, allowing things to happen at the community's pace, and a more contemplative way of working and of valuing silence. As Parton and O'Byrne (2000) write from a constructionist perspective: "Relational reflexivity leads to joining with people in creating the service they want, and worker and user having a joint say in how their relationship is going or needs to go" (77). It was also important for me to see that the assumptions I and the department had about families and family life were culturally determined and didn't fit the indigenous community's experience. Over time, this recognition contributed to changed policy about services both for the indigenous community and non-indigenous families. The indigenous community's valuing of broader family networks rather than a narrow nuclear family definition, for example, contributed to better family practice in general.

Implications for Reflexivity in Teaching and Supervision

Much of my current practice is teaching social work students. This experience reinforces the value of working from what they know, their own experiences, concerns, and questions in small group work. Other writers have also encouraged students to practice reflexivity using their own experience in journaling or other forms of writing (Bolton, 2001; Le Gallais, 2008). Teaching also indicates the value for students and professionals of hearing from other people's experience. Some writers would suggest, for example, that for students, it might be more appropriate to start with hearing about and reacting to others' experiences (Lehmann, 2006). Rather than perpetuating a dichotomy here, it is more realistic to think that both can work. So what seem to be the important elements?

Clearly in this example, I was already connected to the issue of working with the indigenous community; I was motivated and interested in wanting to understand what was happening in this particular example. Students may not be as connected to a particular issue, but are generally motivated to understand when they can see a connection to their future practice. Experiences in the classroom then need to be explicitly related either to the students' own interests or to their future practice, or ideally both. This could apply to learning the process of reflecting or understanding a specific issue, such as the perspective of a client or consumer. This fits with my experience of using critical reflection to encourage students to explore issues of social diversity. Students were asked to share an incident that illustrated an example of discomfort with an aspect of social difference, then to work with this incident first to understand more deeply where they were coming from and then to explore implications for practice, including the development of principles and processes in working constructively with this social difference. Initially, students found it hard to see how exploring a probably embarrassing issue of their own would help with practice. However, once I had modeled the process and the connections became explicit, they became more enthusiastic about the task.

Academic teaching is often seen as purely an intellectual exercise and one that is about objective knowledge. A reflexive approach generates a different attitude to knowledge: more as "an experience," rather than something "once and for all acquired and possessed" (Forbes, 2008: 449). My experience here demonstrates how practitioners constantly face opportunities for new knowledge. This reinforces the need for reflexivity to be part of ongoing learning in practice in a way that involves the whole person—the emotions or feelings, as well as the mind, the capacity to see the implications of the social and the physical. Training social work practitioners clearly needs to involve recognizing feelings and personal reactions and their impact on the practitioner, as well as the client, community, colleagues, and organizations. Thinking reflexively also generates ideas about how the physical environment will impact learning. Teaching environments are often not ideal for encouraging sharing at depth, the usual rows of desks reinforce the authority of the teacher and academic knowledge. While it is important not to be put off by an environment that can't be changed, it is also important to be proactive about seeking spaces conducive to this kind of learning.

What This Means for Practice Using Social Constructionism

Using this incident has demonstrated the value of being aware of our own assumptions, our perceptions of ourselves and others: we must have the capacity to consider the complexity of the part we play in our reactions with others. The interaction with Felicity shows the power of engaging with deeper levels of understanding how we have been and continue to be shaped by our own experiences and constructions and the social context in which we live. The incident also demonstrates the potential value for the practice of working reflexively, enabling the creation of new and more meaningful knowledge of self and others with the recognition that such knowledge will continue to evolve.

I have partly chosen to use this incident because it illustrates a particular way of working with a social constructionist approach: a way of identifying both where I am coming from and what the differing perspectives of the others involved might be where prevailing cultural values are clearly influential. This is very typical of much of my current work and provides a way of reflecting on practice within a critical framework. The particular incident highlights the need for a *critically informed* approach to social constructionism: the ability to name the social context and what meaning that has for those involved. A critical perspective is also vital for highlighting where there are issues of power and implications for social justice. Without a *critical* approach, the danger in this example is that I might continue to perpetuate the injustices already experienced by Felicity and her family, seeing our perceptions of each other as only individual rather than reflecting the influence of broader social issues, collective history, and culture. Bowers' (2005) views about the validity of cultural knowledge and history are relevant here: the need to acknowledge that there is a shared understanding of history and of cultural knowledge, as well as individual socially constructed perspectives. The indigenous community's knowledge of the importance of what in Western culture would be called extended family is vital here, as well as understanding that those who are indigenous would vary in how they felt and what they thought about this knowledge and how they wanted to use it. Holding these different perspectives together in a creative tension is more useful than a more modernist approach of valuing one or the other.

The incident also illustrates both the value and the challenge of using a social constructionist perspective in managing the complexities of working in organizations. Workers need to understand that each person in the organization will have their own understanding or sense of meaning of a particular situation. Clearly, how I was perceived outside the organization was influenced by how the department I worked for was viewed. Within the department, I also had to contend with the differing social perceptions of the indigenous community, from almost exclusively non-indigenous staff, often with limited understanding of indigenous issues. Having a social constructionist understanding can encourage naming of these different perceptions in a way that enables different kinds of discussions: simply acknowledging, for example, that there are many points of view. In this particular incident, naming such differences, including cultural differences, led, over time, to changes in perception and to changes in policies and programs. The Department recognized that it had a very narrow Western view of how to define families and that the indigenous community had a significantly different view. This had clear connections to policy: If the extended family was the "real" family as opposed to the Western nuclear family, children could well move from family member to family member without this being experienced as disruption in the way it might be defined in Western culture.

Changing such views took time and education: This meant valuing the cultural knowledge and history of the indigenous community and their ability to communicate, and teaching it to departmental workers. A critically informed social constructionist view encouraged me to maintain an attitude that it was important to persevere.

One of the challenges of coming from a perspective that says there are many points of view is that this is not necessarily valued by organizations experiencing pressure to be outcome focused or "evidence-based" according to narrow funding guidelines. However, there does seem to be increasing interest in other ways of thinking that are congruent with social constructionism such as the idea of the learning organization or organizational learning, essentially the view that "learning incorporates the broad dynamics of adaptation, change and environmental alignment of organizations, takes place across multiple levels within an organization, and involves the construction and reconstruction of meaning and world views within the organization" (Gould, 2004: 1). Such an approach, which is also aligned with reflective practice or critical reflection, allows for different ways of perceiving organizational life and life outside the organization.

The use of critical reflection in supervision is a means of fostering such organizational learning. Much of my current practice of working with organizations is in running monthly supervision groups and in training those in health and welfare organizations to use critical reflection in their practice and supervision. One of the current tensions for many workers, reflecting the expectations for their organizations, is the pressure to work in a more task-oriented, outcome-focused way (Gardner, 2006). Supervision in such settings can also be very task focused, with individual workers having little emotional support or opportunity to explore the complexity of their experience. This can, in turn, lead to a sense of disillusionment and low rates of retention in such agencies as child protection (Gibbs, 2002). Fostering the use of critical reflection in supervision enables workers to have a safe space within which to explore and identify the social constructions they and their clients may be making: to look reflexively and critically at their and others' assumptions and values. Workers are able to do the kind of work demonstrated in my incident above, which enables them to both work more effectively with their clients and also to work strategically within their organization to seek change. Although such work can be challenging in one sense—it's easier to think there is a solution that will fit all—ultimately working in a way that reflects fundamental values is more rewarding for workers.

Conclusion

My experience suggests that the processes of critically reflecting can help social workers identify social constructions in a way that also recognizes their implicit values and the influence of social context. Practice is never value free, and critically informed social constructionism encourages recognition and naming of what is implicit in the prevailing culture that can perpetuate injustice for individuals and communities, as well as affirming the importance of working in a socially just way. What that means in a particular context will vary, and as the incident used here demonstrates, requires those involved to be prepared to unearth assumptions, values, and perspectives in a way that means new, socially just possibilities emerge.

Notes

1. What I mean by deconstruction here is looking for the underlying meaning in both what I and others say and what we would do. Often, of course, there are many meanings, many ways of constructing what is happening at emotional, physical, and social levels. The language used also needs to be examined carefully: Do we mean the same things in the words and phrases we use and the ways we use them. Deconstruction is also used here as the first stage of exploring a particular experience: seeking to understand at deeper levels the constructs, assumptions, and meanings of what is happening. Once this is understood, it is possible to move to a second stage of reconstructing: exploring how the same incident can be perceived differently—and how understanding the incident more deeply might mean that future perceptions of similar experiences would be differently constructed.

2. I am conscious that in writing about this experience I have benefitted from exploring it as part of a critically reflective process. I had previously used this example in some critical reflection workshops, particularly those focusing on social difference. This experience emerged again at a Transforming Social Work Conference conducted by the Global Partnership for Transformative Social Work (www.gptsw.net) in a group exploring reflexivity in critical reflection. The group decided to use the example to experience a critical reflection process in action. I will concentrate on the findings from this experience and would like to acknowledge the group's contribution.

3. I have changed the details of this for confidentiality.

4. This information about the Stolen Generations comes from the ReconiliACTION Web site: http://reconciliaction.org.au/nsw/education-kit/stolen-generation. It explores the policy of forcibly removing Aboriginal and Torres Strait Islander (indigenous) children from their families. These children became known as the Stolen Generations.

   The forced removal of Aboriginal and Torres Strait Islander children from their families was official government policy from 1909 to 1969. However, the practice took place both before and after this period. Governments, churches, and welfare bodies all took part. The removal policy was managed by the

Aborigines Protection Board (APB). The APB was a government board established in 1909 with the power to remove children without parental consent and without a court order.

Under the White Australia and assimilation policies, Aboriginal and Torres Strait Islander people who were "not of full blood" were encouraged to become assimilated into the broader society so that eventually there would be no more indigenous people left. At the time indigenous people were seen as an inferior race. Children were taken from Aboriginal parents so they could be brought up "white" and taught to reject their Aboriginality.

Children were placed with institutions and, from the 1950s, were also placed with white families. Aboriginal children were expected to become laborers or servants, so in general the education they were provided was very poor. Aboriginal girls in particular were sent to homes established by the Board to be trained in domestic service.

The lack of understanding and respect for Aboriginal people also meant that many people who supported child removal believed that they were doing the "right thing." Some people believed that Aboriginal people lived poor and unrewarding lives, and that institutions would provide a positive environment in which Aboriginal people could better themselves. The dominant racist views in the society and government also meant that people believed that Aboriginal people were bad parents and that Aboriginal woman did not look after their children.

No one knows how many children were taken, as most records have been lost or destroyed. Many parents whose children were taken never saw them again, and siblings who were taken were deliberately separated from each other. Today many Aboriginal people still do not know who their relatives are or have been unable to track them down. The generations of children who were taken from their families became known as the Stolen Generations. The practice of removing children continued up until the late 1960s meaning today there are Aboriginal people as young as their late thirties and forties who are members of the Stolen Generations.

5. When I explored this incident in a workshop, one of the participants asked why in the car? What was it about the rain? What was it about the time or timing? The responses to these questions have to be individual although they will also be influenced by the social context.

References

Allan, J., B. Pease, and L. Briskman (2003). *Critical social work: An introduction to theories and practices*. Melbourne, Australia: Allen & Unwin.

Bolton, G. (2001). *Reflective practice: Writing and professional development.* London: Paul Chapman Sage.

Bowers, C. A. (2005). *The false promises of constructivist theories of learning a global and ecological critique.* New York: Peter Lang.

Brookfield, S. D. (2005). *The power of critical theory: Liberating adult learning and teaching.* San Francisco: Jossey-Bass.

Fook, J. (2002). *Social work: Critical theory and practice.* London: Sage.

Fook, J. and F. Gardner. (2007). *Practising critical reflection: A resource handbook.* Maidenhead, UK: Open University Press.

Forbes, J. (2008). Reflexivity in professional doctoral research. *Reflective Practice,* 9(4): 449–60.

Francis, D. (1997). Critical incident analysis: a strategy for developing critical practice. *Teachers and Teaching: theory and practice,* 3(2): 169–188.

Freshwater, D. (2002). Guided reflection in the context of post-modern practice. In C. Johns (Ed.), *Guided reflection advancing practice* (pp. 225–38). Oxford: Blackwell.

Gardner, F. (2006). *Working in human service organizations: Creating connections for practice.* Melbourne, Australia: Oxford University Press.

Gibbs, J. (2002). *Sink or Swim: Changing the story of child protection: A study of the crisis in recruitment and retention of staff in rural Victoria.* PhD Thesis in Social Work and Social Policy. Bundoora, Australia: La Trobe University.

Gould, N. (2004). The learning organization and reflective practice—the emergence of a concept. In N. A. Gould and M. Baldwin (Eds.), *The learning organization and reflective practice–The emergence of a concept.* Aldershot, UK: Ashgate.

Hertz, R. (1997). *Reflexivity and voice.* Thousand Oaks, CA: Sage.

Ife, J. (1999). Postmodernism, critical theory and social work. In B. Pease and J. Fook (Eds.), *Transforming social work practice,* (pp. 211–23). St. Leonards, Australia: Allen & Unwin.

Iversen, R. I., K. J. Gergen, and R. P. Fairbanks (2005). Assessment and social construction: Conflict or co-creation? *British Journal of Social Work,* 35: 689–708.

Johns, C. (2002). *Guided reflection advancing practice.* Oxford: Blackwell.

Johnson, Y. M. and S. Munch (2009). Fundamental contradictions in cultural competence. *Social Work,* 54: 220–32.

Kondrat, M. E. (2002). Actor-centered social work: Re-visioning "person-in-environment" through a critical theory lens. *Social Work,* 47: 435–49.

Le Gallais, T. (2008). Wherever I go there I am: Reflections on reflexivity and the research stance. *Reflective Practice,* 9(2): 145–55.

Lehmann, J. (2006). Telling stories. . . . and the pursuit of critical reflection. In S.White, J. Fook, and F. Gardner (Eds.), *Critical reflection in health and social care,* (pp. 201–12). Buckingham, UK: Open University Press.

Parton, N. (2007). Social work practice in an age of uncertainty. In S. L. Witkin and D. Saleeby (Eds.), *Social work dialogues transforming the canon in inquiry, practice, and education,* (pp. 144–66). Alexandria, VA: CSWE Press.

Parton, N. and P. O'Byrne (2000). *Constructive social work.* London: Macmillan Press.

Roche, S. E. (2007). Postmodern call and response: Social work education in the modernist university. In S. L. Witkin and D. Saleeby (Eds.), *Social work dialogues transforming the canon in inquiry, practice, and education,* (pp. 299–325). Alexandria, VA: CSWE Press.

Rolfe, G., D. Freshwater, and M. Jasper (2001). *Critical reflection for nursing and the helping professions: A user's guide.* Basingstoke, UK: Palgrave.

Schon, D. (1983). *The reflective practitioner: How professionals think in action.* New York: Basic.

Taylor, C. and S. White (2000). *Practising reflexivity in health and welfare: Making knowledge.* Buckingham, UK: Open University Press.

Taylor, C. (2006). Practising reflexivity: Narrative, reflection and the moral order. In S. White, J. Fook, and F. Gardner (Eds.), *Critical reflection in health and social care,* (pp. 73–88). Buckingham, UK: Open University Press.

White, J. (2008). Family therapy. In M. Davies (Ed.), *Blackwell companion to social work,* (pp. 175–183). Oxford: Blackwell.

White, S. (2006). Unsettling reflections: The reflexive practitioner as 'trickster' in interprofessional work. In S. White, J. Fook, and F. Gardner (Eds.), *Critical reflection in health and social care,* (pp. 21–39). Buckingham, UK: Open University Press.

White, S., J. Fook, and F. Gardner (Eds.) (2006).*Critical reflection in health and social care.* Buckingham, UK: Open University Press.

Witkin, S. L. (1999). Constructing our future. *Social Work, 44:* 5–8.

Wood, G. G. and Tully, C. T. (2006). *The structural approach to direct practice in social work.* New York: Columbia University Press.

6

Thinking and Acting Constructively in Child Protection

NIGEL PARTON

My introduction to social constructionist ideas was very much theoretical and, primarily, sociological via my introduction to the book by Peter Berger and Thomas Luckmann (1966) called *The Social Construction of Reality: A Treatise in the Sociology of Knowledge*. This came towards the end of my social work degree in 1973 when studying a course on social work organizations. One of the key texts was by David Silverman (1970), which provided a very demanding tour of different theoretical perspectives on organizations, in which he outlined an "action frame of reference" and which drew heavily on *The Social Construction of Reality*. A small group of us were determined to try and make sense of the book, and I am not going to pretend we found any of it easy! Increasingly, however, I found the book opened up a way of seeing the world that has informed my thinking and practice ever since. In fact, as the years have gone by, I have found the insights provided by Berger and Luckmann ever more helpful. In particular, the discussions of the relationship between the individual and society and the thorny issue of "agency" and "structure" have tremendously helped me understand the nature of social work and opened up creative ways of thinking and acting for me.

As I understood it, Berger and Luckmann took issue with images of society that dominated social theory in the postwar period and which they saw as excessively rationalistic and functional, giving little room for human agency. They were concerned that most social theories had become overly concerned with explaining the impersonal laws of social order rather than how social order was an outcome of social action.

They set themselves two tasks. First, drawing on phenomenological philosophy, they used a range of concepts in order to frame everyday life as a fluid, multiple, precariously negotiated achievement in interaction. Second, they provided a general theory of the social origins and maintenance of social institutions. Their principal thesis was that individuals in interaction create social worlds through their linguistic, symbolic activity for the purpose of providing coherence and purpose to an essentially open-ended, unformed human existence. Society is neither a system, nor a mechanism, nor an organism; it is a symbolic construct composed of ideas, meanings, and language, which is all the time changing through human action while also imposing both constraints and possibilities on human actors. They saw the relationship between the individual and society as operating in two ways: human beings continually construct the world, which then becomes a reality to which they must respond. In acting in the world, we construct and *externalize* phenomena, which then take on an *objective* reality of their own and which then are *internalized* by us and thus play a key role in the processes of externalization. In this way, the relationship between the individual and society is seen as a dialectic process. Thus, while we are always acting and thereby constructing and changing the world and ourselves, we do so in the context of the institutions and frameworks of meaning handed down by previous generations.

This approach emphasizes the *processes* through which both individuals define themselves and their environments together with the processes whereby social institutions are themselves created. It encourages us to *problematize* the "obvious" and the "taken for granted"; it challenges the view that conventional knowledge is neutral and unbiased and asks us to recognize that the categories we use to make sense of and operate in the world are historically and culturally specific, and therefore vary over time and place, and subject to change. The approach provides a way of relating to the world whereby creative spaces for analysis and intervention are continually opened up.

I have drawn on such thinking over the years to try and make sense of and develop critical analyses and positive interventions at both the policy and day-to-day practice levels. I will look at each in turn.

Thinking and Acting Constructively in Child Protection

The Politics of Child Abuse

When I started as a social worker, the department was experiencing considerable change following the introduction of the newly established departments of social services in April 1971 and the reorganization of local government in England in April 1974. Even so, I felt an excitement and optimism associated with the explicit recognition that social service departments were now large and significant players in local authorities and that the profession of social work was key to its operation and development. It was as if social work had come of age. However, as I commented in the Preface to *The Politics of Child Abuse* (Parton, 1985: ix):

> the period was punctuated by an event which generated enormous interest in, and debate about, social work and social workers, and which seemed of a different order to anything that had happened before—certainly in recent history. It felt as if the death of Maria Colwell[1] and the subsequent inquiry had an impact on social work well beyond the more specific concerns about protecting children from cruel parents, a responsibility which child care officers were well accustomed to.

I was very conscious that the public inquiry into the tragic death of Maria Colwell (Secretary of State, 1974) was not only an inquiry into the way this particular case was (mis)handled but was, in effect, a public inquiry into the newly emerging profession of social work itself and which had seemed to be found so wanting. Rapidly and dramatically, social work and child abuse had become issues of considerable media, and public and political interest and concern (Franklin and Parton, 1991); this has continued ever since (Franklin and Parton, 2001). It was as if the optimism evident in social work had been dealt a major blow by one significant event and policy makers, managers, and practitioners were required to rethink and reorder their priorities and the ways they worked in the light of the new procedures, guidelines, and training that were being introduced. Social workers were being required to take the lead responsibility for responding to a newly discovered social problem—child abuse—which required new skills, new forms of intervention, and new organizational arrangements to deal with it.

However, I was uneasy about what was happening to both clients and social workers. I was especially concerned that the nature of this new problem did not seem as clear-cut and self-evident, as was suggested in most of the training and practice procedures and guidelines that were made avail-able at the time. Nor was I convinced that many of the new policies and practices that were being introduced were as humane as was assumed. They seemed to have a number of unintended consequences that were deleterious for all concerned—not least for many of the children and par-ents who were on the receiving end of the changes being introduced. In-creasingly, I felt the need to develop a more critical analysis of what was happening with the hope of formulating new insights and perspectives as the basis for developing new ideas for taking policy and practice forward.

I wrote *The Politics of Child Abuse* to engage with these issues. The mate-rial was organized into two parts: Part One, *The History*; and Part Two, *A Critique*. Part One built on earlier work (Parton, 1979; 1981) and was con-cerned with trying to explain why the problem of child abuse had emerged as such a crucial one for welfare practitioners from the early 1970s on-wards, what the nature of the problem was, how this had changed, and what the implications were for policy and practice. The analysis drew upon perspectives and concepts developed in the sociological study of social problems since the early 1960s in the United States but which had rarely been used for the analysis of social problems in the United Kingdom. The starting point was that we cannot begin to understand the nature of child abuse without analyzing the nature of the category itself, how this had been constructed and then recognized as a social problem requiring state intervention. The approach offered by Fuller and Myers in 1941 was found instructive, where they differentiated between social problems as *objective conditions* and social problems as *subjective definitions*.

> A social problem is a condition which is defined by a considerable num-ber of persons as a deviation from some social norm which they cherish. Every social problem thus consists of an *objective condition* and a *sub-jective definition*. The objective condition is a verifiable situation, which can be checked as to existence and magnitude (proportions) by impartial and trained observers. The subjective definition is the awareness of cer-tain individuals that the condition is a threat to certain cherished values (Fuller and Myers, 1941, 320, *original emphasis*).

While Fuller and Myers did suggest that the existence of objective con-ditions is insufficient on its own for a phenomenon to be recognized as a social problem, they stopped short of arguing that objective conditions are neither necessary nor sufficient. Yet as Blumer (1971) and Spector and Kitsuse (1973) subsequently argued, a concern with what might constitute the objective conditions may deflect attention from what they felt should be the central focus of the sociological study of social problems—to account for the emergence, maintenance, history, and conceptualization of what is defined as a social problem and what should be done about it. The publication of Spector and Kitsuse's *Constructing Social Problems* in 1977 proved to be something of a watershed in establishing social constructionist approaches as the dominant, though controversial, perspective in the sociological study of social problems in the United States (see for example Holstein and Miller, 1993; Miller and Holstein, 1993). It was this social constructionist approach to social problems that was the primary influence upon the approach to Part One of *The Politics of Child Abuse*.

My empirical work was based on an extensive search for and analysis of published material, including research and policy statements, on child abuse, or "the battered baby syndrome" and "non-accidental injury" to children, as it was usually referred to in the 1960s and 1970s in England. It also included content analysis of newspaper coverage and interviews with a number of key informants who had played important roles in policy and practice developments on the issue in England during the period. It became clear that the key development in the modern "(re)discovery" of child abuse in the 1960s was the publication of the paper by Henry Kempe and his colleagues in Denver, Colorado, in the *Journal of the American Medical Association* in 1962 on "the battered child syndrome."

Clearly the term had been specifically chosen in order to appeal to as wide an audience as possible, including relevant professionals, particularly pediatricians. There was no reference to any possible legal, social, or deviancy implications of the phenomenon—the problem was *medicalized*, so that doctors and medical technologies, for example the use of the X-ray to identify old and otherwise hidden injuries, were seen as key to identifying and *diagnosing* the problem. Not only did the issue receive wide coverage in the United States, but it also attracted the attention of a number of pediatricians in England, as well as the NSPCC (the National Society for Prevention of Cruelty to Children), which in 1968 set up the Battered Child Research Unit to carry out research on the problem and bring it to the attention of professionals in the child care field.

However, I demonstrated that it was the public inquiry into the death of Maria Colwell (Secretary of State, 1974) which was to prove crucial in mobilizing public, professional, political, and, crucially, media concern about the issue, thus establishing it as a major social problem. What became apparent was that it was not so much the death of Maria that attracted attention, outside the local area of Brighton where she lived, but the inquiry which was to transform the case into something of a *cause célèbre* and a national scandal of significant proportions. For example, *The Times* newspaper had very little coverage of either Maria's death or the case prior to the announcement of the public inquiry on May 25, 1973. Between October 10, 1973, when the inquiry opened, and December 7, when it closed, *The Times* carried 320 paragraphs on the inquiry and the problem more generally. This was primarily concerned with providing a detailed coverage of the evidence to the inquiry and more general comment. There was coverage on forty-three days between those dates. The publication of the final report the following year also attracted considerable space (see *The Times*, September 5, 1974) and included 112 paragraphs of the main editorial comment, a summary of the report, and comment articles. The inquiry was as much, if not more, about the failures of health and welfare professionals—particularly social workers—as it was about child abuse per se. In many ways, the inquiry is best characterized as an inquiry into social work policy and practice and in the process catapulted social work into the public spotlight in a way that had never happened before. From this point on in England, the *problem* of child abuse and the *problem* of social work were to be seen and experienced as closely interrelated.

I also tried to demonstrate how these developments could be related to a more general social anxiety that seemed to be developing about the decline of the family, the growth of violence, and concerns that inadequate families and innocent victims were being let down by "woolly do-gooders"—particularly social workers. All of which reflected and fed into changes in the economy and the (welfare) state, which were to become even more significant later in the decade. In the process, I argued that the way the problem was socially constructed depended on a very particular set of assumptions and explanations. The "disease model," as I called it, with its emphasis on individualized identification, prevention, and treatment, was to prove dominant in influencing the way the problem was understood and influencing what was seen as the most appropriate way of responding.

The focus of Part Two of *The Politics of Child Abuse* was to develop a critical analysis of the disease model and outline alternative approaches. I attempted to make the underlying values and assumptions of the model explicit, together with its inadequacies at the conceptual and empirical levels. In this model, child abuse was conceptualized as a pathological phenomenon with its roots in the personality or character of the abusing parent. Social factors were only seen in terms of the characteristics associated with abusive individuals or families. In effect, the model ignored social arrangements and denied that social and economic factors played any significant part. A major focus of Part Two was to draw attention to social context in two ways. First, drawing on a range of secondary data from this country and the United States, it underlined the link between social inequality, poverty, and child abuse. It argued that the stresses, frustrations, and lack of opportunities, for some parents, were major factors in explaining why the incidence of abuse was so much more concentrated in the most deprived sections of society. I argued that the traditional concentration on dangerous individuals failed to consider the significance of dangerous conditions. Second, I argued that this focus on individual causes and manifestations of abuse failed to recognize the way in which the non-individualistic practices of industrial, corporate, and government agencies could and did cause harm to children but in ways which were never defined as child abuse. In effect, arguments about the nature, causes, and consequences of abuse had ignored abuse at the institutional and structural levels.

At the time of publication, *The Politics of Child Abuse* was seen by many as a challenging but somewhat peripheral critique of contemporary policy and practice. However, this was to change as the second half of the 1990s witnessed a major debate in the United Kingdom concerned with "the refocusing of children's services" (see Parton, 1997). The debate was primarily prompted by the publication by the Audit Commission of its report *Seen But Not Heard: Coordinating Child Health and Social Services for Children in Need*, in 1994, and the publication by the Department of Health, the following year, of *Child Protection: Messages from Research*. The latter summarized the findings from 20 recently completed research studies on child protection practice (the majority commissioned by the Department of Health) and their implications for policy and practice. It was to prove key in prompting a major rethink of the most appropriate ways to respond to concerns about child abuse in England since the Maria Colwell case.

The definition of child abuse, or child maltreatment as it was called in *Messages from Research*, is of particular interest. Rather than fall back on more traditional approaches it argued that child abuse was a socially constructed phenomenon, and quoted one of the research studies (Gibbons, Conroy, and Bell, 1995, 12) that:

> Child maltreatment is not the same sort of phenomena as whooping cough; it cannot be diagnosed with scientific measuring instruments. It is more like pornography, *a socially constructed phenomenon* which reflects the values and opinions of particular times (DH, 15, *emphasis added*).

In fact, the study by Gibbons, Conroy, and Bell (1995) referenced *The Politics of Child Abuse* to support and legitimate such a position. It seemed that social constructionist perspectives had moved center stage and that *The Politics of Child Abuse* was implicated in this.

However, there were more fundamental ways in which some of the central themes in *The Politics of Child Abuse* became reflected in emerging developments. Many of the concerns about child protection practice that were first articulated in *Messages from Research* formed the basis of central government guidance in *Working Together to Safeguard Children* (DH et al., 1999; HM Government, 2006). Again, this reflected many of the central arguments in *The Politics of Child Abuse*. It stated that the government wished to shift the balance in the provision of children's services and aimed to promote the central message that child protection work must be placed firmly within the context of wider services for children in need and that children should not be routed inappropriately into the child protection system in order to gain access to services. It argued that many families who find themselves enmeshed in the child protection system suffered multiple disadvantages and that they needed help at an earlier stage to tackle their problems. The approach was based on a "social stress" model of child abuse, whereby it was assumed that if the stresses can be addressed at an earlier stage, child abuse can be averted. Child abuse was conceptualized as lying along a "continuum," so that service responses should be differentiated to meet different levels and types of "need" and the form of intervention should recognize different thresholds of intervention. This assumes that the provision of family support at an earlier stage will not only prevent parents maltreating their children, but that it would divert many cases away from the formalized child protection system. In effect *child abuse* becomes a subset within the overall continuum of *children in need*.

While I was sympathetic to much of what such a refocusing aimed to achieve, I also had some fundamental questions and concerns about some of the changes being introduced. In part these arose from my growing uneasiness about some of the analyses originally developed in *The Politics of Child Abuse*; I now consider these problems to lie at the heart of some of my concerns about the attempts to refocus children's services in England from the late 1990s onwards.

I had become aware that *The Politics of Child Abuse* was inadequate in three major respects: its failure to address sexual abuse; its difficulties in taking into account the dimension of gender; and, perhaps most crucially, its silence in relation to children (Parton, 1990). First, in concentrating the analysis on the ways the problem of child abuse and responses to it had been constructed, I had given insufficient attention to the causes of the original (abusive) behavior and, therefore, to the impact on the child. Second, while helpful in demonstrating the possible relationship between physical abuse and neglect and wider issues of poverty and social deprivation, I had difficulty explaining why abuse occurred in middle-class and affluent families. And, third, I had real difficulty in accounting for sexual abuse, which has little clear relationship with poverty and social deprivation but does have a clear relationship with gender. While a social stress model may be appropriate to develop our understanding of physical abuse and neglect, it has serious flaws in relation to sexual abuse. Thus, in the same way that I have identified significant difficulties in the analysis in *The Politics of Child Abuse*, I have also identified a number of similar problems with current central government guidance as it attempts to operationalize the refocusing of children's services in terms of family support in England (Parton and Wattam, 1999).

Governing the Family

At the time of writing *The Politics of Child Abuse*, the issue of child sexual abuse had barely entered the public and political domains; however, this was quickly to change with the events in Cleveland in the north east of England in mid-1987, which prompted the Secretary of State to set up a major public inquiry, published the following year (Secretary of State, 1988).[2] This was to be a major focus for *Governing the Family* (Parton, 1991). In some respects, *Governing the Family* can be read as simply taking further the story and analysis in *The Politics of Child Abuse*. In other respects, however, it is rather different because, during the late 1980s, a major shift had been taking place in the way the state aimed to prevent harm to children. Rather than focus almost exclusively upon trying to prevent *child abuse* as previously, it now seemed the focus was on a new activity—*child protection*—where the latter tries to combine attempts to protect children from danger while also trying to protect the privacy of the family from unwarrantable state interventions. The aim of *Governing the Family* was to try to understand the nature of these changes.

As I argued in the Preface to *Governing the Family*, in order to make sense of these changes, a rather different conceptual and analytic toolkit was required compared to that used in *The Politics of Child Abuse*:

> Rather than being centrally concerned with analysing the emergence and impact of the problem of *child abuse* as previously, I am here concerned with, on the one hand, discussing a broader range of legal, regulatory, and interventive strategies, while on the other, analysing in some detail the debates, recommendations for reform and the processes of policy change. The book therefore combines both a different conceptual framework and a closer attention to detail in order to explain the emergence of a new discourse focused around notions of child protection and family autonomy (Parton, 1991: ix).

I wanted to understand and explain how certain issues in child welfare in England in the 1980s had been framed in various public and official documents and debates. How were the problems conceived, and what were seen as the best ways of addressing these? In particular, I was keen to identify the key discourses that were being developed to explain and address the problems and the processes whereby these were "made up" and constituted. Again I was involved with interviewing key informants and analyzing newspaper coverage and a whole range of policy documents and inquiry reports as before, but this time it was combined with a more detailed analysis of a range of internal government and pressure group records and discussion papers and a close reading of *Hansard*, the verbatim record of parliamentary debates and committees at Westminster (the U.K. parliament). This time, however, rather than draw only on social constructionist approaches derived from the sociology of social problems, the study was much more influenced by the approaches developed by Michel Foucault (1977; 1991) and Jacques Donzelot (1980) in terms of their analysis of discourse, the "tutelary complex," and the nature of "the social," together with the work of a number of post-Foucaldian scholars working in England, particularly Nikolas Rose (1993) and Peter Miller (Miller and Rose, 1990) who were analyzing the contemporary changing nature of government policy.

Miller and Rose (1990) suggested that an analysis of policy should give primary attention to *discourse* in two respects. First, policy should be located in discussions about what is conceived as the proper ends and means of government and how these are articulated. Second, discourse should be seen as the technology of thought, whereby particular devices of writing, listing, numbering, and computing, for example, make an issue into a knowable, calculable, and administrative object. It was through certain procedures that the "objects" of the family, child welfare, and child abuse were presented in a form that made them amenable for intervention and regulation. Language provided a key mechanism whereby policies and practices are represented, refined, and made subject to action.

The central argument I developed in *Governing the Family* was that the period had witnessed important changes in the relationships and hierarchies of authority between different agencies and professionals in key areas of decision making. While at the time of its modern (re)emergence in the 1960s, child abuse was constituted as essentially a socio-medical problem, where the expertise of doctors was seen as key, from the late 1980s onwards, it was constituted as a socio-legal problem, where legal expertise took preeminence and where the issues were framed in terms of child protection. Whereas previously the concern was with diagnosing, curing, and preventing the "disease" or "syndrome," increasingly the emphasis became investigating, assessing, and weighing "forensic evidence." While social workers and social service departments continued to be seen as the lead agency throughout the period, the focus and priorities of both their work and that of other charitable and statutory agencies in the child welfare field had been reconfigured as a result.

I concluded that the contemporary discourse of child protection could be characterized in terms of its emphasis on the need to investigate and differentiate cases of "high risk," in a context in which notions of working together were set out in increasingly complex yet prescriptive procedural guidelines and in which the work was framed by a narrow emphasis on legalism and the need for forensic evidence. Such a characterization was further substantiated in a subsequent collaborative study, based on secondary analysis of social work files (see Parton, Thorpe, and Wattam, 1997), where it was established that the overriding concern of child welfare practitioners was to try and identify high-risk cases, differentiate these from the rest, and allocate resources accordingly. The research and analysis I carried out for *Governing the Family* also helped me clarify and identify what I came to see as the central tensions that lie at the core of child protection policy and practice. For the question which has to be continually addressed, and which has been a central issue for the liberal state since the mid-nineteenth century, is how can we devise a legal basis for the power to intervene into the privacy of the family to protect children which does not convert a sizeable proportion of families into clients of the state? Such a problem is posed by the contradictory demands of, on the one hand, ensuring that the family is experienced by its members as autonomous and the primary sphere for rearing children, while on the other recognizing a need for intervention in some families in which they are seen as failing in this primary task and in a context in which such laws are supposed to act as the general norms applicable to all. However, the way these challenges are responded to varies at different times and in different jurisdictions. These are significant issues for liberalism, and thus illustrate why they are so sensitive and potentially volatile politically as well as personally and professionally. For liberalism is based on a vision of society in which government is based on the exercise of freedom and in which the relationship between liberty and discipline, freedom and rule, while interdependent, is subject to continual renegotiation and fine balancing. I have subsequently analyzed these issues and their implications in greater detail, including the strategic significance of the idea of risk—its assessment, monitoring, and management—and why it had become so central to policy and practice (Parton, 1996; 1999).

(Post)Modernity, Social Theory, and Social Work

My interest in analyzing the changes in thinking, policy, and practice in relation to child abuse and child protection was, in part, informed by my parallel interest in trying to understand the changing nature and role of social work. Perhaps one of my underlying assumptions throughout has been that the changes in social work in the United Kingdom over the past thirty years have been so intimately related to the issue of child abuse, that in order to understand the former an analysis of the latter is key. Engaging in these projects, I have drawn on a number of ideas and conceptual frameworks derived from social constructionism and social theory. During the 1990s, I pursued these ideas even more explicitly in terms of how a number of debates and developments in social theory might contribute to our understanding of social work directly rather than only through my discussions of child abuse.

The paper which first outlined the possibilities of such analyses (Parton, 1994a) drew upon the theoretical framework and key concepts used in *Governing the Family* but refined to take account of my growing interest in social theory with debates about postmodernity. The discussion of postmodernity and social work was further developed in another paper published the same year (Parton, 1994b). The rationale for developing these ideas about postmodernity were made explicit a few years later.

> Our argument is that such debates provide important insights into helping us to understand and conceptualize contemporary social work in a way which can inform practice itself (Parton and Marshall, 1998, 240).

While *postmodern* perspectives are primarily united by a number of cultural projects that proclaim a commitment to heterogeneity, fragmentation, and difference, it is perhaps their critiques of *modernity* that have proved most influential and contentious. Modernity, as a summary term, is seen to refer to the cluster of social, economic, and political systems that emerged in the West with the Enlightenment in the late-eighteenth century. Unlike the premodern, modernity assumed that human order is neither natural nor God-given, but is vulnerable and contingent. However, by the development and application of science, nature could be subject to human control. The distinguishing features of modernity are seen to be: the understanding of history as having a definite and progressive direction; the attempt to develop universal categories of experience; the idea that reason can provide a basis for all activities; and that the nation state could coordinate and advance such developments for the whole society. The two crucial elements of modernity in the post-Enlightenment period are thus seen to be the progressive union of scientific objectivity and politico-economic rationality. In the modern frame, the goal is to produce knowledge about a chosen aspect of the physical or social world by which we can claim greater certainty. At that point we can confer a sense of truth about that knowledge, and also confer on the people producing knowledge (for example, scientists or professionals) the status of holders-of-truth, and thus experts about that aspect of the world. As David Howe (1994) has suggested, social work was in many ways a child of modernity.

Increasingly, however, in social work and elsewhere, it seemed to me that we were now inhabiting a world that had become disoriented, disturbed, and subject to doubt. The pursuit of order and control, the promotion of calculability, belief in progress, science, and rationality, and other features so intrinsic to modernity were being undermined. In part this is related to the major social, economic, and cultural transformations that have characterized recent times in terms of globalization, the increasing significance of media, and the widening networks of information technology that transform and transmit knowledge, the changes in modes of consumption and production, and the increased awareness of risk and uncertainty.

More fundamentally, however, it is related to changing notions of ontology (who we are and our sense of being) and epistemology (how we know what we know). It seems that modernity's promise to deliver order, certainty, and security has been unfulfilled and, increasingly, it is believed there are no transcendental and universal criteria of truth (science), judgment (ethics), and taste (aesthetics). The rejection of the idea that any one theory or system of belief can ever reveal the truth, and the emphasis on the plurality of truth and "the will to truth," captures some of the essential elements associated with postmodernity. Following Smart, postmodernity, for me, means "living without guarantee, without security and order and with contingency and ambivalence. To put it another way, it means living without illusions and with uncertainty" (Smart, 1999, 16). It was almost as if we were having to come to terms with the full implications of living in and relating to a "socially constructed" world where nothing could be taken for granted.

Postmodernity can thus be characterized by the fragmentation of modernity into forms of institutional pluralism, marked by increasing awareness of difference, contingency, relativism, and ambivalence—all of which modernity sought (and claimed) to have overcome. It is this constant and growing questioning of modern approaches and modern resolutions that I have argued is symptomatic of the postmodern condition; the conception of postmodernity as the condition of modernity coming to its senses, emancipated from false consciousness, is seen as key (Bauman, 1992). Truth thus now takes the guise of "truth" and is centered neither in God's word (as in the premodern) nor in human reason (as in the modern) but is de-centered and localized so that many truths are possible, depending on different times and different places. In the postmodern, there is thus a considerable destabilization of a core assumption of modernism—that the way something is represented closely reflects its underlying reality. For if nothing is inherently or immutably true, nothing is inherently or immutably real. In a world in which everything is increasingly mediated and relayed via complex systems of representation, the symbols that are used have a life of their own and take on their meaning, not on the basis of what reality they are meant to represent, but the context in which they are used.

Thus, and as with social construction, an understanding of language is central to approaches which are sympathetic to the postmodern, for instead of merely being a tool that points to objects, language is seen as mediating everything that is known. Far from having a separate existence, reality is seen as embedded in interpretation so that "truth" is a product of language not reality. An understanding of the part that language plays in the formation of human selves, human thought, and human subjectivity thus underpins postmodern perspectives.

In developing and applying some of these ideas to social work, while I was of the view they could be very suggestive in casting light on the current state of social work and possible ways forward, I was also very conscious of some major potential pitfalls. In particular, such approaches could introduce an unacceptable level of relativism and nihilism into social work, which would have the effect of undermining the enterprise altogether. Further, while it may provide important deconstructive analyses of practice, it is possible that it might never offer anything of a positive nature.

It is in this context that I have found the work of Rosenau (1992) valuable. She has delineated two broad orientations within postmodernism: the *skeptical* postmodernists and the *affirmative* postmodernists. She argues that the *skeptical* postmodernists offer a distrustful, pessimistic, negative, gloomy assessment of contemporary times characterized by fragmentation, disintegration, meaninglessness, an absence of moral parameters, and social chaos—this is clearly of no help if we are serious about trying to make a positive contribution to social work. On the other hand, while the *affirmative* postmodernists agree with the skeptics' critique of modernity, particularly in terms of science and rationality, they have a more hopeful, optimistic view of the possibilities of the postmodern age and are positively oriented towards the importance of *process*. This approach has increasingly informed my thinking in recent years and was first articulated in the paper with Wendy Marshall (Parton and Marshall, 1998). Such an approach is much more open to the potential of practical actions, for it is not just concerned with *deconstruction* but with *construction* and *reconstruction*.

There is a recognition that choice and negotiation are central and that trying to *build* practical and political solutions lies at the heart of everyday life. Recognizing that subject(s) need to be understood in context(s), it thus recognizes the importance of interdependence and the social and political cultures in which we live. It is not the death of the subject but a recognition of the diverse nature of subjectivities which becomes the focus, for it is argued there has been a widening in the constructability of identities from ascriptive and natural (in the premodern), to socially acquired and quasinatural (in the modern), to chosen and socially negotiated (in the postmodern) (Hollis, 1985). It is argued that because there is such an intimate relationship between language and reality, persons are able to influence their own destiny. They are given agency and the potential to construct their own realities in a way reminiscent of Berger and Luckmann's *Social Construction of Reality.*

Postmodern and Constructionist Approaches to Social Work

Thus, while it is difficult to accommodate the skeptical postmodernist perspective, with its nihilistic stance on truth and other absolutes, within social work, I have found the emphasis of the affirmative postmodernist perspective on truth redefinition, rather than truth denying, is potentially very suggestive. Rosenau's interpretation of an affirmative postmodern vision demonstrates that, while it cannot offer truth, it is not without content. It is interpretative, and its focus is receptivity, dialogue, and listening to and talking with the other. It reveals paradox, myth, and enigma, and it persuades by showing, reminding, hinting, and evoking, rather than by constructing theories and approximating truth. It suggests that our focus should be narrative, fragmented fantasies and different stories. Social work takes on the guise of persuasive fiction or poetry.

What such an approach demonstrates is that postmodern perspectives are not necessarily bleak or antisocial work but provide novel and creative insights that clearly talk to a number of themes and approaches which have been associated with social work for much of its history. It almost suggests that social work could be (re)interpreted as being postmodern all along. Many social workers will identify with approaches that blur the difference between fact and fiction, history and story, art and science (England, 1986), and which take the view that what an individual perceives or experiences as her or his reality isn't *the* reality, but a reality capable of change in a variety of ways.

I became aware that there were a number of attempts to develop and apply the positive elements of such an approach explicitly to social work practice. In the process, a number of themes and issues were illustrated which can be widely applied and developed further in different contexts. *Uncertainty* is seen as central, for, as Pozatek (1994: 399) suggests, "the acknowledgement of uncertainty is an essential element of the postmodern practice of social work" and that such a position can push workers to make the effort to understand a service user's experience. A position of uncertainty is seen to represent a more respectful approach to cultural difference, so that social workers should not expect to know in advance what the outcomes of interactions will be. They can, at best, only trigger an effect. A position of uncertainty means that social workers will approach each situation respectful of difference, complexity, and ambiguity. Words are understood by clients according to how they have constructed the reality embodied in the interaction. It is thus essential for practitioners to be aware of this and construct, through *dialogue* with the client, a shared understanding and reality which they agree represents their interaction. It is an approach that recognizes that *language* is crucial for constituting the experiences and identity of both the self and the interaction, and which takes seriously the diverse elements of power involved. It is similarly serious about notions of *partnership* and *participation,* and enables the views of service users to be prioritized. This is not to say, however, that such issues are self-evident and clear-cut. A commitment to uncertainty, indeterminacy, and unpredictability will reinforce social workers' continual need to reflexively consider what they are doing, why, and with what possible outcomes.

Sands and Nuccio (1992) similarly identified a number of themes central to postmodern perspectives which could be drawn on in practice. Thus, rather than think and act according to *logocentrism,* assuming that there is a singular fixed logical order which is "real" or "true," practitioners need to recognize that there are no essential meanings. *Definitions and interpretations are historically contingent and context bound and hence fluid.* Similarly, logocentric thought promotes thinking in terms of binary opposites—male/female, black/white, adult/child, true/false—which are seen as mutually exclusive, categorical, and hierarchical, rather than interdependent. Such categories are usually embedded in language in a way that privileges some experiences and marginalizes others. It is thus important to explicitly recognize the importance, but fluid and changing nature, of *difference* so that the oppressed and devalued can have a voice and we can think and act in terms of both/and *relational* terms.

One way to recover suppressed meaning is through the key operation of *deconstruction*, whereby phenomena are continually interrogated, evaluated, overturned, and disrupted. Deconstruction is a way of analyzing texts, language, and narratives that is sensitive to contextual dimensions and marginalized voices. The process of deconstruction recognizes that, while *multiple discourses* might be available, only a few are heard and are dominant, these being intimately related to the dominant powers/knowledges. When we deconstruct, we do not accept the constructs as given but look at them in relation to their social, historical, and political contexts. Constructs are "problematized" and "decentered." Through deconstruction, the presumed fixity of phenomena is destabilized, and the perspective of the marginalized can be given voice. It involves, amongst other things, helping people to externalize the problem, examining its influences on their lives, and reconstructing and liberating themselves from it. The notion of *possibility* (O'Hanlon, 1993) recognizes that things can be changed. A vision of possibility can be used to mobilize people's potential and competence, and can empower them to reclaim and redefine who they are and how they want to act.

However, we should not assume that postmodern and constructionist perspectives are concerned with giving suppressed subjects a voice in any simple way. The notion of *subjectivity* is itself complex. While, within a logocentric tradition, the individual is autonomous and has an essential subjectivity, identity, personality, and (if healthy) integration, this is not the case with postmodern and constructionist perspectives. In the latter, subjectivity is precarious, contradictory, and in process, constantly being reconstituted in discourses. Accordingly, the subject is multifaceted and speaks in many voices, depending on the sociocultural, historical, and interpersonal contexts in which it is situated.

It is perhaps the emphasis on language and its intimate relationship with knowledge and power which provides the most distinctive message for practice arising from postmodern and constructionist perspectives. A focus on social work as text, narrative, and artistry, as opposed to social work as science, moves center stage. Whereas science looks for explanations and causes, the story or narrative approach is intent on finding a *meaningful* account. As Howe (1993) has demonstrated, via his in-depth analysis of studies of what clients say about what they value from counseling and therapy, the latter is important. Talking not only helps people to understand their experiences but also allows them to control, reframe, and move on. As Howe states, "there are no objective fundamental truths in human relationships, only working truths. These decentered contingent truths help people make sense of and control the meaning of their own experience. This is how we learn to cope" (Howe, 1993: 193). Such approaches emphasize *process* and *authorship*. An open-minded engagement with people's stories and the possibility of helping them to reauthor their lives using more helpful stories can be both an empowering and a respectful way of understanding situations and bringing about change.

I find that in listening to a variety of different vocabularies and developing a curiosity about them we not only open up a whole range of possibilities for the type of relationships we develop with the people we work with but we also recognize—as practitioners, teachers, and researchers—that we do not so much *find* facts as *make* them. If we don't understand what someone is saying or doing, we need to ask them. In trying to educate for uncertainty and in recognizing the limits of our "knowledge," we should thereby increase an emphasis upon compassion, carefulness, and wisdom.

I developed these ideas further with my then-colleague, Patrick O'Byrne, in our attempt to develop *Constructive Social Work* (Parton and O'Byrne, 2000). Drawing on a range of perspectives from postmodernism, social constructionism, and narrative approaches, our aim was to provide a theoretical framework which was usable by practitioners. This took me back to some of my earliest attractions to social constructionism but we aimed to be directly relevant to practitioners in a much more micro/clinical sense.

The term *constructive social work* was chosen for two reasons. First, it reflected our wish to provide an explicitly positive approach. For the core idea of *construction*, from the Latin to the present day, is that of *building* or *putting together*. The *Oxford English Dictionary* defines *construction* as "the action or manner of constructing," while *constructive* is defined as "having a useful purpose; helpful." Second, the term was chosen to reflect the postmodern, discourse, and social constructionist theoretical perspectives that informed it. The *constructive* approach emphasizes process, plurality of both knowledge and voice, possibility, and the relational quality of knowledge. It is affirmative and reflexive and focuses on dialogue, listening to and talking with the other. Social work practice is seen as a specialized version of the process by which people define themselves, participate in their social worlds, and cooperatively construct social realities. It underlines both the

shared building of identity and meaning that is the basis of effective practice, and the positive results for service users that stem from the approach.

Constructive social work is concerned with the narratives of solutions to
problems and with change; instead of providing the practitioner with information about the causes of problems, so that s/he can make an expert
assessment and prescribe a "scientific" solution, the service user is encouraged to tell the story of the problem in a way that externalizes it, giving more
control and agency and creating a new perspective on how to manage or
overcome it. These narratives construct the future and anticipate change;
questions encourage the service user to identify exceptions to the apparently
overwhelming nature of problems—situations in which s/he has done
something that made a positive difference. Constructive social work devel-
ops techniques and thinking associated with solution-focused (De Shazer,
1985, 1991, 1994; Miller, 1997), narrative therapy (White and Epston,
1990; White, 1993), possibility (O'Hanlon, 1993; O'Hanlon and Beadle,
1994; O'Hanlon and Weiner-Davis, 1989), and the strengths (Saleebey,
1997) perspectives. The approach attempts to provide questions that elicit
clear goals about what the service user wants, in the user's own words, and
which involves her or him in doing something in the immediate future
which can launch a new beginning. The practitioner's mode of address is
one of "curiosity and respectful puzzlement" at the service user's unique
way of making things better, rather than expertise in fitting an intervention to a need. Service users are encouraged to repeat successes, to identify
solutions as theirs, and as steps to the achievement of their own goals.

Service users are invited to tell their stories using the cultural resources
of their communities—local language and interpretation of the problem
and the origins of their oppression and exclusion. The language of oppression, domination, subjugation, enslavement, and recruitment is used in
order to try and establish how the problem is dominating the person. The
service user is then encouraged to distance herself or himself from the
problem and to give it an unpleasant name, using their own metaphors.
It can then be externalized and politicized in terms of the forces operating against empowerment and achievement in society, in terms of style,
appearance, class, gender, race, ability, family relationships, or whatever.
Sometimes it is as simple as treating people with respect and referring to
them by the name by which they wish to be known. The approach aims to
defeat the stereotypes of the blaming official organizations, and offers service users new ways of giving an account of their situation in which their

agency becomes central, and they begin to take control. This has the potential for reducing conflict between the practitioner and the service user and prepares the ground for cooperation in trying to reduce the influence of the problem and, constructing possibilities and solutions. None of this reduces accountability for mistakes, offenses, or the abuse of others, although it may challenge beliefs about more fundamental issues of self-worth and potential for change. A key aspect of the approach is thus that it encourages service users to retell their stories in terms of courageous opposition to their disadvantages and heroic resistance to their problems.

Conclusion

This chapter has outlined how I have drawn upon, used, and tried to develop a range of ideas and perspectives associated with social constructionism and, more recently, postmodernism. Much of this is in the context of my particular interests in child abuse and child protection work. While these were initially concerned with critical analyses of policy, they have also been concerned with trying to contribute, much more directly, to practice (see also Gorman et al., 2006).

In my teaching, research, and writing, I have always attempted to introduce an "untimely" ethos to the present and thereby encourage a sense of its *fragility* and *contingency*, thus trying to demonstrate it does not "have to be like this." In the process, we can think about the present differently and act in new and creative ways. The present is not seen as inevitable and homogeneous but as something to be deconstructed, problematized, and acted upon. The *ethos* is thus one of humility and a commitment to uncertainty together with a continual questioning of the present—"what is going on here?" and "does it have to be like this?" The approach adopted is not designed to establish the limits of thought and action but to locate the possible places of their transgression and how things might be done differently.

Most recently this has involved working with a large number of practitioners and first-line managers working in three children's centers in particularly deprived localities in the northwest of England. We are trying to introduce social constructionist ideas in order to develop a constructive approach to work with children, families, and communities. In the process, we have needed to distill what we see as the key elements of such an approach, and this seems an appropriate way to conclude this chapter.

For while there is no one feature which can be said to identify a *social constructionist* approach, a number of themes can be seen to link them together:

- It insists that we develop a *critical* stance towards our taken-for-granted ways of understanding the world, including ourselves. It encourages us to be curious and questioning about the things that we might ordinarily "take for granted," and that also we seek to question "received wisdom" and the assumptions about the way things are and the way things are assumed to work.
- Because the world is the product of *social processes,* it follows that there cannot be any given, determined nature of the world "out there." How we interact with the world does not only impact how we see the world but can act to change the nature of the world itself.
- *Social categories* such as "offender," "abuser," "problem family," etc., are seen as *historically and culturally specific,* and therefore vary over time and place. Particular forms of knowledge are the products of their history and their culture. What is meant, for example, by a "family with additional needs" or a "family with complex needs," for example? Where and how did these terms become invented? How do they differ from other terms and with what implications for the children, families, and professionals concerned?
- Our knowledge and understanding of the world is developed between *people in their daily interactions.* These *negotiated* understandings can take a variety of forms which invite different actions. Crucially, language and all other forms of representation gain their meaning from the ways in which they are used within *relationships.* Thus, *negotiated interactional relationships* are seen as central in day-to-day life and the work that we do.
- Thus, if we wish to make changes, it is important to confront the challenge of trying to generate new meanings and become what Kenneth Gergen (1999) has called "poetic activists." Generative discourses provide ways of talking, writing, and acting that simultaneously challenge existing traditions and also open up new possibilities for change. The term "constructive social work" can itself be seen as an example of a generative discourse.
- A key theme that underlies the constructive approach in day-to-day practice is then that it becomes important to check our assumptions

and also our areas of agreement and difference, with each other as practitioners, with practitioners in other agencies, and with the children, young people, and adults with whom we work. Thus the quality and detail of dialogue and communication between the various parties is crucially interdependent with the quality of the relationships involved. Honest, reflective relationships become central and these will be mutually enhanced by checking out our underlying assumptions in detail at various points. It is through relationships that change is primarily brought about. Our knowledge of ourselves and others is developed through day-to-day interaction and processes.

Notes

1. Maria Colwell died on January 7, 1973, at the age of seven in Hove, Brighton, in the South of England. She was one of nine children born to her mother by that time. She spent over five years in local authority care, being fostered by her aunt, but was returned to her mother and stepfather (William Kepple) at the age of six years and eight months, having been placed on a supervision order to the local authority social services department from that date. The family was visited by a number of social workers over sixty times, and concerns were expressed about Maria by her schoolteacher and neighbors on numerous occasions. However, she died of "extreme violence" at the hands of her stepfather, and was found to weigh only about three-quarters of what would be normal for a girl of her age. William Kepple was convicted of Maria's murder in April 1973, although, on appeal, the charge was reduced to manslaughter, and he was sentenced to eight years' imprisonment. The decision to establish a public inquiry was taken by Sir Keith Joseph, the Secretary of State for Social Services, in May 1973, and the public inquiry took place between October 10 and December 7, 1973, with the report published in September 1974 (Secretary of State, 1974). The inquiry and the report received huge media coverage.
2. The Cleveland "affair" broke in the early summer of 1987 and focused on the activities of two pediatricians and social workers in a general hospital in Middlesbrough, a declining chemical and industrial town in the north east of England. During a period of a few weeks, 121 children were removed from their families to an emergency place of safety on the basis of what was seen by the media and the two local members of Parliament as questionable diagnoses of

child sexual abuse. As a result, a number of techniques for diagnosing and identifying sexual abuse, particularly the use of the anal dilation test, the use of anatomically correct dolls, and disclosure work—were subject to close critical scrutiny. This was the first child abuse scandal in England concerned with the possible overreaction of professionals, the first involving sexual abuse, and the first where the actions of pediatricians and other doctors, as well as social workers, were put under the microscope and subjected to high-profile and prolonged media criticism. The public inquiry was established in the summer of 1987 and reported in 1988 (Parton, 1991; Secretary of State for Social Services, 1988).

References

Audit Commission (1994). *Seen but not heard: Coordinating child health and social for children in need*. London: HMSO.

Bauman, Z. (1992). *Intimations of postmodernity*. London: Routledge.

Berger, P. L. and Luckmann, T. (1966). *The social construction of reality: A treatise in the sociology of knowledge*. New York: Doubleday.

Blumer, H. (1971). Social problems as collective behaviour. *Social Problems, 18*(3): 310–26.

Department of Health. (1995). *Child protection: Messages from research*. London: HMSO.

Department of Health, Home Office and the Department for Education and Employment (1999). *Working together to safeguard children: A guide to inter-agency working to safeguard and promote the welfare of children*. London: The Stationery Office.

De Shazer, S. (1985). *Key solutions to brief therapy*. New York: Norton.

———. (1991). *Putting difference to work*. New York: Norton.

———. (1994). *Words were originally magic*. New York: Norton.

Donzelot, J. (1980). *The policing of families: Welfare versus the state*. London: Hutchinson.

England, H. (1986). *Social work as art: Making sense of good practice*. London: Allen & Unwin.

Foucault, M. (1977). *Discipline and punish*. London: Allen Lane.

———. (1991). Governmentality. In G. Burchell, C. Gordon, and P. Miller (Eds.), *The Foucault effect: Studies in governmentality* (pp. 73–86). London: Harvester Wheatsheaf.

Franklin, B. and N. Parton (Eds.) (1991). *Social work, the media and public relations*. London: Routledge.

——. (2001). Press ganged! Media reporting of social work and child abuse. In M. May, E. Brunsden, and R. Page (Eds.), *Social problems in social policy* (pp. 233–47). Oxford: Blackwell.

Fuller, R. and R. Myers (1941). The natural history of a social problem. *American Sociological Review,* 6(6): 318–28.

Gergen, K. J. (1999). *An invitation to social construction.* London: Sage.

Gibbons, J. S., S. Conroy, and C. Bell (1995). *Operating the child protection system.* London: HMSO.

Gorman, K., M. Gregory, M. Hayles, and N. Parton (Eds.). (2006). *Constructive work with offenders.* London and Philadelphia: Jessica Kingsley.

HM Government (2006). *Working together to safeguard children: A guide to inter-agency working to safeguard and promote the welfare of children.* London: The Stationery Office.

Hollis, M. (1985). On masts and men. In M. Carrithers, S. Collins, and S. Lukes (Eds.), *The category of the person: Anthropology, philosophy, history* (pp. 45–61). Cambridge, UK: Cambridge University Press.

Holstein, J. A. and G. Miller (Eds.) (1993). *Reconsidering social construction: Debates and social problems theory.* Hawthorne, NY: Aldine de Gruyter.

Howe, D. (1993). *On being a client: Understanding the process of counselling and psychotherapy.* London: Sage.

——. (1994). Modernity, postmodernity and social work. *British Journal of Social Work,* 24(5): 513–32.

Kempe, C. H., Silverman, F. N., Steel, B. F., Droegemueller, W., and Silver, H. K. (1962). The battered child syndrome. *Journal of the American Medical Association,* 181: 17–24.

Miller, G. (1997). *Becoming miracle workers: Language and meaning in brief therapy.* Hawthorne, NY: Aldine de Gruyter.

Miller, G. and J. A. Holstein (Eds.) (1993). *Constructionist controversies: Issues in social problems theory.* Hawthorne, NY: Aldine de Gruyter.

Miller, P. and N. Rose (1990). Governing economic life. *Economy and Society,* 19(1): 1–31.

O'Hanlon, B. (1993). Possibility theory. In S. Gilligan and R. Price (Eds.), *Therapeutic conversations* (pp. 88–101). New York: Norton.

O'Hanlon, B. and S. Beadle (1994). *A field guide to possibility land.* Omaha, NE: Possibility Press.

O'Hanlon, B. and M. Weiner-Davis (1989). *In search of solutions.* New York: Norton.

Parton, N. (1979). The natural history of child abuse: Study in social problem definition. *British Journal of Social Work,* 9(4): 42–51.

——. (1981). Child abuse, social anxiety and welfare. *British Journal of Social Work,* 11(4): 391–414.

——. (1985). *The politics of child abuse*. London: Macmillan.

——. (1990). Taking child abuse seriously. In The Violence Against Children Study Group (Ed.), *Taking child abuse seriously: Contemporary issues in child protection theory and practice* (pp. 7–24). London: Unwin Hyman.

——. (1991). *Governing the family: Child care, child protection and the state*. London: Macmillan.

——. (1994a). Problematics of government, (post)modernity, and social work. *British Journal of Social Work*, 24(1): 9–32.

——. (1994b). The nature of social work under conditions of (post)modernity. *Social Work and Social Sciences Review*, 5(2): 93–112.

——. (1996). Social work, risk and "the blaming system." In N. Parton (Ed.), *Social theory, social change and social work* (pp. 98–114). London: Routledge.

——. (Ed.). (1997). *Child protection and family support: Tensions, contradictions and possibilities*. London: Routledge.

——. (1999). Reconfiguring child welfare practices: Risk, advanced liberalism and the government of freedom. In A. Chambon, A. Irving, and L. Epstein (Eds.), *Reading Foucault for social work* (pp. 101–130). New York: Columbia University Press.

Parton, N. and W. Marshall (1998). Postmodernism and discourse, approaches to social work. In R. Adams, L. Dominelli, and M. Payne (Eds.), *Social work: Themes, issues and critical debates* (pp. 240–250). London: Macmillan.

Parton, N. and P. O'Byrne (2000). *Constructive social work: Towards a new practice*. London: Macmillan; New York: St Martin's Press.

Parton, N., Thorpe, D., and Wattam, C. (1997). *Child protection: Risk and the moral order*. Basingstoke, UK: Palgrave/Macmillan.

Parton, N. and Wattam, C. (Eds.). (1999). *Child sexual abuse: Responding to the experiences of children*. New York: Wiley.

Pozatek, E. (1994). The problem of certainty: Clinical social work in the postmodern era. *Social Work*, 39(4): 396–43.

Rose, N. (1993). Government, authority, and expertise in advanced liberalism. *Economy and Society*, 22(3): 283–99.

Rosenau, P. M. (1992). *Post-modernism and the social sciences: Insights, inroads and intrusions*. Princeton, NJ: Princeton University Press.

Saleebey, D. (Ed.). (1997). *The strengths perspective in social work* (2nd ed.). New York: Longman.

Sands, R. G. and K. Nuccio (1992). Postmodern feminist theory and social work. *Social Work*, 37(6): 489–494.

Secretary of State for Social Services (1974). *Report of the committee of inquiry into the care and supervision provided in relation to Maria Colwell*. London: HMSO.

Secretary of State for Social Services (1988). *Report of the inquiry into child abuse in Cleveland.* London: HMSO.

Silverman, D. (1970). *The theory of organisations: A sociological framework.* London: Heinemann.

Smart, B. (1999). *Facing modernity: Ambivalence, reflexivity and morality.* London: Sage.

Spector, M. and J. Kitsuse (1973). Towards a sociology of social problems, social conditions, value judgements and social problems. *Social Problems,* 20(4): 380–395.

Spector, M. and J. Kitsuse (1977). *Constructing social problems.* Hawthorne, NY: Aldine de Gruyter.

White, M. (1993). Deconstruction and therapy. In S. Gilligan and R. Price (Eds.), *Therapeutic conversations* (pp. 43–46). New York: Norton.

White, M. and D. Epston (1990). *Narrative means to therapeutic ends.* New York: Norton.

[7]

Mostly We Played with Whatever She Chose

DEBORAH R. MAJOR

The foyer of the former Catholic elementary school was totally deserted and eerily silent. The school had been converted to office space as private Catholic education became too expensive for immigrant families in the surrounding Chicago neighborhood. The absence of a receptionist or passing custodian seemed odd. I had recently left a business career where customers were never left alone to hunt for their destination. At the same time, there was something soothing about the total silence; silence that brought attention to the sunlight playing through stained glass windows and that bid its own voiceless welcome. As I started to look for the stairwell to the office where I would interview for a job I did not want, a young boy who looked about five opened a door on my left and crossed the foyer. Because of the way we were positioned, I never saw his face. He walked across the room and began pushing against a large wooden door that must have been quite heavy because it did not want to give under his weight. He did not notice my presence, or if he did, he did not turn to ask for help. As I moved closer to help him, the door suddenly gave way, he slipped through, and it closed behind him. As far as I know, I never saw him again. And in that moment, I suddenly changed my mind and thought, "I *have* to work here." I dropped my initial motive to "practice" interviewing and walked the three flights of stairs determined to find work in that place. I would normally second-guess an immediate and radical change of heart bubbling up right before such an important meeting. I certainly would not assume I should follow a directive perceived in that way. Ordinarily, I might have considered such a reversal to be some form of countertransference. But I have never second-guessed that particular change of heart: a wish to help that child push open an enormous, heavy wooden door.

So began my entrance, in 1992, into the world of social work practice in child welfare. That same year little Joseph Wallace, a two-year-old recently returned to the custody of his mother, was found hung from a closet door. At the time I knew nothing about Joseph Wallace, or his mother, and next to nothing about child welfare for that matter. I had not planned to work in child welfare after completing my M.S.W., and so I was quite surprised to hear myself asking to be given a job as a therapist for children in foster care during my first interview for a social work position.

One of my first clients was a six-year-old little girl, Tina, who came into the system together with two older sisters and two younger brothers—the stated reason: neglect (in this case inadequate supervision and homelessness). The case file indicated that the family wandered from place to place, and all of the children were out on the streets "helping" their mother in fights. Tina's mother, whom she called Janice,[1] was described by staff as "strung-out" and "on the streets," and the file documented a long history of investigations for allegations of abuse or neglect, most of which had been "indicated." Since Tina's entry into foster care, the caseworker was often unable to locate Janice to confirm visitation with her children or to offer other services.

Tina was referred for individual therapy to address a variety of behaviors her foster mother found disturbing and reprehensible, including frequent fighting, bedwetting, hyperactivity, and periodically attempting to insert a pencil or other small objects into her vagina. Tina was very quiet and tense during our sessions, and it was quite a while before she would say much of anything to me. Mostly we played with whatever she chose: green play dough kneaded tensely and forcefully with tiny but strong fingers, before she turned it into hamburgers for us to eat. She was sometimes unable to play until she straightened the entire room, repositioning items on every horizontal surface to face the direction she needed them to face. Or sometimes she would just want to stand at the sink washing, washing something—anything: toys, pencils, dolls, her hands. And she was always, always tight and tense. The tension in her hands and arms seemed all wrong for someone so young. She seemed not to be at home in her own body, as if bracing against any possible threat that might take her by surprise. I often found myself thinking, "No six-year-old should have to carry this kind of tension."

Like many of the children with whom I worked, Tina suspected that she was partially responsible for the separation from her mother and her siblings. She had told somebody something about what had happened to her, which started a series of investigations, leading up to her removal. So she had a sneaking suspicion that if she kept her mouth shut (this time) that she just might stem the tide of damage done to her family. I wondered what her play might look like if she didn't experience me as part-therapist/ part-police. I was determined to alter her view of me—determined to help her relax, determined to help her shed the false assumptions of responsibility for her mother's safety and her family's destruction. In retrospect, she probably experienced me as tense and uptight in my determination as I experienced her in hers. Like Tina, it did not help that I had multiple masters to satisfy and that these masters had conflicting goals. Her foster mother did not seem terribly concerned about whether Tina relaxed. She just wanted her to behave and expected me to make that happen. Tina's guardian ad litem[2] wanted to know who had done the dreadful deed that got the child inserting objects into her vagina. The guardian hoped that over time I might be able to unearth this information, the assumption being that if Tina's mother had failed to protect her from a character who frequented the family's space, this was yet another reason that it would not be safe to send her home. I wanted Tina to *not* be kicked out of her placement.

Of course everyone engaged in practice with children wants to protect them. And while it helps to know something about what a child has had to tolerate in her daily life, getting "the facts" may be less important than understanding what meaning the child constructed of what happened to her, and how she might have used that meaning to alter her identity (Saari, 1993, 2002). For children in foster care, much of the conscious meaning they articulate is connected to the separation from their family, and not to the facts surrounding events leading up to separation.

One day when Tina and I were standing at the sink together washing various and sundry toys, she said, "You give my foster mother all that money to take care of me. Why can't you just give that money to my mother? My mother could take care of me if you would give *her* that money." I remember thinking, "What an interesting idea. It has a very interesting logic." She completely surprised me in her understanding of the inequity of a system that would pay a stranger to take care of her, when it would never consider paying her own mother to do so. At the time, I remember thinking that this level of cognitive sophistication around the way payments transfer "ought" to have helped her understand that even if the system could pay her mother, that unless Janice made an effort to address her addiction, Tina was not likely to be the beneficiary of that payment. I decided to say nothing about this, but took a floundering stab at explaining that her caseworker wanted to do what she could to help her mother, but her worker was also having a really hard time finding Janice.

In the few years that I worked with Tina she was moved to several different homes, each foster parent requesting her removal for behaviors that Tina and I could not manage to get under control. Each time she was moved the demand for better behavior was ratcheted up (as she grew older), and the foster parents' views of good behavior seemed more and more out of reach. Of course, it was not clear to me that getting the behaviors under control was a priority for Tina. What she did make clear to me was that she wanted to go home to Janice and her sisters and brothers. Going home remained her top priority; however, this did not occur. Janice's parental rights were eventually terminated due to noncompliance with her service plan. Tina continued to move from home to home.

Stumbling onto Social Constructionism

The families that allowed me into their lives in the role of helper struggled with a staggering combination of environmental and personal concerns, all the while working to regain custody of their children. With few exceptions children also wanted to "go home," to have what they imagined their friends and classmates had, a real sense of being grounded in a family that did not constantly shift, so that Mother's Day and Christmas would build on traditions from prior Mother's Days and prior Christmases. What these children got instead was the tradition of no tradition at all, where the mother on this Mother's Day might bear no resemblance to last year's mother, and the family this Christmas might bear no resemblance to that of last year's Christmas. Such changes during crucial stages of childhood can have deleterious consequences, since we all need some degree of sameness and predictability (both inside and outside) to develop a stable sense of who we are in the world (Nelson, 1985, 1989; Saari, 2002; Sroufe et al., 2005).

Within this context of face-to-face practice with children in foster care, I stumbled into social construction without anyone ever uttering those words. Children in foster care live and breathe a social constructionesque reality in ways that would make most of our heads spin. Little girls and boys who lose foster placements against their will and find themselves placed into new families overnight are often asked to become entirely different little people in those new families. I remember being shocked over and over again to see little girls appear for their counseling sessions looking like completely different little people from one week to the next. And the new families expected change not only in the exterior appearance of the children, but in their insides as well. This sometimes worked to a particular child's advantage, such as when a young boy was moved from a home where his foster parent told me she thought he was "possessed by the devil." Fortunately, his next foster parent harbored no such ideas about him, which seemed to go quite a long way toward freeing him from an extremely negative set of ideas about who he was and who he could become.

Social constructionist ideas are particularly well suited to practice with families in the child welfare system because they emphasize the notion that meaning can only be understood in context. It is critical to adopt an approach that helps us as practitioners do this, since parents in the system are often judged as if they enjoyed every opportunity available to any middle-class family, but that they simply chose to decline these opportunities because they prefer lives mired in chaos, violence, or addiction.

I will never forget meeting a particular parent whose case file reported multiple indications of abuse and neglect. She was often late to her appointments and seemed lacking in motivation to engage, even though she said she wanted her children back. One day she brought me a Polaroid photograph of the apartment she was renting. It showed exposed electrical wires with bare light bulbs and exposed two-by-fours through holes in the ceiling. For weeks her legs were covered with fleabites from flea-infested alley cats that entered the building hallways seeking shelter. She talked about how, as a child, the police recognized her family members' voices immediately by telephone, so often were they called to come in and break up violent disputes between her parents. She described her experience of her mother's hatred, on one occasion waking up during the night to find her mother standing over her with a raised frying pan. In the context of so much familial and societal desecration of her personhood, I began to marvel that she was willing or able to show up at all. I began to ask myself, what kind of parent might I have become in the face of this kind of constant chaos and degradation? I also began to recognize and appreciate her constant exhaustion for what it was, as opposed to the "resistance" that it had initially appeared to be. Taking this parent's social world into consideration required that I suspend some of my assumptions about how the world operates. Social constructionist ideas helped sensitize me to the importance of parents' and children's meaning structures, and their voices and stories. As I learned to listen in a new way, I began to see new possibilities for aligning with her and with other clients that I had previously overlooked.

For instance, I was helped to see and hear why a child might experience subjective distress living in a home that is safer by some objective standards, without viewing this as a maladaptive defense. The child may only recognize himself in his family of origin. This understanding does not inform us with regard to safety recommendations, but these ideas help to make sense of the child's personal feelings about what constitutes subjective safety. These children struggle to live with a foot in two worlds, to manage dual identities, and are asked to do so without causing their caregivers or themselves major headaches, an astounding demand given what we know about the stresses of trying to effectively bridge dissimilar cultures (Chestang, 1972; Furman, 2005; McClain, 1986; Wallerstein, 1987).

So I came to understand the meaning of social constructionist thought and its impact from a view alongside children who were trying to survive either by acceding to demands to reconstruct their identities, or by fighting like hell to resist others' notions of the little people they should be, or who were waiting to be placed in a home with new parents who would just allow them to be.

I think that most of us in the field did not truly comprehend what we were asking of children in these situations. There is a great deal of literature focused on children in foster care and their behavior problems and what a trial it is for substitute caregivers trying to take care of them (Barber and Delfabbro, 2004; Buehler, Cox, and Cuddeback, 2003; Cox, Orme, and Rhodes, 2002, 2003; Newton et al., 2000; Smith, et al., 2001). And of course it is very challenging, especially when children are so confused, frightened, angry, or dissociated that they cannot communicate coherently what it means to them to be separated from their families. We do not seem to fully understand what a trial it is for a child to reconstruct herself as a member of a new family while holding on to a vestige of herself as a member of her first family. Consider, for example, that foster children referred to counseling for fighting, bedwetting, hyperactivity, depression, and other painful symptoms often end up with treatment plans focused on reducing the frequency of tears shed, pants wet, punches thrown, swear words hurled, with little, if any attention paid to the subjective experience giving rise to the behaviors, and the difficulty of being required to reconstruct themselves as members of two (or more) dissimilar families, none of which may offer a permanent home. And while it does matter how people behave in communities, the focus on behavior modification in some settings can feel dismissing when it essentially disregards the part of the child that helps her know herself (e.g., it disregards the child's motives and meaning structures). It may not be crucial in all settings to focus on subjective meaning making, but in child welfare settings this seems a very important part of human functioning to ignore. In fact, it seems akin to professional neglect.

In most cases, even when children had not been safe at home, they still loved their parents (most often mothers), and they just wanted parents to do whatever needed to be done to end the separation. In most cases, children were not focused on whatever incidents triggered the investigation. They were focused on the separation and all of their pain around that. They understood who they were as members of their first family, while they struggled to understand who they were in their foster families. This is not to suggest that we ought to base our decisions on children's understandings, but rather to notice that children prioritize very differently compared to adults, and we must learn to understand how children make meaning, because that is where we ought to do our work with them (Saari, 1991). Of course, the same is true for their parents.

Practice Implications of Using This Approach

From this perspective, "in the trenches" social constructionist ideas seemed a more suitable framework for thinking about how to work in the system on behalf of children and their families. By highlighting individuals' subjective views of their world, this perspective invited me to look for ways to "get inside" a child's or parent's view to develop a deeper and more accurate perspective of how relationships operated for them. I was also invited to understand the particular conditions under which the relationships evolved, in all their social complexity (Saleebey, 1993). This perspective required that I suspend some of my own taken-for-granted, middle-class assumptions about how the world works, and that I reexamine and analyze my personal viewpoints as part of the process. Most importantly, I was invited to consider my role in helping relationships as part of the evaluation process. By incorporating a social constructionist perspective, it became increasingly important to examine the lens through which I viewed my clients, to look *at* my lens while concurrently looking through it, as a way to reflect on the impact of my actions (Millstein, 1993). Drawing myself inside the system under evaluation helped to subject my own values, biases, and assumptions to a higher degree of scrutiny than I might otherwise have done (Tyson, 1995).

Using social constructionist ideas helped me recognize the bias inherent in the privileging of behavior and behavior modification, both for children and for their parents involved in the child welfare system. This is not to suggest that I ever came to see behavior as inconsequential—indeed, it is very important. However, the bias that privileges behavior change (or the appearance of change) presents enormous problems when it ignores relationship motives in favor of motor behaviors that we count. Children feel discounted and disrespected when we dive in to make them change their behavior without regard to the meanings that gave rise to it. This doesn't necessarily mean that children want to explain it to you, or even that they can explain it. But they taught me that it does matter to them that I would want to understand, and it mattered that I would prioritize that knowledge above trying to make them change. The problem with this way of working, of course, is that people really want children to behave, and so in many settings behavior modification is king. Privileging behavior creates the expectation that treatment goals and objectives will be documented in behavioral terms, and that progress or lack thereof will be tracked in behavioral terms. Paradoxically, this focus on behavior often feels dehumanizing to children who struggle with self-regulation, while adults in authority often see this focus as a significant civilizer. For this reason, when working with children, I would often go out of my way to let them know that while their behavior mattered, I would first be interested in hearing what they wanted to tell me and how they understood and felt about what was going on in their lives. Often I could only make sense of their behavior by hearing their side of a story.

For the first couple of years after the death of Joseph Wallace, there was little discussion about sending children home. Since these years were formative in my training in child welfare, they led me to believe that if children were removed, they likely would never be returned. It took a while to recognize that after any high-profile death every worker on the frontlines with these families is shell-shocked and gun shy, and that all policies, from federal laws to agency policies, are interpreted through a lens of apprehension and heightened caution.

In some states, reliance on a rehabilitative service plan and its successful completion as the barometer of a parent's readiness to regain custody of children is a double-edged sword. On the one hand, we must establish some benchmark as a way to assess parents' understanding of what went wrong and how they might take action to prevent the reoccurrence of events resulting in their children's removal. However, the constellation of factors contributing to family separation is usually multidetermined and so complex that putting a service plan in place that operationalizes required behavior changes, without regard for the wider context that gave rise to the problems in the first place, is reductionistic and a bit like plugging a dike with a wad of bubble gum.

Trust in rehabilitative service plans rests on the assurance that if we can successfully modify parents' behavior via completion of a number of services (parenting classes, drug treatment, anger management, individual or family therapy, etc.), that children will be safer in their care. Parents "get" these messages and come "to treatment" saying, "I just have to complete these services, and then I can get my kids back. How many times do we have to meet?" Caseworkers, children's guardians, public defenders, and judges all tend to get swept up in the service countdown. Everyone wants to place their faith in those aspects of the process that they can see, touch, and count: number of classes attended, certificates received, services completed. Court systems, which are focused on parental accountability and responsibility, prefer to see changes in black and white, and so behaviors and behavior change at the individual level becomes the default unit of analysis. The same is often true for children in the system. Most foster children are referred for behavior problems of one sort or another. In my experience, only rarely were children referred for depression, anxiety, or for some experience of subjective distress where these children were creating more problems for themselves than for those in the environment. Those kinds of difficulties were often not noticed.

In addition to detracting from a deeper understanding of parents' caregiving motives, this reductionistic focus on their behavior often serves to detract from a clear and much needed examination of the social environment, the surrounding community, and whether the community has within it the support systems, resources, and services that will help shore up the parents' caregiving motives, or instead harbors forces that will conspire to obstruct them. So materialist, reductionist ways of working with parents and children most often detract us from looking both deeper inward to see who the person truly is, and also detract us from looking outward to the larger context, and we need to look both deeper and wider in our work with children and their families.

So how might a social constructionist-informed approach open up a social worker's ideas and shape a practice? It may be more challenging to consider what this would look like in work with parents where children have been seriously injured. While we know that there are no universally accepted definitions of abuse or neglect (Agathonos-Georgopoulou, 1992; Hong and Hong, 1991; Korbin and Spilsbury, 1999), when children have been injured most of us are inclined to agree that it becomes quite difficult to see certain kinds of injuries as social constructions. In working with a parent who has been accused of inflicting a potentially fatal injury, as for example, a subdural hematoma, is there any possible way to see what happened through the eyes of the parent? Is there a way to "work with" the parent's understanding of the incident and still help the family create and sustain adequate safety for children? And even more risky, is it possible to work with "nonadmitting" parents—parents who deny having caused the injury?

A Case of "Nonadmitting" Parents

Child welfare cases where parents are believed to have caused children's injuries, but will not admit to having done so, are very difficult to work with and to resolve satisfactorily. In cases involving serious injuries, when parents cannot offer coherent explanations for how children were injured, the process of regaining custody can be stalled right at the outset. Every case involves working with the parent's version of what took place, which can be at odds with the case document filed by the investigator. But there are comparatively few cases where parents claim to have no real understanding about the injury.

One advantage of taking a social constructionist approach is that it gives temporary permission to set aside the official document and hear first from the parent how they saw events unfold, which can lend some legitimacy to an alternative viewpoint. When parents know that you are sincere in wanting to hear their side of the story, this stance often helps to develop a working relationship. However, parents need to know that while you are sincerely interested in their view, significant differences between their version and what is contained in the file may become a serious roadblock in court. To help engage the process of radical listening,[3] I would sometimes intentionally avoid reading the case file until after I had met the parent. Doing so helped me to suspend judgment and to give parents the benefit of the doubt. It was always interesting to notice how much more difficult it was to believe parents if I already had the official version in mind. It was also interesting to notice differences in my body when I was able to stay open as compared to when I was second-guessing much of what they had to say.

In this case, I did not have the opportunity to hear from the parents first. I had been briefed at a staffing and asked to serve as therapist for the mother of an infant who had suffered a potentially fatal head injury at three months of age. The parents were quite young, recently married, and parenting their first child, who had been born premature and had spent the first few weeks following birth in the hospital. Both parents insisted that they had done nothing to injure their baby. Interviewed separately by the investigator, they told basically the same story about how the child could possibly have been injured. During the staffing, the caseworker and supervisor referring the parents pointed to multiple "red flags," including medical records documenting that the injury could not have been accidental. By the time I met Beth (the baby's mother), I had read the entire case file, and I had been fully updated about the child's current condition (now a year after the incident), the current placement, and the parents' attitudes about the situation in which they found themselves. Frank, a social work colleague, had been assigned to work with Beth's husband, Tim.

Because of the way this case was transferred to the department, there was considerable suspicion from the outset that these parents were colluding to protect each other. Physicians on the child protection team insisted that the only way this particular constellation of injuries could occur was child abuse; it could not have been an accident. This information was relayed to me before I ever set eyes on Beth. Frank and I began with two young parents who were angry and frightened, but who insisted that they had not caused their baby's injury. When parents are referred under such circumstances, is there any good way to proceed?

This certainly did not seem a good way to begin, but it is not usual for the enormous document trail in child welfare cases to hit the social worker's desk before meeting the client. I asked myself how I might set opinions aside, meet this young mother with fresh eyes, listen openly to her perspective with an attitude of not knowing, and try to consider all possibilities (Anderson, 1997).

As with all cases involving serious injury to children, I explained to Beth that her confidentiality was compromised from the outset. Parents are informed that in the interest of child protection, officers of the juvenile court must receive pertinent information regarding parents' progress in treatment, without which there is no way to gage the parent's readiness to resume a protective parenting role. This typically means anything that will clarify the parent's ability to recognize and accept responsibility for the incidents that brought children into care, and what parents are willing to do to mitigate risks and increase protective factors. The first step focuses on the parent's understanding and admitting their responsibility, in the absence of which parents may be stuck on first base.

It did not help that Beth told me in the first session that she would be willing to lie to get her child back and that she had other relatives who would also be willing to lie on her behalf. However, when Beth said she would be willing to lie, she meant lie and admit that she had hurt her baby, when in fact she insisted that she had *not* done so. In many ways, this case seemed doomed from the start: a child who had sustained life-threatening injuries that parents' explanations did not explain; one parent saying she would be willing to lie if that was the only way to get her child back; physicians and investigators who believed the parents were already lying to cover themselves and prevent criminal charges. Where was the truth? And was the only path to progress to locate this truth first? I wondered if there was a way to move forward in the absence of knowing. Could I develop a therapeutic alliance with Beth, while all of these confounding factors swirled in the foreground? If such an alliance could be created, would that make any difference in the truths that emerged? What view would the guardian and the judge take of a decision to try and work with parents who continued to deny responsibility—parents referred to in case law as nonadmitting?

Frank and I suspected that if we moved forward with this couple, the judge would likely view us as ineffective, biased, and essentially unable to present reliable information as to the either parent's progress, and hence unable to make any reasonable recommendation about their readiness to regain custody. Every word we said and every document we produced would receive the highest scrutiny.

I could have taken an immovable stance with Beth, but if I did I knew that we would begin on an adversarial footing, and I could see that she was preparing herself for just such a relationship. From the very outset, Beth complained about her caseworker, about how she couldn't trust her and wanted her case transferred to someone she could trust. On a process level, I heard her expressing her distrust of me as well. She complained about her own mother (her child's relative foster parent), and how she resented the way her mother was caring for her child. I suspected that I had inadvertently joined a long line of women in authority with whom this young parent did battle, and by whom she felt unjustly accused and dismissed. I conferred with Frank, who had met with Beth's husband, Tim, for an assessment, and who was convinced that Tim was totally innocent. Despite our lengthy discussions about this case, my colleague's certainty made no sense to me. From my perspective there was uncertainty all around. But accepting uncertainty meant including the possibility that there just might be a way to work with the couple without insisting that they start by admitting guilt. I considered what might help my client to feel more at ease with the process. Beth seemed fearful and resentful that she and her husband were seen separately, and she felt that we had been intentionally attempting to encourage one of them to implicate the other. Frank felt that there was truly nothing more to be learned from seeing his client individually, and so despite the judge's court order for individual work, we brought the couple together to see if we could co-create a new dynamic that would help to get the case "unstuck."

There was a significant shift in the dynamic when we brought the parents together. Beth appeared to feel much more at ease than she had been when alone with me. Frank and I checked in with them about this, and Beth admitted, somewhat apologetically, that she did not feel that I was always hearing her side of things. I was relieved at her openness, thanked her for telling me, and confirmed that it was really good that she could share this with me, and that the more she could let me know when she felt that I was failing to stay with her would really help. During this session,

Beth also began to talk about her life in a way that she had not done before. She spoke at length about her frustration and feelings of isolation as she tried to care for her baby alone while Tim was at work. She admitted that she had had to give herself "time-outs" from caring for Chris when she would cry inconsolably and there was no one around to help. So in this first session of bringing Beth into the room with her husband, the nature of her talk shifted such that she was more open about the losses she experienced in trying to care for her child alone.

After reviewing my initial counseling assessment, the state's attorney called to ask if I were operating under the premise that the parents "did it" or "didn't do it," and that if the parents had stipulated to the facts that the injuries were caused by abuse, then *why* had I failed to create a treatment goal of having the parents accept responsibility for having caused the injuries; and if this was not currently a goal of treatment, then when *would* this become a treatment goal? The state's attorney also asked *if* I were working from the premise that the adjudication order was accurate, then *what evidence* existed that the parents were making any progress as documented in my initial assessment? The state's attorney seemed convinced that I was biased in favor of the parents, and that my biases were clearly getting in the way of seeing the facts.

When Beth read my initial counseling assessment, she was furious because it did not say what she thought it should say, and she told me angrily that she did not think people without children should be allowed to work with parents since they *could not possibly understand anything* about having a child! She was very frustrated that the case was not moving forward, and she was sure that I was standing in the way by what I had written. Beth was also angry with her mother for saying certain things to me about the way she parented during the visits, even though she had asked me to call and talk with her mother prior to the court date.

So on the one hand, Beth was angry because I had failed to represent her in a more positive light. And on the other hand, the state's attorney was convinced that I was representing Beth in a way that was biased in the direction of making her look too positive because I did not begin by making her admit guilt and responsibility.

After the first court date, Frank and I explained to Beth and Tim that the court was not satisfied that they fully recognized the risks to their child's safety; nor had they taken sufficient steps to address these risks. We saw the wedge as the focus on the balance of risk and protective factors, and if the parents could demonstrate that they recognized the risks, the part they played, and most importantly their role in identifying protective factors and garnering sufficient supports to put protective factors in place, then *perhaps* there would be a way to balance working with the parents while also assuring the court that their child could be protected going forward.

The Process of Co-Creating Mutually Accepted Goals

In a collaborative effort, we asked the couple to partner with us to flesh out the risks to their baby's safety and to consider carefully every offsetting protective factor they could possibly bring to bear to mitigate these risks. When they bristled at the court's assessment of risk, we invited them to do their own research on risk factors for child endangerment. Beth and Tim had never done such research, and they were quite eager to check behind us, hoping to demonstrate how the pediatric child protection team, the court, and Frank and I were all overreacting, since they were focused on their child's current state of significantly improved health. When they objected to our suggestions of what we thought would help their case, we gave them the freedom to come up with their own ideas about what they were willing to do to address any risks they could identify (DeJong and Kim Berg, 2001). We repeatedly invited them to present their perspective and to tell us what was important to them, and we spent a considerable amount of time listening and affirming their perspective, although we could not always agree with them.

When Beth and Tim did their own research on risk factors for child abuse, they were able to take a step back and see things from more than one perspective, and they admitted that there were indeed gaps in their ability to protect their baby. With this knowledge, Beth began to see that the purpose of identifying these gaps was to close them and not to blame her for them. We invited them to come up with any ideas they were willing to consider to close these gaps, and we offered to join them in brainstorming and to have them say what they thought of our ideas.

The process of coming to a meeting of minds around treatment goals began with helping Tim and Beth to discuss openly what they noticed as they conducted their own research (DeJong and Kim Berg, 2001). They noticed a number of factors that made it more likely that others would see risk, rather than the view of themselves they thought they were portraying: Beth revealed her own childhood history of abuse and neglect and a brief period of being in foster care. They discovered additional factors, such as their social isolation, lack of knowledge about child development, and risks that often accompany premature birth that are often considered potential risks to their baby's safety. Beth also disclosed frustration with Tim for failing to understand what she was going through at home alone, as well as frustration with her mother for judging her. She admitted that her frustration had made it difficult to attend to Chris when they had first brought her home from the hospital, and that the first few weeks of being separated from her had affected her ability to bond, and now she felt frustrated that everyone was putting all the blame on her. As Beth heard us convey that her frustration was completely understandable, she began to experience us less as adversaries.

Once the shift occurred where they no longer felt judged, Beth and Tim began to consider steps they were willing to take to address several risk factors that they could see operating in their lives, including their lack of knowledge about child development, a parent-child bond that was not as strong as they had hoped it would be, a general sense of isolation from social support systems, and a negative relationship with the relative caregiver, Beth's mother. They also became more amenable to considering other ideas that would demonstrate their commitment to their child's safety and healthy development. For example, we discussed the importance of developing a stronger bond with Chris, which would mean visiting her more often, even if that meant visiting individually, something Beth had firmly objected to early on. We asked them to consider what it would mean for the relationship with Chris if at least one of them visited frequently by comparison to having both of them visit together infrequently. They were able to recognize that infrequent contact with Chris would compromise her ability to develop a strong attachment to them, and they both said that they wanted to strengthen the attachment. They also recognized the importance of gaining more knowledge of child development, particularly about toddlers, since Chris was nearing her second birthday and was already having difficult tantrums during their visits. Frank and I had some concerns about their lack of understanding of this important developmental stage. We suggested that they do some reading about early child development and that they try journaling about how they responded to Chris during their visits, reflecting on her needs and development, as well as their feelings about the relationship with her. They responded by saying that they did not like the book Frank suggested and that they would look for their own material. They did agree to try journaling when they had visits.

After these discussions, we were able to agree on several treatment goals that included strengthening the parent/child bond, increasing their understanding of Chris's behavior and child development, and decreasing Beth's isolation by increasing her social support systems. Beth also began to be more aware of her reactions to stress and how she responded to everyone when she was angry. Some of this she identified as related to stressors in her family of origin, since her mother was Chris's primary caregiver and stressors in the relationship with her mother impacted the quality of visitation, as well as her motive to visit in the first place. Once Beth noticed how interrelated these concerns were, she saw the benefit of addressing the stressors in her relationship with her mother and her own tendency to become very angry when stressed. These seemed to be goals that Beth felt supported her personally, but they also supported an improved relationship with Chris and with her mother. In the co-construction of treatment goals, Beth began to recognize that Frank and I were invested in her progress and in favor of supporting the possibility to regain custody, as long as she and Tim could address the risks and follow through on strengthening protective factors.

Noticing Signs of Progress

There were several signs of progress developing as we continued to meet over the next few months, among them that Beth was more engaged in the counseling sessions and began to relate to Frank and I more as allies who could think *with* her about whether she was responding during visits with Chris the way she intended. As a result, she grew increasingly open about how she handled many things with her child and offered her own views about disciplinary techniques, such as how she felt about the use of "time-out." As Beth began to be more open, she could see that the space was there for her to reflect on *her own* motives and for her to be listened to without judgment. This awareness of the relational space, combined with the experience of being heard, seemed to bring about a positive shift in the direction of fewer angry reactions and more reflection.

I compared this increased ability to reflect to earlier reactions when Beth bristled and became very angry with us about the judge's refusal to grant unsupervised visitation. Initially, whenever she received news that she did not want to hear, she would respond angrily with, "This is dumb!" followed by shutting down, and turning her face away in a scowl. In the face of these disappointments, she at first had a tendency to interpret what she heard in a negative way. For example, when the judge refused to grant unsupervised visits, she assumed that Frank and I had written something or said something to the judge to bring about this ruling. This experience of loss tended to be followed by reactions akin to paranoia, and on more than one occasion Beth called her husband at the office to tell him that I had said she would never get Chris back. She spent a day or two thinking that I was covertly working to undermine her. It sometimes took an intervention from Tim to convince her that her impression was unwarranted. But as Beth began to make progress, her responses to loss began to shift in perceptible ways, as for example, when she received disappointing news from the court, she was able to be more reflective about the meaning of that news and did not automatically assume that anyone was out to get her. So by contrast with her initial responses to disappointments from the court, as she progressed, when the judge denied the unsupervised visitation that she and Tim had hoped for, she was able to see that the concern was for Chris's safety.

Another important sign of progress was that Beth started to show a deeper investment in her relationship with Chris, as evidenced by an increased willingness to visit her child alone and of her own accord. Whereas initially she had refused to visit Chris without her husband, after agreeing on the centrality of improving the bond with her, she began to visit Chris weekly and stayed longer, even if Tim had to work. Also, the tenor of her discussion about these visits changed markedly. Whereas initially these discussions sounded very flat and perfunctory, over time Beth began to speak in an animated and joyful way about the pleasure of being with her child. She began to think much more about things from Chris's point of view and about the impact of her choices, as for example, her use of "time-out," which she began to find distressing as she identified more with her child's feelings. When Chris would cry about being placed in time-out, Beth began to wonder if Chris was thinking that she wanted to create that distance between them and if that *motive* of intentionally creating distance hurt Chris even more than the actual punishment. As she visited her more often, Beth began to think more and more about her child's feelings and perspectives on what they did together.

Over time, Beth's response to a variety of losses noticeably shifted in the direction of increased reflection and a willingness to consider what was happening, without automatically responding as if the unwanted event was a personal criticism. Gradually, Frank and I noticed that when Beth experienced a loss she would try to listen and understand why something was being said about her. A notable example was her response to unflattering comments made about her in a bonding assessment performed by an outside examiner. Rather than becoming defensive, she expressed curiosity about what she had said that could have conveyed this impression. Compared to her responses ten months earlier, this availability to consider others' opinions represented significant progress. It appeared that this shift was in part the result of a relational process, whereby Beth had the experience of being cared for in a way that was gratifying to her and that represented a departure from earlier relationship experiences where she felt routinely demeaned or dismissed. The relationship process appeared to strengthen her motives to care for herself, such that Beth could recognize her prior shutting down as not offering the kind of protection she used to believe it offered, and she could then recognize that staying open to hear what people had to say would result in a more satisfying outcome for her and for her entire family. Some treatment models might describe this kind of change as demonstrating improved coping skills and better reality testing.

Beth also began to invest more initiative in her own progress by addressing other goals we had agreed upon as important to her parenting. To address her social isolation, she decided to reach out to another young parent in her neighborhood, forming a supportive friendship, and she located a parent support group near her home. She also became more aware of a relationship dynamic in her family of origin that had previously felt quite normal, but that she now wanted to change because she started to experience it as toxic. She described the dynamic as one where family members engaged in excessive verbal criticism, followed by "tuning out" in a way that "silenced" the critical person. When asked, Beth explained that this way of relating had been the norm in her family for "decades," as she recalled her grandparents and her mother interacting this way when she was a young child. She began to wonder if this old dynamic might be part of the reason her mother criticized her parenting so much. In addition, Beth began to notice that this was not just a dynamic that she fell victim to, but it was also a tactic that she used with other family members, again showing more openness and increased self-awareness. As her trust of the counseling process increased, Beth also began to be more open about the impact of such problematic communication patterns on the quality of her marriage with Tim, and also on their parenting. She noticed and talked openly about how she and Tim also engaged in this "tuning out" tactic to avoid addressing painful topics.

At ten months, it appeared that Beth experienced the counseling process as a legitimate source of personal and family support, and that she recognized the importance of having support as a way to strengthen the important relationships in her life and to shore up her parenting ideals. In general, I noticed less defensiveness and more openness to a range of opinions and perspectives from others, but also more tolerance and openness to her own internal processes, feelings, thoughts, and awareness of responses to others. These changes could be felt in the way the dialogue changed between us and also in the way that the dialogue changed between Beth and Tim during the counseling sessions. Early on in the process, Beth was often angry and distancing; she often closed down or backed away in a huff. She talked about her suspicion of people without children and how she didn't think they could be trusted. She talked about how she wanted a change in caseworkers (indirectly referring to the treatment relationship as well). But at the ten-month period Beth showed much stronger motives to stay engaged even during difficult times. She talked about good moments and difficult moments she had with her child and with her husband. She smiled and giggled when she was pleased. She asked for advice or input about things that were important to her. And when she felt upset or frustrated, she shared those feelings without suggesting that it was someone else's fault that she was feeling them. Over time being with her felt more like a dance we were all engaged in, and much less like walking on eggshells, as it had in the beginning.

Twelve months after our initial meeting, many differences seemed evident including a significant increase in Beth's desire to be both physically and emotionally available to her child; an increase in empathy for her child, particularly when she felt hurt or upset; a desire to use Chris's motives for care and comfort as the regulating guide for her caregiving responses; and an increased awareness of the parent/child bond and the painfulness of being apart. Other significant differences included Beth's motive to seek help with marital conflicts, as evidenced by a desire to talk openly about communication problems she and Tim experienced during disagreements.

She voluntarily asked for help with their tendency to shut down and then later blow up and distance themselves from each other, because she believed that their relationship would be stronger if they could change this dynamic. In seeking help with these communication problems, Beth said she now believed that asking for help was not a sign of personal deficiency and that being able to do so *improved* their parenting and interpersonal communication. She reported that they were better able to "hang in there" with each other and talk through difficult issues in less defensive ways, and were much less likely to walk away and tune each other out. She also expressed a wish to be able to communicate in a more conflict-free way with her mother, and she asked if we could help her improve that relationship as well.

Shortly after their twelve-month progress report, Beth and Tim asked to have the service transferred to a location closer to her mother's home so that visiting Chris would not involve such a long commute. They also asked if we could intervene to have her mother participate, as they recognized that Beth's mother continued to treat her as if she were still the rebellious teen she had once been. She identified wanting to have a better relationship with her mother as important and thought it would be important to have some help addressing some longstanding negative relationship patterns with her mother.

Evaluating Treatment

At this point, Frank and I invited Beth and Tim to review the work we had done together, to identify how they felt they had been helped, or what they thought was different from when we began. As usual, Beth did most of the talking. In evaluating the service, Beth said she thought they were both more open now to admitting when they needed help, and they were better at asking for help and not feeling that asking meant that they were bad parents. They had come to believe that asking for help actually enabled them to be *better* parents. Beth also said they were better at addressing issues between the two of them and admitting that they needed to work on their relationship, which they had never done. Prior to treatment they would simply not talk and then would periodically blow up at each other, and that had greatly decreased. They noticed that they had not had any big fights in a long time. They both said that they had learned more about how to take care of Chris and how to handle her tantrums without getting into big power struggles.

Beth said she thought that they had learned a lot about risks for abuse and that they had addressed most of the risks for abuse and neglect. She giggled as she said they believe that they worked on all the treatment goals, sometimes without really meaning to. They agreed that they hated being told what to do, and they felt that what we had said at first was dumb, but they now saw that it really wasn't dumb and that it had actually helped them. Beth also talked about how she used to get really mad and just shut down, and now she was able to listen to criticism more without getting as mad as she had before. They both seemed pleased to reflect on their progress and what they had accomplished over the year of working together.

Issues and Challenges

Managing Institutional Challenges and Service Users' Expectations

In work with parents whose children have been removed, officers of the court tend to be skeptical when treatment providers take an approach that deviates from a legal understanding of what constitutes successful resolution of the situation that brought children into care. Judges and guardians want to hear testimony from treatment providers about the parents' understanding of problems that led to the separation, and most importantly they want to hear that parents' have clearly accepted responsibility for what went wrong. They insist on having evidence that the original conditions have been thoroughly "addressed" in the treatment, that parents recognize and are prepared to prevent any further risks, and that they have built in sufficient protective factors to ensure children's safety.

Judges may not think about case resolution in black and white terms when off the bench, but official testimony does not welcome shades of gray. This is understandable given that children's safety is on the line, and no one wants children to sustain further injury after returning them to their families. It is also important to keep in mind that judges and guardians hear similar cases for months (sometimes years) on end, and the never-ending flood of abuse and neglect cases naturally affects how they see parents. So guardians tend to ask questions about parents and treatment progress in terms that may conflict with the way treatment has actually taken place, or with the way parents and treatment providers have been thinking about it. In addition, testimony has to be given in a kind of legal language, so treatment providers must have a clear understanding of the legal expectations and may need to translate the work that has been accomplished into language the court understands. This can feel subjectively discordant to parents and treatment providers, since it means taking a constructionist understanding of the case and sifting it through a different categorical, less forgiving lens. It is important to keep in mind that the legal system is intentionally adversarial and in the courtroom treatment providers advocating for parents may be viewed with skepticism or even demeaned unless they are skilled in speaking about the case in legal terms. Further, it is impossible to remove all elements of risk given that most parents in the system are very poor and live in poor (and sometimes crime-ridden) communities that carry significant risks for *all* residents. And while this is obvious to service providers and to clients, explaining to the court that some risks will always be beyond the client's control is not likely to be helpful since the legal system prefers that all possible risks be resolved.

With these tensions in mind, it is important to understand that what helps clients in the treatment setting and what may help them in court can be entirely different things, and workers must be prepared to respond differently according to the setting (Wood and Tully, 2006). In the case presented, and in most child welfare cases, there is an ongoing tension between agency clients and officers of the court who often disagree about the nature of the problem, the facts of the case, and what constitutes case resolution. The court environment and that of the family are very different worlds. The need to ensure that children will be protected means that there will continue to be court oversight, and this means that the court and its officers (the guardian, the state's attorney, and the judge) are also service users and should be considered as such. Professional training means that legal officers generally rely on an adversarial process and a history of case law that they do not view as negotiable even as it shifts with the rulings on new cases. Most often they try cases in black or white: The parent is either guilty or innocent, in need of rehabilitation or not, and in the absence of a confession they are convinced that children will be at great risk. The parents' experience is anything but black and white. Parents in the system are often navigating a confluence of very difficult waterways: insufficient financial resources, insufficient social support, unsafe neighborhoods, family histories of abuse, addiction, domestic violence, and sometimes their own addiction.

Child endangerment is rarely intentional, but is more likely when parents are negotiating these multiple streams with insufficient resources and insufficient supports. The demand on the worker is to understand the nature of these very different worlds and to find a way to navigate between them, to be conversant in both of them concurrently, to translate between them, and to try to find a way to enrich the parents' social environment on multiple levels such that risks to children are decreased. Of course, the resources workers can garner on behalf of these families are rarely enough to satisfy their needs, and the time constraints allowed for case resolution generally demand early evidence of parents' behavioral rehabilitation over and above enrichment of the parents' social environment and economic situation. The expectation that parents will make rapid behavioral changes, in addition to reducing risk by improving neighborhood contexts or finding more and better resources within chronically impoverished neighborhoods, brings significant stressors into the treatment setting. Some parents become overwhelmed by the magnitude of expectations, and many give up trying.

Social constructionist ideas provide workers with a framework for viewing and understanding these colliding viewpoints and social realities without reifying any one of them, which is essential given that the juvenile court has substantially more power to determine the parents' fate with regard to reunification. In the absence of a framework for assessing the relative merit of multiple viewpoints (and indeed the value of considering them concurrently), the tendency would be to espouse one specific frame for analyzing a case. Social workers come into the field of child welfare with very strong motivations to help, and so depending on one's view of what constitutes help, one can easily be co-opted by the power inherent in the legal system to determine what constitutes legitimate child protection. But it is just as easy to be won over by a parent's extreme vulnerability. One does not have to work in the field very long before it becomes painfully obvious that parents have often experienced difficult childhood histories of deprivation and loss similar in many ways to those undergone by their children. Sadly, some case files document multiple generations of the same family having spent time in foster care. It is imperative that workers recognize and understand multiple, colliding truths, those that lie within the judge's frame of reference, within the parent's, within our own, and whenever possible, within the child's. These viewpoints are not likely to line up in a seamless way, and so it behooves us to step back and ask, "Given the multiplicity of perspectives, including a comprehensive assessment of risk, what constitutes good help in this particular situation?"

In the case presented here, my colleague and I believed it worth the risk to challenge the notion that child safety could not be achieved in the absence of parental confession. We could not know in advance what direction the parents would take, but over time we came to believe that their increased openness, decreased defensiveness, and personal choice to bring more history and more relational issues into the treatment space suggested that they were serious about improving the relationships across their lives, including their parenting. So our court documents continued to push this perspective. The ability to document the parents' progress in the absence of a confession helped the judge to consider our viewpoints while concurrently listening to the guardian ad litem. Meanwhile, the child's guardian objected consistently and unrelentingly to our recommendations, and the judge agreed with her right to the end and publicly admonished us for failing to determine whether the parents had "directly addressed the injuries" that brought Chris into care. The judge stated that he was not obligating the parents to admit guilt, but that he needed evidence that they accepted responsibility for their child's injuries, and he did not see this evidence. Despite the parents' refusal to admit responsibility for the initial injury, the judge granted the agency discretion to increase parental visitation, while continuing to express his displeasure about the shortcomings of our treatment choices. He insisted that he wanted the new therapists picking up the case to be clear about his imperative that these parents accept responsibility for the child's injuries. The judge also emphasized that he wanted a return to individual counseling for both parents because the case had never been about communication between the parents. In this ruling, it is easy to see how the court discounted the impact of marital harmony and communication on the couple's parenting and on their functioning as individuals.

This case is in no way intended to present a recipe or template for how to help parents who refuse to admit, nor should it be used as a template for how to assess risk, although my colleague and I were very intentionally assessing risk every time we met with this couple. There is an ever-growing body of literature addressing risk assessment in child welfare practice (Baird and Wagner, 2000; Baumann et al., 2005; English and Pecora, 1994; Gambrill and Shlonsky, 2001; Schwalbe, 2004, 2008; Shlonsky and Wagner, 2005). Indeed, the tension between camps preferring actuarial assessments and those preferring consensus-based or clinical assessments has mounted to the point where these debates are being conceptualized as war (Baumann et al., 2006; Johnson, 2006). All risk assessment concerns the attempt to identify situations where children are in danger and to determine the appropriate type of intervention. Actuarial instruments attempt to estimate the probability of future maltreatment at the point where Child Protective Services closes an investigation and must decide whether to open the case for additional services or close it altogether. And despite the mounting evidence on the efficacy of actuarial risk assessments, I think that we will never escape the necessity (and the risk) of using our informed judgments, in part because interpreting the meaning of complex situations is what social workers are inevitably called to do. This is because the processes and skills that breathe life into the principles we entered the profession to use demand some dialogic flexibility that allows us to pay very close attention and to respond to the unique needs and strengths each person brings. Is client empowerment a possibility if we close ourselves off to our own judgment?

While it is valuable to understand the risk debates, it is also important to avoid being consumed by them, because they tend to focus our attention narrowly on the relative merits of either method, and in so doing we are distracted from broader concerns. So for example, if we focus our attention on which method more accurately predicts future maltreatment or the likelihood that a report will be substantiated, are we not being distracted from assessing the neighborhood, community and cultural contexts, and how these contextual variables might support adaptive family processes or conspire to undermine them (Garbarino, 1995; Garbarino and Barry, 1997)? Do the risk assessment debates help us to ask the questions, "What do these parents (indeed all parents) need to take the best care of their children, and how can we help them to access these resources? How can we create the resources that poor families need to care for their children? How do we as social workers and as a society move from an environment where we are narrowly focused on child protection crises to one where we can address more broadly defined child welfare issues and the system's goal of improved family and child well being?"

Future Directions

The Case for Prevention

Nearly twenty years ago, my first social work supervisor said, "There is an endless stream of children coming into the system." While there are fewer children in the child welfare system today than there were in 1992, there are still many factors operating that make his words seem tragically prophetic. State budget allocations for child welfare services far outstrip allocations for prevention programs. Neglect and abuse are strongly associated with family and neighborhood poverty, and the numbers of families living in poverty-stricken communities continue to rise (Dworsky et al., 2007; Gourdine, 2007). In large measure, we as a nation hold fast to a view of child abuse and neglect as problems that arise within individual families, and our interventions are primarily focused at the level of individuals, although we would likely make far more progress if we could convincingly recast this problem as a public health concern. Such a shift in thinking does not seem likely to happen in the near future.

The guiding objectives of the child welfare system are safety, permanency, and family and child well-being. To the extent that the system focuses on narrow definitions of child safety and permanency, and struggles to articulate and flesh out a meaningful understanding of family and child well-being, we are not likely to see real changes in how the system responds to children and families in need of assistance. Given the crisis-oriented state of the child welfare field and the adversarial nature of the legal system, it is likely that workers will continue to find themselves in situations similar to the one represented in Beth's case. And since we know that foster care is by no means a panacea for the multiproblem situations that land children and families there, we need to look in many directions for possible ways to prevent children's placement, and to ameliorate the family situation. This requires advocacy and action on multiple levels (individual, community, agency, and policy).

When we as social workers find ourselves working with individuals, one avenue will be honing the skills needed to engage involuntary parents in collaborative ways, including those who may initially resist discussions of how children were injured when signs suggest that parents may have played a role in their injuries. Social constructionist principles help engage parents who are mandated to treatment because its processes attempt to depathologize clients' situations and to bring their voices and perspectives to the fore (DeJong and Kim Berg, 2001). These ideas remind us not to stand in the role of expert, to listen with a "not knowing" stance, and to question which stories receive credibility and which are institutionalized (Anderson, 1997). They also remind us to look to broader systems for their contributions to the problem and to the solutions, to look for client strengths and ways that the family has managed to survive, and to co-create interventions that will address the problems on multiple levels (Wood and Tully, 2006).

Current Trends

The current trend in the field of child welfare is to demand greater state accountability via the creation of national standards designed to assess states' performances with regard to child protection and child welfare outcomes. States are expected to be in substantial conformity with these standards as evidenced by the degree to which they meet certain performance outcomes (Courtney et al., 2004). Conformity is determined by matching specific quantitative indicators of child safety and permanency (e.g., rates of maltreatment recurrence, the incidence of abuse or neglect in foster care, foster care entries and re-entries, length of time to reunification or adoption, and stability of foster placements). The data, submitted to automated reporting systems such as CFSR (Child and Family State Reviews), AFCARS (Adoption and Foster Care Analysis and Reporting Systems), NCANDS (National Child Abuse and Neglect Data Systems), and SACWIS (Statewide Automated Child Welfare Information Systems), focus on narrow indicators of child safety and permanency and, since it is collected at the program level, is often limited in its ability to tell us how children actually fare. For example, the demand to reduce the number of placements a child has could translate into workers feeling pressured to keep a child in a particular home even if the home is a poor fit. At the program level, the data represented by the stability of this placement looks like success, but tells us nothing about the viability of that foster relationship and how it contributes (or fails to contribute) to the well-being of the child or foster parent. Further, the demand that workers in the trenches spend more time documenting this information means they have less time to deliver services, which can lead to situations where workers know less about how children fare. As successfully meeting the national target indicators comes to be seen as good performance, the indicators themselves start to shape our understandings of child welfare in ways that may say little about the actual welfare of system clients. In other words, contrary to being objective barometers of good performance, they too are social constructions (Tilbury, 2004). This is not meant to say that the data are unimportant, but the data should not be accepted as the primary barometers for how the system is meeting its goals, particularly the goal of improving family and child well-being.

The demand for accountability is surely a good thing when it means evaluating child welfare practices on multiple levels to determine whether or not we are actually improving the lives of children and families. However, if the manner in which we do so leaves no space to consider the goal of family and child well-being more broadly defined, and if the data collection processes constrict the meanings we construct about the nature of child welfare practice such that it is reduced to a system surrounding mandated reporting, abuse investigations, and foster care, then we need to ask to what degree we have lost the ability to consider more broadly what child welfare practice could otherwise mean. If social workers employed in the field of child welfare were allowed to allocate some portion of their work week to thinking creatively about how to improve the welfare of children and families, perhaps the research about these workers would be about the intrinsic rewards of this work instead of the high levels of burnout and the constant struggle to retain skilled workers. Given more freedom to think with fewer restrictions about clients' needs (in lieu of casework documentation demands), families might throw open their arms and greet us with enormous smiles when we identify ourselves as child welfare workers. If we were given the freedom to think broadly and creatively about child welfare, wouldn't social workers engaged in this work be some of the most popular people on the planet? When their doorbells ring, parents in need might respond, "Thank goodness the child welfare worker has finally arrived! I've been waiting for you! What on earth took you so long?" Child welfare workers do not receive that kind of welcome—and are more typically greeted with suspicion by families, and with disdain or even pity by the larger community. When I interviewed to embark on my doctoral education, and told the interviewer how long I had been working in the field of child welfare, she shook her head and said, "That's a burnout job. How have you managed to survive?"

Unfortunately, the trend toward creating large automated databases that can track system outcomes has not translated into the development of better programs or healthier communities for disadvantaged families. Anecdotal information from agency administrators who have worked in the field of child welfare for thirty years or more suggests that families entering the system today have more problems and are doing considerably worse compared with families that needed these services thirty years ago. Research supports these anecdotal reports of families in the system having more severe needs in recent years (Hohman et al., 2003; Marsh et al., 2006; Spratt and Devaney, 2009). We need to ask ourselves why this is the trend and what indicators would tell us that we are making progress solving that problem.

Possibilities

If creating national indicators of safety and permanency and demanding that states document progress toward meeting them has not resulted in recognizable benefits for children and families, perhaps we should consider changing what it means to be accountable. Why not change the indicators to reflect more comprehensive priorities, for example, those known to be key indicators of children's well-being, especially poverty, education, and healthcare (www.childstats.gov)? What would it mean to shift the focus in child welfare practice from a crisis response to large-scale prevention in the interest of supporting the well-being of all families? Would it really cost more than what we spend today? Some researchers think not (Foster et al., 2008). What would it take to house programs in communities that respond to families and neighborhoods in ways that preempt crises (Fernandez, 2007)? And how might we engage other institutions (e.g., law and education) to help our professional colleagues understand this shift and its practical implications as we endeavor to make it? How might we move the field from one that is focused on families that are stigmatized to one that is focused on asset-based community capacity building and family support (Mannes, Roehlkepartain, and Benson, 2005)? When we evaluate our progress toward these kinds of goals, we will know we are moving in the right direction when the language being spoken by workers and administrators in public child welfare agencies is a language of hope that centers on the enhancement of health, happiness, and the general well-being of children, families, and communities. Shouldn't that be what we mean when we talk about child welfare?

Notes

1. All names in the document have been changed to protect the identities of children and parents whose lives are depicted here.
2. Guardian ad litem is a Latin term used in most U.S. juvenile courts to designate the child's legal representative.

3. Radical listening refers to a process of inviting and attending to all aspects of the client's story in order to understand their unique meanings. The worker focuses entirely on what the client is saying, listening for what is said and for what is not said, and tries to get into the client's subjective experience of himself or herself in his or her world. The worker should try to listen without imposing diagnostic categories and other filters of cultural, generational, and sociopolitical differences (Wood and Tully, 2006).

References

Agathonos-Georgopoulou, H. (1992). Cross-cultural perspectives in child abuse and neglect. *Child Abuse Review*, 1: 80–88.

Anderson, H. (1997). Client voices: Practical advice from the experts on how to create dialogical conversations and collaborative relationships. In H. Anderson (Ed.), *Conversation, language, and possibilities: A postmodern approach to therapy* (pp. 132–165). New York: Basic.

Baird, C. and D. Wagner (2000). The relative validity of actuarial and consensus-based risk assessment systems. *Children and Youth Services Review*, 22: 839–871.

Barber, J. H. and P. H. Delfabbro (2004). *Children in foster care*. London: Routledge.

Baumann, D. J., J. R. Law, J. Sheets, G. Reid, and J. C. Graham (2005). Evaluating the effectiveness of actuarial risk assessment models. *Children and Youth Services Review*, 27: 546–490.

—— (2006). Remarks concerning the importance of evaluating actuarial risk assessment models: A rejoinder to Will Johnson. *Children and Youth Services Review*, 28: 715–725.

Buehler, C., M. E. Cox, and G. Cuddeback (2003). Foster parents' perceptions of factors that promote or inhibit successful fostering. *Qualitative Social Work*, 2(1): 61–83.

Chestang, L. (1972). The dilemma of biracial adoption. *Social Work*, 17(3): 100–105.

Courtney, M. E., B. Needell, and F. Wulczyn (2004). Unintended consequences of the push for accountability: The case of national child welfare performance standards. *Children and Youth Services Review*, 26: 1141–1154.

Cox, M. E., J. G. Orme, and K. W. Rhodes (2002). Willingness to foster special needs children and foster family utilization. *Children and Youth Services Review*, 24: 293–318.

—— (2003). Willingness to foster children with emotional or behavioral problems. *Journal of Social Service Research*, 29(4): 23–51.

DeJong, P. and I. K. Berg (2001). Co-constructing cooperation with mandated clients. *Social Work*, 46(4): 361–374.

Dworksy, A., M. E. Courtney, and A. Zinn (2007). Child, parent and family predictors of child welfare services involvement among TANF applicant families. *Children and Youth Services Review*, 29: 802–820.

English, D. J. and P. J. Pecora (1994). Risk assessment as a practice method in child protective services. *Child Welfare*, 73: 451–473.

Fernandez, E. (2007). Supporting children and responding to their families: Capturing the evidence on family support. *Children and Youth Services Review*, 29: 1368–1394.

Foster, E. M., R. J. Prinz, M. R. Sanders, and C. J. Shapiro (2008). The costs of a public health infrastructure for delivering parenting and family support. *Children and Youth Services Review*, 30: 493–501.

Furman, F. K. (2005). The long road home: Migratory experience and the construction of the self. *Journal of Prevention & Intervention in the Community*, 30(1–2): 91–116.

Gambrill, E. and A. Shlonsky (2001). The need for comprehensive risk management systems in child welfare. *Children and Youth Services Review*, 23: 79–107.

Garbarino, J. (1995). *Raising children in a socially toxic environment*. San Francisco: Jossey Bass.

Garbarino, J. and F. Barry (1997). The community context of child abuse and neglect. In J. Garbarino and J. Eckenrode (Eds.), *Understanding abusive families: An ecological approach to theory and practice* (pp. 56–85). San Francisco: Jossey-Bass.

Gourdine, R. M. (2007). Child-only kinship care cases: The unintended consequences of TANF policies for families who have health problems and disabilities. *Journal of Health and Social Policy*, 22(3–4): 45–64.

Hohman, M. M., A. M. Shillington, and H. Grigg Baxter (2003). A comparison of pregnant women presenting for alcohol and other drug treatment by CPS status. *Child Abuse & Neglect*, 27(3): 303–317.

Hong, G. K. and L. K. Hong (1991). Comparative perspectives on child abuse and neglect: Chinese versus Hispanics and whites. *Child Welfare*, 70: 463–475.

Johnson, W. (2006). The risk assessment wars: A commentary. Response to "Evaluating the Effectiveness of Actuarial Risk Assessment Models" by Donald Baumann, J. Randolph Law, Janess Sheets, Grant Reid, and J. Christopher Graham, *Children and Youth Services Review*, 27: 465–490. *Children and Youth Services Review*, 28: 704–714.

Korbin, J. E. and J. C. Spilsbury (1999). Cultural competence and child neglect. In H. Dubowitz (Ed.), *Neglected children: Research, practice and policy* (pp. 69–88). Thousand Oaks, CA: Sage.

Mannes, M., E. C. Roehlkepartain, and P. L. Benson (2005). Unleashing the power of community to strengthen the well-being of children, youth, and families: An asset-building approach. *Child Welfare*, 84(2): 233–250.

Marsh, J. C., J. P. Ryan, S. Choi, and M. F. Testa (2006). Integrated services for families with multiple problems: Obstacles to family reunification. *Children and Youth Services Review*, 28: 1074–1087.

McClain, L. (1986). *A foot in each world: Essays and articles.* Evanston, IL: Northwestern University Press.

Millstein, K. H. (1993). Building knowledge from the study of cases: A reflective model for practitioner self-evaluation. In J. Laird (Ed.), *Revisioning social work education: A social constructionist approach* (pp. 255–279). Binghamton, NY: Haworth Press.

Nelson, K. (1985). *Making sense: The acquisition of shared meaning.* Orlando, FL: Academic Press.

——. (1989). *Narratives from the crib.* Cambridge, MA: Harvard University Press.

Newton, R. R., A. J. Litrownik, and J. A. Landsverk (2000). Children and youth in foster care: Disentangling the relationship between problem behaviors and number of placements. *Child Abuse & Neglect*, 24: 1363–1374.

Saari, C. (1991). *The creation of meaning in clinical social work.* New York: Guilford Press.

——. (1993). Identity complexity as an indicator of health. *Clinical Social Work Journal*, 21: 11–24.

——. (2002). *The environment: Its role in psychosocial functioning and psychotherapy.* New York: Columbia University Press.

Saleebey, D. (1993). Notes on interpreting the human condition: A "constructed" HBSE curriculum. In J. Laird (Ed.), *Revisioning social work education: A social constructionist approach* (pp. 197–217). New York: Haworth Press.

Schwalbe, C. S. (2004). Re-visioning risk assessment for human service decision making. *Children and Youth Services Review*, 26: 561–576.

——. (2008). Strengthening the integration of actuarial risk assessment with clinical judgment in an evidence based practice framework. *Children and Youth Services Review*, 30: 1458–1464.

Shlonsky, A. and D. Wagner (2005). The next step: Integrating actuarial risk assessment and clinical judgment into an evidence-based practice framework in CPS case management. *Children and Youth Services Review*, 27: 409–427.

Smith, D. K., E. Stormshak, P. Chamberlain, and R. B. Whaley (2001). Placement disruption in treatment foster care. *Journal of Emotional and Behavioral Disorders*, 9: 200–206.

Spratt, T. and J. Devaney (2009). Identifying families with multiple problems: Perspectives of practitioners and managers in three nations. *British Journal of Social Work*, 39(3): 418–434.

Sroufe, L. A., B. Egeland, E. A. Carlson, and W. A. Collins (2005). *The development of the person: The Minnesota study of risk and adaptation from birth to adulthood.* New York: Guildford Press.

Tilbury, C. (2004). The influence of performance measurement on child welfare policy and practice. *British Journal of Social Work,* 34(2): 225–241.

Tyson, K. B. (1995). *New foundations for scientific social and behavioral research: The heuristic paradigm.* Boston: Allyn & Bacon.

Wallerstein, J. S. (1987). Children of divorce: Report of a ten-year follow-up of early latency-age children. *American Journal of Orthopsychiatry,* 57: 199–211.

Wood, G. G. and C. T. Tully (2006). *The structural approach to direct practice in social work: A social constructionist perspective.* New York: Columbia University Press.

[8]

Shedding Light on the Expert Witness Role in Child Welfare Work

The Value of Social Constructionism

TRISH WALSH

My words fly up, my thoughts remain below;
Words without thoughts never to heaven go.
—Claudius, act 3, scene iii, of *Hamlet*

Since my move from social work practice to social work education in the mid-1990s, I have retained a small practice base as an expert witness and independent social worker in public law child protection cases. These cases primarily involve care proceedings taken by the Irish authorities (often referred to as social services) under child welfare legislation in cases of child maltreatment but have also included assessments of relatives (as potential carers) of Irish children in care in the English system.

In this chapter, I will describe my work in this role and how I have found a social constructionist perspective to be invaluable in illuminating not only the position I hold but also in expanding the potential of the work I do with families, courts, and child protection workers. A Foucauldian analysis of power relations (1979, 1980) drawing on the relationships between power, knowledge, and discourse is central to my effort to unsettle established practices and specifically the role of the "expert" witness, in order to open up possibilities for creative practice with families.

A Journey of Discovery

My practice biography runs from the late 1970s, when I qualified as a social worker in Dublin, through a ten-year period of work in London, both in child welfare and mental health, before a return to Dublin in the early 1990s and a move into social work education on a fulltime basis fourteen years ago.

Along the way, I completed advanced training in mental health social work with children and families at the Maudsley Hospital in 1989, where my interest in systemic work and family therapy deepened. At the same time, I was introduced to solution-focused therapy (SFT) (de Shazer et al., 1986; de Shazer et al., 2007) through the work of Chris Iveson and colleagues at the Marlborough Family Service in London (George et al., 1990). Having previously co-worked with Chris and his colleagues at the Marlborough (we were all social work employees of the same local authority), I was already impressed by not only their very effective work but also their respectful and collaborative approach to clients. When they offered their first three-month training course in SFT in 1989, I jumped at the chance. Initially I struggled with some of the central concepts, especially the (at the time) radical notions of clients as experts on their own lives; of reframing the worker as facilitator and collaborator rather than problem-solver; and of the concept of "not-knowing," being provisional in one's assessments, and focusing more on the here and now and the unfolding of knowledge through dialogue and relationship than on the confirmation of suspicions or hypotheses. More of these five concepts in relation to court work later. For now, back to the journey.

It felt like a significant leap of faith to embrace this new approach. Having spent years in generic, community-based social work services, I was just finding my feet as an "expert" in family therapy and now this new idea had come along to tell me that I was not an expert—and furthermore, that thinking I was an expert was downright dangerous! I became more intrigued about the meaning of concepts, such as knowledge, therapy, change, expert, and power. Although SFT has its critics and can be viewed (particularly in its original formulation for clinic-based practice) as a formulaic, strategic approach far from the social justice mandate of "real" social work, for me the core concepts, especially the belief in people's ability to build better lives, the hope that underlies the approach, and the emphasis on really listening to how clients experience their own lives was both humbling and exhilarating. SFT became, for me, a vehicle of change—an approach that fundamentally challenged my assumptions about, and ways of doing, social work.

The change of heart that a social constructionist approach invoked for me is captured in the following excerpt from an earlier publication in which I tried to articulate what is needed on the part of the practitioner to embrace SFT:

> This approach starts from the position that clients are the experts on their own lives, and that the best therapy is done when people work towards goals they have identified. . . . For practitioners to use this method, they need to feel comfortable with not knowing the answers. They need to feel okay about giving the client a lot of control, and they need to maintain an interested but open-minded curiosity about what might emerge in this piece of work with this client. They must overturn a lot of the received wisdom about social work: social workers do not need to know all the answers; the less we think we know the answers to other people's problems, the better. Each situation is so uniquely different in any case that creativity is always required, rather than technical rationality (Walsh, 1997: 80).

Questions of epistemology and philosophy came later. My starting point was a growing awareness that for my work with clients in social work, solution-focused concepts and principles offered hope, release from a self-imposed impossible task (of always needing to be right or always able to solve problems), and a real sense of a different quality of engagement with clients. These were not insignificant advantages over existing expert practice methods, especially given my specialty in child welfare and mental health. For me, my work was energized and my confidence raised that change could happen. The burden was lifted because "SFBT suggests a much more equal partnership between client and therapist, one in which the client does as much or more 'heavy lifting' as the therapist. With this shift also can come a more relaxed connection to clients. *It's easier to be an interested and compassionate companion for someone on the road to change when you don't feel burdened with the responsibility of their change"* (de Shazer et al., 2007: 163–164, my emphasis).

For me, SFT is social constructionist in the very real sense that it is "based on the concept that reality is an intersubjective phenomenon, constructed in conversation among people" (Wetchler, 1996: 129). As de Shazer developed his ideas further, the influence of Wittgenstein's philosophical work on language became more obvious, although de Shazer firmly states that Wittgensteinian philosophy is not a grand theory underlying SFT; rather he sees a parallel between Wittgenstein's view that the philosophical problems that concerned him involved traps or knots that are inherent within language and the therapeutic process, which also contain such traps and knots, so that "therapists and clients are subject to falling into the same and similar traps, and to getting all tied up in the same kinds of knots . . . language must be used to resolve muddles and to get us out of the traps and knots inherent in language" (de Shazer et al., 2007: 101).

My interest in social constructionist and strengths-based approaches deepened after I had managed the major paradigm shift from expert-led to client-led practitioner (more of this later). This deepening interest led me to take on research studies into the momentum for change in the helping professions, which had built throughout the 1980s and 1990s, and the philosophical traditions of constructivism and postmodernism, which combined with social constructionism and underpinned the emerging new practices of narrative and solution-focused therapy. So far, this journey has led to a completed Ph.D. thesis on the Diffusion of Innovation—a case study of the introduction of solution-focused therapy to Irish social workers (Walsh, 2002); a first publication on how Irish child welfare workers were using it in practice (Walsh, 1997); and a continuing journey of discovery about both the value and limitations of experts and expert systems and the potential for therapeutic change in regulatory social work practice (Walsh, 2006; 2010). But what do SFT and social constructionism mean to me, and how are they linked?

Social Constructionism

Perception is the subjective and relational experiences that shape the meanings and understandings we develop about the world we inhabit and also shape the manner in which we engage with it and each other. A social constructionist viewpoint (Payne, 1997) accepts the varied experiences that different people may have and acknowledges the importance of subjective experience. A key distinction for me lies between constructionism/ constructivism and positivism. Positivism is concerned with "formal scientific and intellectual knowledge"; social constructionism with "everyday knowing, the perceptions of reality that form our daily behavior and relations with each other" (Payne, 1999: 36). Iversen et al. (2005) make an important distinction between constructionism and constructivism in emphasizing that the former is essentially relational whereas the latter "locates the process of construction in the mind" (690). When applied to social work, social constructionist thinking "requires the inclusion of reality and self-consciousness . . . because social work activity does not merely seek to explain and account for but to interact and change the context of social constructions" (Payne, 1999: 36–37). For me, the possibility of interacting with—and changing—the context of social constructions is particularly inviting in my work at the interface of social work and legal systems.

Adopting a social constructionist mindset means that I remain wary of the tendency to label, to essentialize experiences and acts, and I try to avoid being reductionist in my thinking. It does not mean adopting a position whereby "anything goes" or that either cultural or moral relativism should shape the parameters of social work practice. Values and ethics of social work and the helping professions need to continue to inform practice. But stories, explanations, and understandings remain important, both as causal narratives and as subjective realities. It is, however, in the dialogical process that both client and professional narratives can be exposed and explored. A social constructionist viewpoint allows this to happen because there is no search for an ultimate truth (although this does not mean that there is no need for an ultimate understanding), rather there is an examination of perspectives, beliefs, and hopes within a respectful relationship. And this includes the need for ongoing reflection on the part of helpers, a self-consciousness that allows us to be reflexive, to consider how we impact others, how we present to others, how we are perceived, and that includes the context within which we engage, as well as our role and specific mandate. Remaining solution-focused but extending its reach into social work practice means making some adjustments. Parton and O'Byrne (2000) outline a social constructionist framework for social work practice which incorporates both solution-focused and narrative concepts and techniques. Their constructive approach ". . . emphasizes process, plurality of both knowledge and voice, possibility and the relational quality of knowledge . . . An ability to work with ambiguity and uncertainty both in terms of process and outcomes is key" (184).

For me, social constructionism crucially emphasizes language as communication which can at times restrict and oppress, but which can also expand and liberate. As noted by Hartman (1991), words create worlds. The philosopher, Ludwig Wittgenstein—best known for his work on language and its importance in shaping our worlds—influenced therapists as attention in psychology and the therapies became focused in the 1980s towards constructivism and an increased emphasis on how people create meaning systems and beliefs about their experiences. The "constructivist turn" began to influence family therapy in the 1980s (Family Therapy Networker,

1988; Burck, 1995) as the work of McNamee and Gergen (1992), Saleebey (1992), White and Epston (1990) also began to focus on the negative effects of language in pathologizing and labeling clients. Both narrative and solution-focused practitioners are interested in mining these concepts and releasing their potential for more empowering forms of practice based on dialogue, an exploration of narrative and meaning, and a search for more hopeful and positive frames of understanding and action. For me the vehicle into this new paradigm was initially that of the work of Steve de Shazer, Insoo Kim Berg, and their colleagues at the Brief Family Therapy Center in Milwaukee, Wisconsin. Their seminal article (de Shazer et al., 1986) in *Family Process* for some time accompanied me on every social work appointment.

The Bridge Between Solution-Focused Therapy and Social Constructionism

In the early 1990s, solution-focused therapy (SFT) was part of a new generation of social constructionist-inspired models within the family therapy field. Applied to family therapy, I view social constructionism as "ideas, concepts and memories [as] arising from social interchange and mediated through language" (Hoffman, 1991: 8). SFT and social constructionism appear to fit each other, with the exception of the fairly prescriptive specific *strategies* used by the worker adopting a solution-focused approach. Although the metaphor of a conversation may now be used to denote the therapeutic encounter, to signal the changes towards a more equal relationship between client and worker, and to indicate that both have contributions to make, there is a limit to how far the metaphor can be taken if the worker is also to fulfill his or her professional and ethical obligation to offer some expertise in how problems may be solved or solutions constructed. Not only in SFT but in its closest relative within the social construction field—narrative therapy—specific tools *are* used to help clients make changes. Tools include the Miracle Question, scaling and exception-finding questions, and externalizing the problem and identifying "unique outcomes." In accepting that social workers use influence to help people to change and use these "tools" to help them to do so, I think that we need to explicitly restrict the extent to which the metaphor of "conversation" can be used to depict the helping encounter, especially when workers have legal mandates which can restrict freedom and choice.[1] Nonetheless, at this intersection between influence and change, I find a social constructionist mindset most useful, and as I will explain further in relation to my work in court systems, the question of who is expert in what way about what matters becomes a central debate in the work that I do, and how I approach it.

Limiting the use of the metaphor of "conversation" does not preclude holding the position that clients are expert on their own lives; rather it allows for an acknowledgement that professional helpers do also hold (and use) expertise and that both forms of knowledge are important elements in co-constructing change. Similarly the concept of "not-knowing" used by de Shazer (and therapists of other persuasions) has been developed further to embrace the notion of the "expertise of knowing and not-knowing" (Gaiswinkler and Roessler, 2009). Following an action research project with social workers trained to use the solution-focused approach with homeless clients in Austria, Gaiswinkler and Roessler used qualitative analysis of video recordings of social worker–client interactions to differentiate between different forms of knowing and not-knowing:

> There are two kinds of expertise that are of vital importance in social work; on the one hand, social workers must have expert knowledge about, for example, legal questions, claims procedures, responsibilities of agencies or further relevant matters concerning these agencies. This kind of expertise is generally called "expert knowledge", or, as we call it, "expertise of knowing". However, this expertise of knowing is not enough: Social workers are also experts in goal-oriented counselling, which is a communicative expertise we suggest could be called "expertise of not knowing" or "expertise of communication in the alternative paradigm (2009: 221–222).

These Viennese researchers found both sets of expertise in successful social work interventions (using client feedback on what was most useful). They conclude that both forms of expertise are also necessary to develop a good working alliance. "The expertise of not-knowing has to build the framework, and the expertise of knowing (specialist knowledge) is guided by the expertise of not-knowing" (223). This very useful distinction has a resonance in the work I do carrying out assessments for courts.

The social constructionist emphasis on the importance of language is developed and actively mined in SFT through the use of several interventions, including the technique of reframing. Reframing is a familiar term to therapists as it predates the development of SFT, but it has been less developed in social work practice. Described as "an opportunity to describe a situation or behavior from a different, more hopeful and optimistic perspective" (Trevithick, 2000: 130), it is often used to shift stuck or negative perceptions or behaviors through changing the meaning ascribed to them. In technical terms, this is achieved through "re-wording" a set of facts and placing them in a different context or frame in order to change the entire meaning (Trevithick, 2000). In practical use, it is more of an art than a technique—an art that relates back to the Wittgensteinian concept of using language to free ourselves from the traps and knots that language-use creates. Taking an example from a piece of work I carried out as a child protection social worker with a young mother of two children who was at risk of losing care of her children due to her problems resisting the powerful hold her incestuous father maintained over her, it was possible to alter her perception of herself from that of a passive victim into a person with agency and choices. The reframed goal for our work of helping her to achieve an independent existence apart from her father was that of "practising staying strong" (Walsh, 2006). By drawing on concepts of social construction combined with a solution-focused future orientation and belief in her ability to make change, the subtly reworded goal was one she could subscribe to without needing to reject all of her past emotional ties to her father. Reframing, used respectfully as a social constructionist intervention, brings alive the assertion that in helping encounters, there is a wide-ranging repertoire of possible meanings which worker and client can explore and develop in order to create new understandings and possibilities.

Solution-focused work is probably distinctive in its heavy emphasis on the future—plans, hopes, and dreams. The worker concentrates on helping clients work out first how to envision their preferred future and then how to build on small steps of change towards it. Underpinning it is an essentially optimistic view of people's capacity to make positive changes in their lives, and that change is not only possible but inevitable. This connects with the Buddhist notion that change is always happening (de Shazer et al., 2007).

The value of solution-focused thinking and techniques has for me stretched beyond direct (or explicit) therapeutic work with clients into a broader frame of reference that now underpins my work in education, training, and consultation. In my work as an expert witness, I tend to use reframing with both professional workers and client families as an antidote to the often stigmatizing and negative perceptions that develop through immersion in an adversarial legal system. I might explore with client families how they can help child welfare workers "do their job" as opposed to listening in silence to them depicting individual workers in negative terms. I will reflect back overly negative summaries of parental deficits in less loaded terms to workers, perhaps by declaring my amazement at how a parent has continued to struggle to do "their best" for the children despite facing adversities x, y, and z, and how well they are coping with the essentially shaming experience of having official interventions into their private family lives. Iversen et al. (2005), in their analysis of assessment using a constructionist critique, remind us of how often "assessment tools carry an overarching and inherent emphasis on client 'problems,'" thus prioritizing a deficit-based discourse as opposed to a language of "potentials" (695) and cast the practitioner as a technical "expert." Within the narrow risk-focused confines of contemporary child welfare practice, this tendency is amplified; once court proceedings begin, the emphasis is on winning the case on technical points. Contextualized knowledge is not often valued here as a means to winning the case! An expert witness who works within a constructionist frame can, however, work to reinsert it in the final reckoning.

Social Work, Child Protection, and the Law

Michel Foucault, the celebrated French philosopher, challenges us to look beyond the importance of language itself to the relationships between power, knowledge, language, and discourse. His ideas have been drawn on by many to highlight the linkages between expert knowledge and power, regulatory practices and systems of thought in modern societies, and the capacity of discourse (institutionalized and/or accepted ways of thinking and doing that are communicated through language and practice) to create new forms of control and surveillance. One discourse that for me has been of enduring interest is that of "child protection," a form of practice which emerged and developed into the dominant frame for social work with children and families in the United Kingdom and Ireland in the 1980s and 1990s. It is a subject I have written about (Walsh, 1999), as my experience has been that it has developed into a particularly punitive and repressive ideology which fundamentally changed the nature of the contract between social workers and families in need to the detriment of both. While it is true that "power and power relations are an inevitable feature of professional social work as an expert strategy" and that "at a most basic level, there is the power of the profession to use language to define social problems in a certain manner" (Skehill, 1997: 193), it is the discursive reframing of child welfare social work as "child protection" that risks pitting workers against parents and carers. Not that I believe that social workers should never intervene formally when children are exposed to abuse and neglect, but rather that authoritative work is possible within a more respectful and constructive frame than that allowed by the contemporary child protection ideology currently governing practices in the United Kingdom and Ireland.

Child protection practice is arguably one of the strongest regulatory forms of social work practice in modern Western societies, and one of its key features is a heavy reliance on the legal system to adjudicate between families and professionals and an increase in legal regulations governing the relationship between social worker and family. Legal proceedings taken under child welfare legislation, in countries and contexts where an adversarial court system is in place, can place parents and social workers in diametrically opposed corners, and locate the child as a passive object to be fought over, rather than an active participant in the process. Necessary as state intervention sometimes is, both to protect children from immediate harm of injury or abuse, and/or to ameliorate the effects of longer-term neglect or emotional abuse, the impact of current child protection systems "underlies the centrality of social workers in providing social assessments of 'risk' and 'dangerousness'. . . . [and] decisions in child care are now carried out in a more legalized context where the need for forensic evidence is prioritised" (Parton, 1996: 11).

With the shift to a legal arena for the determination of what is in a child's best interests, the complex nuances and provisionality of social work assessments can be lost in the search for certainty and in the mandate to establish a case that justifies official intervention, that identifies harm and future risk, and that proposes action to manage the risk and prevent future harm. In this recasting of the social work role much is lost: "No longer are social workers constituted as caseworkers drawing on their therapeutic skills in human relationships, but as care managers assessing need and risk and operationalising packages of care where notions of monitoring and review are central" (Parton, 1996: 12). While it is also important that social workers exercising such strong statutory powers as removing children from their families are accountable and need to justify their actions to independent bodies such as the courts, too often the adversarial court system involves a search for those to blame but also often includes a demand for complete compliance on the part of the parents or carers. Given these conditions, the risks of positions becoming polarized and of all involved reaching an impasse are high. In such situations, calls are often made for an independent assessment to be carried out—for an expert witness to be recruited to advise the court. So, can social workers and other professionals operating in the role of expert witness recast the die and use their position to open up, if possible, potential "win-win" situations?

The Role of the Expert Witness

"Outside the legal field the court itself has no expertise and for that reason frequently has to rely on the evidence of experts. Such experts must express only opinions which they genuinely hold and which are not biased in favour of one particular party" (Pizzey and Davis, 1995: 59).

Many of the provisions of Irish child care law are similar to those of the British system, and the role of the expert witness is one such example. Solicitors (also known as attorneys) representing either parent, the child welfare service, or the child can make a request to have an independent assessment carried out; the judge may also initiate such a request. The expert witness is asked to carry out an assessment or an examination (if of a medical nature) or offer an opinion based on a letter of instruction, which must "clearly set out the context in which the expert's opinion is sought and define carefully the specific questions the expert is being asked to address" (Pizzey and Davis, 1995: 58).

So far, so crystal clear! You are not alone if you are now thinking that this leaves the role rather broad and yet tightly specified. Yet, the ways in which this role is embodied and the manner in which individuals choose to enact these responsibilities are manifold. One consequence of the increasing legalization of child welfare has been the cleaving of assessment from intervention; the fear that if one were to follow therapeutic principles during an assessment, evidence would be contaminated. Yet, happily there are increasingly voices of dissent, resisting this rigid practice (Mantle et al, 2008; Ruegger and Neil, 2009). Many skilled practitioners recognize that in the crisis of public intervention into private family life, of removal of children from their homes, there can also often be opportunity for change. "It is our experience that the event of care proceedings renders parents more amenable to change than they are before or after due to the crisis they produce through the threat to the integrity and the very existence of the family unit. . . . It is our premise that access to resources at a time when families are psychologically available offers a unique opportunity for a variety of effective therapeutic interventions to be employed" (Ruegger and Neil, 2009: 142).

Some of the questions I ask myself when embarking on a court-ordered assessment are as follows: Do I need to amplify and consolidate the child protection expert system unquestioningly, participate as another guard on the panopticon of child protection? (And sometimes this is the case where extreme dangerousness exists in families, and there appears no feasible hope for change in the foreseeable future.) Or can I through the adoption of a social constructionist perspective examine the seemingly objective "facts" of this case to show how human subjectivity has imposed itself on those facts—to highlight how positions of perspective and power have shaped certain interpretations into privileged facts while other versions and views have remained submerged or subordinated? Furthermore, how can I do this while remaining true to my own expertise and wisdom from years of practice as a social worker with children and families? How do I hold onto my own ethical perspective and acknowledge it without becoming yet another actor in this scenario with too much to lose if I am proved wrong?

An Example Based on Practice Experience

Let's take a case and illustrate how social constructionism can inform court-ordered assessments.[2] Baby Sean was taken into care by social services at the age of six months following a diagnosis of non-accidental injury by the local pediatric hospital. His mother brought him to the local general practitioner and was then referred on to the hospital after his arm "cracked" while she changed his nappy that afternoon. She had just returned from work; Sean and his four-year-old sister Nicola had been in the care of their father all day. X-rays taken at the hospital indicated that there were three healing fractures involving both shoulder joints and the right lower leg, possibly all of the same age. Further investigations took place while Sean remained in the hospital. A child protection case conference was called and, in the absence of any satisfactory explanation from the parents regarding the source of these injuries, non-accidental injury was suspected. The parents agreed to place Sean in foster care (with daily access) while social services and the police continued to assess and investigate the situation.

Some four months later, another case conference confirmed physical abuse and made a decision not to return Sean to his parents because "the perpetrator has not been identified" and so risk to the baby remained. Additional expert medical opinions on the injuries confirmed the original doctors' views: one declaring that "The events were highly suggestive of inflicted injury"; the other that "The appearance of three separate fractures in a child of this age is suspicious and raises the strong possibility of non-accidental injury." Both medical experts also discounted the possibility that vigorous play (for example, being swung by the arms and one leg) could account for the injuries, a possible explanation which the parents had forwarded. Underlying causes or vulnerabilities such as brittle bone disease were also ruled out.

The situation at this point appeared to reach an impasse, with Sean remaining in foster care for a period of thirteen months and social services refusing to return him yet unable to elaborate how his parents could satisfy them as to his future safety. In desperation, the parents' legal advisors applied to the courts for his return home, and an independent social work assessment was requested and granted. A guardian ad litem was also appointed to report on Sean's best interests.

Following a short but intensive assessment involving joint and separate interviews with both parents, observations of family time in the home both with their older child and in the foster home with Sean and his sister, and reviews of all documentation and interviews with the social workers involved, it appeared that a stalemate existed in relation to this young child's future. The impasse had been reached because of the weight of the medical expert opinions, the case conference finding of confirmed physical abuse, and the position taken by social services that in the absence of a "confession" and identification of "a perpetrator," they would not take the risk of returning Sean to his parents. Yet, the social workers, foster parents, public health nurses, school teachers, GP, and all professionals involved with the family agreed that there had been no concerns before Sean's hospitalization or since regarding the parents' capacity to care for their other child, nor had Sean's care in itself been of concern. The parents had continued to comply fully with all that was demanded of them by social services, they visited Sean daily, and they remained actively distressed by his continuing absence from their care.

Both the guardian ad litem and I reached the conclusion that there was no significant reason for Sean to remain out of home, especially given the family's willingness to comply with any monitoring or ongoing treatment required. Sean was returned to the care of his family some six weeks after the initial court hearing, and he continues to do well in their care.

Reflections

In this piece of work, a rigorous assessment of the documentation about the original injuries and causes of concern was coupled with an assessment of present family functioning, parenting styles, and an evaluation of family dynamics. Crucially, this not only concentrated on elements of risk and dangerousness but also incorporated a more holistic assessment of not only the deficits but also the strengths in both the environment and the family (Cowger, Anderson, and Snively, 2006). This assessment highlighted and developed the extent to which this family demonstrated resilience in their handling of this situation (Benard, 2006) as well as a steadfast commitment towards their child and a persistence in seeking his return home.

The medical opinions, while they voiced considerable concern about the possibility of non-accidental injury, were not definitive. Uncertainty remained as to how Sean had received these injuries (there had been a large family gathering over a weekend in the time-frame when the injuries occurred, when Sean had been in the care of older teenage cousins, unsupervised). It was an isolated incident without precedence or sequel and one which had occurred in the context of an otherwise caring and well-functioning family. In stating this position quite strongly in my report, in acknowledging that uncertainty would remain about how Sean had been hurt, in accepting that there may be no answers about this, it was possible to avoid the danger of making a judgment about the injury itself. By detailing the areas on which there was no evidence of problems usually associated with child abuse or violence (history of violence or anger management problems; alcohol or drug misuse; mental health problems; discordant relationships), and also by detailing the nature and extent of the positives (both parents with childhood and adolescent histories unmarked by extreme trauma or disruption; both parents with steady work records; strong extended family supports on the maternal side; strong positive parenting skills and practices; full cooperation with social services and foster carers), it was possible to shift the focus from the past to the future. *What now?* became the central issue to be resolved, rather than *What happened?*

The judge found himself freed up to move the focus to Sean's overall welfare and the increasingly detrimental impact of remaining in foster care at such a young age, especially when there were clear signs that Sean was beginning to attach to his foster carers and increasingly confused about the different adult carers in his life. Social services were also freed up to accept that a return home needed to happen and to do so quickly.

A solution-focused approach with both family and social workers enabled a shift in thinking away from past risk and towards future plans, and in particular the construction of a plan for ongoing monitoring when Sean returned home. Both Sean's parents and the social workers were able to develop a picture of how to best handle the transition home and to support each other in this goal. An analysis of the situation informed by social constructionism allowed for an acceptance of the different perspectives the professionals and the family members held on the situation. Sean's parents could understand that the social workers would continue to have worries for some time, and so Sean's parents accepted their role in needing to reassure them and accept their involvement for some time. An appreciation of the importance of language and the value of reframing helped in articulating the real concerns felt in a more hopeful and future-focused way. The goal for the parents became one of building and demonstrating safe parenting practices for Sean and his sibling. The goal for the workers became one of helping to rebuild these parents' confidence in their parenting abilities. In my report to the court, I was able to uncover and highlight hidden areas of competence and strength such as the parents' strong relationship, which had withstood the stress of a long period of time separated from their son and under suspicion for child abuse; their initiative in making a referral themselves to a local service to receive assistance on their parenting practices; and their maturity in accepting the various social work assessments and interventions, despite not agreeing with the need for them all.

Finally, a Foucauldian analysis allowed for an appreciation of how child protection practices operate as disciplinary forces with an unequal gaze: an appreciation of the supremacy of the medical discourse and expert medical opinion and an awareness of the need to counteract this with an equally strong evidence-based opinion, in this case relating to the risk factors most strongly associated with physical abuse (and their complete absence in this situation). In addition, the reframing of the core task as being as related to child welfare as it was to child protection enabled a shift back to a focus on this child's overall welfare.

My Approach to the Work

Finally, I share some of the principles, informed by a social constructionist frame, which I have found useful when carrying out such work:

READ EVERYTHING!

Invariably, your cases come with a large bundle of files, records, reports, and observations. In the rush and haste of current practice realities, social work students have sometimes told me that they "had no time" to read case files before meeting with clients; practitioners sometimes tell me the same. In such ways, workers risk adopting a surface approach to practice, denounced by Howe (1996) as ahistorical. "Clients arrive, in effect, without a history; their past is no longer of interest. It is their present and future performance which matters. Present behaviour. . . . is now assessed in terms of future expectations. The lack of depth in the social work assessment is therefore both spatial and temporal" (89). Yet, if I am to "make sense" of an injury, an accident, a history of alleged neglect or abuse, I need to know the meaning of the events, of the reactions to events, of how past experience has helped to shape these perceptions. This does not mean an essentialist approach, as will be explained later. Constructionist ideas privilege the importance of both historical and contextual elements of knowledge-construction and attempt to "elucidate the sociohistorical context and ongoing social dynamic of descriptions, explanations and accountings of reality" (Witkin, 1990: 38, quoted in Iversen et al., 2005: 694). Written representations of our clients' lives are especially powerful because they endure over time. Once the author of such a representation is no longer at hand, control is lost on the future interpretation of written "facts," and no mediating influence is possible.

UNDERSTAND YOUR ROLE AND, SPECIFICALLY, WHAT IT IS
YOU ARE BEING ASKED TO COMMENT ON.

If I don't understand the directions I receive from a judge or attorneys in a case, or if I think I am being asked to address the impossible, I return for clarification. Sometimes, such letters of instruction are framed in difficult if not impossible terms: "Please advise the court on the likelihood of the child being injured or harmed in the future." At times, it is such a search for an impossible certainty that boxes both social workers and parents/carers into rigid straitjacket solutions, when instead a search for a reframed realistic and more achievable goal may be successful in finding a new formula for moving forward. So, for example, "Yes I am willing to advise the court on the child's welfare, in the context of potential stressors, supports, and potential for change in this family" may be a reframe of the initial request outlined above, which social workers, parents, and the courts will be happy to see addressed. Iversen et al. (2005) suggest that using a constructionist lens, assessment tools are capable of "transcending their own origins" (699) to develop transformative outcomes. One such is that of challenging existing realities. By reframing impossible demands for certainty, it is possible to challenge the presumption that such certainty exists.

DISTINGUISH BETWEEN WHAT IS KNOWN (AND HOW)
AND WHAT IS NOT KNOWN AND CANNOT BE.

In several situations of suspected non-accidental injury, I have been struck by the ways in which the demands of the child protection expert system stretch social workers' assessments beyond what is realistically answerable. For example, you may have a child who has a broken limb, a child who is too young to injure herself in this way, or a child who is maybe not yet walking; you may have two or three or more adults who all had care of this child during the days before the injury is diagnosed in the time-frame that the doctors determine was the time it was inflicted. Who injured the child? In cases where it is an isolated incident, where finding the culprit is literally anyone's guess, instead of relying on prejudice, hunches, and unreliable interpretations of eye-contact, body language, or other nebulous "evidence," I will declare it: I do not know. Instead of over-reaching either my level of expertise or the "facts" as they are known, in my reports, I emphasize the unknown. This, in my experience, can free up the judge, lawyers, and child welfare workers to look beyond the isolated injury; it can also free up parents and carers to talk about what stresses they are under that they would like to address in the future, what help they need, and what changes they will make, while accepting that a level of monitoring and supervision will be necessary for a time because "nobody knows." But instead of this declaration paralyzing everybody, its very articulation can help people to move on. In so doing, it is possible to work towards realizing new realities, a second form of transformative outcome identified by Iversen et al. (2005) as a potential outcome from use of a constructionist approach.

MAKE CENTRAL TO THE ASSESSMENT THE KEY QUESTION:
HOW DOES THIS FAMILY WORK?

Like any other parent, I come to this work with some pretty strong opinions of my own on what are acceptable and unacceptable parenting practices. These can be hard to set aside. Rather than pretend that I come to the role as a neutral, scientific, objective, value-free observer, I will declare this position and make clear what is opinion and what is "fact," based on observations, conversations, and beliefs. Some facts and opinions will be based on direct experience and some on professional literature. In addition, *How does this family work?* is the central question that directs my engagement with every family. Taking a position of informed curiosity, I explore this question with all family members, not only the nominated responsible parent (most often the mother or female carer is cast in this role). I also explore different meanings of family and family life with the family group, or a parenting couple, or a parent and child if they are interested in engaging and working with me on this. In this way, both assessment and creative possibilities can co-exist. My assessment may raise some new ideas, some changed meanings, and some potential for change. "In bringing new realities into being, dialogue may be focused on new resources, images, metaphors or narratives, each serving as a lattice for alternative courses of action" (Iversen et al., 2005: 702). In the work with Sean's family, cited earlier, it was important not to gloss over some adverse family circumstances which Sean's father had experienced but to consider these in the light of his commitment to his own children and his desire to make a better life for them. Using the theme of how resilience can be developed through the experience of overcoming adversity, it was also possible to build in suggestions for further attention to these experiences with the goal of helping both parents work more closely together in their parenting.

DO NOT PRESUME THAT A REPORT-WRITING ROLE PRECLUDES INTERVENTION.

Mantle et al. (2008) describe how, in their British research with court-appointed welfare officers, the primary report-writing function was often accompanied by actual interventions where it appeared, to the individuals involved, such interventions were warranted. So, too, with the role of the expert witness. While the primary function may be to advise the court on the best possible course of action for the child or children involved, this assessment is best viewed as an intervention in itself and one which can therefore confirm and/or reinforce existing positions and perceptions or which can potentially reframe some of the supposed certainties to create new possibilities. Remaining mindful both of time frames (and the need for children not to be left "waiting" unnecessarily) and of role definition and boundaries does not preclude also seizing opportunities to renegotiate, reframe, and reformulate both the extent of the issues involved and possible alternative solutions.

Constructionist ideas give voice to this potential in recognizing that assessment is essentially dialogic in nature: "Constructionist texts also invite us to see the assessment device not as an instrument for *finding*, but for *making*, i.e., not as a means of determining what is the case, but of creating visions of our world." (Iversen et al., 2005: 703, original emphasis). In my work in the case example cited earlier, in assessing Sean's best interests and welfare, I was able to create an alternative view of Sean's situation and possible solutions by broadening the focus from the issue of protection to wider concerns about welfare and long-term interests.

SHARE THE ASSESSMENT WITH THE FAMILY. INCLUDE THEIR FEEDBACK AND RESPONSE AS PART OF THE FINAL REPORT. WRITE IT WITH THEIR EYES OVER YOUR SHOULDER.

It is surprising how often families do not know what is contained in official reports until they appear in court on the date of the hearing. This should not happen. Sharing the report with the family beforehand is only one small way in which you can use your dominant position in a less oppressive way. Sometimes reports do not contain the recommendations that the family would wish; sometimes I have not accepted their views and proposals for change;

but I will still meet with them beforehand and let them know what is in it and I will share my thinking with them. When there is strong opposition to my proposals, I will redraft and leave the final decision to the judge: in such cases, I will make clear the pros and cons of different courses of action using care in my choice of language. If I pose the dilemmas as such, pointing out that "On the one hand, this could be tried but. . . . On the other hand, this could be put in place. . . ." a subtle challenge is also taking place to the notion that there is only one correct course of action; that there is a guarantee of a particular outcome or of a child's future, either remaining in the care system or being returned home or to relatives, is a one-dimensional decision.

Continuous dialogue is the third and final form of transformative action that Iversen et al. (2005) identify. In the role of expert witness, there are three potential sites for such collaborative inquiries to take place: the family and child, the professional system, and the court. For all: "As new constructions are grasped, and their implications played out in practice, they now become candidates for 'the real'" (Iversen et al., 2005: 704). In the case example outlined earlier, once the possibility was raised that Sean could be returned home despite the absence of an answer (to the question, *What happened?*), the social workers became energized around how this might work out in practice. A momentum developed, and it appeared as if they were freed to bring their own doubts about the need for Sean to remain in care out into the open. Hence, by the time of the court hearing, they were enthusiastic advocates for this course of action.

Conclusions

In the following excerpt from the famous Shakespearean play *Hamlet,* the power of our thinking to shape experience with relatively positive or negative connotations is apparent.

HAMLET: What have you, my good friends, deserved at the hands of Fortune, that she sends you to prison hither?

GUILDENSTERN: Prison, my lord!

HAMLET: Denmark's a prison.

ROSENCRANTZ: Then is the world one.

HAMLET: A goodly one, in which there are many confines, wards and dungeons, Denmark being one o' the worst.

ROSENCRANTZ: We think not so, my lord.

HAMLET: Why, then, 'tis none to you; for there is nothing either good or bad, but thinking makes it so. To me, it is a prison.

Hamlet, Act 2, scene 2, 239–251

Adopting a social constructionist framework while working as an expert witness in child welfare cases has for me many advantages over a form of thinking which would have me carry out my function in a less critical and reflective manner. "Rather than branding assessment as an inherently re-actionary/modernist process, a constructionist alliance enables assessment to become a collaborative inquiry into transformative possibilities" (Iversen et al., 2005: 704). In a nutshell, social constructionist thinking gives me flexibility, allows me to set aside unanswerable or unhelpful questions, allows me to reframe concerns in ways that promote joint work rather than conflictual positions, and allows me to search for new solutions before legal interventions restrict these options. Social constructionist ideas do not in themselves address the complex economic, environmental, psychological, and interpersonal factors which contribute to problems of child maltreatment, but they can provide a strategy for rendering less rigid the demands of expert-led child protection and legal systems.

Notes

1. In a noteworthy shift of position, de Shazer et al., in their posthumous publication (2007), altered their view on the relationship between helper and client from one of equality to one of hierarchy: *"SFBT therapists accept that there is a hierarchy in the therapeutic arrangement, but this hierarchy tends to be more egalitarian and democratic than authoritarian"* (3–4).
2. While this scenario is based on practice experience, the details have been changed to protect anonymity.

References

Benard, B. (2006). Using strengths-based practice to tap the resilience of families. In D. Saleebey (Ed.), *The strengths perspective in social work* (4th ed.), (pp. 197–220). Boston: Pearson.

Burck, C. (1995). Developments in family therapy in the last five years. *ACPP Review*, 17: 247–254.

Cowger, C., K. Anderson, and C. Snively (2006). Assessing strengths: The political context of individual, family and community empowerment. In D. Saleebey (Ed.), *The strengths perspective in social work* (4th ed.) (pp. 93–115). Boston: Pearson.

de Shazer S., I. K. Berg, E. Lipchik, E. Nunnally, A. Molnar, W. Gingerich, and M. Weiner-Davis (1986). Brief therapy: Focused solution development. *Family Process*, 25: 207–221.

de Shazer, S., Y. Dolan, H. Korman, T. Trepper, E. McCollum, and I. K. Berg (2007). *More than miracles: The state of the art of solution-focused brief therapy.* New York: Haworth.

Family Therapy Networker. Special Issue on *The constructivist eye.* Sept/Oct, 1988.

Foucault, M. (1979). *Discipline and punish: The birth of the prison.* Harmondsworth, UK: Penguin.

——. (1980). Two lectures. In C. Gordon (Ed.), *Power/Knowledge: Selected interviews and other writings, 197–1977* (pp. 78–108). Brighton, UK: Harvester.

Gaiswinkler, W., and M. Roessler (2009). Using the expertise of knowing and the expertise of not-knowing to support processes of empowerment in social work practice. *Journal of Social Work Practice,* 23(2): 215–227.

George E., C. Iveson, and H. Ratner (1990). *Problem to solution-brief therapy with individuals and families.* London: Brief Therapy Press.

Hartman, A. (1991). Words create worlds. *Social Work,* 36: 275–276.

Hoffman, L. (1991). A reflexive stance for family therapy. *Journal of Strategic and Systemic Therapies,* 10(3–4): 4–17.

Howe, D. (1996). Surface and depth in social-work practice. In N. Parton (Ed.), *Social theory, social change and social work* (pp. 77–97). London: Routledge.

Iversen, R. R., K. J. Gergen, and R. P. Fairbanks (2005). Assessment and social construction: Conflict or co-creation? *British Journal of Social Work,* 35: 689–708.

McNamee, S. and K. Gergen (Eds.) (1992). *Therapy as social construction.* London: Sage.

Mantle, G., I. Williams, J. Leslie, S. Parsons, and R. Shaffer (2008). Beyond assessment: Social work intervention in family court enquiries. *British Journal of Social Work,* 38: 431–443.

Parton, N. (Ed.) (1996). Introduction in *Social theory, social change and social work* (pp. 4–18). London: Routledge.

Parton, N. and P. O'Byrne (2000). *Constructive social work.* Basingstoke, UK: Macmillan.

Payne, M. (1997). *Modern social work theory* (2nd ed.). Basingstoke, UK: Macmillan.

——. (1999). Social construction in social work and social action. In A. Jokinen, K. Juhila, and T. Poso (Eds.), *Constructing social work practices* (pp. 3–25). Aldershot, UK: Ashgate.

Pizzey, S. and J. Davis (1995). A Guide to ad litem in public law proceedings under the Children Act 1989. London: HMSO.

Ruegger, M. and M. Neil. (2009). *Care proceedings: The window of opportunity for therapeutic interventions during assessment.* Unpublished paper presented at British Association for the Study and Prevention of Child Abuse and Neglect (BASPCAN) 7th National Congress, Swansea, South Wales.

Saleebey, D. (Ed.) (1992). *The strengths perspective in social work.* New York: Longman.

Skehill, C. (1997). *The nature of social work in Ireland.* Lampeter, UK: Edwin Mellen Press.

Trevithick, P. (2000). *Social work skills: A practice handbook.* Buckingham, UK: Open University Press.

Walsh, T. (Ed.) (1997). *Solution-focused child protection: Towards a positive frame for practice.* Occasional Paper No 3. Department of Social Studies, Trinity College, Dublin, Ireland.

——. (1999). Changing expectations: The impact of "child protection" on Irish social work. *Child and Family Social Work,* 4: 33–41.

——. (2002) *The introduction of brief solution-focused therapy to Irish social workers: A case study of innovation diffusion.* Unpublished PhD thesis, Trinity College Dublin Library, Dublin, Ireland.

——. (2006). Two sides of the same coin: Ambiguity and complexity in child protection work. *Journal of Systemic Therapies,* 25(2): 38–49.

——. (2010). Therapeutic options in child protection and gendered practices. In B. Featherstone, C. A. Hooper, J. Scourfield, and J. Taylor (Eds.), *Gender and child welfare in society* (pp. 273–299). London: Wiley.

Wetchler, J. (1996). Social constructionist family therapies. In F. Piercy, D. Sprenkle, J. Wetchler, and Associates. *Family therapy sourcebook,* 2nd ed. New York: Guilford Press.

White, M. and D. Epston (1990). *Narrative means to therapeutic ends.* New York: Norton.

Witkin, S. L. (1990). The implications of social constructionism for social work education. *Journal of Teaching in Social Work,* 4: 37–48.

[9]

Family Therapy with a Larger Aim

DAN WULFF AND SALLY ST. GEORGE

After many years of working therapeutically with families, we have recently been developing some practices within our work that attempt to address larger social ills simultaneously with helping families change specific troubles that bring them to therapy (Rojano, 2004). Our family work has always been an integration of family therapy and social work; we regularly address basic needs (e.g., adequate housing, effective childcare, good nutrition, and supportive medical care) along with presenting problems, and now we are bringing what we call the larger societal discursive influences on families, that is, those scripts or messages about how one should conduct his/her life that we learn from growing up within specific communities/societies, into our therapy with them (St. George and Wulff, 2008).

We have each begun incorporating specific themes in our work that address the larger social problems of gender imbalances, unfairness, and violence among people. I (Sally) have found some ways of conversing with client families that help them solve/resolve/dissolve their presenting issues, while simultaneously raising the issue of discrimination and unfairness in gender relationships within their own family system. My therapy includes examining and re-visioning families' lived gendered relationships and how those arrangements may impact the issue(s) that brought them to therapy. The family becomes part of a process of seeing themselves and their troubles as connected to influences shared by all persons in their community, that they are not alone. Seeing themselves as connected to other families and their larger world encourages a sense of togetherness, as opposed to a sense of isolation and privatization of their troubles which often happens with the structural design of traditional therapies around confidentiality and working with families separately (Wulff, St. George, and Besthorn, 2011).

I (Dan) have taken up working with families in ways that address their concerns with violent behaviors of their children while avoiding reinscribing the use of violence (verbal and/or physical) as a parental response. A great deal of family therapy and family intervention literature has encouraged, in varying degrees, the importance of a parent or parents exercising their legitimate hierarchical control over their unruly or defiant children (e.g., Minuchin, 1974; Nichols and Schwartz, 2004). This process of establishing a hierarchical system whereby the parents occupy a position of authority may be inadvertently misinterpreted as a call to exercise domination and power. Being responsible and accountable for children can be developed by a parent creating a dependable "presence" without incorporating power tactics of fear and intimidation (Omer, 2000). Instead of aggressive tactics, methods of nonviolence, such as those that have been employed by Mahatma Gandhi and Martin Luther King Jr. on a larger scale (e.g., sit-ins, going on strike, consistent nonparticipation), can be adapted to the family context. The connection between this way of working and the larger aim of resisting aggression and violence on a community or societal level is based in the belief that violence is supported and expanded by the individual performances of violence in our daily lives, even within our most intimate familial relationships. These efforts within my practice of family therapy represent a grassroots initiative to teach and mentor client families to resist the all-too-prevalent invitations to include aggression and violence in our lives and relationships.

In both of these initiatives, we hope to demonstrate how social workers, family therapists, and potentially all helping professionals can perform their therapeutic work in ways that promote social justice. Working with families in ways that challenge gender inequalities or families' overreliance on violent or dominating practices constitute approaches that some refer to as *subactivism* (Bakardjieva, 2009), that is, actions in everyday life that have the potential to collectively impact larger social concerns or systems.

Subactivism includes those experiences in the everyday flow of life that can be understood to have a political or ethical frame of reference (or both) (Bakardjieva, 2009). They are personal and interpersonal events or relationships that reflect or support preferred ways of being that may uphold societal discourses and preferences *or* may deviate from them. They could include preferred ways of practicing one's job, one's role as a parent, or one's position in a neighborhood or social network that reflect some fundamental values or beliefs. One could go so far as to say that all our behaviors are built upon values and beliefs. We continuously reinforce or contradict values and beliefs by our choices of behaviors, but we may not be cognizant of this process or of the values and beliefs we favor. As a social worker or family therapist, one could practice professionally from a position that tends to support nonviolence (or re-inscribes violence), tends to support gender equality (or upholds hierarchical gender relationships), or tends to support emotionality (or privileges intellectualizations), and so on. These allegiances are not absolute—it is unlikely that any practitioner can behave *completely* in accordance with any of the above-mentioned positions consistently. But the point here is that we tend to gravitate to one side more than the other.

In our view, it is not enough just to perform our therapeutic work without having that work address social problems that plague our communities and societies in which that therapeutic work occurs. Further, we believe that whether we are aware of it or not, our therapeutic practices emanate from positions on these societal and communal values and beliefs—we do not operate in a vacuum. One risk of this kind of work may be a tendency for a practitioner to use the therapy situation to proselytize for a social cause, neglecting the family's original reason for coming. We think this balancing of functions/actions can be effectively nurtured and maintained to provide high-quality family therapy while deliberately working toward challenging social problems. This blending of therapeutic work and activism presents a challenging new frontier in how we might imagine clinical practice.

Social Constructionism

As social workers and family therapists we have long approached our work with philosophical and theoretical ideas that are commonly understood as postmodern or social constructionist (Becvar and Becvar, 2009). For us, these ideas have been, and still are, a preferred foundation for our therapeutic work because of their constructive and generative impact in helping us help families and also their coherence with the principles by which we live. We think it is important to live out the collaborative principles more generally in our lives than we espouse in our therapy approach (St. George and Wulff, 2007).

The affiliation of these ideas with the term "social constructionist" is not our motivation in embracing them. In fact, the oft-cited debates between social constructionism and positivism seem, in our view, to detract from considering more directly how ideas and their associated practices influence behaviors and relationships.

That being said, we are pleased to present some notions that we have been working with that share much with the ideas that resonate with other literature under the label, social constructionist. In particular, we appreciate working from a position that openly acknowledges and values that "the realities we live in are outcomes of the conversations in which we are engaged" (Gergen, 2009: 4). This quote represents some key ideas that we center our work around, namely: Realities are plural (not singular), language is crucial, relationships are central to our lives, and life (and our understandings of it) is fluid.

Each of us will describe how we have developed some ways of working with families that are built upon these ideas. We include some illustrations of our experiences with these ideas-in-action, and what these experiences suggest to us now regarding next steps or new avenues that we might pursue to further the aim of helping social workers and family therapists find ways to more positively impact our communities and society.

Women Supporting Women

"Women supporting women" is a phrase that I (Sally) used as an antidote to the discouraged and heartsick feelings I experienced as a result of working with a number of families in which mothers and daughters were seemingly at war with each other. It is a phrase that captured the spirit of gendered expectations and resistance to repeating the languaging, hierarchies, and experiences that women and girls are vulnerable to in interactions at the workplace, in school, and other social situations. It has become a code phrase (1) for noticing the ways in which women are covertly treated as second-class citizens in the world and (2) as a warning for women to not succumb to reenacting such behaviors inside the home, particularly between mothers and daughters. It flows from social constructionist ideas that Ken Gergen speaks of in *The Saturated Self* (1991) summarized below:

> We create the *realities* of our relational lives.
>
> What we think of as the *individual* evolves from the confluence of all our relationships.
>
> Together, we are creating a different reality of living together in ways that are more satisfying for the mother and her daughter (or of working together in therapy).
>
> The individual self is thought about and talked about in relationship, between mothers and daughters, between family and their society.

In the last two years, I have seen many families consisting of single-parent mothers and adolescent daughters. The conversations that are occurring in family therapy sessions between mothers and daughters are filled with anguish, anger, self-righteousness, blaming, threat, and confusion. I have heard daughters accusing their mothers of being "stupid" and "failures" and mothers calling their daughters "whores" or "inconsiderate losers." Often they are both so angry that the only solution they can think of is to have the daughter leave the home. In talking with other colleagues in the field, I found that I was not the only one who was trying to deal with and counteract such situations in daily practice. Therefore, my purpose is to share the directions that my experiences and thinking have taken me in working with families who are experiencing major conflict between mothers and daughters.

This is a work-in-progress and contains three ideas I am developing and using in working with mother-daughter conflict from a social constructionist stance and incorporating a kind of *gentle gender* talk. The first is a shift from problem or solution talk to what I call *philosophical* talk in session. The second idea is centered on encouraging mothers to reposition themselves from a "power over" or "overpowered" position to one of guiding and preparing their daughters for womanhood in our society. The third idea is involving a community of women and men who are all invested in the growth and development of our daughters. As illustrations of these ideas, I will share some stories of success and challenge.

Philosophical Talk

A long time ago I read *Plato not Prozac* (1999) by Lou Marinoff. My intention in reading that book at that time was to look for conversational alternatives to the language of deficit and diagnosis, to bring forth different metaphors and focus to therapy and supervision. In the last two years, I have again been drawn back to philosophy, not a formal study of philosophical thought per se, but to the ways of living or worldviews that we live by as we face crises, change, excitement, danger, opportunity, and globalization in daily living.

When mothers and daughters begin fighting in session as I try to learn the nature and location of their distress, the last thing I want to sort out are the facts about coming in late, who reneged on a promise, who used a certain tone, who made what threat, who lied more often. We know from the principle of *reciprocal causality* (Becvar and Becvar, 2009) that each action is in reaction to what has already transpired and to sort out the truth or the beginning will be futile—all behaviors are responses to other behaviors before them. What I prefer to do is to see how things "make sense"—how behaviors and interactions that are upsetting may be traced back to good intentions and efforts that maybe have deviated from what the participants had hoped. Perhaps the intentions that got so far off-track actually contribute to the interpersonal anger and frustration. I am finding that I can get the conversation to move in that direction if I use some open and relevant questions to generate possibilities for more effective ways of talking and listening. Let me offer the following composite synopsis formed from several different first sessions.

2:00 p.m. Greetings and introductions among Sally; mother, Sandy (age 42); and daughter, Shannon (age 15).

2:05 Sandy begins by telling about all the therapy they have attended and that things are worse because "my daughter is hanging around with undesirable people and will not tell me where she is going and she won't answer her cell phone. Furthermore, she is engaging in risky sex and won't listen to me about taking precautions because she thinks I don't know what I am talking about. I believe in therapy but she doesn't, so I don't even know if this is going to be helpful."

2:07 Shannon doesn't wait for a question inviting her to offer her perspective; instead she immediately jumps in fiercely staring at her mother, saying, "What difference does any of this make? You never listen to me. Nothing I can say will change your mind. And why would I answer my cell phone? You call every ten minutes trying to tell me what to do and what not to do. Plus, I know my friends much better than you do and at least they are not liars, and at least, I don't lie—like you do. You need therapy; I don't. You and my father are both liars and you both need therapy!"

2:10 I am thinking at this moment "Is there any graceful or inviting exit from this array of accusations on the table to a different kind of conversation?" With hope I offer, "It seems like you both are very sensitive to having important principles in your lives violated. But sometimes with a listing of the complaints, we lose sight of the philosophical principles that we were trying to live by. What I mean by philosophical principles are those important values you are trying to live by or live up to—the main ideas of how you want to live and how you want to be understood and treated. And I have a feeling that you two have fought this round before. Is that so?" (They agree so I continue.) "Would it be OK to switch the conversation for the next few minutes into a more adult-to-adult, woman-to-woman form and examine the principles you are trying to defend with one another? And then if you want to return to the things that you were listing a few minutes ago, we can. But for now could we make this slight shift and go in this other direction?"

2:13 Shannon is doubtful that her mother has any principles, but she would "love to have an adult, and especially womanly, conversation." Sandy is ready for anything that is different; she admits to being exhausted from the fighting.

2:15 I ask them, "What philosophical principles are so important to you that you are willing to fight for them?" They begin to list them individually, not jointly. Sandy says "cooperation and respect," and Shannon says "honesty and freedom to be an individual." I then ask, "When you are arguing and calling out each other on faults or missteps, which of the principles are you trying to uphold?"

2:20 What ensued was a discussion of what each was trying to achieve—Sandy was working hard to get Shannon to be cooperative and respectful so that Sandy can feel close and give Shannon all the attention and things she would love to give her. Shannon just wanted her parents to be honest with her about the nature of their relationship. (Shannon suspected that both were having affairs and she felt left out and very uncertain.)

2:30 We are about halfway through the session and the tone is different with fewer accusations and more regard for the other. In addition, anything that is said or offered for the next portion of the session is discussed in relation to the fidelity to their claimed philosophical principles of living. When they leave, I note that we are talking as women supporting women; they are smiling and agree that talking philosophically was a new, more womanly (speaking to each other as women more so than as mother with power and as daughter challenging authority), and less distressing way to converse.

In some cases, this first session was enough of a start that mother and daughter could carry-on together at home in this manner without my direct participation. In other situations, they have come back telling me that they have begun thinking more about their philosophical stance and that they are more cognizant of being a woman who supports other women as they interact with each other, as well as other family members, workmates, and even in making big and small decisions.

Of course, changing the discourse to one that is more philosophical is not foolproof, but it is often a viable option. In another therapy session, while a daughter refused to talk, she did not disrupt her mother from conversing with me about her philosophical stance as a mother. Some of the questions that I had asked her were:

- What are the principles that you had hoped for and expected to uphold as you prepared to be a parent?

- Now that you have had some parenting experience, which of those principles do you still hold near and dear?
- Which aspects of your philosophy of being a woman in this society do you see your daughter accepting? Which ones does she seem to reject?
- How does your philosophical position help you to be true to the kind of mother you most want to be, regardless of what your daughter does?
- How does your philosophical position help you to act as a woman who is supporting a young woman?

Most of the times when I have this kind of conversation with mothers in the presence of their daughters, their daughters are listening intently as evidenced by their gaze, by nonverbal signs of disagreement, or when they re-enter the conversation. I suspect it is more listenable for daughters because the focus is on the mother's thinking rather than the daughter's behavior or the interaction.

Power and Repositioning

One of the things that I have noticed with mothers and daughters coming to therapy is their particular version of "power struggles." It seems that they are caught up in a competition in which one person is a winner and one is a loser—they even use these words in describing their interactions. Mothers and daughters are both frequently worried about "giving in" and "losing" and thus they hold tightly to their positions, even when it is unpleasant and unproductive. I am increasingly alert to the limitations of discourses of competition in family life, which I see as a dominant societal discourse representing male-gendered behavior and socialization. In response to this type of discourse, I purposefully try to move the conversation to one in which mothers embrace the role of guiding their daughters toward successful adulthood and in which daughters can focus on learning to be women in our society. I ask mothers to tell me about the responsibilities they feel in regard to raising their daughters. They usually respond with a sense of duty to teach and prepare their daughters to be productive and good adult women and citizens. Then I ask daughters to tell me about the confidence they have that this process of preparation is on track, that they are on their way to becoming productive and good adult women.

One of the sticky points I have noticed of late is that many of these daughters sound like adults in terms of their criticisms, certainty, and demands (although not adult-like in terms of responsibility to others). It seems that when adults hear adult-like talk from their children, they expect the full range of adult behaviors and skills that adults hold, such as understanding long-range consequences, reasoning, and logic about who else might be affected, or the ways in which events or situations might not go as planned. I think this is the place in which the talk at home often breaks down—the presumption that the daughters hold an adult stance because they use adult-like claims as well as sarcasm and other tones that adults use to achieve power.

To help mothers counteract this urge to treat their daughters as full-fledged adults/women and understand the presumptions they hold, I ask them what they believe their daughters still need to learn in order to be an advantaged woman (one day) rather than a disadvantaged woman. By advantaged woman, I mean a woman who understands the traps and turmoils of gendered expectations, unspoken rules, rights, and possibilities, as opposed to a woman who accepts the world and her expected role as it is prescribed by society. Many times the daughters think they are already in the knowing position, but I encourage the mother-daughter pair to examine their positions for the merits and limitations inherent in any position. I can do this with the mothers individually or with their daughters, helping mothers with some new languaging to continue to guide their daughters, especially in the face of a daughter's resistance. I use some of Haim Omer's (2004) ideas about nonviolent parenting (which Dan will discuss in more detail later in this chapter) that invite mothers into some more fruitful forms of conversation with their daughters. In this way, we are using language to open possibilities to more effective ways of talking and listening. I am very active in sessions giving examples and illustrations. But those are just that—examples and not prescriptions—and are often in response to the request for concrete strategies for change.

For example, to counteract some of the predictable patterns they identify occurring at home (e.g., the power struggles), I ask mothers about their stances regarding what they think their daughters yet need to know in terms of what is happening or going to happen. These items that they may need yet to know are not small nagging items about rules, chores, or privileges, but rather the big learnings. Additionally, this is not about coercing a daughter to follow traditional norms that perhaps the mother experienced. Chances are these items are major issues that the mother and daughter may likely agree with in principle—their divisiveness may stem from just how to reach those goals or principles. From this I add a distinction between consistency and predictability. It seems to me that children need consistency, that is, they need to know that they will be cared for and supported no matter what happens. But they do not always need to be able to predict or know in advance exactly what will happen as a result of an interaction, that is, how the mother will feel and what she will do to take care of a situation. When all of this is too predictable or thought to be scripted, daughters seem to plan ahead to oppose their mothers' efforts. In the face of a daughter's protest, I coach a mother to say something like:

"I will have to think about that . . . I was thinking . . . we'll have to put it aside for now and think more about it tomorrow."

or

"That's one way of looking at it . . . and there are others, but that is one way."

or

"I'd love to, but I'm not in a position to."

In a sense these responses add a degree of complexity to these situations that the daughter is often trying to minimize. The daughters appear to want the decision to be simple and favorable. When a parent introduces added complexity into a situation, there is another important learning moment for the child. For example, a daughter came in extremely late without calling home and her mother was very worried and started making calls to everyone she could think of who might have information about her daughter's safety. The daughter also wanted to guarantee a weekend outing and so she did some cleaning and her homework for a couple of days. Then when the outing came, the daughter asked her mother for permission and a ride. When the mother replied no, the daughter launched into a tirade about how she has done everything that was asked, expecting that a short time of compliance should balance out her transgression of deceit and irresponsibility. She made no connection between the lack of responsibility and her being told no, nor did she take into consideration the other person in the situation, thinking her solution would do for both parties and anything other than acceptance of her solution was unfair and stupid. Attending to complexity is another social constructionist idea that helps me honor the difficulty of the situations and open possibilities for creating a difference (Gergen, 2009; McNamee and Gergen, 1999). It helps me help mothers teach their daughters some things that will be useful in the daughter's adult future. It is not about a parent gaining compliance— rather it is about teaching about relational complexity. This can change the whole mindset of the involved parent.

I have identified a prevalent (although largely unsatisfying) teaching strategy all of the mothers I have spoken with in this situation have utilized. It is repetition and each mother has reported it to be exhausting for them as well as their daughters. The repetitions may vary, but they usually progress from polite requests to threatening demands. I have come to understand or frame this as an interaction that has evolved in which the mothers sense that they are not being taken seriously by their daughters. When I have asked the daughters when they know they should take their mothers seriously, they can oftentimes give me a precise number or signal such as "on the fifth time she says it" or "when her voice lowers and there is anger" or "when she stands with her hands on her hips." Part of the goal then becomes to help the mother and daughter to develop a new pattern in which the mothers are serious on the first time they say something and the daughters take them seriously on the first time as well (or at least work toward that).

What distresses me about this interaction and what I share with clients is that I see it as an enactment of what many adult women often face in the workplace or in other societal contexts—that they are not taken seriously until they express themselves angrily or forcefully (most mothers have agreed). This discourse of not paying attention until one is threatened can be seen on the front page of world politics as well as in interactions in intimate relationships, in effect encouraging violence toward one another (a theme taken up by Dan in the second part of this chapter). To counteract this I try to develop ways with mothers that they can be taken seriously without needing to escalate or explode, helping them to add another truth about effective parenting. I urge them to say what they want and mean very clearly and fully and yet succinctly, *once*. We talk about saying more with less, while sending a clear message and in the face of resistance to employ language along the lines of:

"I think you already know what the expectations are for you."

or

"I don't want to insult you by repeating something you already know."

Daughters are often caught up in repeating their views or wishes far too many times. In my experience, it seems much more productive and efficient for both mothers and their daughters to find ways to not repeat what they say to one another. It is oftentimes the act of repeating that is most annoying and angering in stressed relationships.

Sometimes the emotions and the stakes rise as mothers are faced with daughters who continue to use threats and violence that invite their mothers to confrontation. For example, when a daughter does not get her way she may threaten or attempt to leave. While many mothers' impulses are to physically restrain their daughters, they know they cannot and they feel desperate to do something to keep them safe. I think it is an untenable situation, and mothers cannot physically force their daughters: if for example, a daughter yells, "then I am leaving" as a tactic, I advise mothers to say something short and pointed (and truthful) like "that's unfortunate," or "leaving will create a dilemma for us." It seems that at these intense moments of escalation and possible confrontation, the tendency to become repetitive is at its strongest. Even at these junctures, being clear, while being nonrepetitive, is a productive path.

One other thing I ask of mothers is to describe the kind of mother they want to be, and I encourage them to continue to strive toward that kind of mother. Again, all of the mothers want to be generous with time and money and share good times with their daughters but they feel constrained because often they have determined that their daughters are not worthy (based on their behaviors). I urge the mothers to be generous on *their* terms and to get the fun, to be as loving as they wish to be and to not violate their own parenting philosophical principles. This relates to Omer's (2004) proposition that negatively escalating relationships cut out the positive aspects of our relationships—the trouble crowds out the good stuff. Mothers can be kind and generous with their daughters any time they wish to be—it is not necessarily limited to when the daughter is compliant or worthy.

These are suggestions for different ways to guide daughters by modeling good adult and womanly communications that are loving, truthful, and clear. In this way, mothers can maintain their stance as guides, enhance the relationship with their daughters, and be the kinds of mothers they would like to be because they love their daughters and their daughters need them and deserve the best of what their mothers have to offer—they are women supporting women. Mothers have not resisted this kind of conversation, even when their view is that the daughter "is the problem" or is the one who "has a problem." My focus has been on mothers and daughters, but there are strong father-son connections that could be developed in particular, focusing on how fathers hope to encourage their sons to be responsible adult men. The risks of boys growing up into manhood in ways that create hardship and pain for them and those around them is high, and working with fathers to be more effective guides and mentors could work well, just as my initiative has approached work with mothers and daughters.

Community Support

Community in this context means a specialized group of people who are invested in the success of the family with whom I am engaged therapeutically. Usually the family's problems are so frightening and overwhelming that to try to tackle them by staying within the parameters of the family and/or therapeutic system could easily defeat a sense of hope and chance of change.

It does not take long to ask families: "Who is not in this room and yet is invested in the success of this mother-daughter team?" Ironically the most common first answer is "no one" or "we are on our own." In spite of this negative answer, I persist. I might ask them to name someone who they interact with regularly without conflict and follow with this question: "If I asked [the people just named] directly, 'Would you want to see [names of mother and daughter] be healthy and successful as a family,' what might they say?" Alternatively I might ask, "Who in your world is invested in thirteen-year-old girls not being expendable or exploited?" With these prompts, mothers and daughters can usually create a list of those who are invested and to whom they could turn for support and help. Often aunts and uncles, grandparents, friends, co-workers, ex-spouses, stepparents, and school personnel are identified, even those at a physical distance, whom mothers and daughters could turn to when the situation seems so exhausting or without the possibility for change. I encourage them to think of ways in which they might turn to their community supporters, and, when available, these people are encouraged to come to therapy with the family, provided that the family thinks that would be useful and is willing to ask these additional people. Most frequently, I have had local aunts, grandparents, and other helping professionals attend sessions and pledge their help. To involve school personnel, I frequently travel to the school to have a joint meeting with the school person(s) identified along with the family.

The Western social discourse and philosophical stance that privileges individualism as one of the highest goals, as described by Gergen (2009) or Stevenson (1998), has taught us to believe that families should be able to handle their own problems without "outside help." Even during moments of despair or being in the failed repetitive patterns of criticizing and defending (Tomm, 1991), there remains a resistance to inviting others into the fray. I have to remind my families (and me, too) that, "You're exhausted—time to call in supports. We cannot handle this on our own. It is far bigger than the three of us."

What I have found important in recruiting and involving other people is that we become clear about the specific ways they might be called upon or what they can offer. For example, one pair of jet-setting grandparents who had not really been aware of the depth of the trouble their daughter and granddaughter were having offered to have "spa weekends" at their house, in which both mother and daughter could stay over at their luxury home to get massages, homemade meals, and generally have a weekend of pampering and playing games and a reprieve from fighting (that was a condition of the weekend—no fighting). In another example, a mother turned to her co-workers whenever she was exasperated and out of ideas and held a type of focus group, investigating things that the average mother could say and do in order to not lose her daughter to life on the streets. One of my favorite examples is the mother who, whenever she was having an escalating argument with her daughter, would call "the girls' team" consisting of two aunts and two friends who lived nearby. The call would go out via text with a coded message that translated into "come now if you can," and a portion of the team, if not all, would come over to listen, to calm down the mother and her daughter, and help create a new or useful resolution. This team was called upon quite a bit in the first month; after that their involvement was lessened, though their emotional and supportive investment remained high. There have been times in which the support network needed to be called together to discuss fatigue or ways to support the support network. A meeting with a focus on progress and a reexamination and perhaps a re-working of the original plan has been sufficiently helpful. The act of help-ing one another also has a component of being uplifting for the persons helping—it feels good to be able to help another. So helping does not only use resources, it replenishes.

Talking about stretching or extending the network of help is an oppor-tunity for me to occupy the role of inquisitive caregiver (Anderson, 1997) in its purist form. Because I do not know the nominees of support, I can only ask questions that I hope will generate answers. For example, I ask, "What makes this person a good support?" or "How do you come to call this person a dependable support?" or "What tells you this person is safe to ask and will hold your best interest centrally?" The other piece of approach-ing the dilemmas in this fashion is that the daughters become full partici-pants—they frequently have many ideas about who could be supportive to both themselves and their mothers—supports for the relationship! One daughter suggested one of her friends and her friend's mother to bring in both points of view when things had gone awry. The daughter's mother did not know the friend's mother very well, but with some encouragement from me, that is, seeing some possibility in this suggestion, agreed to call her and talk with her and offer her a bilateral agreement to protect both of their girls from the pitfalls that single mothers with daughters face as well as the harsh gendered realities that women often face in their lives—an-other example of women supporting women.

Working Nonviolently

My (Dan) attentions in therapy have been upon the prevalence of violence and domination on the parts of parents and children and, all-too-often, from the helping systems. I have found that families who use violence tactics have frequently been involved with police, courts, and other governmental services. Living in today's world provides constant reminders of the perva-siveness of violence—in wars, in gangs, in schools, in sports, in the envi-ronment, in advertising, in economic policies, in our homes. Violence has become embedded in our societies, so much so that its presence may be

overlooked. Our attentions are drawn to global scale violence such as terror-
ism and war, and consequently we may consider interpersonal acts of hostility or aggressiveness as found in our homes, schools, or neighborhoods as
not real violence—just isolated acts of frustration that do not merit concern
like militaristic or terroristic forms. It is my concern that downgrading interpersonal violence in homes among family members as not as serious
as mass killings or tortures plays into the view that tends to minimize the
more local and smaller-scale examples of violence. This minimization tends
to excuse or hide the consequences of these actions.

My work at the Calgary Family Therapy Centre centers largely on families experiencing parent–child conflict, frequently including physical and
verbal violence or threats of violence from children/adolescents toward
their parents, siblings, and/or classmates. Parental response to this aggressiveness often resorts to heavy-handed tactics to try to assert their control
over the threatening young person, oftentimes at the behest of therapists
and social workers, and additionally by society in general. Society expects
that parents are responsible for their children; when faced with serious
breaches of conduct, a parent is expected to regain control and ensure the
child becomes compliant. The means by which a parent is to gain control are not specified—there is a principle that says that the child should
not be harmed, but there is also a principle that says that a parent *must*
gain control over the child's unruly behavior. Research has indicated that
matching violence with violence in families often leads to an escalation in
violence, rather than its reduction (Omer, 2001). Withdrawing or ignoring
the violent overtures also is ineffective. Despite the ineffectiveness of these
responses, parents are often at a loss for what else they can do.

Responding to children/adolescents in strong and domineering ways
may be an understandable response, but one that may actually re-inscribe
our society's already well-developed allegiance to violence and its tactics
without any resultant diminution in the violence that prompted the action.
So how do we break the cycle of violence in these frontline client situations
in a way that undermines the use of violence by all?

Connecting to the social constructionist notion that behaviors are best
understood within a relational context, I have been focusing on sociological
approaches rather than psychological ones, a bit of a departure from most
psychotherapeutic traditions. Interventions/approaches that are built upon
sociocultural theories (such as nonviolent resistance) rather than psychological theories (in which behaviors are understood as more individual in

nature) have significant potential to impact the violence in relationships that comes forward in therapy as well as violence seen in the larger social world.

Adapting ideas of nonviolent resistance from Gandhi and Martin Luther King, Jr., families (as well as schools and communities) can learn to effectively respond to violence. Haim Omer (2001, 2004), from Israel, has demonstrated how specific nonviolent resistance practices can be employed by families and has provided some research results indicating the effectiveness of this approach.

Overview

From an understanding that behaviors emanate from relational patterns (McNamee and Gergen, 1999), violent words and deeds are contextually understood. Violent actions stem from a network of relationships rather than from an autonomous self. This does not absolve responsibility for one's actions—rather, it points us toward ways of responding to violence in ways that enhance the possibility for reducing the continuance of violence. It fundamentally shifts our understanding from one of independent and autonomous actors in competition with one another for dominance to one in which an understanding of our interconnectedness as persons invites us to choose from a set of responses that can serve to either encourage or discourage interpersonal violence. The culprit is violence itself, not the individual actors who engage in the violent relationship. The mutual engagement in violent encounters provides the opportunity for all participants to join in an effort to turn away from that way of relating. This is a form of *externalization* as Michael White and David Epston (1990) have outlined. This way of relating to violence provides a space in which any and all participants can join efforts to eliminate this interactional pattern. While a collaborative effort would be most advantageous, if one or more persons engage in this undertaking (and some do not), it can still pose a strong resistance to the continuance of violence.

With this viewpoint, parents and others can respond to violence from a child/adolescent with various responses, some more likely to continue the violence and others that contradict the continuation of violence. I encourage families to respond to violence in ways that emanate from nonviolent approaches. Consider the following message that a parent or parents might use with a violent child/adolescent:

Violence has made life unbearable for us. We cannot and do not want to live like this any longer. We will do all we can to change the situation—except attacking you physically or verbally. To this end, we decided on the following:

- We shall be consistently present in your life.
- We shall no longer remain alone with the problem but shall appeal to relatives and friends, tell them openly what is going on, and ask for their help and support.
- We shall determinedly oppose the following behaviors: _____ [usually specifies the violent behaviors of concern]
- We have no intention whatsoever of subduing you or gaining control over you. This message is not a threat, but an expression of our supreme duty as parents and human beings (Omer, 2004: 52).

This sample response is an example of a nonviolent response from parents in the face of violence from their child/adolescent. This is a challenging statement for parents to make. They typically have responded to violence with efforts to control and perhaps have used violence (or threats of violence) to try to curtail the child/adolescent's violent or oppositional behavior. As you can see, this statement takes a decided position against the violent behaviors, but not in a manner that uses violence in the process. It expresses a clear and decided opposition to the violence, but also includes a commitment to oppose without aggression or attack. This nonviolent statement and approach stands in stark contrast to what most of us have experienced within our own families of origin, and even when parents see the logic and value in this stance, they find it extraordinarily difficult to employ in their own family situations.

The following points (Omer, 2001) highlight the reasons why the typical parental efforts to control their children fail:

- When parent(s) and/or children conceptualize their conflict in terms of winning and losing, the possibility of escalation increases. The structure of their relationship is cast in a dichotomy of being either a winner or a loser, and faced with that forced choice, the desire to be a winner makes the choice rather easy.

- When parent(s) and/or children become emotionally charged in a conflictual situation, the risk of escalation becomes higher. When emotions are running high, the ability to consider the variety of options available is hampered. Escalation, as an option, seems to be fueled by a high emotional charge and a lack of being able to step back to evaluate.
- Parental exhorting, entreating, and apologizing increase the risk of complementary escalation. Attempts by the parents to appease or please the child who is acting in aggressive or violent ways lead to escalating violence. One might think that if a parent tries to soothe, calm down, or give the child what he/she wants, the child would calm down in similar proportion. But the evidence suggests it does not have that effect; parental arguing, threatening, blaming, and screaming increase the risk of reciprocal escalation. The choice of challenging or dominating a child who is behaving aggressively or violently also results in escalation, this time by a process of one-upmanship—the more you "fight fire with fire," the more the child feels justified in escalating.
- Constant hostile interchanges tend to narrow the parent–child interaction to conflictual issues and conflictual patterns; this, in turn, reduces the options of conflict avoidance or of successful conflict resolution. The development of an escalating pattern of aggressive or violent interactions tends to limit the parents and children from imagining or engaging in nonhostile relating. The hostility pattern rises in importance and can hijack the entire parent–child relationship, making it very difficult to imagine a different kind of relating.
- A key element of working with these nonviolent ideas is finding ways to encourage parents to step away from traditional parenting approaches that do not work. Despite parental inability to make the kind of differences that they want, there is a reluctance to step away from those failed practices. For years, there have been vigorous debates regarding whether or not physically disciplining one's child is good or bad, effective or not. The debates are often emotionally charged and difficult to organize in a way to have a serious consideration of the issue.

An example often given is one where a parent responds to his/her child who hits his/her sibling by hitting the offending child, and then exhorting him/her to not hit. Is it possible that this parental reaction re-inscribes the violence that the parent is trying to oppose? Or, is this a false comparison? Regardless of one's viewpoint on this, I think it is crucial for parents to engage in this type of reflection when choosing parenting strategies. All too often, parenting decisions are made by default, harkening back to some experiences "when the parent was a child" without making a deliberate evaluation as to what option the parent wishes to choose.

Violence exhibited by one's child is alarming on several levels: (a) concern for the child's safety and the consequences (short-term and long-term) for him/her; (b) concern for the parent's own safety (or others around them); or (c) worry about this behavior as a sign of parental failure and the resultant feelings of blame or shame. The distress of this situation can also lead a parent to feel a sense of disbelief that this is happening and an unrealistic desire for this problem to just go away on its own.

Let me describe some applications of these ideas that I have tried. I have discussed using nonviolent methods with parents who have become extremely frustrated, bordering on hopelessness. After repeatedly attempting more conventional strategies of behavioral management of their children, including boundary setting, reward systems, consistency, tolerance, firmness, and emotional appeals, they have a readiness to trying something new. My efforts to begin working with parents using nonviolent strategies (before they have tried all of the other more commonsensical methods) is oftentimes viewed by parents as insufficient, weak, and maybe even capitulation to the child. This early tendency by parents to want to control the child supports my belief that discourses of control and domination are firmly rooted in our societal belief systems. Parents accept the belief that they must control their child at all costs and diligently follow that mandate, even when they engage in behaviors with which they personally disagree.

Once parents have the sense that they have exhausted all conventional parental strategies and approaches, the way is cleared to discuss the possibility of utilizing nonviolent strategies. The theoretical, as well as pragmatic, case is made to the parents as to the potential of this approach in achieving what the other more customary approaches could not. Without this foundational understanding, the efforts to consistently use nonviolence will likely wilt under the child's uncooperative or even hostile reactions to this way of responding. Children are also convinced of the value of violence as suggested by the societal discourses, so when faced with a nonviolent parental response, their initial response is likely one of disbelief and/or scorn for the parents for using this approach. If the parents are uncertain or unsupported in this new way, the frustration of not seeing quick results and the verbal abuse forthcoming from the child may encourage them to reenact their conflictual dance.

This radical refiguring of the family interactional patterns highlights that parent–child interactions are constructed. They can be configured in a variety of ways. When relationships are not problematic, we usually do not consider our roles in constructing them. It is when they seemingly fall apart that we are given the opportunity to revisit and revise them and can more readily see how relationships can shift by our efforts. Deconstructing our practices allows us to see more clearly how they function and to assess whether or not they should be continued. This knowledge can be comforting and reassuring when we are having doubts about the possibilities of our social world changing.

One set of parents who had just begun this process of using a nonviolent approach with their physically threatening sixteen-year-old son reported back to me that their son "laughed at them" and told them that they were "weak." These comments shook their resolve, and they became verbally aggressive in return. They felt that they had failed. The history of nonviolent approaches on large societal levels (Sharp, 2005) (along with parenting approaches in general) has shown us that perfect applications of strategies cannot be realistically expected. A misstep in consistent parenting does not ruin the effort. I encouraged them to regroup their thinking, reflect on his response, and plan for how to continue their effort as now wiser parents than before. His challenge to their new approach conveniently provided them with more information from which to more ably continue on their new path.

Their persistence in using nonviolent strategies in the face of his scorn or ridicule had an impact on him. He had been used to derailing his parents' parenting efforts, and their determination with this approach caught his attention. In fact, this approach to parenting was much more agreeable to him on a certain level, because they were not overtly challenging him in his strength (his power showed in his loud voice and threatening behaviors). They remained calm and did not escalate with him (which he had come to expect). They maintained their resolve to not accept his aggressive behaviors but did not engage with him in forceful interchanges where they demanded his obedience.

One of the elements of this approach flies in the face of psychological understandings; rather than respond with consequences to a misbehavior close in time to the unwanted behavior, this nonviolent approach suggests that responses that stand in opposition to the violence should occur when the emotions associated are cooled down. So rather than "strike while the iron is hot," the idea here is to "strike while the iron is cold" (Omer, 2004). This principle worked well with this family—the boy was more able to carry on a conversation about his behavior when he was not in the "heat of battle." The possibility of having a discussion with him about his behaviors was much greater when they spoke with him in a nonagitated state. He was often able to reflect upon his behaviors in ways that indicated to the parents that he at least understood the outrageousness of his actions, even though his ability to refrain from periodic outbursts was limited.

One of the most disconcerting aspects of this family's violent situation and their long history of failure in changing it was that the parents were unable to be the kind of parents they had wanted to be with their son. The violent interactions had generated a conflict zone where they could not be nurturing, supportive, loving, or even appreciative of their son. The parents felt that they had been cheated out of being the kind of parents they most wanted to be, instead becoming the kind of parents that they most did *not* want to be. When I asked these parents, "Are these the behaviors, thoughts, and feelings the ones you had hoped to have as a parent?" the result was silence and then tears. This type of question invites parents to step back and reflect on their hopes and dreams, similar to Sally's earlier point of engaging her clients in a type of philosophical talk.

With this question, I was inviting them to imagine the kind of parent they once hoped to be and to compare it to the present. They described many of the things they had hoped to do with their son and felt that those experiences were now unavailable to them, in large measure due to a need to follow a parental script that was handed to them by society, by tradition, by expectations outside of them. They had come to believe that they had no choice—they were trapped by the violence of their child/adolescent and were forced to either try to dominate in return or simply to "take it."

The violence that their son exhibited had been a shameful experience for the parents that led them to want to hide that aspect from their rather large extended family. They would often skip family gatherings or leave early if they sensed that the violent behavior might be noticed. In my work with this family, I encouraged the parents to no longer keep this a secret. In fact, I asked them to deliberately discuss the situation with extended family members in order to receive support and perhaps some new ideas on how to deal with the situation. Several extended family members stepped forward to volunteer to have the boy stay with them for weekends or even longer stays, providing respite for the parents as well as offering some direct help in dissuading the boy from violent interactions. While these times living with other relatives did not eliminate the violence, it gave the boy and his parents some much-needed time apart and some other perspectives on what was happening to them. These short stays with relatives were mostly peaceful, not going on long enough to develop the kind of testiness and raw feelings that the parents and their son had experienced together. Had the visits with relatives been longer, it is very possible that those relatives could have encountered similar forms of disagreeable aggression and violence.

Exposing the "secret" was a relief for the parents (although it involved some initial embarrassment for the son), and the pressure that was present due to the need to keep this hidden from the rest of the family was relieved. Being able to confront the influence of violence in one's family by talking about it openly with one's family, extended family, and others in one's social network is a significant step in cracking the influence of violence. By naming it and openly rebuking its influence in one's life, it mounts a successful point of resistance, and to the degree that it is shared with others may stimulate others to follow likewise.

They used the strategy of a "sit in" whereby they sat in his room and when he asked them why they were there, they stated that they were opposed to his aggressive and violent behaviors and were planning on sitting to think and discuss what might be done to stop the violence in the house. (He was invited to participate if he wished—he declined.) They performed the sit-in repeatedly, thereby emphasizing their commitment to change even though the exact plan on how to change was unknown.

Probably the most noticeably nonviolent method they used was persistent noncompliance with his invitations to escalate. As they developed their skills in nonviolence, they became more able to simply resist/refrain from his overtures to escalate angrily and aggressively in return to him. He initially tried to bait them into anger (and it sometimes worked), but they became increasingly adept at sidestepping these invitations. He began to try to provoke them less in return—another sign that their initiative was being noticed and having an impact.

Early research results suggest that this way of working has had only a modest ability to curb the violent behavior of the child/adolescent (Weinblatt and Omer, 2008), but a noticeable outcome has been that parents are able to "find themselves" again. They recognize that they can stay within the bounds of what being a good parent means to them, irrespective of whether or not their child/adolescent changes. This seems to be a key development for the parents. It re-establishes their own self-control and allows them to behave in accordance with their principles rather than feel controlled by the child/adolescent. This serves as an invitation to the child/adolescent into a new kind of dialogue with the parent leading by example.

In my work with this particular family, the son's behavior has continued to be at times violent and threatening, but less often. The biggest improvement has seemed to come from the parents recapturing a sense of themselves as parents. They now feel as though they are not wholly dependent on their son and his moods. The escalating behaviors they used to engage in daily with him are not as frequent. They also feel that they can do fun or kind things with or for him when they feel like it. The "dark cloud" that hung over their relationship with him has lifted somewhat and they are no longer held hostage by his moods or behaviors. This change is very significant because persons under threat of violence often feel that their whole life is eclipsed by the angry relational partner—their entire life is subject to the angry feelings of the other. To not be chained to the other's moods/behaviors provided this couple with a sense of liberation in their own lives, which had an overall positive impact on their relationship with their son. This ability to be less hopeless and disconsolate probably contributed in a positive way to their son's disposition as well.

A positive aspect of this approach is also to reduce the sense of frustration and feelings of unhelpfulness for the therapist. To work with families with this level of violence is worrisome for the therapist—there is a strong desire to try to improve the situation quickly (just like the parents feel). To be able to see some relief in the parents, irrespective of the child/adolescent's progress in reducing his/her anger/violence, provides some optimism for the therapist as well. Too often, therapists tend to look only at the reduction or elimination of the presenting problem as the only marker of therapeutic progress. In this case, the parents' growing sense of optimism and relief for the reclaiming of their own self-agency was a significant development. In fact, this development may have been most advantageous in terms of curbing the use of violence in this family. The parents have refrained from those tactics and their son has seen a parental example of not resorting to violence to deal with violence. This living example of turning away from violence affords the child the opportunity to see what it takes to say "no" to violent tactics. In the spirit of nonviolent resistance efforts throughout history, the goal is not to attack or defeat (in this case, violence)—it is rather an opportunity to claim a nonviolent behavior as one's own in an effort to support what you believe in.

In this way, the parents turning away from using violence in relationship with their son decreases the overall use of violence—by two people. Hopefully, their son might be able to join this nonviolent path, but for now, the violent interaction of three people is cut from three to one. If violence can be reduced or rejected by more and more people, perhaps this might eventually impact the larger society's overall investment in violent ways. At this point, this idea is only a proposition, but, in my view, one worth believing. In the early stages of any movement, the efforts to resist some negative influence are usually small and are oftentimes considered insignificant. These decisions to behave nonviolently are based upon principled behavior and are worth it because the means used to pursue some goal must be congruent with the principles we espouse.

Beyond the value for the families to desist from violent parental strategies, an important point in this example is having professional helpers paying attention to the values and beliefs that they uphold in practicing their profession. A more deliberate knowledge of, and effort to develop, those principles we believe in can be built into the ways in which we help people. Social action is not only something that is done in protest marches and letter-writing campaigns; in very significant ways, the everyday practices of family therapists speak loudly in supporting or challenging the preferred societal practices of family life.

Conclusion

In discussing our projects in which we use front-line therapy work to try to impact larger social ills, we see common points. In our practices, we promote a position of asking parents to *not* use force or overt domination with their children as they try to deal more effectively with the troubles their children pose for them. Actively using nonviolent strategies makes sense both from a moral position as well as a way of most effectively conversing with the other.

Another intersection was the conversations asking the parents to return to their original hopes and intentions for becoming a parent. In both of our projects, we encourage the parents to reclaim their hopes for parenting and to find ways to bring them to fruition. This reconnection to their personal wishes and dreams raises their optimism level. What they had considered lost and irretrievable is discovered to be still available.

The third commonality is the importance of breaking the code of secrecy that surrounds the family trouble. The shame and blame associated with these situations drives the parents to secrecy and fosters feelings of isolation and hopelessness. As with all these common points, they can be enacted by the parents by simply rethinking their ideas and their behaviors. They are able to unilaterally stop being violent or threatening, they can reclaim their dreams of how they want to be a parent, and they can break out of isolation. In the face of disagreeable relationships with their children, they can turn the tide—not by making their children be different, but by altering their own behaviors. The feelings of victimization that come with being parents in these very troublesome situations can be impacted by parents who re-think their ideas and decisions and make adjustments.

Many professions are well-positioned to have an impact on our world beyond the stated objectives of the profession. The ways we enact our roles serve to support or challenge pervasive understandings within our societies. From our perspective, we cannot *not* contribute to our societal ways of being. When we revisit social constructionist ideas, we are reminded that we are constantly remaking our relationships in all our interactions. The ways we have come to understand gender and the associated roles, and violence and its consequences, are not automatic, and they are not beyond our influence. Developing ways of conversing or dialoguing about the ways these aspects of our lives impact us provide us with an opportunity to make changes in our lives that have an impact on others around us. Given this, we believe that one should consciously consider these larger societal issues and how one might fit these into daily practice to make a difference in society. In our situations, we have taken stands in support of gender equality and in nonviolence. We have illustrated our ways of enacting our roles as family therapists in ways that support these larger societal initiatives to make our worlds better places within which to live.

References

Anderson, H. (1997). *Conversation, language, and possibilities: A postmodern approach to therapy.* New York: Basic.

Bakardjieva, M. (2009). Subactivism: Lifeworld and politics in the age of the internet. *The Information Society,* 25: 91–104.

Becvar, D. and R. Becvar (2009). *Family therapy: A systemic integration,* 7th ed. Boston: Pearson.

Gergen, K. (1991). *The saturated self: Dilemmas of identity in contemporary life.* New York: Basic.

Gergen, K. (2009). *An invitation to social construction,* 2nd ed. Los Angeles: Sage.

Marinoff, L. (1999). *Plato not Prozac! Applying philosophy to everyday problems.* New York: HarperCollins.

McNamee, S. and K. Gergen (1999). *Relational responsibility: Resources for sustainable dialogue.* Thousand Oaks, CA: Sage.

Minuchin, S. (1974). *Families and family therapy.* Cambridge, MA: Harvard University Press.

Nichols, M. and R. Schwartz (2004). *Family therapy concepts and methods.* 6th ed. Boston: Pearson.

Omer, H. (2000). *Parental presence: Reclaiming a leadership role in bringing up our children.* Phoenix, AZ: Zeig, Tucker.

———. (2001). Helping parents deal with children's acute disciplinary problems without escalation: The principle of nonviolent resistance. *Family Process,* 40(1): 53–66.

———. (2004). *Nonviolent resistance: A new approach to violent and self-destructive children.* New York: Cambridge University Press.

Rojano, R. (2004). The practice of community family therapy. *Family Process,* 43(1): 59–77.

Sharp, G. (2005). *Waging nonviolent struggle: 20th century practice and 21st century potential.* Boston: Porter Sargent.

Stevenson, J. (1998). *The complete idiot's guide to philosophy.* New York: Alpha.

St. George, S. and D. Wulff (2007). Collaborating as a lifestyle. In H. Anderson and D. Gehart (Eds.), *Collaborative therapy: Relationships and conversations that make a difference* (pp. 403–420). New York: Routledge.

———. (2008). *Community-minded family therapy.* Unpublished manuscript.

Tomm, K. (1991). Beginning of a HIPs & PIPs approach to psychiatric assessment. *The Calgary Participator,* 1(2): 21–22, 24.

Weinblatt, U. and H. Omer (2008). Nonviolent resistance: A treatment for parents of children with acute behavior problems. *Journal of Marital and Family Therapy* 34: 75–92.

White, M. and D. Epston (1990). *Narrative means to therapeutic ends.* New York: Norton.

Wulff, D., S. St. George, and F. Besthorn (2011). Revisiting confidentiality: Observations from family therapy practice. *Journal of Family Therapy,* 33(2): 199–214.

10

Opening a Space for Hope in a Landscape of Despair

Trauma and Violence Work with Men Who Have Sexually Abused Minors

MARIE KEENAN

The concept of hope is not often evident in public or professional discourses on child sexual offenders—the language of pathology, evil, or risk manage-ment more often to the fore. If you consider the lives of the "residents" of Coalinga Mental Hospital in California,[1] you gain a sense of how little real hope darkens the door of this and other regimes of containment and treatment for men who have perpetrated child sexual offenses. Explanatory theories of child sexual offending offer the personality of the perpetrator or gendered relations of power and control as the main protagonists; medico-legal paradigms or the feminist alternative provide the relevant evidence for such perspectives. Within medico-legal perspectives, the identity of the perpetrator is recast as a new species of pedophilic being, while the gender alternative offers all men as possible suspects.[2] Within such a context, the search for meaning seems almost as futile as hope is the domain of the "naïve." But within this context, my work in relation to trauma and vio-lence, love and abuse takes place.

It is impossible to discuss men who have sexually offended without re-ferring to the children and young people whom they have abused; however, the primary focus of this chapter is my work with men who have perpetrated such offenses. That work is influenced by and, in turn, influences my ther-apeutic work with individuals who have experienced sexual violence and sexual abuse in childhood. In some cases, the man who has perpetrated the abuse has also experienced trauma and abuse at another time in his life.

This chapter illuminates the varying influences on my trauma and violence work with men who have perpetrated sexual abuse against minors—an area of professional activity that is conducted under the gaze of an ever-vigilant and concerned public and professional community. An ethic of social justice informs this work. I also point to a number of ways in which a social constructionist perspective enhances my practice. The first part of the chapter focuses on the theoretical underpinnings, philosophical influences, and personal inspirations on my work; the second part illuminates some of the practice ideas.

Context

My mother was a central character in my life. Formally uneducated but with an insight into the human condition that none could teach, I, the first of her five children, was to be the benefactor of a depth of wisdom that flowed effortlessly as she and my father coached their five children from childhood to adulthood in an Ireland that was undergoing great social change. Here, the lessons that I now see as resonating with social constructionist thought began: Rules are manmade and meant to be questioned; never judge a book by its cover; never underestimate the power of the human spirit; trust your instinct, but always remember that your "view" is not the only one; do not fear those in authority, such as doctors and clergy, and never take as "gospel" what they tell you; doing what you think is right often involves risks (of rebuttal or rejection); tread gently for life is difficult. Within the parameters of this humble working-class enclave, I learned "to avoid isolation" and "refuse indifference" (Weingarten, 2007: 15) and that by doing so lives and worlds can change. In these early years, I also learned the importance of having allies in life, people who were interested in standing with me in solidarity as I navigate the journey that is my life.

I am currently employed as an academic at the School of Applied Social Science, University College Dublin. While most of my teaching involves masters students of social work, I also teach modules to undergraduate students on a range of perspectives relating to crime and the "justice" system. In moving into academia from practice as a systemic and forensic psychotherapist and formerly as a social worker, I committed myself to responding to former clients and their families, should they ever need to consult me in the future. This work, alongside some organizational consultations, keeps the practice side of my professional life strong but not overwhelming. My research and practice also involves Roman Catholic clerical men who have perpetrated sexual abuse against minors,[3] and this work has brought me into dialogue with many Catholic clergy and Church leaders and into witnessing some of the practices that are involved in the institution that is the Roman Catholic Church. In 1996, I was one of three people who set up a community-based program in Dublin for individuals who experienced sexual abuse in childhood and for those men[4] who had committed such offenses (and both sets of families). In recent years, influenced by the failure of current practices that divide individuals into victims/offenders, good/bad, and innocent/guilty, and the socially sanctioned marginalization and oppression that results from such dichotomies, I have turned my attention to attempts to find other more useful ways forward in the area of sexual trauma and violence work, partly influenced by ideas of justice (Sandel, 2009) and based on restorative and redemptive principles.

My Introduction to Social Constructionism

My primary training as a social scientist, later as a social worker, and later still as a systemic and forensic psychotherapist, equipped me with the intellectual skills to undertake my professional life and to evolve and expand my intellectual horizons over what is now a period of more than thirty years. The myriad clients whose lives intertwined with mine gave shape to that learning, teaching me the small but important lessons in what it means to be a compassionate and courageous worker. In translating compassion and courage into activities that fight against isolation and indifference and work on behalf of inclusion and concern, I learned to welcome folks, to be hospitable, to avoid labels, to be humble but not self-effacing, to lead and be led, to listen carefully to what people said, to honor silence, to be skeptical of certainty, and to take risks[5] (Foucault, 2001: 11–24). The more I learned about clients' lives the more the distinctions between "us" and "them" became increasingly untenable. "They" were "us" and "we" were "them"—connected by more than what divided us. This became increasingly clear when both worker and client managed to "show up"[6] and particularly when the dialogue moved to the sphere of hopes, dreams, values, and intentions for life.

Speaking and writing about these reflections in relation to my work with men who have committed sexual offenses, and in suggesting that the distinctions between "us" and "them" are far thinner than many would care to accept, has indeed drawn its own caste of critics and skeptics. Beyond the accusation of my "naivety" or the suggestion of their "manipulation"—marking me out as another of their victims—I am invited by the literature and the academy to take certain stances that will help me become a "good" and "effective" social worker and psychotherapist.

I am invited to listen for difference rather than similarity, especially with men whose behavior is universally abhorred and whose personhood is recast as embodied evil. I am invited to pit the innocence of childhood against the guilt of adulthood and to render invisible the adult-child as though the abusive adult never had childhood. I am invited to privilege "behavior" and ignore "intention," and if intention must be noticed, one melody must apply—"bad action always speaks to bad intention." I am invited to punctuate my conversations with men who have perpetrated violence and abuse with invitations to responsibility, but I am to ignore the manner in which violence and abuse get replicated by the very social processes and therapeutic practices designed to prevent and treat them in the first instance, such as when individual identities are reduced to descriptions of "abuse perpetrator" or when men who were once abusive are run out of their homes or their country [as happens in Ireland] without so much as a peep from the political caste, religious elite, human rights defenders, or the psy-professionals, all of whose silences serve to condone such practices. Ultimately, I am invited to correct, discipline, and punish through socially sanctioned "corrective" and "therapeutic" measures, by keeping the gaze on this therapeutic "other." By means of community management of such subjects who become objects, I am invited to believe that I am behaving ethically. In navigating such terrain, social constructionism has been an ally.

As I reflect back on my introduction to social constructionism proper, three important forces came together in the early 1980s and one in more recent times to sway my life and work in that direction: my work as a probation and welfare officer[7] in a Dublin prison, my training as a systemic therapist in the first family therapy program in Ireland, and my introduction to the narrative work of Michael White. The more recent influence has come through my meetings with Art Fisher who runs a program in Nova Scotia for responding to love, hurt, and violence in families.[8]

While the work in the prison offered humbling evidence of embodied resilience and marginalized despair in the men whose lives had taken them into confinement, my systemic training offered a questioning site of much new learning. Foucault's (1991) *Discipline and Punish: The Birth of the Prison*, which combined both, had a profound and lasting effect— taking its place alongside Goffman's (1961) *Asylums*, C. Wright Mills's (2000 [1959]) *The Sociological Imagination*, and Virginia Axline's (1990[1947]) *Dibs in Search of Self*. These texts would be returned to again and again. Run by Imelda McCarthy, Nollaig Byrne, and Philip Kearney of the Fifth Province Associates,9 the systemic family therapy training program also provided support and challenge as my exposure to the philosophy of social constructionism took hold. Imelda and Nollaig, who were to become lifelong friends and mentors, were also unknowingly to become the guardians of my new social constructionist and systemic home, as I learned to witness and meet with imprisoned men and those who loved them. The work of Michael White led me to consider the multiple meanings of "imprisonment" and the "life sentences" imposed by Western psychiatric practices. Having worked in adolescent and adult psychiatry, I developed skepticism towards the promises offered by psychiatric practices, for example as pathways to liberation from emotional pain, which contrasted with the stigmatized identities and side-effects of medication that often came instead. I learned that diagnostic classification systems are instruments of power that mask the power relations involved in their very construction (Foucault, 1991, 2004). I concluded that diagnostic classification systems served interests other than those of the so diagnosed.

All of these experiences compelled a professional coming-of-age and a wake-up call from which there was no return. Going forward, all taken-for-granted ideas and truths, particularly in the human sciences, became "truth in parentheses" and just one version. No longer could truth claims in the social sciences be accepted as outside of the context of their creation (Foucault, 1991, 2004), which included the sphere of influence of vested interests, ideology, and power relations. Going forth, all taken-for-granted truths in the "soft" sciences would have to be deconstructed and challenged, in the name of ethical practice, and any suggestion that certainty or truth could be arrived at through "scientific" methods, "objective" instruments, and "objective" researchers was no longer acceptable. Grand theory would have to be "held lightly" (McCarthy, 2002). In its place came my interest in the omnipresence of power, ideology, and emotion and the influence of this trio on the creation of knowledge and on how human beings live. I also became interested in the power of language and in the stories that get told and that people tell about themselves and their lives. It was also during this time that I committed myself anew to working *with* the people who sought my help rather than *on* them. I decided that the only way forward was to offer *with-ness* work (Shotter, 2005), *with* those imprisoned men whose life met with mine, rather than *aboutness-work* or *on-ness work* that engaged the men as object-subjects. I also committed myself to joining with the individuals who consulted me in the search for meaning. My belief and subsequent experience was that in the creation of such conversational and human meetings that lives and worlds can change.

Acknowledging that no one life represents a linear event and that the complexity of the inspirational factors on one's life cannot easily be narrated in a simple linguistic representation, my understanding of the period described above and the confluence of factors that came together during this time is that they were to determine and influence the course of my professional life and have continued to do so until today.

Social Construction: Core Ideas and Spheres of Influence

Since my introduction to social constructionism, several of its core ideas are always close at hand to disturb complacency in my work and in my life, acting as propellers against indifference. That is the thing about social constructionism—used as critique it disturbs everything! It moves the "subscriber" from the security of foundational knowledge of human phenomena, to the uncertainty of a multiplicity of truths; it questions essentialist notions of interior self (with all its ramifications for emotion, gender, race, and ability), in its place giving birth to a narrative self, created through dialogue; it exposes traditional *visible* power practices based on intentional oppression, top-down violence, and social control over people as only one expression, and instead construes modern power practices as invisible and omnipresent, manifest in the social control that is exercised through normative practices and normative surveillance. Following Foucault (1991, 2004), social constructionism establishes a link between power and the creation of knowledge, destabilizing the hegemony of certainty in the social and human sciences and rendering somewhat inane those scientific discourses that proclaim objectivity in methods and interpretations.

In this context, social scientific disciplines, unhappy with the current "soft" status, see the production of empirical "data" on individuals, preferably achieved by means of the gold standard, randomized, controlled trials, as evidence of their worthiness for membership of the elusive "pure" science club (Seto, 2005; Seto et al., 2008). The language of evidence-based is used in this aspiring new "science."

Measuring and categorizing individuals and subjects in a manner that reduces them to objects or numbers renders invisible the power relations that are at play in these consensus-building exercises that emerge in the name of science. Measured and judged as pathological objects, the social impact of this new "science" and its "findings" on the individuals so evaluated is rarely the subject of "empirical" or reflective evaluation. The aspiring "new" scientists who call for evidence-based answers to the problems of living and for outcome studies as the only reasonable measure of worthiness for all that we do, are rarely seen to debate and evaluate the social and political "effects" of their work and pronouncements on the individuals and groups who are caught in their web of influence. The men in Coalinga again come to mind. While I am not arguing against the importance of empirical and large-scale research into sexual abuse and violence, including that which is grounded in positivist thought, I am arguing for reflexivity and critical approaches to all that we do in our practices in the social sciences. It is here that the philosophy that is social constructionism offers sanctity and respite, giving a critical edge to research and therapeutic practice by providing distance from essentialist notions, totalizing descriptions and the lure of "objectivity" by instead putting "reality" in parentheses, inviting attention to power relations, ideology, and emotion and to the processes by which modern consensus is achieved.

My understanding of social work and psychotherapy is that they stand as activities of hope that center on the possibility of change within a social justice commitment. However, the focus of the change largely depends on how the problem and the problem's nature are formulated. The construction of the problem against a background of what is regarded as normal sets the stage for all social intervention. Understanding the politics of problem construction and of social research is, therefore, one of the contributions of a social constructionist perspective in the social sciences.

Measuring and Assessing Men Who Have Abused Minors—The New "Science"

Positivism and notions of scientific certainty generally influence much of the psychological literature on men who have perpetrated sexual offenses against children. The primary focus of much of this research is an individual one, with a strong emphasis on understanding the psychological and personality factors that might lead an individual down a sexually abusive path (Hudson, Ward, and McCormack, 1999). The psychiatric literature is equally framed by truth-claims and notions of scientific certainty, and the aim of the psychiatric perspective is to measure and quantify and identify the predictive personality variables that are seen as playing a causative role in creating the phenomenon (Berlin and Krout, 1986; American Psychiatric Association, 2000, *DSM-IV-TR*). Individual biological and psychological factors are generally privileged in accounting for sexual crime in much of this research. In effect, the predominant focus of the psychiatric and psychological literature is one of individual limitation and personal failure, giving rise to professional discourses based largely on ideas of deviance, deficit, and individual pathology.

Within such a perspective, the child sexual offender is classified as a pedophile (Berlin and Krout, 1986; American Psychiatric Association, 2000, *DSM-IV-TR*) or conceptualized as suffering from a host of psychological dysfunctions, such as "cognitive distortions" (Abel et al., 1984, 1987; Mann and Beech, 2003), "deviant sexual attraction" (Hanson and Bussière, 1998), or "poor emotional regulation" (Keenan and Ward, 2000). At any rate, he is conceptualized as different from "normal" men; belonging to a different "class" or "type"; a member of a class apart. This construction of the sexual offender has been challenged by some scholars within the psychological discipline (Marshall, 1996; Marshall et al., 2000; Freeman-Longo and Blanchard, 1998). However, despite this challenge, the power that these professional disciplines exercise in the creation of knowledge appears to be rarely questioned. Instead the "scientific" journals are filled with disputes about which findings are more "scientific" and whose version can claim to be closer to the truth. In all of these deliberations, the "gold standard" of randomized controlled trials is proposed as the only valid way of speaking with authority. Those researchers who are interested in more "local" narrative, including the voices of clients who are living through the situations under investigation, are marginalized along with their "findings" as merely "qualitative." If allowed at all, qualitative work can be used to support the "real," "scientific" authorities.

Given the power of "scientific" research findings to influence how one version of a problem is played out and given truth-status in the public and professional sphere, my concerns center on a number of issues: (1) The results of such theorizing can serve to marginalize and stigmatize; (2) within a context in which much psychological and psychiatric research is created and portrayed as objective and unbiased truth, the risk for oppressive and discriminatory practices is omnipresent; and (3) the findings of such research, which are subsequently reinterpreted by the popular press, have implications for shaping the public discourse in which child sexual abuse is narrated. By framing the problem as one of individual deviancy and pathology and neglecting the social context in which the problem comes to be, men who have abused are seen in singular terms and viewed as "other." Their identities are totalized as "sexual predator." Such a focus sets men who have abused apart, and it totalizes the identity of people who have experienced this trauma as "victim,"[10] thereby setting up binary constructions that do justice to none of the participants in this unhappy sphere of human activity. Totalized identity descriptions are hard to find release from. The social and personal consequences for the marginalized and alienated cannot be underestimated. This is not to say that psychological discourses of pathology create this marginalizing situation, but rather that they unintentionally contribute to it.

The Discursive Constitution of Social Phenomenon

Social constructionism as critique raises different issues from those addressed in the psychological or psychiatric literature. Rather than privileging individual personality features in understanding sexual crime, the complex relationship between the individual and the social, and the language used in bringing forth certain phenomenon, is under review. The social constructionist perspective brings together the individual and the contextual dimensions of the problem in a web of interacting dynamics and relationships that are brought forth in understanding, through particular forms of language. Social constructionists want to understand the context and circumstances in which sexual offenses occur, and they also want to understand how some actions become defined as deviant (Foucault, 1991; Hacking, 1999: 27; Jenkins, 1998: 7; Best, 1995a: 2; Berger & Luckmann, 1966: 39; Kincaid, 1998: 5; Johnson, 1995: 22). The political and cultural context in which the abuse takes place and the professional discourses which give form to the subjects that emerge from these scenarios are kept in view (Mercer and Simmonds, 2001; Haug, 2001; Cowburn and Dominelli, 2001). The social constructionist focus questions the role that knowledge plays in the creation of a problem's definition and in what core features will become taken-for-granted as central to the problem's depiction (Hacking, 1999: 27; Jenkins, 1998: 7; Best, 1995a: 2; Berger & Luckmann, 1966: 39; Kincaid, 1998: 5). This is especially so when one is confronted with abuse that goes to the heart of what most adults appear to abhor.

Social constructionism raises questions about the positioning an author, researcher, or worker will take, either inside or outside of the realm of the crime that has been committed. Where will a worker position him- or herself in relation to the other, especially when the other is socially reviled? Related to this question is the possibility of creating a "them and us" distinction. The social constructionist critique raises questions about whose truth is important and whose truth can claim to be final? Should the perpetrator have a say in telling his story or should he only be listened to through a lens of assessment, judgment, and objectification? Do such "subjugated knowledges" (Foucault, 2004: 44) have a place in contextualizing the abuse and in helping towards explanatory understanding? These questions are important in the context of working towards avoiding isolation and refusing indifference within a social justice ethic. While social constructionism does not offer prescriptive maps regarding how to work with men who have perpetrated sexual abuse and violence towards children, its offerings, which I experience in the shape of invitational questions and cautions for the worker, are no less powerful in their effect.

Jenkins (1998: 9) argues that none of the words or concepts that are often used in relation to child sexual abuse represents universally accepted objective realities. Rather, many of the words used in relation to this problems definition, such as *sexual abuse, victim, survivor, pervert, pedophile, and molester,* are rooted in the attitudes of a particular time and each carries its ideological baggage. It seems impossible to write on the topic of child sexual abuse without using language that appears to accept the ideological interpretations of a particular time. In so doing, it forecloses the exploration of other avenues of interpretation. This is particularly challenging for social constructionist practitioners, many of whose practices are influenced by social constructionism, except for when it comes to sexual violence. It often appears to me that even those workers who consider themselves as influenced by social constructionist thought return to normative and uncritical ideas and to traditional views of visible power in relation to sexual abuse and violence. Power as domination is the only version of power considered. Dominant discourses of sexual violence, particularly against children, invite workers to define the person who has abused as the problem, respond by educating him about the effects of the violence on the other, take a position towards him that is influenced by ideas of management and risk, and do all of this in the name of community values of safety, child protection, or professional care (Fisher, 2008; 2009). Where is social constructionism in this formulation?

Adopting a social constructionist perspective for trauma and violence works invites critical exploration of the web of conditions that might favor what we are calling child abuse. Kincaid (1998:9) argues that Western culture has "enthusiastically sexualised the child while denying just as enthusiastically that it was doing any such thing." Child pageants and the sexualizing of children in the realm of the pop music industry and in the advertising of certain goods provide the evidence for this thesis. For Kincaid, a society that regards children as erotic, but also regards an erotic response to them as criminally unimaginable, has a problem on its hands. In his opinion, the extent of the abuse of children is still denied because the complexities involved in the interplay of childhood, sexuality, and adulthood are also denied, while attention is focused on the "monster" (Kincaid, 1998: 20). The logical conclusion is that a change in the discourse is necessary if a society wants to work towards a safer society for children and all adults—including men. The discourse must change to one in which the problem of child sexual abuse is located within the general adult population and not with a few individuals who are identified as monsters. Ultimately, a better understanding of the complexities of adult and child sexuality is required.[11]

Foucault's (1998) analysis of power and sexuality helps the social scientist to refocus his or her view from deviant individual to particular institutions—such as the family, the fate of the body, and how it relates to desire when thinking about child abuse and violence. Foucault's work also helps the social scientist to be cautious when it comes to accepting pathologizing or totalized descriptions of individuals. This is not to say that individuals are not accountable for their actions. Rather, the social scientist is invited to move cautiously around normative discussions of child sexual abuse; always mindful of the fact that at best we only ever have a partial perspective of the complexities involved. The dichotomous thinking that abounds this subject may ultimately not serve children or adults well. "Them" and "us" distinctions may serve only to alienate and marginalize, rather than embrace the problems of living within the shared human community. In Kincaid's (1998: 6) view, many children suffer in the current situation: those children who are sexually abused and those who are denied a nurturing relationship with adult men. Men who have ever abused a child suffer, too, when they are sentenced to live their lives as "evil monsters" by an unforgiving adult public.

The Practice: The Fifth Province Provides a Space in Which to Speak

As well as providing a mentoring environment for my introduction to social constructionist thought, the Fifth Province Associates, mentioned earlier, also enormously influenced my approach to therapy with men who had sexually abused minors. As well as forming a team to provide family therapy training in Ireland, they focused their clinical work and research in the areas of incest disclosures, poverty, and gender inequality (Byrne and McCarthy, 2007, 1999, 1998, 1995, 1994, 1988; Colgan, 1991; Hydén and McCarthy, 1994; Kearney, Byrne, and McCarthy, 1989; McCarthy, 2002, 1994, 1990; McCarthy and Byrne, 1988). They developed this work in a department of child psychiatry in a large general University Hospital in Dublin[12] and they were influenced in these processes by the work of four Milanese psychiatrists, known as the Milan Team (Prata et al., 1988). An ancient Irish allegory was adopted by the Fifth Province Associates as the guiding allegory for their work and it is a story that must be told in order for the power of the allegory and its importance for my practice to be appreciated.

During the 1970s and 1980s in Ireland, two Irish philosophers, Mark P. Hederman and Richard Kearney, co-edited a biannual journal, *The Crane Bag*, in which they attempted to create a forum for the expression of diverse and sometimes divisive points of view on a large range of topics in Irish thought: economics, the arts, history and politics (Hederman and Kearney, 1977: 10, 11; McCarthy and Byrne, 1988: 181). In the creation of the forum, Hederman and Kearney (1997: 10) invoked the allegory of the Fifth Province from ancient Celtic mythology, because they felt it symbolized what their forum was all about—"a neutral ground where things can detach themselves from all partisan and prejudiced connections and show themselves for what they really are." According to Hederman and Kearney, the Fifth Province was a province of imagination, an archetypal imaginary meeting place where even the most ordinary things could be seen in an unusual light. The Fifth Province represented "a place where a new understanding and a new unity might emerge . . . [a place] where all oppositions were resolved . . . where unrelated things coincided. . . . This province, this place, this centre" was not "a political or geographical position" but it was "more like a dis-position" (Hederman and Kearney, 1977: 10, 11; McCarthy and Byrne, 1988: 181). Within the Fifth Province, apparently varying competitive and disqualifying views could be held and honored, allowing new connections and understandings to emerge. "The metaphor is a remembrance of duality transcended and of pragmatic concerns transformed" (McCarthy, 2002: 10).

While for Hederman and Kearney (1977:10-11) the Fifth Province represented a province of imagination, for others it was believed to have been an actual geographical location in the very center of Ireland (Woods, 1907: 242; Colgan 1991:125). Ireland is known to be divided geographically into four provinces (Ulster, Munster, Leinster, and Connacht) and the ancient myth of the Fifth Province tells a story of how it was created. According to the ancient Celtic myth, during the first century, one of the ancient Irish High Kings, King Tuathal Teachtmar, erected a palace in the center of Ireland, at the Hill of Uishneach, in County Westmeath. Around the hill he cut off tracks of land from each of the existing four provinces, thereby creating the geographical site for the new province—the Fifth (Woods, 1907: 242; McCarthy and Byrne, 1988: 181). The legend suggests that the leaders of the four provinces came to this Fifth Province to sort out grievances and to receive counsel (Woods 1907: 242; Colgan, 1991: 125). The Fifth Province was not part of the existing four provinces, but it was not an unrelated domain either. It incorporated the four provinces and transcended them at the same time (Colgan, 1991:125; Hederman and Kearney, 1977: 10, 11; McCarthy and Byrne, 1988: 181). Inspired by this ancient Irish story the Fifth Province Associates adopted this allegory for their systemic consultations with families and agencies involved with families disclosing incest. Inspired by the work of Fifth Province Associates, I adopted this allegory also as guiding the allegory for my work with men who had sexually abused minors, albeit in a different way in the direct clinical situation.

In my work with men who had sexually abused minors, the allegory of the Fifth Province allows for the existence of an expansive speaking site, one that is not constrained by policing the form of talk that men utter. Rather, the men are facilitated in speaking their truth [as one of a multiplicity of truths] and their intentions and preferences for life, and through these lenses come to understand their actions and evaluate their consequences. This conversational space incorporates the dominant discourses and transcends them at the same time, bringing forth multiple perspectives on sexuality, power, violence, childhood, adulthood, and justice, in the project of creating a safer world for children, women, and men. By drawing on the allegory of the Fifth Province as the metaphorical site for my work, the conversations that take place are not restricted to the public or professional normative prescriptions of what "should" be discussed in relation to the problem that is defined as child sexual abuse and sexual violence. However, it is not a disconnected domain either, cut off from normative ideologies or the "real" world. Crucially within this conversational space child sexual abuse is seen as material reality yet prejudiced by the dichotomous binaries that constrain and limit its true exploration as expressions of living, with all the consequences of trauma, pain, and harm. Child sexual abuse is seen as both real and socially constructed. My experience is that sometimes the full exploration of how it comes to be that some men [and women] engage in these practices is often constrained by discourses that delineate what is permitted to be spoken and what is proscribed—even within the therapeutic conversational context.

Dialogue in relation to the "wrongness" of sexual contact with children is often encouraged in much therapeutic practice with men who have abused minors, when the men's words are monitored for evidence of "distorted thinking," which are in turn challenged or "corrected" by the worker. I often notice how some men in therapy for sexual violence are interested in letting me know about the wrongness of these activities and how these activities represent an aberrance. However, I am of the view that unless I am willing to enter into the man's understanding of how sexual contact with children "fitted" in his life at the time of his abusing and may in some senses have even made "sense" [no matter how inappropriate this may now appear], that a whole area of useful and meaningful exploration is ignored. I also believe that most human beings do what "fits" for them in a particular context at a particular time, and I am more interested in exploring this with the men with whom I work. By exploring the man's understanding of how the abuse fitted for him at the time of his offending [often a conversation that workers and clients can find difficult, for the truth-telling that it involves] and simultaneously exploring the high possibilities that these activities were intrusive for the child who was abused [who cannot give consent by definition], my experience is that a process unlocks, creating with it new visions for responding to life in respectful and non-abusive ways. It is important that the events of the abusing are explored not in a manner of excuse-making or justification, but as a means of meaning-making in the context of the socially available structures of life.

By locating the therapeutic conversations in the imaginary site of the Fifth Province, a space is created in which it is possible to speak about this highly complex and emotionally charged subject in a manner in which all points of view get expressed, and the integrity of no one is challenged. The language of "denial" does not even enter the room. Through such conversational meetings, the male participants get to speak about their lives and times, actions and inactions, hopes and dreams, intentions and motivations, achievements and failings. They also get to discuss the relational networks they inhabit and the children and adults whom they hurt by their violence. All experiences of suffering and cruelty can co-exist in this conversational space, one neither serving as explanation for another (such as, your experience of A caused you to commit B) nor disqualifying another (such as, by committing B your right to acknowledgement of your experience of A is disqualified). The need for a type of clarity that reduces one "reality" to make room for another is not part of the project. Rather, the multiple and complex realities of the human condition can be explored and shared and new pathways for living forged.

Much research has demonstrated the futility of "confronting" men who perpetrate abuse into ways of being better citizens (Marshall, 2005; Marshall and Serran, 2004). Shaming strategies have also shown themselves to do more harm than good (McAlinden, 2007). Instinctively, some of the "responsibility" work in this area (Jenkins, 1990) leaves me uncomfortable for reasons to do with the limited construction of responsibility that is often in play. In "responsibility" work with men who have abused, I am more interested in discerning and unpacking the dichotomies shaping the plots of responsibility/irresponsibility and what it means to be individually and socially accountable. My aim is that within the imaginary site of the Fifth Province that multilayered rich descriptions of storied lives are given time to be told and retold, and in the reshaping of life stories, men's values and commitments have time to emerge (White and Epson, 1990).

Within this conversational space, there is time to attend to the complications of children's experiences of trauma, violence, and silencing; women's experiences of trauma, violence, and silencing; men's experiences of trauma, violence, and silencing; and adults' violence towards the less powerful (Fisher, 2008). There is also time to attend to experiences of re-traumatization that occur, sometimes in intervention and therapeutic practices. There is an honoring of and support for the men's desires for directions in their lives that do not include inflicting violence on others. No premature punctuations in the evolving stories are marked with professional "diagnoses" or "assessments," and nothing needs to be pinned down. The therapeutic space becomes a conversational milieu that allows for the complexity and messiness of life to emerge and expression given to all conflictual and contradictory thought.

My experience is that the witnessing and meaning-making that emerges in such situations can be transformative for all participants, including the workers. However, the challenges are immense—primarily the call of the "shoulds" and "oughts" and the relentless invitations for the worker to interrupt the clients' narratives with his or her "better" knowledge of life and his or her "expert" knowledge in what it means to be a non-abusive individual or live a non-abusive life. Despite the moral weight that bears down on workers to adopt such a professional stance, this invitation might better be resisted, as its "shoulds" or psycho-educational features rarely come without shame for our clients, no matter how mild a dosage or how well camouflaged, often foreclosing opportunities for real therapeutic engagement. Instead, a therapeutic space in which clarity and un-clarity can co-exist is important so that explanations and meaning-making can emerge and the emotional, relational, and social conditions that give rise to what we call child sexual abuse can be explored.

The allegory of the Fifth Province inspires a spiritual or mystical sense for complex human work and it also inspires a political space in which all voices, utterances, and perspectives in a divided political landscape can be held and honored (Byrne and McCarthy, 2006). It offers a metaphorical or imaginary site from which to work to avoid dualities in conversations with individuals, while at the same time to embrace all normative and "provisional divisions and disputes" (McCarthy and Byrne, 1988: 189). The Fifth Province offers a way of being both apart from and a part of all voices involved in complex human problems (Colgan, 1991: 10). By its attachment in imagination to all voices and domains, it creates a space where new connections and encounters between apparently disparate understandings, explanations, and experiences can become possible (10). At the same time, it facilitates possibilities for going beyond the constraints of one's starting position and point of view (10).

My learning from this kind of work is that men who have come to perpetrate sexual abuse and acts of violence against children do not need psycho-educational lessons in how to take responsibility for the wrongs they have done, or in how to stop offending. Rather these commitments come through conversational activities that allow the complexities of the men's histories and stories and preferences and values for life to be rendered visible. Paradoxical as though it may seem to individuals who think of men who have perpetrated sexual violence in terms of absolute dichotomies, such as bad not good, or abusive not loving, many of these men value safety for children and value respect, justice, and love in life. However, the complexities of these values and the context of their expression in the men's lives and in the social structures available to them often need unpacking. The accounts of these experiences are told and received in microdetail, bringing to the fore what the men themselves already know about responding to love and abuse, trauma and violence (Fisher, 2008). In some therapeutic practice, many of these skills and knowledges are drowned out by dominant story lines of abuse perpetration.

Finding a Place to Stand

Men who come to therapy for sexual offending are often experts in shame and personal failure, and finding a place to stand, other than in shame and personal failure, is key to their "able-ity" to do the work (Fisher, 2008). If shame is the only available site from which to speak (Byrne and McCarthy, 2006) and shame becomes the medium through which they must be engaged, it is likely that they will exit prematurely from the therapy process, in spirit if not in body. Men in therapy for sexual offending know the difference between being defined and being heard. They also know the difference between being judged and being received. They know what it is like to be defined by others, and they often have developed skills in protecting themselves in order to make things safe. Disengaging is often an option. No matter how otherwise well-intentioned, if workers enter the therapeutic relationship with a partially closed heart and a closed mind, clients who have experienced shame and trauma will be highly skilled at noticing any ambivalences towards them, no matter how well-camouflaged. They will also have skills at noticing workers' absences of transparency and mystifications of power, saying one thing while believing another (Fisher, 2008). As one of Fisher's clients observed to him, "You seem nicer than most but you're still clever."

Having a space to stand (Fisher, 2008), or a site from which to speak (Byrne and McCarthy, 2006), other than shame or personal failure, allows participants in therapy for sexual offending to achieve a little distance from the immediacy of the problems and an opportunity to see the problems in a new light. For this reason, my group-work with men who have perpetrated abuse and violence always begins with life-story work, including intentions, hopes, and dreams—and not with offense-specific work, as is preferred by workers who are not of the same persuasion (Wyre, 1996). Some therapists do what they call self-esteem work, before engaging men in therapy for sexual offending, as another way of helping them find an alternative site to shame and personal failure from which to do the work (Marshall et al., 1997; Marshall et al., 2000). In my context, the allegory of the Fifth Province allows for such possibilities by creating a welcoming safe space, a space beyond dualities and a space of possibilities (Colgan, 1991). The "doing" of hope through *with-nessing* in dialogue and silence becomes part of the therapeutic imperative.

Taking a Stance Against Totalizing Identities

Within some professional discourses the self is theorised as an essential or interior self, capable of being thought about as a separate entity. In these discourses the self is seen as something to be discovered; something that is fixed and autonomous and something that is internal to the individual (Burr, 1995). Social constructionism theorizes the self in rather different terms; here the self is conceptualized as relational, as a self-in-action, always fluid, always being created and re-created in relationship with others. Such a way of conceptualizing self gives rise to the concept of a narrative self, a self that may have a core, a physical and emotional embodiment, but which is primarily storied and constructed in language and in relationship with others (Flaskas, 2002: 87; Gergen, 1992; Ward and Marshall, 2007: 2; White, 2004a).

According to White (2004a: 121), individuals living out of a negative self-identity are more likely than those who live out of positive identity descriptions to live unfulfilling lives. Abusive behavior is more likely to occur in individuals who hold negative identity conclusions (Marshall et al., 2000: 48–50). It is therefore important to consider the impact of labels, stigma, and social rejection on the narrative identity of individual men who come to commit child sexual offenses and to take a stance against such practices in the work. In most cases, the actual offending behavior of men who abuse minors occupies a very small portion of their lives. Based on the analyses of the very detailed diaries of a predatory child-sexual offender, who had abused over four hundred boys, over a twenty-year period, Marshall (1996: 318) estimated that this man spent 8 percent of his time offending (including planning and arranging). For many child sexual offenders, the time spent offending is much less than 8 percent. However, when sinister motives are attributed to all of a man's actions and his actions are seen as evidence of a pathological or deviant identity, the effects may be disintegrative in nature, in that there is little or no effort made to affirm the basic goodness of his character or to reinforce his membership in the community of law-abiding citizens, long after he has served prison terms and fulfilled community sanctions (Garfinkel, 1956). The primary relevance of stigmatization is that it shuns the offender, keeping him as outcast—a situation some scholars hypothesize can lead to further offending (Karp, 1998: 283; Maxwell and Morris, 1999; Soothill and Francis, 1998: 288, 289). Many men who have abused minors often end up with "sexual offender identities" in which no other identity descriptions are permitted (Hudson, 2005:1, O'Malley, 1998:1). The extent to which such sexual offending identities influence any further offending is the subject of ongoing research.

As a social constructionist-informed practitioner I am aware of the potential cul-de-sac that is encountered when we lend support for explanations that are based on "naturalistic" accounts of individual identities and of certain social problems (White, 2000: 51). Naturalistic accounts, which are premised on an understanding of the individual's "nature" and on "the nature" of things, dominate many contemporary understandings of individuals' identities and of certain events (White, 2000: 51). The dominance of such naturalistic accounts renders it difficult to think outside of them.

By contrast, the refusal to accept naturalistic accounts, or at least to subject them to critique and question, opens the door for endless possibilities
and curiosities about how things came to be the way that they are and to
the complexities of the skills and knowledges, hopes and intentions that
human lives comprise. In effect, "too much is obscured by explanations
that defer to the rules of human nature" (White, 2000:49).

The practices involved in the work that I am describing are very different from responses to the problem of violence and sexual abuse that are
based on predefined socially available definitions of "the problem"[13] and
the person who acts, and it is in line with the work being carried out by
Fisher (2008, 2009) and his colleagues in Nova Scotia. This approach differs from those which focus on the problem-only stories of a man's life—
such as "distorted thinking," "inability to regulate emotion," or "deviant
sexual interests," which then become the focus of the treatment. This approach instead keeps open a space for consideration of the points of ambivalence and contradiction that exist in the area of love and violence, care
and abuse, which are rendered invisible by descriptions of love and abuse
as dialectically opposed, with all the social ramifications that follow. The
complexities involved in paradigms of justice (Sandel, 2009) are also honored in this conversational milieu.

Turning the Discursive Gaze onto the Worker's Practice

Fisher (2008) observes in his work with men who have perpetrated violence
that workers must always be conscious of the positions they are invited into
by dominant discourses, particularly in relation to their clients. He suggests
that it is no longer acceptable to maintain the questioning gaze on the client's life but rather that all therapeutic practice must also be subjected to
the same critical optics; the absence of which can lead to therapeutic abuses.
In addition it must be recognized that power relations in the room shape
the politics of "possibilities" (Colgan, 1991; Fisher, 2008).

For Fisher (2008), this reflexive work is given form by means of a
number of reflexive questions, which cover more than individual or group
conversations and extend far beyond the interview room, to the way that
people's lives are documented in case files and in reports. The reflexive
questions broadly take the following form: What socially available forms of
problem definition am I invited to find compelling, promising, or productive?

What socially available ideas about "effects" of the problem am I being asked to privilege? What socially available forms of judgment am I invited to impose? What socially available identity conclusions am I being invited to come to? Unless the worker turns the reflexive lens onto his own practices and professional discourses then the possibility exists for unreflexive and potentially oppressive work to be carried out by workers (even those who may label themselves as social constructionists), which is presumably not something that they intend.

Fisher (2008) also cautions workers against complacency and against adopting a belief that their practice offers the best or only right way forward. Violence and trauma work that are inspired by social constructionism must sit alongside many other practices as just one way. There is little room in the area of sexual trauma and violence work for contentment or certainty than any one group of workers or individual perspectives will provide all the answers. In effect, either/or thinking might usually be replaced by both/and perspectives.

Practicing Vigilance Against Social Violence and the Violence of Misrepresentation

The use of shaming mechanisms is not new, nor is the use of public humiliation and social disgrace in order to exact punishment for an offense. Such strategies can be state-led, as well as popular responses to sexual offending; both have the same disintegrative or stigmatizing effects. These strategies, designed to shame offenders into greater respect for the law and to create a powerful deterrent to reoffending (Karp, 1998), can also be seen as strategies of social or institutional violence—a violence that we have not begun to address in the Western world. While some of the state-led examples of social violence in the United States, England, and Ireland can include registration and notification schemes, which are a response to populist calls for punitive responses to sexual crime (Bottoms, 1995), other schemes are much more violent in their impact. In the United States, mandatory self-identification, which mandates the offender to personally inform his neighbors that he is a convicted sexual offender, or community notification schemes, which give the police the power to release details of convicted sexual offenders via the Internet or on posters, are in effect strategies of public exposure and humiliation, although the intent may be to protect the public (Karp, 1998:

281). There are numerous examples of shaming strategies imposed in the Western world, which are all designed to bring the crime to the attention of the public so that they may respond with shaming. While part of the intent is to warn potential victims of the potential dangers that an offender may pose, the risk of stigmatization attached to such penalties is very high (Kelley, 1989: 775).

At a more community-based level, public humiliation and shaming strategies are also in evidence, often with the help of the media. The 2000 *News of the World* "name and shame" campaign in England, which also spilled over to Ireland, centered on the "outing" of suspected and known men who had sexually abused minors, by printing their photographs, names and addresses, and details of their offending histories in the public press. The aim of this campaign was to name and shame all the child sexual offenders in Britain and to pressure government into adopting an equivalent of Megan's Law from the United States, in Great Britain, which would provide for a greater degree of community notification than had previously been in existence. The media campaign provoked widespread hysteria and vigilante activity, culminating in demonstrations outside of people's homes, forcing several families to flee, one man to disappear, and two alleged child sexual offenders to commit suicide (Ashenden, 2002: 208). Its effects in Ireland were that some men lost their employment, some were run out of their homes, and some out of their country.

Far from protecting the community and adding to greater community safety, such strategies of social violence only serve to label and stigmatize individual offenders and isolate them from their communities (Winick, 1998: 539). Such strategies work against the rehabilitative ideal and ultimately may drive many sexual offenders underground (Soothill and Francis, 1998: 288, 289). While the aim ought to be to invite sexual offenders or potential sexual offenders to come forth and to seek help, in effect such strategies may have the exact opposite result. Social violence renders crucial stories about abuse perpetrators' lives invisible, their motivations and intentions bad, their personalities damaged, and their good works suspect. Within the modern day technologies of power, nobody is accountable for inflicting such social violence and social trauma. The challenges involved in working against such oppressive practices are ever mounting as the new punitiveness and the culture of control (Garland, 2001) continue to gain their foothold in what is becoming regarded as the Atlantic Alliance—the United States, England, and Ireland—at least in how it attends to sexual crime.

Whose Side Are You On?

A short story tells of the complexities of the conversations that take place when one is working with individuals for whom trauma and violence, love, and abuse and their intricacies form part of the life histories. My client, Tom[14]—a man who had abused a number of adolescent boys in the context of his work as a teacher—was taking part, prior to sentencing, in group therapy in a community-based program of which I was the co-facilitator. He recounted many stories of his life, including numerous accounts of how he was sexually abusive to adolescent boys. One such young boy, Alan,[15] who had experienced abuse by Tom, and who had discovered that Tom was in treatment in my program, requested a meeting with me. Having secured the necessary permissions and considered that this was something meaningful for Alan, I agreed to the meeting. Alan wanted to know if Tom had remembered him. Did Tom remember exactly what he had done? Did Tom show remorse? Did Tom have any sense of how his actions had impacted Alan's life?

One of the difficult aspects of this scenario was that Tom had no memory of Alan, but because he had abused a number of boys he would plead guilty to this offense, too, believing that Alan must be telling the truth. Alan's description of the abuses that had occurred fitted largely with the pattern told of Tom's abuse by other boys, now men, and by Tom himself. However, Tom's plea of guilt was insufficient consolation for Alan, and he needed a more personal kind of acknowledgement of the events that had occurred and of their impact on him.

Over the course of two and a half hours, Alan and I spoke of these and other matters. I was deeply sorry for Alan that Tom found it hard to remember him. We wondered about injustice on top of injustice—and Tom's lack of memory of Alan was located in the realm of adding insult to injury. We considered ways of helping [or forcing] Tom to remember—and we considered how this could be best done. In the end, we had exhausted so many options that seemed to offer such little promise (much had already been tried with Tom), that we came to wonder why we should be so concerned with Tom's remembering—as maybe it was Alan's life and remembering (White, 2000, 2004a, 2004b) that should matter most for Alan now.

We moved to consider power and agency and the small but powerful child strategies that Alan used to fight against the abuse that was occurring and the options and strategies available to individuals who have suffered abuse at taking back power. We evaluated the responses that Alan had made in his life to the events that had occurred and how he had worked to turn his tragedy into something that made him an even greater human being in the world. We made a long list of the skills and knowledge that had come to Alan in life through his tragedy. And we discussed his future hopes and dreams. Overall, I found this to be a most moving, sad, and precious conversational space.

As we moved towards the end of our meeting I offered to help Alan in any way I could in the future, if he had any ideas of how that might take shape, especially given my ongoing contact with Tom. Alan, who was having therapy with another worker, who knew he was seeing me on this occasion, said he would let me know if anything arose. We got up to leave together and I walked with him to the door. As we said our goodbyes and were just about to part company, Alan paused and said that he had just one more question. Looking at me straight in the eye, Alan asked: "Whose side are you on?"

In all my time of doing trauma and abuse work in all its complexity with men and women, I had never been asked this question before, although it often hung unlanguaged in the room. Being systemically trained in the tradition of the Milan School[16] and being utterly familiar with the debates concerning the concepts of neutrality in therapeutic positioning (not moral neutrality) which the Milan School reauthored as "curiosity," because of the inflamed debate that the concept evoked in the literature, I immediately thought of the systemic calling to neutrality. However, I declined this as inadequate. Instead my reply was to be indelibly printed on my mind and heart forever. "Fifty-one, forty-nine," I answered. "Fifty-one percent on your side—you are innocent, you were the child. Forty-nine on Tom's side, and this is so because I have come to know him well and know about his life. I feel I have glimpsed his soul. I know that he is working never to hurt a child again and I know that he is truly sorry for what he has done." Silence followed for a few moments. Alan thanked me. He appeared happy with this reply, and so was I, and we left the room together.

Back in the therapy group on the following week I reported to Tom the account of my meeting with Alan (as agreed with Alan), and I included in my account Alan's final question to me: "Whose side are you on?" I also recounted the answer that I had given to Alan, articulating the logic propelling my reply. Tom said he understood, and my impression was that he was grateful to be "a forty-nine." Other men listened intently, and nobody commented. And so we carried on with the work. Alan never did call me. I assumed he didn't have a need.

One year later, Tom was still in the therapy group and was active in his participation, deconstructing his life and its stories and considering all aspects of the abuse that he had perpetrated. Although he had mentioned some time along the way that he had experienced abuse in adolescence by a number of school teachers, on this particular day that I will never forget, his narrating of the story caught my attention and that of the other participants in a way that it had not done before. This time, the small details of the story were overwhelmingly sad, such as the first abuse that he suffered occurring at the age of eleven years, on the week of his return to school following the sudden death of his father. The detail of the story had the whole room spellbound, including myself.

As I listened with my heart, a shaft of light beamed from my consciousness and it carried on it a single message, the strength of which I could not ignore—"fifty-one, forty-nine." I could not believe what was happening.

When Tom finished speaking and had received support from the other men and the other worker, I asked for permission to say what had occurred for me during his telling of his story. This included my account of the beam of light which carried the message that merely said "fifty-one, forty-nine." The group participants and Tom afforded me such a luxury. I now wanted to articulate the following to Tom (and later to Alan) in that spontaneous occurrence. "Last year when I met with Alan and he asked me "Whose side are you on?", if you remember I responded by saying "fifty-one, forty-nine." At the time, I explained to you the logic of my reply. Now I want to say something else, and I hope this is okay with you." I told Tom about the beam that shone light on my consciousness when he was talking, and I went on to say the following. "I want to tell you that for me today "fifty-one, forty-nine" feels really inadequate, and I want to change my answer to that question." I paused for a moment to keep pace and breath with the heaviness of the heart that was beating and then I continued: "I want now to let you know that I am on the side of *all* human beings who are trying to live their lives, in the only and best way that they can, a life that is often difficult and messy and complex. I am *against* abuses and violence of all kinds, in all their dirty and rotten manifestations and in the multitude of ways they get expressed in the world. I also want to tell you that I am on the side of people who are trying to live their lives with the resources that they have in the only and best ways that they can and I am against oppression and injustice in all its nasty manifestations. I feel I need to tell you that just now." Nobody spoke. My utterance had come from deep within my being, visible to all by the voice that gave it expression.

Tom began to cry inconsolably. Apart from Tom's tears, no sound could be heard. Individuals gave witness in silence. These were Tom's first tears to be shed in twenty months of group conversations, and a river of tears was cried on that afternoon. Lumps filled eight other men's throats, and a lump filled one woman's throat on that day, too. The silence lasted for a long time, broken only by Tom's voice: "When you said fifty-one, forty-nine on that day following your meeting with Alan, and I was forty-nine, I accepted that fully, because what could I expect? I was the guilty one, and I knew that. I was grateful not to be much lower on the scale, and I knew what you were saying. But now I can tell you that on that day I was also very sad and in a way a little part of me died, too. You see it was a secret hope. You see I have always wished that someone could really love me and that someone could really know me, and you were as close as anyone had come to knowing me ever. When you said forty-nine that day, I came to the realization that I could never be loved, that it was never going to happen, and that, that was my lot." Tom cried again, crying that was held in the silent witness of me and the other men. His voice then uttered the following words: "Now when you have said what you have just said, I am just overwhelmed. Thank you."

But this is not the end of the story, for at the very least there was Alan to consider and my reflections on the journey of learning that accompanied these events. Life brought the opportunities for both.

During the course of Tom's sentence hearing I was asked to give to the court an account of Tom's therapy and my witnessing to that. Alan gave the court an account of his life before and since the abuses that he had suffered. Here Alan and I met again in a small but bright courtroom, with eight people listening and witnessing to the sadness and heroics of the lives that were being shared. Tom accepted his culpability and was sentenced to a number of years' imprisonment. He was taken away to the holding cell by the officers of the court, following brief moments of good-bye. I promised to visit and to keep in touch.

At the back of the courtroom, Alan and I shook hands. I asked him if he was okay. He said it was hard. I agreed. We spoke briefly about this and that and I asked him if he remembered our conversation of one year ago. He said that he did. I asked if he remembered my saying something about fifty-one, forty-nine and about taking sides in these issues. He said that he did. I said to him that I have come to another realization about that since the time of our last meeting and I offered to share my thoughts with Alan if he wanted. He said that he did. As I had done with Tom in the group therapy program, I described in similar language the realizations that had come to me (as described previously) in response to the question "Whose side are you on?" I also added that "I will continue to work against violence and abuse."

Having listened in these halls of lawful justice, Alan looked at me intently and said that he had come to realize that there are no winners in these situations, but that maybe we are not losers either. He concluded that all we have got is what we have got, and we all have to live—only one life. He expressed a hope that this day, when the man who had abused him as a child was met with the rigors of the law and held accountable for the abuses that he had perpetrated, would mark another milestone in that which was Alan's life. I added that I hoped this day would bring whatever it was that Alan desired and required.

We chatted some more before we left the courtroom, and I wished him well. I have not had further contact with Alan. I still have contact with Tom, who survived prison and is retired. He contacts me from time to time. To my knowledge he has not abused a child in over twenty years. It is thirteen years since we first worked together. I will leave it to the reader to speculate about the personal learning that may have emerged for me from this work in relation to the forms of problem definition that I relied upon, what I privileged, the judgments I made, and the identity conclusions that resulted. I will simply say that these men helped me realize more fully than I had previously that there is another part to the current problem of sexual abuse by children; one that is beyond the obvious and to which we are all recruited. It is the unhelpful idea that sides must be taken for or against individuals in situations of sexual abuse, and in the process compassion must be rationed or even withheld from certain individuals. I refuse this invitation to ration compassion.

Future Directions: "Doing" Hope in a Landscape of Despair

A life without hope is no life at all. Life without meaning is a life not worth living. So what must it be like to be exiled in a meaningless, hopeless place of existence in which no one wants to understand and few appear to care?

Experiences of loneliness and abandonment are common features of the stories of many men and women who have experienced trauma and abuse. The men who are in effect warehoused in such institutions as Coalinga Mental Hospital in California after serving their prison sentences again come to mind in this regard. They are not alone. This homeless place of no-man's land is what many men in Ireland who have perpetrated abuse and violence also describe in the wake of the disclosures of their sexual offending, when some are run out of their homes and some out of their country (Keenan, 2007). The absence of hope and the prevalence of despair contribute in no small way towards the webs of human misery and suffering that surround this very topic.

Western ideas of hope view it as a feeling—an achievement of the individual alone. From this perspective, responsibility for its achievement rests with the individual (Weingarten, 2007: 14). However, such a perspective does not always bring the desired effect. Expecting people to achieve hope when they are marginalized and low of spirit seems not only foolish but may also be downright irresponsible (14). Despair is a likely outcome, based on the isolation of the position and failure in achieving the goal. An alternative perspective of hope, conceptualized by Weingarten (2007: 14), is predicated on the idea that hope is something we "do" with other people, and far from being the responsibility of individuals, "doing" hope is the responsibility of the community. Within this perspective there are hope tasks for the hopeless and tasks for those who witness their despair. Individuals who feel hopeless must resist isolation and those who witness despair must "refuse indifference" (15). The moral imperative is to stand in witness to those people whose lives are blighted by trauma and violence and to build communities of support for their preferred ways of living.

Living in a global village, injustice and oppression are much in evidence. In cultures predicated on fear, anger, and hatred, hope is in short supply (Weingarten, 2007: 15). Yet it is necessary. Standing together to resist hate represents a way of doing hope together (20). The imperative is for groups of individuals to work together to diminish fear and resist the powerful pull of hate. In this all human beings stand to win.

This is not to suggest that we blindly ignore the re-offense potential of men who have abused minors, or that we do not work to protect children. It is, however, to suggest that we move the lens through which we view the problem; we need to move it from individual to community, from fear and hatred to hope, and we need to seek solutions that will provide good and meaningful lives for all. Central to this activity is an understanding of the problem in all its complexity, based on deep introspection, honest dialogue, and the concept of justice for all. Michael Sandel, the Harvard-based political philosopher, enticed his academic audience over the last few months with an entire lecture course about "Justice," subtitled "What's the right thing to do?" (Sandel, 2009). Sandel raises questions about what exactly constitutes a good life. He asks what exactly its purpose is, and he reminds us of the role that values, purpose, and meaning have in life. He encourages us to think about what our purpose is as a society, what holds it together and why we should care. We are not just a loose assembly of individuals in which everything is mediated through or determined by market forces. Sandel's argument forces us to think about the common values that we are striving for, even as we dispute some finer aspects of how we should live. He shows that deliberation about the ends is important in itself since a preoccupation with means can lose sight of our purposes.

Conclusions

I recognize that social workers and psychotherapists cannot work outside of a normative structure, by definition, as the very act of intervening with men who have perpetrated sexual offenses can be conceptualized as a normative move in itself. However, at the same time, the power of normative and dichotomous structures to replicate the very violence and abuses which they purport to work against must not be underestimated. As societies go on alert in their desire to stamp out abuse of children and the populace becomes increasingly sensitized to the possibilities of abuse, we develop categories that reduce the complexities of life to simple binaries, such as abusers and victims, which in turn become the means by which we index many other aspects of social life (McNamee and Gergen, 1999: 50). In effect, we develop a dichotomous structure in which we look for and see abuse everywhere. Events that require more elaboration, unpacking, and deconstruction are reduced to simplistic descriptions and explanations. As McNamee and Gergen (1999:50) observe, "our indignation creates the very conditions for constructing a world in terms of abusers and victims." The work that I have described in this article represents an attempt to problematize such dichotomous structures in therapeutic practice and to replace them with a linguistically ambiguous[17] space that leaves room for exploration of the complexity and messiness of life that includes love and violence, trauma, and abuse.

I propose a way of thinking about the problem of trauma and violence that offers a futures framework for the work that is not dominated by a preoccupation with the past alone. This does not imply that the offenders' past offenses are not considered, but rather that the methodology involves a constant movement back and forth between past, present, and future, in which past, present, and future are constantly interwoven between people, through conversation and through their imagining, envisioning, and anticipating (McAdam and Hannah, 1991: 224; Lang, 2003). Rather than focusing on trying to prevent bad things from occurring, a futures focus emphasizes future possibilities (Lang and McAdam, 1997; Lang, 2003; Ward and Stewart, 2003). The movement is from positive action to positive outcome. The futures orientation of this approach is supported by research in the psychotherapy literature, which confirms the importance of hope, expectation, and a belief in possibilities for bringing about positive therapeutic outcome (Hubble, Duncan, and Miller, 2005: 419; Snyder, Michael, and Cheavens, 2005: 181).

As Kathe Weingarten (2007: 22) tells us, "[h]ope is a resource. We hoard it at our peril. . . . It is a human rights issue. Just as food, water, and security must be equitably distributed, so too, must hope. Whether we offer or receive, co-create or imagine, we can all participate in doing hope." Mandela had it right when he advised that a nation should not be judged by how it treats it highest citizens, but by how it treats those who are seen as its lowest. In current times in the English-speaking world, there are few who are seen as lower than men who have sexually abused minors.

Notes

1. Coalinga State Hospital is owned and operated by the State of California. The institution houses more than 500 convicted sex offenders, most of whom have already served prison sentences for their crimes but are deemed too dangerous to release back into the community. Since Jessica's Law was passed in the United States of America in 2005, men who have sexually abused children and who have come to the end of their prison sentences can be deemed mentally ill and put up in Coalinga indefinitely. Although the official aim of the hospital is to rehabilitate offenders, up to 70 percent of the inmates or

"patients" refuse therapy, in some cases as a means of protest. Of the hundreds of individuals treated at Coalinga, up until April 2009 only 13 men had been approved for release into the community, with a few more being released with the help of their lawyers. Commenting on his documentary "A Place for Paedophiles" shown on BBC2 in the United Kingdom on April 19, 2009, Louis Theoreux remarked, "If therapy was really being embraced by a lot of the patients it would seem workable, but there wasn't a lot of therapy going on as far as I could see. Because so many of them refuse to engage, it means Coalinga is basically a very expensive, luxury warehouse to keep these people off the streets for the rest of their lives." (Singh, A., *The Telegraph*, April, 20 2009.) Most of the men are sent to Coalinga as compulsory patients, where they can either participate in the therapeutic programs that the hospital offers or resign themselves to an indefinite stay. But the majority know they're going to be there a very long time indeed. According to the director's message on the hospital's Web site, this facility is a critical part of Governor Arnold Schwarzenegger's goal to protect Californians from sexual predators. When the facility is fully operational, it will be the largest employer in the Coalinga area with an annual operating budget of $152 million and more than 2,000 staff. (http://www.dmh.ca.gov/services and programs/state_hospitals/coalinga/default.asp)

2. Whilst feminist theory has made a huge contribution to contemporary understanding of sexual violence, the limitations of the feminist argument come from its conceptualization of power as only one form—power as domination and control—and its under-theorizing of other forms and exercises of power, such as in the creation of consensus discourses (see Lukes, 2005).

3. In August 2011, my book, *Sexual Abuse and the Catholic Church: Gender, Power Organizational Culture*, will be released by Oxford University Press.

4. Of course, women also sexually abuse minors.

5. I like Foucault's work on risk which he elaborates in Foucault (2001), *Fearless Speech*, 11–24.

6. Showing up means more than the body showing up. Rather it means that the person, with their skills, knowledge, intentions, pain, and vulnerabilities, show up and allow themselves to be seen and heard in dialogue with others (Fisher, 2008).

7. Probation and welfare officers in the Irish jurisdiction are generally social workers who have therapeutic functions over and above statutory and monitoring responsibilities ascribed in legislation.

8. Art Fisher is director of Alternatives, a program in Nova Scotia working with trauma and violence. For further information the reader is directed to http://www.alternativesinstitute.com.

9. The Fifth Province associates were comprised of Dr. Nollaig Byrne, a child psychiatrist, Dr. Imelda McCarthy, a social worker and university lecturer at University College Dublin, and Philip Kearney, a social worker. They formed a team for their clinical work and research with families disclosing incest and they also developed the first family therapy program in Ireland.

10. In circumstances where an individual wishes to identify him or herself as a victim, that is perfectly acceptable and the prerogative of the individual concerned. However, I have concerns that in the context of sexual violence some individual identities are constructed in which people who have experienced sexual violence are totalized as victims, which marginalizes other aspects of the individual's identity, including his or her resistance to the violence that was perpetrated.

11. A full discussion of this subject is beyond the scope of this chapter. For a fuller treatise of this subject see Foucault (1990, 1992, 1998), Haug (2001), and Bell (2002). I also give the subject due regard in my book by Oxford University Press (2011).

12. Mater Misaecordiae Hospital in Eccles Street, Dublin, Ireland.

13. I am here interested in Fisher's work (2008, 2009) on trying to unpack socially available definitions of "the problem" and his thinking on the complexity of what gets called "violence." In essence, Fisher is thinking of violence as a practice that signifies many complexities of intention, knowledge, skill, agency, and positioning within the socially available structures that are available to individuals. The "problem" may have many aspects for the individual who acts in this way—and to fail to unpack these complexities by merely describing the behaviors as "the problem" is to miss something of significance in context. Fisher invites the worker to see the complexity of intentions, knowledge, skills, and agency in what gets called "the problem."

14. Tom is not the client's real name, and some features of his biography are altered in order to preserve his anonymity.

15. Alan is not the man's real name, and some features of his biography are altered in order to preserve his anonymity.

16. The Milan School of Systemic Therapy was interested in the concept of neutrality to describe the positioning of workers in the therapeutic conversation. The concept of neutrality was not intended to imply a moral neutrality on the part of the worker but rather a positioning towards each of the participants in the dialogue that privileged no-one (Prata et al., 1978). However, following critique in the literature and the accusation that the concept of neutrality was gender and power blind, the Milan team reconfigured their concept of neutrality and adopted instead the idea of curiosity as that to guide the positioning of the worker.

17. By creating a linguistically ambiguous space, I wish to create a space in which all complex thought can emerge. I am certainly not suggesting that the worker adopt a morally ambiguious position with regard to the wrongness of sexual violence for children.

References

Abel, G. C., J. V. Becker, and J. Cunningham-Rathner (1984). Complications, consent, and cognitions in sex between children and adults. *International Journal of Law and Psychiatry*, 7: 89–103.

Abel, G. C., J. V. Becker, M. Mittelman, J. Cunningham-Rathner, J. L. Rouleau, and W. D. Murphy (1987). Self-reported sex crimes of non-incarcerated paraphiliacs. *Journal of Interpersonal Violence*, 2(1): 3–25.

American Psychiatric Association (2000). *Diagnostic and Statistical Manual of Mental Disorders: IV-text revised*, Washington DC: American Psychiatric Association.

Axline, V. (1990). *Dibs in Search of Self.* London: Penguin.

Bell, V. (2002). The vigilant(e) parent and the paedophile: The *News of the World* campaign 2000 and the comtemprary governmentability of child sexual abuse. *Feminist Theory*, 3(1): 83–102.

Berger, P. and T. Luckmann (1966). *The social construction of reality. A treatise in the sociology of knowledge.* Harmondsworth, UK: Penguin.

Berlin, F. S. and E. W. Krout (1986). Pedophilia: Diagnostic concepts, treatment, and ethical considerations. *American Journal of Forensic Psychiatry*, 7(1): 13–30.

Best, J. (1995a). Typification and social problem construction. In J. Best (Ed.), *Images of issues, typifying contemporary social problems* (pp. 1–16). New York: Walter de Gruyter.

——. (Ed.) (1995b). *Images of issues: Typifying contemporary social problems.* New York: Walter de Gruyter.

Bottoms, A. E. (1995). The philosophy and politics of punishment and sentencing. In C. Clarkson and R. Morgan (Eds.), *The politics of sentencing reform* (pp. 17–49). Oxford, UK: Oxford University Press.

Burr, V. (1995). *An introduction to social constructionism.* London: Routledge.

Byrne, N. O'R. and I. C. McCarthy (1988). Moving statutes: Re-questioning ambivalence through ambiguous discourse. *The Irish Journal of Psychology*, 9(1): 173–182.

—— (1998). Marginal illuminations. A fifth province approach to intracultural issues in an Irish context. In M. McGoldrick (Ed.), *Re-visioning family therapy: Race, culture and gender in clinical practice* (pp. 387–403). New York: Guilford Press.

—— (1999). Feminism, politics and power in therapeutic discourse: Fragments from the fifth province. In I. Parker (Ed.), *Deconstructing psychotherapy* (pp. 87–102). London: Sage.

—— (2006). Personal communication. University College Dublin, Ireland.

—— (2007). The dialectical structure of hope and despair: a Fifth Province approach. In C. Flaskas, I. McCarthy, and J. Sheehan (Eds.). *Hope and Despair in Narrative and Family Therapy: Adversity, Forgiveness and Reconciliation.* London: Routledge.

Colgan, I. F. (1991). *The fifth province model: Father-daughter incest disclosure and systemic consultation.* PhD thesis, University College Dublin, Ireland.

Cowburn, M. and L. Dominelli (1998). Moving beyond litigation and positivism: Another approach to accusations of sexual abuse. *British Journal of Social Work*, 28(4): 525–543.

—— (2001). Masking hegemonic masculinity: Reconstructing the paedophile as the dangerous stranger. *British Journal of Social Work*, 31: 399–415.

Fisher, A. (2008). Power and practices of documentation in working with clients, especially those involved in family violence. Three day intensive workshop held in Maynooth, Ireland.

——. (2009). Leading-edge developments in narrative practice responding to violence. Workshop given at the European Conference of Narrative Therapy and Community Work, Brighton, United Kingdom.

Flannery, T. (2009). *Responding to The Ryan Report.* Dublin, Ireland: Columba Press.

Flaskas C. (2002). *Family therapy beyond postmodernism: Practice challenges theory.* New York: Brunner-Routledge.

Flaskas, C., I. McCarthy, and J. Sheehan (Eds.) (2007). *Hope and despair in narrative and family therapy: Adversity, forgiveness and reconciliation.* London: Routledge.

Foucault, M. (1988). The dangerous individual. In L. Kritzman (Ed.), *Politics, philosophy, culture: Interviews and other writings 1977–1984* (pp. 125–151). New York: Routledge.

——. (1990). *The care of self: The history of sexuality: 3* (trans. Robert Hurley). London: Penguin.

——. (1991). *Discipline and punish: The birth of the prison.* London: Penguin.

——. (1992). *The use of pleasure. The history of sexuality: 2* (trans. Robert Hurley). London: Penguin.

——. (1998). *The will to knowledge. The history of sexuality: 1* (trans. Robert Hurley). London: Penguin.

——. (2001). *Fearless speech.* Edited by Joseph Pearson. Los Angeles, CA: Semiotext(e).

——. (2004). *The archaeology of knowledge.* Translated by A. M. Sheridan Smith. (First published in 1969; first published in English in 1972). (6th ed.). London: Routledge Classics.

Freeman-Longo, R. E. and G. T. Blanchard (1998). *Sexual abuse in America: Epidemic of the 21st century.* Vermont: Safer Society Press.

Garfinkel, H. (1956). Conditions of successful degradation ceremonies. *American Journal of Criminology*, 61: 420–424.

Garland, D. (2001). *The culture of control: Crime and social order in contemporary society.* Oxford, UK: Oxford University Press.

Gergen, K. (1985). The social constructionist movement in modern psychology. *American Psychologist*, 40: 266–275.

——. (1992). Social constructionism in question. *Human Systems*, 3: 163–182.

Goffman, E. (1961). *Asylums*. New York: Anchor.

——. (1990/1963). *Stigma: Notes on the management of spoiled identity*. London: Penguin.

Greer, C. (2003). *Sex crime and the media: Sex offending and the press in a divided society*. Devon, UK: Willan.

Hacking, I. (1999). *The social construction of what?* Cambridge, MA: Harvard University Press.

Hanson, R. K. and M. T. Bussière (1998). Predicting relapse: A meta-analysis of sexual offender recidivism studies. *Journal of Counselling and Clinical Psychology*, 66(2): 348–362.

Haug, F. (2001). Sexual deregulation, or the child abuser as hero in neoliberalism. *Feminist Theory*, 2(1): 55–78.

Hederman, M. P., and R. Kearney (1977). Editorial, art and politics. *The Crane Bag: Book of Irish Studies, 1977–1981*, 1(1): 10–12. Dublin, Ireland: Blackwater.

Hubble, M., B. Duncan, and S. Miller (2005). Introduction. In M. Hubble, B. Duncan, and S. Miller (Eds.), *The heart and soul of change. What works in therapy* (pp. 1–32). Washington, DC: The American Psychological Association.

Hudson, K. (2005). *Offending identities: Sex offenders' perspectives on their treatment and management*. Devon, UK: Willan.

Hudson, S. M., T. Ward, and J. McCormack (1999). Offence pathways in sexual offenders. *Journal of Interpersonal Violence*, 14: 779–798.

Hydén, M. and I. C. McCarthy (1994). Woman battering and father-daughter incest disclosure: Discourses of denial and acknowledgement. *Discourse and Society*, 5(4): 543–565.

Jenkins, A. (1990). *Invitations to responsibility: The therapeutic engagement of men who are violent and abusive*. Adelaide, Australia: Dulwich Centre Publications.

Jenkins, P. (1998). *Moral panic: Changing concepts of the child molester in modern America*. New Haven, CT: Yale University Press.

Johnson, J. M. (1995). Horror stories and the construction of child abuse. In J. Best (Ed.), *Images of issues: Typifying contemporary social problems* (pp. 17–32). New York: Aldine de Gruyter.

Karp, D. R. (1998). The judicial and the judicious use of shame penalties. *Crime and Delinquency*, 44(2): 227–294.

Kearney, P. A., N. O'R. Byrne, and I. C. McCarthy (1989). Just metaphors: Marginal illuminations in a colonial retreat. *Family Therapy Case Studies*, 4(1): 17–31.

Keenan, M. (2007). *The "good clergy man": A study of Roman Catholic clergy who have sexually abused minors* (Unpublished PhD thesis). University College Dublin, Ireland.

——. (2009). "Them and us." The clergy child sexual offender as 'other'. In T. Flannery (Ed.), *Responding to the Ryan Report* (pp. 180–231). Dublin, Ireland: Columba Press.

Keenan, T. and T. Ward (2000). A theory of mind perspective on cognitive, affective, and intimacy deficits in child sexual offenders. *Sexual Abuse: A Journal of Research and Treatment*, 12(1): 49–60.

Kelley, R. K. (1989). Sentenced to wear the scarlet letter: Judicial innovations in sentencing. *Dickinson Law Review*, 93: 759–788.

Kincaid, J. R. (1998). *Erotic innocence: The culture of child molesting*. Durham, NC: Duke University Press.

Krugman, R. (1996). The media and public awareness of child abuse and neglect: It's time for a change. *Child Abuse and Neglect, The International Journal*, 20(4): 259–260.

Lang, P. (2003). Putting children beyond risk and perpetrators beyond suspicion. Workshop held in Department of Social Policy and Social Work, University College Dublin, Ireland.

Lang, P. and E. McAdam (1997). Narrative-ating: Future dreams in present living. *Human Systems: The Journal of Systemic Consultation and Management*. A special issue, 8(1): 3–12.

Lukes, S. (2005). *Power: A radical view*. London: Palgrave Macmillan.

McAdam, E. and C. Hannah (1991). Violence—Part 2: Creating the best context to work with clients who have found themselves in violent situations. *Human Systems. The Journal of Systemic Consultation and Management*, 2(3–4): 217–226.

McAlinden, A.-M. (2007). *The shaming of sexual offenders: Risk, retribution and reintegration*. Oxford, UK: Hart.

McCarthy, I. C. (1990). Paradigms lost: Remembering her-stories and other invalid subjects. *Contemporary Family Therapy*, 12: 427–437.

——. (1994). Abusing norms: Welfare families and a fifth province stance. In I. C. McCarthy (Ed.). *Poverty and Social Exclusion*, a special issue of *Human Systems*, 4(3/4): 229–239.

——. (2002). The spirit of the fifth province: An ancient metaphor for a new millenium. In *Celebration of the Fifth Province, Feedback: The Magazine of the Family Therapy Association of Ireland*, 9(2): 10–13.

McCarthy, I. C. and N. O'R. Byrne (1988). Mistaken love: Conversations on the problem of incest in an Irish context. *Family Process*, 27: 181–199.

McNamee, S. and K. Gergen (1999). *Relational responsibility: Resources for sustainable dialogue*. Thousand Oaks, CA: Sage.

Mann, R. and A. Beech (2003). Cognitive distortions, schemas and implicit theories. In T. Ward, R. D. Laws, and S. M. Hudson (Eds), *Sexual deviance: Issues and controversies* (pp. 135–153). Thousand Oaks, CA: Sage.

Marshall. W. L. (1996). The sexual offender: Monster, victim or everyman? *Sexual Abuse: A Journal of Research and Treatment*, 8(4): 317–335.

——. (2005). Therapist style in sexual offender treatment: Influence on indices of change. *Sexual Abuse: A Journal of Research and Treatment*, 17: 109–116.

Marshall, W., D. Anderson, and F. Champagne (1997). Self-esteem and its relationship to sexual offending. *Psychology, Crime, Law*, 3: 161–186.

Marshall, W., D. Anderson, and Y. Fernandez (2000). *Cognitive behavioural treatment of sexual offenders* (2nd ed.). Chichester, UK: Wiley.

Marshall, W. L. and G. A. Serran (2004). The role of the therapist in offender treatment. *Psychology, Crime and Law*, 10: 309–320.

Maxwell, G. and A. Morris (1999). *Understanding re-offending*. Wellington: Institute of Criminology, University of Wellington, Victoria, Australia.

Méndez, C. L., F. Coddou, and H. Maturana (1988). The bringing forth of pathology. *The Irish Journal of Psychology*, A Special Issue, 9(1): 144–172.

Mercer, D. and T. Simmonds (2001). The mentally disordered offender. Looking-glass monsters: Reflections of the paedophile in popular culture. In T. Mason, C. Carisle, C. Walkins, and E. Whitehead (Eds.), *Stigma and social exclusion in healthcare* (pp. 170–181). London: Routledge.

Mills, C. W. (2000). *The Sociological imagination*. (First published in 1959). New York: Oxford University Press.

O'Malley, T. (1998). Opening remarks. *Conference on Treatment of Sex Offenders*. (Unpublished paper) Irish Penal Reform Trust, Dublin, Ireland.

O'Reilly, G. (2009). *Sexual offender treatment and recidivism*. Paper presented at the Annual Conference of the Association for Criminal Justice, Research and Development, Castleknock, Co. Dublin, Ireland.

Prata, G., G. Cecchin, L. Boscolo, and M. S. Palazzoli (1978). *Paradox and counter paradox*. Lanham, MD: Jason Aronson.

Sandel, M. (2009). *Justice. What's the right thing to do?* New York: Farrar, Straus & Giroux.

Seto, M. (2005). *The evolution of sex offender treatment: Taking the next step*. Paper presented at the 24th Annual Research and Treatment Conference of the Association for the Treatment of Sexual Abusers, Salt Lake City, Utah.

Seto, M., J. Marques, G. Harris, M. Chaffin, M. Lalumiere, M. Miner, L. Berliner, M. Rice, R. Lieb, and V. Quinsey (2008). Good science and progress in sex offender treatment are intertwined: A response to Marshall and Marshall. *Sexual Abuse: A Journal of Research and Treatment*, 20(3): 247–255.

Shotter, J. (2005). Goethe and the refiguring of intellectual inquiry: From "about-ness" thinking to "with-ness" thinking in everyday life. *Janus Head*, 8(1): 132–158.

Snyder, C., S. Michael, and J. Cheavens (2005). Hope as a psychotherapeutic foundation of common factors, placebos and expectancies. In M. Hubble, B.

Duncan and S. Miller (Eds.), *The heart and soul of change: What works in therapy* (10th ed.) (pp. 179–200). Washington, DC: The American Psychological Association.

Soothill, K. and B. Francis (1998). Poisoned chalice or just deserts? *The Sex Offender Act 1997. Journal of Forensic Psychiatry,* 9(22): 281–293.

Ward, T., S. M. Hudson, L. Johnston, and W. Marshall (1997). Cognitive distortions in sex offenders: An integrative review. *Clinical Psychology Review,* 17: 479–507.

Ward, T., T. Keenan, and S. M. Hudson (2000). Understanding cognitive, affective, and intimacy deficits in sexual offenders: A developmental perspective. *Aggression and Violent Behaviour,* 5(1): 41–62.

Ward, T. and W. L. Marshall (2007). Narrative identity and offender rehabilitation. *International Journal of Offender Therapy and Comparative Criminology,* 6(51): 279–297.

Weingarten, K. (2007). Hope in a time of global despair. In C. Flaskas, I. McCarthy, and J. Sheehan (Eds.), *Hope and despair in narrative and family therapy: Adversity, forgiveness and reconciliation* (pp. 13–23). London: Routledge.

White, M. (2000). Re-engaging with history: The absent but implicit. In M. White, *Reflections on narrative practices: Interviews and essays* (pp. 35–58). Adelaide, Australia: Dulwich Centre Publications.

White, M. (2004a). *Narrative practice and exotic lives: Resurrecting diversity in everyday life.* Adelaide, Australia: Dulwich Centre Publications.

White, M. (2004b). Working with people who are suffering the consequences of multiple trauma: A narrative perspective. *International Journal of Narrative Therapy and Community Work,* 1: 45–76.

White, M. and D. Epston (1990). *Narrative means to therapeutic ends.* New York: Norton.

Winick, B. (1998). Sex offender law in the 1990s: A therapeutic analysis. *Psychology, Public Policy and Law,* 4(1–2): 505–570.

Woods, J. (1907). *Annals of Westmeath: Ancient and modern.* Dublin, Ireland: Sealy.

Wyre, R. (1996). Personal communication on a visit to The Lucy Faithfull Treatment Programme, Birmingham, United Kingdom.

11

Narrative Supervision and Professional Development for School Teachers in Hong Kong

WAI-FONG TING

Deconstructing Anonymity: Writing as Social Construction

When Stanley Witkin sent out his invitation to prospective contributors of this book, he attached a special request—write something about yourself so that the readers would have a sense of who you are and where you come from. "Yes," I thought to myself, "that is a reasonable request"—especially when this book is about social construction-informed practice. However, though the request was sensible, I had little idea how to pack a half century of me into less than five hundred words. This was my first challenge in writing this chapter. Fortunately, I love a challenge!

I am the first generation of locally born Chinese in Hong Kong, a British colony for more than a century and a half (1842 to 1997). My parents came to Hong Kong from the southern part of China in the 1930s, prior to the Japanese Occupation (of Hong Kong) and the outbreak of the Second World War, hoping to seek "protection" from the British rulers. The British did not put up a fight with the Japanese, thus most of Hong Kong people's lives, unlike their counterparts' in Nanking, China, were spared from the devastation of the Japanese "invasion." After the chaotic 1940s, my parents celebrated the peace that finally came in the 1950s and gave birth to five children, and I was the youngest among them.

Growing up and educated in a colony, my knowledge of my mother country was poor. As I have once confessed (Ting, 2004:28), I knew and had felt more for England than China throughout the first twenty-some years of my life. While we all speak a local dialect in Hong Kong in our daily encounters, English is *the* language that we had to master if we ever wanted to "achieve" in life. Given the importance of language to our life and identity, as underscored by social constructionism, this piece of personal/cultural/social history certainly impacted my evolvement into the "me" I am today.

It was not easy to find means to feed five hungry mouths in post–World War II Hong Kong. My parents coped by adopting a "non-interventionist" approach in bringing up their children. For a long time, I believed that my current life circumstances had nothing to do with my parents as they literally did not intervene in my life. With this "freedom," I thought that I could craft a life independent of them. This turned out to be a myth, as my parents, especially my mother, contributed a lot to my life story and my identity (Ting, 2005: 16).

Thanks to my proficiency in the English language, I was among the 3 percent selected for university study in the late 1970s. I started my career as a social work practitioner in the early 1980s and began a teaching career in social work in the late 1980s, after failing to become a film director and a journalist. Having engaged in social work education for more than twenty years, I find myself "directing" social work programs and journalizing a lot. So I achieved all three goals in one career! However, when I eventually got acquainted with social construction and, in particular, narrative practice, I finally understood the commonality of all three career choices—people's lives and identities can be changed through stories and narratives, because both life and identity are socially constructed.

My Acquaintance with Postmodernism and Social Construction

My encounter with social constructionist ideas dates back to the mid-1990s when I was pursuing my PhD. My social work programs in the 1970s taught that there is an "underlying" cause to every social phenomenon and that it took a trained and competent professional to get to the "root" of the problem. With these expert understandings, intervention programs could be developed to help or emancipate troubled persons. My original thesis was to understand the phenomenon of teenage suicide and to devise a program to "salvage" these youngsters from their predicament. In order to get to the root of the problem, I reviewed a large volume of literature about the causes and the "risk factors" that led to teenage suicide. After diligent reading and note taking, I noticed that the findings generated from all those scientifically conducted research studies added little to what I already knew. I also noticed that this literature expressed the voices of experts while those of the young people studied were by and large silent. Often the young subjects in these studies supplied answers to questionnaires that reflected the researcher's theoretical frame. This marginalized the young people who were supposed to be at the center of these studies. As I did not feel right about this approach to research, I began to explore alternative ways of developing knowledge. This led to my encounter with postmodern and social constructionist ideas.

My introduction to the postmodern turn in the social work realm began in the early 1990s with my "accidental" review into the work of two social work educators, Peile and Heineman-Pieper (Heineman-Pieper, 1985, 1989, 1991; Peile, 1988, 1994). In their work, they wrote about how social work as an applied discipline long aspired to the supreme status of natural science and thus paid allegiance to positivistic science in both research and practice. To these authors, the dominant positivistic paradigm has suppressed creative and heuristic practice in social work research. Although much of what they wrote about positivism was alien to me, I fervently desired to learn. So in 1994, I started studying topics having the "post" prefix (e.g., postmodernism). The more I looked into this postliterature and its critique of positivistic inquiry, the more I felt caught up in an academic fraud. Although the spread of positivism in social sciences was meant to enhance its academic status, the consequences from my perspective were disastrous. I felt that I had spent nearly two decades studying and teaching in a deeply flawed paradigm. The anger I felt was not small.

A second group of authors, namely the relational psychologists,[1] showed me how to question authoritative, psychological knowledge. One example can be found in the work of Gilligan (1982: 64), who, as a student of Kohlberg, dared to challenge the dominance of his theory on moral development. Their work was groundbreaking in its questioning/challenging of the long-standing truth status of the individual psychology that was so prominently professed by the "four kings," namely Freud, Erikson, Piaget, and Kohlberg. The theories they proposed were being taught to social workers in

Hong Kong as "the" knowledge that crucially underpinned practice. While acknowledging their contribution to psychology, Gilligan's work reminded me to take each of these theories as just one way, but not the *only* way, to explain human development. It also encouraged a skeptical stance when using these theories to make sense of the lives and experiences of people with whom we work, as the concepts they used were historically, culturally, and socially specific rather than universally true.

Although these two groups of writers were not generally regarded as postmodernists, their effort and courage to challenge mainstream knowledge inspired me to look for alternative ways of understanding social phenomenon and human experiences. Moreover, I was eager to look for a model of practice that would help me align my epistemology and practice. In 2000, I participated in a two-day workshop in Hong Kong in which Michael White introduced his practice of narrative therapy. Halfway through the workshop, I remember telling myself "this is it." Since then, I have been studying and practicing narrative therapy.

Taking up the Postmodern Position of Challenge

The postmodern position of challenging dominant and taken-for-granted ways of thinking and acting fit well with my personal beliefs and commitments. First, the challenge to rationality as the only or superior means of understanding appealed to me because reasoning is again "just one" but not the "only" or superior way of understanding.

Second, I supported the challenge to expert knowledge and practice. Expert or professional knowledge is one source of knowledge that needs to be complemented by many others. I also believe that the people with whom we work in our practice are the genuine experts of their own lives and experiences.

Third, challenging the belief that self-identity is fixed and unified helped resolve the perplexity I often encountered in practice: Is there a real or true self? I remember in the early days of my practice with "at-risk" youths, I was often reminded by other professionals such as teachers, policemen, and educational psychologists that the young people who I befriended, trusted, and respected were not showing me their "true selves" but trying to please me and get resources. In other words, they were showing me a "false self" in exchange for my attention and service. From a postmodern perspective, there is no true self; identities are multiple and fluid. The search for a "true" identity is futile as identity is a social product. Since young people maintain different social relationships with their teachers, parents, friends, and social workers, each of us can only "see" their identity in the context of that relationship. When the relational context changes, so does the identity.

Fourth, challenging "grand narratives" was another appealing aspect of the postmodern turn. When I was a student first of social science and then social work, I was taught that there was one best way for human society to develop and prosper. This "one best way" was also possible and indeed desirable for any individual in society. As a student, I did not see the problem associated with having one grand narrative in a given society.[2] My suspicion of the grand narrative began to brew when I started working with groups of young people who did not subscribe to this grand narrative (and paid the price of being labeled "losers" and "failures" in our society). I started to realize this "one size fits all" grand narrative was by and large totalizing and left no room for the development of an alternative way of living. When I was finally exposed to the postmodernist ideas that challenged this grand narrative, I immediately felt that I was not alone in my search for alternate ways of living and being.

Core Assumptions of Social Construction

No single description adequately represents the wide range of writers who call themselves social constructionists (e.g., Burr, 2003: 2). For me, Kenneth Gergen's writings have been the most stimulating and relevant to my practice. In the following sections, I highlight the central assumptions of social construction that Gergen proposes, discuss their relevance for social work practices, and illustrate their expression in an extended practice example. Others who hold these assumptions may develop congruent but different practices (see, for example, Parton and O'Byrne, 2000: 118).

Critical Reflection on Our Taken-for-Granted Worlds

This assumption that we need to critically reflect on our taken-for-granted worlds is particularly significant to social work practitioners. As an applied social science profession, social work takes on theories from other disciplines for use in practice—for example, psychological and sociological theories. This technical-rational model of professional practice (Schon, 1987: 8), which views practice as based on the application of specific methods, has a long history in social work. Within this tradition, social workers seldom question the origin of these theories and its relevance in working with a particular group of people or community located in a historical, social, and cultural context different from those in which the theory was developed. As such, Gergen's (2001: 18) advice for us to "question tradition" as "every tradition closes the doors to new and alternative ideas and practice" is particularly relevant for those of us working in an Asian culture while using theories that originated primarily from the Western world. In the subsequent description of my practice, I have located one such tradition in which schoolteachers are trapped: the "global tidal wave of marketisation and managerialism in education" (Chan and Mok, 2001: 21). I had to challenge this tradition before I could contribute to reconstructing a practice in which the participating schools and teachers would be able to "re-author" a new narrative, story, and identity.

There Is Nothing Real out There, Unless We Agree There Is

For me, the central and most intriguing part of social construction is the assumption that everything we can know is socially constructed. This denial of a knowable objective reality challenges many truth and morality claims. Although some interpret this as also denying the reality of social problems such as violence, poverty, or oppression, I do not think that is the case. Rather, I see social construction purporting that the ways we understand our world, our relationships, our experiences, and our identities are agreed and sustained by historical, cultural, and social processes. For example, the concept or phenomenon of child abuse did not even exist thirty years ago, although the actions we would call child abuse today probably existed for centuries. While social workers "celebrate" the "social construction" of "child abuse" as protecting children (at least by law) from violence, there can be other kinds of unwelcomed consequences associated with this social construction, such as the application of a "victimhood" discourse to children in need, which strips them of the agency or ability to protect themselves (White, 2005, 10). Understanding the social

world as social construction creates space to construct alternative understandings. As my extended case example illustrates, understanding the
grand narratives of marketization and managerialism as social constructions, not an objective reality, enabled schoolteachers to construct alternative worlds that expressed their educational endeavors more fully and
meaningfully.

Our Understandings of the World Are the Outcomes of Relationships

Gergen's remark that "our understandings of the world are achieved
through co-ordinations among persons—negotiations, agreements, com-
paring views and so on" (Gergen, 2009: 6) reminds us of the vital role
that the "social" plays in our construction of the world. Although as social
workers we are no strangers to this notion, I provide an example that illustrates my understanding of the above statement. The movie *Gua Sha*
(English title: *The Treatment,* 2001[3]) portrayed a Chinese family consisting
of two working parents and a young boy living in United States. The boy's
grandfather came to visit from China and helped take care of the boy. One
night when the parents were still working, the boy had abdominal pain. As
the grandfather could not understand the English labels on the medicine
bottles, he resorted to giving the boy "gua sha"[4] (a traditional Asian healing
technique practiced in both the clinical setting and in homes) to relieve his
pain. This treatment always leaves patches of petechia[5] on the skin for several days. Later that night, the boy was taken to the hospital by his parents
for "proper" medical treatment. The medical practitioners of the hospital
"discovered" the "sha" (petechia) and inferred that the boy was being physically abused. This resulted in the parents being investigated for suspected
child abuse and losing custody of their son to the child protection agency
and the bewildered grandfather fleeing back to China.

This story highlights how two different traditions, namely Western
medicine and the Asian healing traditions, arrived at two completely different understanding of the same symbol—the petechia. For the grandfather
and the parents, the petechia, although not pleasant to look at, is more
than a symbol of illness/health. It also carries messages of love and care
for and among family members. In contrast, the Western medical practitioners, investigating and interpreting the same symbol, concluded that the
petechia was a sign of abuse. To bring the discussion further, the message

of love and care as symbolized by the "sha" is not uniquely held by this particular family, but by many other Chinese and Asian families. Likewise, interpreting the petechia as a sign of abuse is also not unique among the Western medical practitioners, but among social workers and legal professionals in the child protection system. This "gua sha" story vividly illustrates the meaning of Gergen's statement that "scientific truths can be viewed as outgrowths of communities, and not observing minds" (2009: 8). As such, we cannot make claims to universal truth. As Gergen remarks, "truth claims are specific to particular traditions" (2009: 8), which in turn are embedded in particular cultural and historical traditions.

Constructions Gain Their Significance from Their Social Utility

Following the above assumption that social relationships are pivotal to our understanding of the world, it becomes apparent that there can be multiple constructions for any situation. As illustrated in the "gua sha" example, different communities of people (and thus social relationships) construct different versions of reality. Gergen suggests that these socially constructed versions of reality can only "gain their significance from their social utility" (Gergen 2009: 9). This implies that through ongoing practices and usages based on the rules of a particular "game" (e.g., a system of child protection or Asian healing tradition), a particular version of reality (e.g., the petechia as a sign of abuse or as a symbol of healing) could become a "true" statement according to the social convention of certain groups (Gergen, 2009: 10). This notion is particularly relevant to social work practice as we now understand that together with members of a community (or social convention in Gergen's term) we can construct (or reconstruct) a reality which would become more meaningful and "real" because of its "social utility."

In the practice example I describe, the schoolteachers found themselves situated in two different versions about what education should be. While practicing in compliance with the "managerial version" is expected (by many stakeholders), the teachers' "heartfelt" version is being marginalized. Having a strong sense of helplessness, teachers would not even talk among themselves about the kind of education they wanted for their students. Inspired by ideas of social constructionism, we attempted to resurrect the marginalized and suppressed version of education that the teachers found to be closer to their dream and vision of their professional practices. In the two-year period of the project, we constructed a collective vision of education which was substantiated by a new "language" that describes their educational practices and a range of operational measures to be implemented in their daily encounters with each other and with students in the school community. Through this "social utility," their own version of "reality" has taken a strong hold and become meaningful and real to the teachers.

In Language Practice We Fashion Our Future

Our understanding of the world is constituted by language practices that express discourses or grand narratives and cultural traditions. These language practices fashion our behavior and actions in the world and in relationships. For example, social workers who work with families are familiar with the many discourses surrounding the "operation" of a "normal" family such as, "proper parenting," "desirable developmental pathway for young people," and the popular discourse of "stress and storm" that depicts teenagers as necessarily rebellious. Although purporting only to describe and explain, these discourses function as prescriptions for a particular mode of life and parent–child practice. As a result, social workers who participate in these discourses contribute to these understandings and practices. Awareness of these processes has had an impact on my practice by generating new possibilities to "fashion our future." For example, the teachers who participated in my project were influenced (as noted previously) by the discourses of managerialism and marketization. As such, being a "good" and "competent" teacher meant one had to be effective, efficient, and have good professional and managerial performances. Despite this long list, not many of these actions were considered by the teachers as their core practice of education. As such, the implication of Gergen's assertion "as we describe and explain, so do we fashion our future" (Gergen, 2009: 11) for our practice is immense. If the teachers do not want to be fashioned in the way they are now, they can start "changing" by altering the way they talk about their educational practices and create a new set of language or local discourses that fit better with their goals and preferred mode of educational practice. As will be shown in the project, through the use of the various narrative practice maps developed by White (2007: 5), teachers can re-author the story of their educational practice in a way that is more fulfilling and meaningful to them.

An Overview of Narrative Therapy

Social construction can find expression in the practice of narrative therapy. In the following section, I provide a summary description of the major theoretical tenets and practice repertoire of narrative therapy so as to pave the way for the description of my practice, which is the main thrust of this chapter.

Initially developed by Michael White and David Epston (1990: 15), narrative therapy is now practiced all over the world. According to White, it is through "story" that we make sense of our life, experiences, relationships, and identity. In other words, this "storying" provides us with a sense of continuity and meaning in our lives. As this self-narrative determines which aspects of our experiences get expressed and thus become intelligible, these stories actually shape and constitute our lives, not just in the present but also in the past and the future. The decision that people make about what life events would be storied is not at all an autonomous experience but is heavily shaped by dominant discourses that prevail in particular historical-social-political-cultural contexts. As such, both the dominant story that persons hold about themselves and their identity are socially constructed. Life story and identity, therefore, are products of the prevailing dominant narratives. However, no matter how tight-knit the plot of these dominant narratives or personal stories are, there are always "gaps" or indeterminate zones in which we can maneuver. White (2007: 23) suggested we can make changes or subvert problematic stories by identifying "unique outcomes" or counter-plots and re-author a new, alternate, and preferred story.

White (2007: 26) used his famous "trick" of externalization to deconstruct dominant or problem saturated stories. In this practice, the problem is "personified"[6] and its intentions and technologies are exposed and challenged. The separation of the person from the problem relieves the person from the burdens induced by the long-standing problem. Although the practice of externalization often begins with a problem, it always leads the person to examine the "things" that are important to him/her and the kind of life that s/he prefers. With the acknowledgement of one's goal and commitment in life, the person can make a choice between the problem saturated story and the new story in which s/he can pursue the life goals. It is not an exaggeration to say that 99 out of 100 persons who consult a narrative therapist choose the new, alternative, and preferred story. Having this commitment to leave the old story behind for the new one, the person is assisted with many other narrative practice maps that help him/her to further develop and thicken the new story and the new identity (Carey and Russell, 2002: 19; White and Epston, 1990: 38).

As persons are separated from their internalized, dominant, and "totalizing" stories, they can attend to aspects of their experiences that contradict these original stories. These contradictions or unique outcomes are essential gateways to "alternative stories" that are ever present and must be identified by the persons concerned. Facilitated by the questions of Landscape of Action and Landscape of Identity,[7] the gaps of people's dominant stories are filled and distinctly named; alternative stories are thickened and found to be deeply rooted in one's history (White, 2007: 78).

At times, persons are assisted to explore issues that relate to their personal sense of failure—a negative identity conclusion induced by the dominant problematic story. Using the Failure Conversation Map[8] to address these "personal failures," persons are assisted to unravel and challenge the dominant discourses that define them as "failure." The most important part of this conversation is to expose the ethical foundation upon which actions are founded. As such, they will see that they are not the one who fails, but it is the "modern power"[9] that fails to recruit or discipline them. While acknowledging their resistance to the modern power, narrative therapy opens up alternative landscapes where people can view/review the desires, values, and beliefs they have about life and relationships (White, 2002b: 33).

When persons' new stories and identities begin to bud, it is imperative to gain acknowledgement from the members of their community. White suggested that our life is like a "club" that is full of members, some of whom we like and others we don't; some make significant contributions to our life and identity while others have been dishonorable and disrespectful to us (White, 1997: 39). With the Re-membering Conversation Map, persons are not just assisted to remember or recall these members in their life but also to review and make changes to their status according to their contribution. In doing so, persons may be able to gather those significant members to acknowledge their new development in life. Subsequently, their contribution to "the club members'" lives and identities is also acknowledged so their lives are linked around shared values. This life linking can serve as an antidote to the isolated and segregated form of self and existence common to the contemporary era (Carey and Russell, 2002: 27; White, 1997: 53).

Oftentimes, people who consult therapists have very negative beliefs about their identity and relationships. Rather than seeing self and identity as transfixing, narrative therapists take on the poststructuralist position in asserting that "identity is a social and public achievement" (White, 2000: 63). As such, it can be negotiated within social institutions and within communities of people. White, drawing on the work of Myerhoff, proposed using the Definitional Ceremony and Outsider-witness practice to address people's "spoiled" identity. According to Myerhoff: "Definitional ceremonies deal with the problems of invisibility and marginality; they are strategies that provide opportunities for being seen in one's own terms, garnering witnesses to one's worth, vitality and being" (1986: 267).

It is in the context of Definitional Ceremony that people's identity is powerfully acknowledged and authenticated by the responses of the out-sider-witnesses who present. It is also through this practice that the alignment of a person's sense of self and identity claims is achieved (White, 2000: 63; 2007: 165; 2009: 204).

It is apparent from this overview that many postmodernist and social constructionist ideas inform the practice of narrative therapy. This understanding of narrative therapy guided my work with secondary school teachers in Hong Kong. Although based on narrative therapy, it was never meant to be "therapeutic" in the sense that teachers needed "treatment." Instead, I would frame this model of practice as narrative supervision that deals with issues of professional identity and commitment.

Social Construction-Informed Practice in Hong Kong

A central theme of social construction is that knowledge is historically and culturally specific. I will first describe the landscape wherein the educational practice of the secondary school teachers is located. Against this background, I will highlight the predicaments or problem-saturated stories that teachers were having about themselves and their practice. These descriptions account for the context where my practice of narrative supervision was located.

The Landscape of Hong Kong's School Education in the Past Two Decades

The ex-colonial government of Hong Kong had introduced an elitist system of education from the very beginning of its reign.[10] Up until the end of its rule in 1997, only 18 percent of youth could get a place in the government-funded universities. This situation remained very much the same after the handover of the sovereignty of Hong Kong to the government of the People's Republic of China (PRC). Although this provision of education service seems meager compared to other developed economies, it already takes up the largest portion of the public expenditure of the Hong Kong government, both before and after 1997.

Being an international metropolitan city, Hong Kong has always been susceptible to the influence of globalization, one of which is the "tidal wave of marketisation" in education (Chan and Mok, 2001: 21). Internationally, the post-war period witnessed the inclination towards the leftist ideology in terms of large-scale government intervention into many domains of citizens' lives. In the late 1970s, this "big government" mentality was challenged as "morally wrong" (Habermas, 1976: 68; Offe, 1982: 7; Le Grand and Robinson, 1984: 1) and financially unsustainable. These cries from the ideological and fiscal fronts led to the introduction of the New Public Management (NPM) movement in the public sector in the 1980s. Central to this NPM was the belief that "the public sphere of services, organizations and institutions would be improved by the application of public choice theory, business values, micro-economics and market mechanisms" (Norris and Kushner, 2007: 3). Going hand in hand with NPM is the introduction of privatization, marketization, and managerialism into almost every sphere of the public sector. Education as an institution is an integral part of the public sector and, inevitably, it was targeted and impacted by this "tidal wave."

Advocates of NPM in the education sector in Hong Kong believe that strong government intervention into schools and universities is stifling potentials and initiatives and subjugating them to become ineffective, inefficient, and incapable of responding to the rapid social and economic changes worldwide (Chan and Mok, 2001: 21). As such, advocates believe that the government needs to adopt a market strategy for the allocation of public resources. As such, in 1997, the Hong Kong Special Administrative Region Government[11] (HKSAR Government) published a report entitled *Quality School Education* (Education Committee, 1997) to embark on unprecedented educational reform. As remarked by Chan and Mok (2001: 28), the rhetoric or discourses conveyed in this and many other subsequent reports are ". . . quality, quality assurance, management initiatives, accountability, competitiveness, diversity, performance indicators, efficiency, effectiveness, standards, parental choices, teacher appraisals, input-process-output model, value-addedness, areas of excellence, school-based management, autonomy, transparency, quality assurance inspection. . . ." Hong Kong's schoolteachers were obviously subjugated to this "language game" and had to get themselves ready for the "quality drive."

The "technology" of this "modern power" (White, 2002b: 33), using the language of narrative therapy, is plenteous, one of which is the measurement of schools' and teachers' performance by using a standardized set of "performance indicators." According to the Education Committee, all schools are subject to assessment in four domains: management and organization; teaching and learning; support for students and school ethos; and attainment and achievement. As a yardstick of these assessments, schools have to demonstrate "value-added" achievement in both school and student performances. In this "value drive," students are taken as "input materials" to be "added to in value"; both students and the teaching and learning process are reified, or numericalized, and the outcome of the education process is commodified (Chan and Mok, 2001: 32). In this kind of educational regime, schools are like factories, teachers are the factory workers, and students are products to be compared and assessed for their competitiveness. The pursuit of efficient and effective services, through increasing quantification and measurement enhancement, restricted the personal agency and autonomy of teachers resulting in feelings of dehumanization and alienation (Chan and Mok, 2001: 21).

On top of their daily teaching, teachers face numerous top-down reforms and demanding tasks in curriculum changes, teaching and learning methodologies, professional development, external and self-assessments of student/school achievements, staff appraisal, promotion and marketing, anxieties about their performance as measured by the 230 indicators, as well as the school's relative competitive position. Most worrying of all is whether their school will have sufficient student enrollment to keep the school going as the birth rate in Hong Kong has been declining over the last two decades.

So how well or poorly are Hong Kong schoolteachers doing amidst this tidal wave? Findings of two studies (Hong Kong Professional Teachers' Union, 2003, 2008) on the teachers' work-related pressure and psychiatric illnesses reported that more than 13 percent of teacher respondents reported suffering from anxiety attacks and nearly 20 percent from depression. These figures are much higher than the general population. Teachers also reported that their average daily work day is 11.5 hours, with 85 percent of them working between 10 and 15 hours per day. In addition, only 6 percent of teachers reported having a 5-day work week, with the vast majority working between 5.5 days and 7 days per week. With regard to the sources of their work pressure, 78 percent reported it originated from the external/self-assessment; 68 percent from the new secondary school structure; 67 percent from competition among schools; 64 percent from decline in student enrollment; and 63 percent from assessment of teachers' language proficiency. Despite this highly stressful work environment, we were amazed to find that 91 percent of teachers still liked the teaching profession and only 20 percent were thinking of leaving the profession via early retirement or changing jobs.

This background depicts the social and institutional contexts within which many schoolteachers in Hong Kong are located. It was at this historical point of time that I had the opportunity to develop a model of practice that I thought could help address some of the concerns of schoolteachers in Hong Kong.

Narrative Supervision and Professional Development for Secondary Schoolteachers in Hong Kong

Narrative therapy is most often practiced with people (either individually or in groups or families) who are "trapped" in a story that allows insufficient space for the performance of the preferred story or identity. Moreover, these people have to actively participate in performing activities that are required by the dominant stories, and the resulting experiences are understandably unsatisfying and dead-ended. As such, an expected outcome of the narrative encounter would be for the persons to identify and generate alternative stories that enable them to perform new meanings and stories that they find satisfying and open-ended. But how is such a framework relevant to professional supervision and development for schoolteachers in Hong Kong? In the following, I attempt to answer this question by describing a model of practice that is based on narrative therapy for the professional development of secondary school teachers.

The upsurge of marketization and managerialism in the education sector made it difficult for schools and teachers to follow their professional ethics in their daily practice. For instance, because schools have to look good on hundreds of performance indicators, teachers are required to carry out tasks that are irrelevant to "education"; for example, promoting and marketing their school among parents and the community so as to make sure they have sufficient enrollment to keep the school going. To the teachers, this is more business than education practice. Moreover, a culture of accountability that prevails in the managerial regime drives the teachers to spend increasing time on reporting at the expense of addressing the holistic development of students. They are "trapped" in a story that does not allow them the space and the agency to perform their preferred identity. Day in and day out, they have to perform activities that they find unfulfilling, unsatisfying, meaningless, and dead-ended. While some teachers have insight into the structural aspects of their predicaments, many see the problems as residing within themselves, e.g., poor time management, lack of professional competence, inability to multitask. The more they cannot "manage" the situation, the more time and energy they devote to their work. Viewed from the story metaphor perspective of narrative therapy, many schoolteachers in Hong Kong are trapped in a story in which they cannot perform their preferred identity—the kind of teacher that they have pledged to be—nor can they satisfactorily perform activities that they consider "genuine" education.

Despite the pressure and various symptoms of stress, the majority of teachers are still "functional" and performing what is asked of them. Some have quit, others want to quit, but most stay on. Those who remain work hard to "close the gap" that exists between what is required of them (the standard) and their present performance. While a sense of personal failure is widespread among schoolteachers, the very fact that they stay on, not giving up, not quitting the job, tells us that they still have hope, no matter how dim it is (or that they see no alternatives). Exploring these issues might open up new resources for the teachers to use in the face of marketization and managerialism. As such, our Narrative Supervision and Professional

Development project endeavored to support the teachers to explore new territories, new stories, and new identities.

Origin of the Project

Against this background, I came across the secondary school MOSSJSS[12] in early 2007. MOSSJSS was founded in 1996 by a group of dedicated Catholic teachers who, in turn, were inspired by a very charismatic principal. The first decade witnessed the hard work of this group of enthusiastic educators who made the school excel among others in the territory. Sadly, the principal died in 2004 leaving the group of teachers shocked and distraught. However, faced with unprecedented education reform, there was barely time to grieve their beloved leader, not to mention to review, reflect, and to re-story their identity as teachers amidst the "tidal wave" in the education sector. Thus, behind the many achievements of the school was a group of weary teachers on the brink of professional burnout.

In late 2006, I was approached by an ex-student who was the social work supervisor supporting the work of a school social worker at MOSS-JSS. Both of them requested that I provide some help to the school and teachers, especially in the area of grief counseling, with the use of narrative therapy. Although I was hesitant to play the role of an expert who heals, I was interested to learn more about the schoolteachers' unique "his-story" and to negotiate a collectively consensual goal on where the narrative encounter would land. Meetings were set up with the key school personnel including the new school principal and two deputy principals. After listening to the story of their past and present, I immediately felt for them. I reiterated my role was not the expert who came from nowhere and claimed expertise to "heal" the wound and devise a developmental blueprint for the school. Instead, I, as an outsider, would take on a "de-centred but influential" (White, 2002a) position and engage the teachers to work collectively as a group to:

- articulate their unique story amidst the grand narrative/education reform;
- discuss among themselves whether this story could speak for their professional identity;

- see if they wish to review or re-author a new story in which they could find alignment between their daily practice and their life/ professional commitment; or
- map out their own strategy that could help them actualize their life/professional commitment, not as an individual achievement, but as a group/collective one.

This was how I framed this practice as a project of narrative supervision and professional development. In the following sections, I describe in greater detail this two-year-long narrative journey as an illustration of social construction-informed practice. After consulting with the school principal and the key staff (who later became the first core group members), the objectives of the project were to provide space for the teachers to:

1. re-view one's commitment in education in the company of fellow colleagues/teachers;
2. re-member the significant others who have contributed to the development of one's professional identity, knowledge, and skills;
3. re-member the contribution one has made to other people's identity projects as well as the development of knowledge and skills of living;
4. give witness by acknowledging each others' new identity and journey in their vocation as teachers;
5. develop strategies for their educational endeavors that align with their renewed vocational commitment.

The Project: Start from Our Hearts

The project was implemented in three phases from March 2007 to June 2009. In each of the three phases, one group (the Core Group) of senior or more experienced teachers would take up the group leader's role to facilitate and implement the activities participated in by another younger and less experienced group (the Focus Group) of teachers. In order to support their role as group leaders, I provided "training" to the Core Group in each of the three phases and then acted as a resource person when the Core Group implemented the activities with the Focus Group. Altogether, I provided three rounds of "training" and served as a resource person throughout the three phases of the project. Tables 11.1 and 11.2 summarize the basic details

Narrative Supervision and Professional Development for School Teachers

Table 11.1 Structure and Organization of the Project

Phases	Core Group	Focus Group
First	There were nine members in the group, including the school principal, two deputy principals, three subject leaders, a social work supervisor, and three social workers. After the "training" sessions, they became the group leaders of the Focus Group. Except two younger social workers, all members of the core group personally knew the founding principal personally and had developed a very deep relationship with him.	There were 12 teachers whose experiences in teaching ranged from 10–15 years and who took up middle management work in addition to teaching. Five of them became the group leaders of the second phase. Most of them were recruited by the founding principal either when the school was first launched or during the beginning days of the school. They all had substantial knowledge and experiences in working with the founding principal.
Second	Five teachers were members of the Focus Group in the first phase, including the Panel chair of the disciplinary team. After the training, they became the leaders of the Focus Group.	There were 28 teachers whose experiences in teaching ranged from 5–10 years. Some of them were recruited by the founding principal but not all of them had an in-depth relationship with him.
Third	Five teachers from the second phase Focus Group became the group leaders of the third phase Focus Group.	There were 27 newly recruited teachers. Most of them were fresh graduates from university and none of them had a personal relationship with the founding principal.

of the project, including the objectives, structure, organization, and content of the project.

As can be seen from the tables, the Project has extensively utilized the various narrative practice maps that White (2007) developed to facilitate re-authoring one's story. I used these maps to facilitate teachers of the various groups to get in touch, once again, with the values, dreams, and hopes that had once led them to take on this journey in the field of education. Some of the teachers had a strong sense of personal failure and wondered whether they were cut out or suitable to be a teacher. I remembered there was a

Table 11.2 Objectives and Content of the Project

Groups	Objectives	Content
Core Group	• introduce the theories and practice of narrative supervision; • re-view and exchange with each other one's philosophy, value, and belief and the journey one has travelled in the profession of education; • re-member the contribution of significant others in their commitment to the vocation in education;	• explain the framework of the project and the theory and concepts of Narrative Supervision; • journey back in time—one's journey in education, who/what inspired the teachers to take up this journey? • what were the dreams/hopes the teacher had in taking this journey; • were these dreams/hopes shared by his/her colleagues? • if these dreams/hopes were upheld, what kind of school education would be provided for the students of the school? • how would this "dream" education be reified as daily educational practice (including teaching and encounters with students outside the classroom)?
Focus Group	• promote interaction among teachers and team building; • re-view and exchange with each other one's philosophy, value, and belief and the journey one has walked in the profession of education.	• using externalizing conversation to help teachers externalize the work-related problems they encountered; • using re-authoring conversation and the scaffolding map to assist teachers to re-view and re-story their philosophy, value, and belief in education; • using re-membering conversation to re-aggregate significant others' who have contributed to the development of one's professional identity, knowledge, and skills; • using the definitional ceremony and outsider witness practice to facilitate teachers to acknowledge each others' professional identity and journey in their vocation as teachers; • using therapeutic documents to circulate the dream school and dream education of MOSSJSS.

female teacher who had been teaching domestic science to junior forms[13] in MOSSJSS for seven years. When I invited her to tell a story that she found most troubling during these years of teaching, she related the following story.

Box 11.1

When I was in my second year of teaching, I was the class teacher* of Form 1. I remember there was a boy in my class who came from a single-parent family. As his father was a policeman and was very preoccupied with his work, the boy was staying in a children's home. It was in late September that year that I wanted to give him a box of moon cake to celebrate the Mid-Autumn (or Moon) Festival.† As the children's home he was staying in was on Shatin Ngao Road, quite near the school, I went there on a Monday after work. But I then found out that I went to the wrong address and thus couldn't meet him. I went back again two days later; I was only free to go after work and dinner. When I got there, it was ten o'clock in the evening, well past the visiting hour, so I missed seeing him again. Then I went back the third time; this time I got my father to take me in his car. Finally I was able to give the moon cake to the boy.

I told you this story because I always felt that I was such a failure; not because I missed him twice, but . . . this boy dropped out of school a year later . . . and three years later he committed suicide. After I learnt about his death, I kept asking myself if I could have done more, I could have probably prevented his premature death! I couldn't help but blame myself, thinking what a failure I was.

*The class teacher takes care of the administrative and logistic matters of a particular class of students. For example, if a student takes sick leave, he/she has to hand in a parent's letter or medical certificate when he/she returns to school. The class teacher is the one who needs to collect and verify this certificate.

†The Mid-Autumn Festival has been celebrated for over seven hundred years in China. One particular emphasis of this festival, like Thanksgiving in the USA, is the gathering of family members for a family dinner. Sometimes the metaphor of moon is used to represent a happy union of family members.

Obviously, this young teacher had formed a negative identity about her suitability to be a teacher, as she considered herself not able to care for the student. However, the story also revealed her "standard" of a "good teacher": someone who does more than just transmits knowledge, but who cares for the well-being of students as persons. The curiosity I had about her "action" led me to continue the following conversation with her.

Box 11.2

Wait a minute; you said you visited this student three times within a week after work, right? But you were his class teacher and you met with him every day in school. If you wanted to give him the moon cakes, you could have done so during the day. Why did you have to bring them to his place of residence?

She was obviously surprised by this question, but was able to tell another story that helped me better understand her view of a good teacher. On an earlier occasion, she gave a small gift to a student to acknowledge his achievement in front of the class. This action resulted in that student being teased by his peers as the "teacher's pet" which, according to the norms of students, was something of a stigma. From then on, she took care not to cause unnecessary trouble to her students.

Box 11.3

I see, so you took care when you "delivered" the moon cakes. Once, twice, and three times, you took care and did not give up, you kept going. How do you describe a person who did what you've done. . . ?

How to describe. . . ? Stubborn maybe. . . ? But it's the kind of stubbornness with a reason, a principle . . . a principle of doing good!

Stubbornness with a principle of doing good . . . , would that be a description that fits with your sense of identity; an identity of a teacher?

I . . . think so. Yes, I think so!

Which do you prefer: a teacher who's incapable of caring for her student or a teacher who's stubborn with a principle?

Oh, of course the stubborn one; the one with the principle to do good!

The above conversation gives a glimpse of the work that I did with many teachers in MOSSJSS. While I was having this conversation with the teacher (the Telling), a group of three to four other teachers were sitting beside us and listening as outsider-witnesses. At the end of the conversation I invited the other teachers to give witness (the Re-telling) to the teacher whose story was at the center by using the Outsider-witness Practice Map. Oftentimes, these were the moments when one person's story strongly resonated with other teachers. In narrative practice, we call this "the linking of lives around shared themes and values." In these resonances that rippled back and forth, teachers found that they were not alone in the uphill journey of holding on to be the kind of teacher they wanted to be right from the beginning of their career. These companions were their comrades who worked shoulder to shoulder and back to back every day in the school. These companions, whether they were older or younger, more experienced or less experienced, were all having the same dreams, hopes, and commitment to education.

Two other stories illustrate that oftentimes it is not the "incentive" instituted by "managers" that motivates the teachers; instead, it is the significant people who had made important contributions that inspire and support the teachers to strive on amidst a hostile environment.

I interviewed another male teacher who was handpicked to join MOSS-JSS by the founding principal in 1996. He was a member of the first Core Group with whom I worked in the first phase before the 2007 summer break. When we met again after the summer, I invited him to tell me of recent developments and his plan for the new academic year. He then told me that he had started to do some running in the summer and had registered to run a local 10K event a few months later. He explained that he had decided to "shape up" because a healthy body would enable him to give more to his students and his daughter. This was a new development as he had never dreamt of running such a race. I then asked what this new development told me about the kind of person he was, i.e., his identity. He pondered for a while and said this reflected that he was the kind of person who was determined to take action for a good cause. I was curious about this change and asked if there was anything or anyone that had triggered him to take on this development. He gave me this "don't you know" look and said he was influenced by me.[14] Huh! That was an embarrassing moment! However, I continued asking if there was any member in his "club of life" who would not be surprised to learn that he had this new development and identity. He immediately said that the founding principal would be the first one to notice his change and the first one to endorse his new development. By this time, he was a bit speechless as he was sobbing with tears running down his face. I was curious about what these tears stood for, so I did not give him a break, but just passed him some tissues in case he wanted to wipe the tears. He answered me softly but firmly that it represented his love for the principal and how he had missed him after his death.

I also learned that following completion of the first Core Group training, the teachers had successfully petitioned the school board to hold a memorial service annually for the founding principal to commemorate his life and his contribution to the school and education. When private reverence turned public, the teachers of MOSSJSS did not find their prolonged grief or mourning "pathological." Instead of "saying goodbye" to the founding principal, teachers were encouraged to "say hello" (White, 1997: 76) to him and resurrect his commitment, values, and beliefs in education (Ting, 2005: 16). These were the values that had originally attracted many of them to join hands in making MOSSJSS a community school for the young people, a school that treasures love over discipline; the well-being of students over grades; cordial and caring collegial relationships over competitive and distrustful relationships.

By the end of the third phase of the project, there was a whole school gathering to celebrate the birth of a new set of values which highlighted "a people-centered approach, genuineness, and cooperation" as the guiding principles for everyone in MOSSJSS. Moreover, a book was published and distributed in June 2009 to widely circulate this new set of values of the school. There are many more stories, but these highlight some representative outcomes of the project.

In the current educational environment that emphasizes efficiency, effectiveness, and value-addedness, teachers have to rush from one task to another, or be preoccupied with tasks that are not relevant to education. Seldom do they have the time to slow down and reflect on their commitments in life and in education, nor listen to each other "speaking from the heart." This project provided valuable space and a platform where teachers who have known each other for years could share stories, worries, and miseries, dreams and hopes. Being witness to each other's story and identity in turn had strengthened their renewed commitments and educational journey.

Re-creating a caring community as initially promulgated by the founding principal was a valuable resource for the teachers and contributed tremendously to the confirmation/reconfirmation of their professional identity. As every teacher in the school had participated in this project, they collectively professed a set of values and goals that served to unite every one of them. This set of values and goals was later adopted as the developmental "blueprint" for the school for meeting the challenges of the next decade. This "ethical baseline" in fact served the school best in resisting the externally set standards. Although they still have to complete reports, they can differentiate between "paperwork" and the educational standards to which they have allegiance.

As noted above, the project obtained strong support from the school "management" as well as frontline teachers. Seeing that it was a project that addressed issues of professional burnout, the school board and principal were keen to support its implementation. When the principal and key school board members personally participated, they experienced the power of the narrative approach to re-author one's life and work. They became enthusiasts who made sure all teachers in the school participated. In fact, the book documenting this journey was entitled *Start from Our Hearts: Narrative Supervision—the Miracle Journey of MOSSJSS*. Ironically, this project was financially supported by the Quality Education Fund (QEF) that operates under the auspices of the Government's Education Bureau and several committee members of the QEF paid a visit to one of our Core Group training sessions in the second phase of the project. It illustrates how such practice can "subvert" the power structure with its own resources. We were all amused by the thought of it.

Challenges and Future Direction

A challenge to projects such as this one may come not only from those who favor managerialism and marketization but, ironically, also from those strongly opposed to it, particularly those wishing to overturn the entire NPM movement. This latter group might view the present project as a palliative that does not address the structural problems, oppressive ideology, or dehumanizing managerial measures. In response, I draw upon White's discussion of traditional versus modern power (White, 2002b: 33). Based on Foucault's approach to power, which sees power as exercised rather than possessed, White suggested we shift attention from "who possesses power" to "how power can be exercised" (Healy, 2005: 193). Rather than seeing power relations as an effect of macrostructures, power is now seen as being produced in microcontexts, in this case the school's and the teachers' daily practices. Following this, the "power center," which is habitually thought of as residing with traditional power sources such as the education committee or the government, is now redefined as exercised by local agents (in this case, the teachers). As such, rather than seeing teachers as "victims" of social structures, they are seen, in this framework of power, as autonomous agents who can exercise power and resist the domination of modern power. Although advocating this particular mode of practice does not exclude any other mode of practice, assisting teachers to develop their local story of professional practice helps to counter the effects of any "grand narratives," including those proposed by the more radical camp.

Burnout is all too common among human service professionals. My experiences with and subsequent to this project suggest that this model of practice may be useful to other human service professions like medicine and nursing.

The Way Forward

There is one last message I would like to share with readers. The ethos of social construction suggests that we not only challenge existing traditions of understanding but also offer new possibilities for action (Gergen, 2009: 12). This ethos is particularly and vigilantly expressed in the work of Michael White. We would benefit from more practitioners like him who deconstruct many of the taken-for-granted practices in "professional helping," and develop new ways of practice that replace the dysfunctional traditions with creative and compassionate alternatives. In the practice I described in this chapter, I have tried to express this mode of practice. I hope that readers will be incited to "cook their own meal with their own recipe."

Notes

1. This group of psychologists including C. Gilligan (1982); L. Brown (1989); C. Lyons (1990); and S. Hekman (1995) were discontented with the paradigm of "bounded self" in traditional psychology in addressing the human development, especially in the moral domain. Instead, they proposed a relational paradigm in which self is conceptualized not as a separate entity, but as an interconnected and interdependent entity that is emergent in a relational context.

2. Every society has its metanarrative surrounding the development of young people. Hong Kong, taking pride in having a mature capitalistic economy, has

prescribed for its young people the most desirable developmental path in which studying hard—getting into university and graduating with a degree and getting a well-paid job preferably in the lucrative financial sector so as to sustain a luxurious materialistic life—are all the more important milestones for young people to achieve. At a university, I was beyond doubt a beneficiary of this metanarrative.

3. This movie is produced by Mark Byers and directed by Zheng Xiaolong, 2001.

4. Gua sha is an ancient therapeutic practice that began in China many centuries ago and is now commonly practiced in China, Hong Kong, Vietnam, Taiwan, Indonesia, and many parts of Southeast Asia. *Gua* means to scrape or rub while *sha* is a reddish and slightly elevated skin rash. In these cultures, gua sha is used to treat and prevent acute conditions, such as common cold or flu, asthma, and bronchitis, as well as chronic problems involving pain and "blood stagnation" (http://calmspirit.net/guasha/guasha.htm).

5. When gua sha is applied, a round-edged instrument is used to rub the patient's skin in downward strokes until the petechia (a tiny purplish red spot on the skin caused by the release into the skin of a very small quantity of blood from a capillary) of that surface is completely raised.

6. By "personified," Michael White meant that the "problem" that the person encounters is treated as if it is a human being that has a life, a personality, and most important a plan for the person concerned.

7. The Landscape of Identity and Landscape of Action questions are two major categories of inquiry that White (2007) used in *Re-authoring Conversations* which he developed based on the work of Brunner, J. (1986) *Actual minds, possible worlds*. Cambridge, MA: Harvard University Press.

8. White used "journey" as the metaphor to describe the therapeutic process he undertook with the people who consulted him and "map" as the metaphor that guided the therapeutic journey.

9. Michael White incorporated Foucault's conception of power into his understanding of the modern discourses that prescribe human life and identity. According to White (2002b: 45), "modern power" recruits people's active participation in the fashioning of their own lives, their relationships, and their identities, according to the constructed norms of culture—we are all a consequence of this power, and a vehicle for it.

10. This system, which is in line with the British system, has been implemented for many decades in Hong Kong. It required young people to complete six years of primary and seven years of secondary school education before taking up study in university.

11. The name of the government that demarcates its sovereignty is the People's Republic of China since 1997.

12. The full name of the school is Mo On Shan St Joseph's Secondary School (MOSSJSS).
13. In Hong Kong's education system, "form" is used to denote the year of study in secondary school. Altogether there are 7 "forms," in which "form 1" refers to the first year of study and "form 7," the last year. Junior forms refer to forms 1 to 3, which is approximately equivalent to grades 7 to 9 in the U.S. system.
14. During our encounter in the Core Group before the summer break in 2007, he learned that I was a regular marathon runner since 2004.

References

Burr, V. (2003). *Social constructionism*. New York: Routledge.
Carey, M., and S. Russell. (2002). Externalising: Commonly asked questions. *International Journal of Narrative Therapy and Community Work*, 2: 24–48.
Chan, D. and K.-H. Mok (2001). Education reforms and coping strategies under the tidal wave of marketisation: A comparative study of Hong Kong and the mainland. *Comparative Education*, 37: 21–41.
Education Committee (1997). *Education Commission Report No. 7 Quality School Education*, http://www.edb.gov.hk/index.aspx?langno=1&nodeid=570 (accessed October 21, 2009).
—— (2000). *Reform Proposals for the Education System in Hong Kong*, http://www.e-c.edu.hk/eng/reform/index_e.html (accessed October 21, 2009).
—— (2002). *Progress Report on the Education Reform* (1), http://www.e-c.edu.hk/eng/reform/report_pdf_eng.html (accessed October 21, 2009).
—— (2004). *Progress Report on the Education Reform* (3), http://www.e-c.edu.hk/eng/reform/progress003_pdf_eng.html (accessed October 21, 2009).
—— (2006). *Progress Report on the Education Reform* (4), http://www.e-c.edu.hk/eng/reform/progress004_pdf_eng.htm (accessed October 21, 2009).
Education Department (1998). *Quality assurance in school education: Performance indicators*. Hong Kong: Government Printer.
Gergen, K. J. (2001). *Social construction in context*. London: Sage.
——. (2009). *An invitation to social construction*. London: Sage.
Gergen, K. J. and M. Gergen (2003). *Social construction: A reader*. London: Sage.
—— (2004). *Social construction: Entering the dialogue*. Chagrin Falls, OH: Taos Institute.
Gilligan, C. (1982). *In a different voice: Psychological theory and women's development*. Cambridge, MA: Harvard University.
Habermas, J. (1976). *Legitimation crisis*. London: Heinemann.

Healy, K. (2005). *Social work theories in context: Creating frameworks for practice*. New York: Palgrave Macmillan.

Heineman-Pieper, M. (1985). The future of social work research. *Social Work Research and Abstracts*, 21: 3–11.

——. (1989). The heuristic paradigm: A unifying and comprehensive approach to social work research. *Smith College Studies in Social Work*, 60: 8–34.

——. (1991). Science not scientism. Paper presented at the Conference on Qualitative Methods in Social Work Practice Research, Albany, New York.

Hong Kong Professional Teachers' Union (HKPTU) (2003). *A survey of working pressure of teachers in 2003*, http://www.hkptu.org/stresssurvey/index.htm (accessed October 21, 2009).

—— (2008). *A study of working pressure and mental health of secondary and primary schools' teachers in Hong Kong*, http://www.hkptu.org/ptu/director/pubdep/ptunews/547/mo1a.htm (accessed October 21, 2009).

Kuhn, T. S. (1996). *The structure of scientific revolutions*. Chicago: University of Chicago.

Le Grand, J. and R. Robinson (1984). *Privatization and the welfare state*. London: George Allen & Unwin.

Myerhoff, B. (1986). Life not death in Venice: Its second life. In V. W. Turner and E. M. Bruner (Eds.), *The Anthropology of Experience* (pp. 212–259). Chicago: University of Illinois Press.

Norris, N. and S. Kushner (2007). The new public management and evaluation. *Advances in Program Evaluation*, 10: 1–16.

Offe, C. (1982). Some contradictions of the modern welfare state. *Critical Social Policy*, 2: 7–17.

Parton, N. and P. O'Byrne (2000). *Constructive social work: Towards a new practice*. Basingstoke, UK: Macmillan.

Peile, C. (1988). Research paradigms in social work: From stalemate to creative synthesis. *Social Service Review*, 62: 1–19.

——. (1994). *The creative paradigm: Insight, synthesis and knowledge development*. Aldershot, UK: Avebury.

Russell, S., and M. Carey (2002). Re-membering: Responding to commonly asked questions. *International Journal of Narrative Therapy and Community Work*, 3: 25–48.

Schön, D. A. (1987). *Educating the reflective practitioner*. San Francisco: Jossey-Bass.

Ting, W.-f. (2004). The roads of Hong Kong: Where are your taking me? *The International Journal of Narrative Therapy and Community Work*, 1: 28–30.

——. (2005). A research journey to "re-member": the development of a personal narrative in the research with adolescent girls' life situation in Hong Kong. *Reflections: Narratives of Professional Helping*, Fall: 16–28.

White, M. and D. Epston (1990). *Narrative means to therapeutic ends.* New York: Norton.

White, M. (1997). *Narratives of therapists' lives.* Adelaide, Australia: Dulwich Centre Publications.

——. (2000). *Reflections on narrative practice: Essays and interviews.* Adelaide, Australia: Dulwich Centre Publications.

——. (2002a). Workshop Notes. http://www.dulwichcentre.com.au (accessed October 21, 2009).

——. (2002b). Addressing personal failure. *International Journal of Narrative Therapy and Community Work,* 3: 33–76.

——. (2005). Children, trauma and subordinate storyline development. *The International Journal of Narrative Therapy and Community Work,* 3–4: 10–21.

——. (2007). *Maps of narrative practice.* New York: Norton.

——. (2009). Narrative practice and conflict dissolution in couple therapy. *Clinical Social Work Journal,* 37: 200–213.

[12]

When Woman-at-Risk Meets Youth-at-Risk

Engaging the Discursive Practices of the Nation-State

MARTHA KUWEE KUMSA

In this chapter, I share autoethnographic stories of my deepest struggles with social construction and weave them into a case illustration from my community practice. I especially highlight the inseparable interwovenness of the personal and the political, the individual and the collective, the ethnic and the national, the local and the global, the past and the future, the conscious and the unconscious. . . . I invite you to follow me through the surprising twists and turns as I peel away the notion of social construction layer by layer. Beware—I don't define concepts! I simply tell you the stories of how I know what I know and invite you to make your own meanings. I also invite you to think reflexively as you read and figure out how the little pieces all fit together and where you yourself fit in these stories.

Woman-at-Risk

I was running away from my homeland, going into the depth of the uncertain. I had taken my three children out of their boarding school for the weekend, but I knew I was not going to take them back. We were fleeing the country of our people. I could not leave them in danger and run for my own life, but my secret schemes were not working. The weekend was coming to an end. I would soon be forced to take them back to school. Time was running out so we had to run—and run as fast and as far as we could. I did not utter a word to them, did not tell them why or where we were going. What if they wanted to say goodbye to their friends and what if the word got out? Nor did I tell my family and friends. What if . . . It was April 1991. Globally the Soviet Union was coming apart; locally the communist military regime in Ethiopia was in its final death throes. Its militias were running around like mad dogs, biting anybody they ran into. They were so threatened they would kill anybody discovered doing anything subversive. And running away *was* subversive! Telling anyone would risk our lives—mine, my kids', and others'.

When we started out, my kids knew that something was not quite right and that they were not on their way back to school. We were going in another direction. They asked and grumbled a bit, but then they trusted me blindly and followed me without a word. Quiet indignation, perhaps? So we left, running in the dark by night and hiding in the bush by daylight. A sudden gush of breeze, a rustle of leaves . . . *Oh my God! We're busted! The militia! They're gonna kill us all! Oh God, why did I take all my kids with me?! Why did I not leave them behind?! They would be alive, if not safe! Oh God I know I didn't believe in You! But these are desperate moments . . . please take care of my kids. They are innocent.*

Tears welled in my eyes. The kids looked at me inquisitively. I looked away. They probably knew I was scared stiff, but I shouldn't show them I was capable of fear. What about their trust in me? For them, I was the pillar of strength! Hussshhh. . . . Don't talk! Don't cough! Don't breathe! Hussshhh, my pets, hussshhh. How many days was it? Days were harder to count because they brought paralysis and terror. Nights brought little sleep, but they were better since they brought the hope of escape, of running as far as our little feet could take us. How many nights, then? Fifteen nights of hopeful terror! Until, in the end, terror receded and hope came to the foreground of our landscape. We were in safe hands in two weeks!

Crossing the border into Kenya meant safety. I knew all along that people from Amnesty and PEN[1] International were working with other people on my behalf on the other side of the border—if only we could get there alive! For ten years, they had been fighting for my release from the Ethiopian dungeon, where I was kept and tortured. They believed that I was a prisoner of conscience, imprisoned and tortured because I was an Oromo journalist and because the communist military regime did not like my political views and my Oromoness. When I was finally released, I did not have a place to come home to. My children were scattered, as were many children of other *counterrevolutionaries* at that time. The irony was that I did not consider myself a *counterrevolutionary* at all. Indeed, I saw myself as a revolutionary of the finest kind! The regime *was* against popular revolution!

In my absence, international human rights activists had worked out a way by which someone secretly collected my kids and put them in a boarding school where they could be cared for. When I was released, I wanted to start where I left off and raise my children, but journalism slammed its door in my face. I went back to the university but that too was closed down, and students were conscripted into the military to fight for their revolutionary motherland. The crumbling regime was scrambling to take down with it everyone in its path. My life was in peril once again. If I went to the training camps, I would be killed as a counterrevolutionary. If I refused, I would be hunted down and killed as a fugitive. There was no escape. If I had to die, I told myself, I would die running for dear life. That was when I pulled my kids out of the boarding school and hit the road.

As soon as I came to safety in Kenya, I became a refugee. *A refugee? Was that what was happening to me? I was simply running for my life!* Looking at the thousands languishing in refugee camps for years, it was hard to accept the fate. *Worse still, have my children become refugees, too? Oh no! They did not choose to come! I made that decision for them! Oh God, that would burn me for the rest of my life.* Although I felt terribly guilt-ridden for the thousands who were left in the camps, for us, the process of resettlement was swift because I was deemed a *woman-at-risk*. Friends told me that the *woman-at-risk* program was created by the United Nations to protect women facing danger. Soon Amnesty and PEN brought me to Canada under the government's *Woman-at-Risk* program.

So I was a woman-at-risk? I was so busy living the experience, I had no time to name it. But I loved *woman-at-risk* and embraced it dearly when others named it for me. I told everyone that I was a *woman-at-risk!* It was a protective cocoon, and I wore it comfortably because it brought me to Canada, my sanctuary. It meant an acknowledgement that I was in imminent danger and needed protection. That was the meaning I took to my studies in social work. My *woman-at-risk* identity inspired my passion to help others *at risk*. I did my doctoral study and continued my community work with refugee youths who I believed were *youth-at-risk*—until one day my cherished "at risk" came into a sharp conflict with their disdain for the label. The tension prompted me to critically examine my unexplored assumptions about my coveted *woman-at-risk* identity. And what I found was shocking to me.

Social Construction

I know *woman-at-risk* as a social construction. It is a social category created by the United Nations, after all! And I am no stranger to the notion of social construction; it has been with me in one form or another since my teenage years. However, my relationship with social construction is a relationship full of surprises. This is because the contours of social construction have been a shifting ground where theories are formulated and reformulated as the contextual ground shifts. It is also because social construction is so textured and layered that the depth of its meanings is revealed to me piecemeal—encounter by encounter and milieu by milieu. I assume everyone's trajectory in making sense of this is as unique as their personal stories. Let me share my unique relations with social construction, focusing on the discursive practices of nation-states. Being a *woman-at-risk* did not just drop from the sky for me. I was constructed as one—not just as an individual, not even in one generation of collectives. It took global and local, delicate and blatant, historical and contemporary processes.[2] It is deeply tied up with how Ethiopia was constructed as a nation-state through the Othering of Oromos, a people put *at-risk*.

Being Oromo in Ethiopia

I am an Oromo born and raised in Ethiopia. Being Oromo in Ethiopia positions me on a specific historical trajectory. Until 1974, Ethiopian historiography wrote Oromos into the world by a derogatory name, Galla, although the people called themselves Oromo. Ethiopianness and Oromoness were national identities competing on a playing field steeply skewed against Oromos. Even my naming was imbued with these struggles. My grandmother gave me her cherished Oromo name, Kuwee. But I was christened Martha, and that became my official name to protect me from the oppression many Oromos faced in Ethiopia. Martha Maxwell was the name of the American missionary nurse who delivered me when I was born. My parents loved her so much that they named me after her. They loved her because she dared to go against the grain and treat Oromos like equal human beings. She went to their homes and welcomed them to hers. She valued their teaching and taught them what she valued. Above all, she learned their culture and language and spoke with them in Oromo, even when most other missionaries followed the rules and spoke down to Oromos through interpreters.

At the time, nation building was at its peak in Ethiopia. Although it was the language of a minority ethnic group, Amharic was being instated as the official language of Ethiopia. My birth in 1955 coincided with the year the emperor proclaimed a new constitution, consolidating earlier decrees and ordering all forms of public speech and instruction, including local sermons, to be in Amharic. That was a huge blow to my parents' generation who worshiped God and taught schools in their own Oromo language. Although Oromos constituted a numeric majority and the Oromo language was the language that the majority of peoples in Ethiopia spoke, it was banned from all public use. Abyssinian[3] colonization was inching towards consolidation. Most American missionaries had to respect the law of the land and ban the Oromo language from their activities. The brave Martha Maxwell and a few earlier missionaries were exceptions to the rule.

American Missionaries

My father documents (Kumsa, 2009) that the first American missionaries came to his Sayyo area in 1919 as doctors and nurses to help victims of the Spanish Flu that was ravaging the world at the end of WWI. The first Abyssinian gun-carrying settlers arrived in Sayyo just a year ahead in 1918 to subdue and incorporate Sayyo Oromos into the new country being forged as Ethiopia. Before that time, Oromos were an independent people who had their own indigenous religion woven into their egalitarian self-governance structures known as the *gadaa* system. Although Ethiopia was created by default as an entity left over from the European Scramble for Africa in the latter half of the nineteenth century, its direct rule had not reached Sayyo until the end of WWI (Kumsa, 2009; Holcomb and Ibsa, 1990). Notwithstanding, today Ethiopia sits in the atlases and maps of the world with distinct borders—seeming timeless, ahistorical, and reified as if it has always been there. The new country has also stolen the ancient Greek naming of biblical Ethiopia to secure the reification. Now biblical Ethiopia coincides and doubles up with Ethiopia of the colonial carving of the twentieth century.[4]

Most missionaries reinforced this colonial process by taking on the civilizing mission to incorporate the heathen Galla into the Christian kingdom. Ironically, many Sayyo Oromos resisted the mortifying disruptions of colonial aggression and attempted a new dignified way of life by taking refuge in the American mission itself. When the Ethiopian theocratic state used fire and sword to convert Oromos to Orthodox Christianity, Sayyo Oromos refused and converted to the Protestant religion in mass, just as the Oromos in other areas converted to Islam in mass. That was a profound act of protest against the aggressive repression of the colonial state. My father was one of the first few Oromos ordained as Protestant pastors. He documents stories of their intense persecution, the burning down of their churches, and the imprisonment and torture of believers (Kumsa, 2009). While being Oromo in Amhara-dominated Ethiopia marked one for persecution, being Oromo and Protestant in Orthodox Ethiopia was a double jeopardy. As an Oromo elder and Protestant pastor, my father took the brunt of his community's persecution and torture and spent half of his life in and out of prison.

Although they introduced the Protestant religion, American missionaries refused to intervene on behalf of the suffering communities of Oromo Protestants. Church elders assumed that the missionaries were caught in a dilemma between their loyalty to the Oromo church and their loyalty to the Christian state. But they expected the missionaries to seek help from the U.S. government. Since the U.S. loved the emperor, a little diplomatic help would go a long way in soothing the suffering of the community. However, the missionaries refused to do even that. They simply stood aside and watched the intensifying persecution. Baffled and feeling used and abandoned, the communities banded together to resist state repression. To add insult to injury, the suffering community realized that indeed the United States and other Western countries supported the emperor even in the brutal repression of his subjects. They learned the hard way that the Ethiopian nation-state was being created and maintained by much bigger global powers. However, this did not dampen the spirit of the suffering community. With tears and broken hearts, they prayed to the Almighty God and continued their struggle against injustice.

Peeling the Surface Layer

I was raised in this spirit of community resistance, inheriting their struggle against injustice but choosing a different gospel. I took on the social gospel and looked to the east of the Cold War divide with so much hope. I turned away from the West that I believed wreaked havoc and resentment among my people. My break with my parents' God was not as clean, however. It happened in ebbs and flows, and the Christian values I internalized so deeply continue to surprise me even now, after four decades. At the time, however, I was blissfully revolutionary. I rejected everything that had to do with any kind of God! So many atrocities and injustices were committed in the name of God. Ethiopian emperors said they were elects of God and used God to denigrate and oppress my people. My parents continued to pray to God for deliverance even after living the atrocities committed in his name. I agreed with Karl Marx; religion was definitely the opiate of the oppressed. I saw it with my own eyes! When we talked about the Oromo national liberation struggle, my parents said there was no liberation outside the will of God. They truly believed in their people's liberation from the Ethiopian colonial yoke, and they sacrificed a lot in the struggle to achieve it, but they tied it all to the will of God.

The Ethiopian theocratic state came tumbling down when over a century of oppression and injustice exploded into popular revolution in 1974. For me, that was a radical break from the bondage of God and religion, a blissful encounter with social construction. What happened was a radical social transformation. Regimes are not put there by God! It is not the will of God that the oppressed masses suffer injustice. Kings and kingdoms and nation-states are creations of the human imagination. No social reality is given; reality is what we make it. It is a social construction. We can create it, and we can change it through social action. Indeed, for the first time in the history of Ethiopia, the derogatory name Galla was officially banned and changed to Oromo. Oromo echoed throughout the country from state and private media. Galla was a social construction. There was no denigration in the nature or culture of the people. Denigration came through social encounters and Galla was changed into Oromo, the name the people liked to call themselves, through social construction. I agree with Karl Marx again. We become who we are through work, through history and action, through what we do and not by some God-given quality—virtue or vice.

That was the surface layer of my social construction. I lived it as a social gospel liberating from the cruel grips of kings and gods and religion. Indeed, free at last, I became a journalist, reclaiming my personal stories and my people's history. I wrote newspaper columns and produced and broadcast radio programs in the Oromo language and in my Oromo name, Kuwee. *Who cares about Martha? Let it sit in the official files and rot there! I am Kuwee, and my people are Oromo.* Gone were the injustices of the Galla days! We were rejecting dehumanization and reclaiming our authentic humanity as individuals and as collectives, our true human potential repressed and stunted by inhuman practices of injustice.

To the utter dismay of my parents, I translated and published the first Communist Manifesto in the Oromo language—when I was only 19! Workers of all countries unite! That was so energizing. All these boundaries created among peoples of different countries were created by the bourgeoisie to oppress and exploit the proletariat. All nationalism was bourgeois nationalism designed to isolate workers and protect bourgeois interests. All national boundaries will be dismantled and the workers of all countries will unite. Long live proletarian internationalism! We have nothing to lose but our chains! That also resolved my cognitive dissonance between the mythical Ethiopia and the real Ethiopia in which I grew up. I rejected the grand narrative of mythical Ethiopia: Ethiopia with 3,000 years of freedom and continuity; Ethiopia, the land of harmony and homogeneity; Ethiopia, the Christian Island. I replaced it with Ethiopia, the colonial carving of the twentieth century; Ethiopia, the prison house of nations; Ethiopia, built by the West on the ruins of over eighty nations and nationalities; and Ethiopia, the land of heterogeneity, conflicts, and struggles. We fight against all forms of oppression!

Facing Brick Walls

"Ssshhhh . . . Don't talk about Oromo oppression," said my comrades in my Marxist student study circles. Why not? Isn't it a form of oppression? Being Oromo in Ethiopia hurts! National oppression hurts! "Ssshhh! Don't say that; not while the imperialist monster is out there! This is divisive; it creates conflict within the revolutionary camp. We will come back to that after we defeat the capitalist monsters out there." But Ethiopia is a colonial carving! It is oppressive to so many! What about the national colonial question?

The response was a shock: "Even the Organization of African Unity (OAU) accepts colonial boundaries! The national colonial question is a Pandora's Box; we cannot open it now. Leave that for later. In the meantime, the motto is Ethiopia First!" *What? The very Ethiopia I just spat out of my mouth? Am I to lick that off the ground? No way! Somebody's gotta be kidding me! Amharas are not real revolutionaries. They want to continue the same story when it comes to their interests. Are we really in this together?*

I drifted to the Oromo national liberation struggle. Sister socialist countries were behind the anti-colonial national liberation movements in the entire world. What an inspiration! Local and global leaders like Amilcar Cabral, Baro Tumsa, Che Guevara, Frantz Fanon, Ho Chi Minh, and Mao Zedong became my heroes. *But wait a minute! They are all men!* Here I could shout about Oromo oppression to the top of my lungs. And I did. Here the brutal hushing up came down on issues of gender. It did not take me long to realize that my male Oromo comrades were not as hot about real gender oppression within the struggle as they were about the national oppression out there, despite the motto: *There is no liberation without the emancipation of women.* "Ssshhh," they said, "don't raise that; not while the Abyssinian monster is out there! It is divisive; it weakens the Oromo struggle now. We will come back to it after liberation." But gender hurts now! Being a woman in the Oromo struggle hurts! Gender is an issue of liberation! I screamed on deaf ears and drifted away again, this time to journalism. I claimed journalism as my personal space to fight against all forms of oppression, class, national, gender, etc. Alas! The dismal consequence was a decade of prison and torture (Kumsa, 2005).

In Canada where injustice continues in other forms, I chose social work as the frontline of my struggle against all forms of oppression. I sought out welcoming spaces that would nurture my anti-colonial approach and found less radicalized, mild, and watered-down forms of *anti* struggles against injustice. I assumed, as a *caring/helping* institution of the liberal nation-state, that's how radical social work could get. I did find a somewhat comfortable home in the anti-discriminatory, anti-oppressive, and anti-racist practices. However, as an anti-colonial revolutionary who lived through two revolutions and got disillusioned by both, I realized that these *anti* forms of reactive politics and oppositional struggles were becoming burdensome fetters on my continuously evolving sense of Self. I felt increasing unease and discomfort with oppositional binaries that I believed contributed more to hardening positions than creating transformative spaces.

Peeling the Deeper Layer

Attention! Innocence is about to be lost! Social construction is about to reveal a deeper reflexive layer. This time it struck right at the very core of my
being. This was an affront on my long held belief about my sense of Self,
a simultaneous assault on my personhood and peoplehood. I was doing
my doctoral research. Social construction was coming at me from all sides,
or was I going at it? Perhaps we were seeking each other out but this time
construction was pointing to me, not to something out there. *I am a social
construction!?* I know Martha is a social construction. Global powers introduced it to my people, after all. But Kuwee feels like my authentic Oromo
name! It reflects my authentic Oromoness. Now even my authentic Self is
called to question! I know Ethiopia is a fiction created by global powers and
local despots. But Oromo is an authentic nation colonized along with 80
other nations and nationalities and herded into a prison house of an empire
called Ethiopia. Now they say Oromo is fiction!? I am not real!? *No way! This
is annoying! Nonsense! I'm reading too much of Western nonsense! Come on,
Kuwee! You're authentic! Your people are authentic! They are real! Their colonization is real! You paid a hefty price for it! Just remember why your kids suffered,
why you lost your loved ones, why you were jailed and tortured! Trust your own
experience! Don't let Western nonsense take away your truth!*

The earth was shaking from under me. The solid ground on which I stood
was quickly dissolving away. I found myself in quicksand with nothing left to
hold on to. I was coming apart and falling apart! *Somebody wants my absolute
death! No way would I allow them to do this to me! Or to my people! I will fight
them tooth and nail! It's an issue of survival! I have survived so much and I can
survive much more!* As a way of survival, I joined the debate. Did nationalisms
create nations or did nations create nationalisms (see, for example, Anderson, 1983; Armstrong, 1982; Bhabha, 1990; Connor, 1994; Gellner, 1983;
Hall, 1996a, 1996b; Hall and DuGay, 1996; Held, 1996)? Are nations and
states coterminous or are there nations without states? I embraced the notion of nations without states (see, for example, Guibernau, 1999; Kristeva,
1993) as it fit the situation of my people. We are a nation though we don't
have a state. I viciously attacked those who argued on the constructionist side
or even hinted at the notion that my Oromoness was a fiction (Kumsa, 2002;
Sorenson, 1996; Gow, 2002). Fiction meant not real. I know I am real and
my people are real! *Come on! From the time I learned how to speak, I grew up
reckoning my ancestors and counting back my genealogy up to fifteen or sixteen*

generations. I know who I descended from! I belong to the Oromo nation by blood and ancestry, not only by history and culture! And that's authentic!

I defended my last stronghold with all the might I could muster. Oromos are a nation, just like Abyssinians, Germans, English, and French. *Although many call us a tribe. A people over forty million strong, a tribe?! Something's wrong with the world.* Ethiopia is built on the blood and tears of many nations, just like Australia, Canada, and the United States. These are all settler colonial states, not nations. English are English, whether in Europe, America, or Australia. So are Oromos; we remain Oromo wherever the cruel world throws us. We remain one authentic nation from across the geographies of time and space and culture. But the assault continued, not just from outside of me; this time something was melting from deep within me as well. My last two defenses, the notions of the *nation* and of blood and ancestry, were being shaken. I learned that the term nation itself was a European invention. In earlier days, Europeans used to call themselves tribes and used nations to refer to Others they considered barbarians. With bourgeois revolution, they claimed nations for themselves and gave tribes to their Others (see Anderson, 1983). I identified so deeply with Frantz Fanon's agonizing cry (Fanon, 1967). *So I have been fighting all my life for something imposed from the outside, all the while believing it was authentic?! Okay, forget the naming! What about blood and ancestry? Is that fiction, too?*

I found some consolation in that fiction did not mean unreal. It just meant it was the product of human imagination but it is real. Well, I knew that much for Ethiopia; I just could not take it when it came to Oromo. I could point construction outward so well but not inward to myself. Okay, I learned that social categories create reality; they don't deny reality. *Or perhaps people's realities create social categories? That doesn't even occur to ardent constructionists, does it?* My birth, my blood, my ancestry are all objective, genetic facts. But it takes on meaning only through language, through discourses and symbols and metaphors, as my people make sense of the fact and convert it into truth. Fact doesn't speak for itself until people interpret and make it truth. The name Kuwee is itself a social construction created through language. *But I know that more than just language is involved here. My grandfather was a local Ayantu—a local astrologer prophet who named children by watching the various constellations of stars and by listening for the spiritual signals of the times.* Naming is not just born out of language; it creates language as well. I refuted this linguistic reductionism fiercely but embraced the partial role of language in creating reality.

If we could refrain from reducing everything to essence or construction, we would get to a deeper layer of social construction where essence becomes construction and construction becomes essence. And these are simultaneous relational processes, intimately and inseparably interwoven. We become subjects through delicate social processes by which our likes and dislikes are woven into our sense of Self and get lodged in our bodies. They become second nature, the external speaking from deep within us, and we may not even be aware of them (see, for example, Bourdieu, 1977, 1990, 1998; Bourdieu and Wacquant, 1992; Merleau-Ponty, 1999; Butler, 1990, 1997; Foucault, 1979, 1980; Giddens, 1984). Here, I was forced to turn my eyes inward and find this internalized external, *to my horror!* I am no stranger to reflection, but critical reflexivity is radically different from what I was used to. When I look inside in reflection, I see Self, and when I look outside, I see Other. Self and Other are reified entities apart from each other. Looking reflexively, I see Other inside and I see Self outside. More aptly, I see Self and Other as inseparably intertwined relational processes. As a person who constructed my identity around my oppression and always looked outside for oppressors, it is hard, indeed painful, to look inside and find the oppressor within myself. And, for me, this is the most deeply hidden face of social construction.

Now I understand why my Amhara Marxist comrades didn't see anything wrong in their own camp and why they looked outside for the imperialist monster. They could not see the imperialist monster deeply entrenched within them. I know why my Oromo nationalist comrades did not see the gender oppression within our struggle but looked outside for the Abyssinian monster. They could not see the Abyssinian monster deeply entrenched within us. I understand why some Americans fiercely hunt for the terrorist out there. They could not turn those eyes inwards to find the terrorist in themselves that wreaks havoc around the world in their name. I can understand why some feminists could not see any other form of oppression but gender. I see why human rights activists so fiercely point away from themselves towards Others when it comes to human rights violations. I see why anti-racist and anti-oppressive practitioners sternly point outwards for the racist and the oppressive. I know why, as social workers, we are comforted by identifying as helpers, and not as violent oppressors. It is especially hard to look inside when we are activists out to get the culprit from out there. We spend so much time and energy looking for the enemy out there that we fail to find it inside.

Indeed, there is a good reason why this face of social construction is invisiblized and why it is so difficult to reach deep down and face that hidden face of our Self. Making it visible is also unmasking the structures of power and privilege. But with this awareness comes tremendous responsibility. I am deeply pained by the fact that I am implicated in the oppression of many Others, and turning blind eyes does not make the pain go away. I cope with it by taking this awareness to my practice and working to redress the injustice. The surprises of social construction continue to be woven into my sense of Self, encounter by encounter and thread by thread. I will conclude this chapter with an illustration of one such encounter.

An Encounter with Youth-at-Risk: A Case Illustration

I remember the deep sorrow and gnawing pain I took into this case. It was May 2005. A young Oromo was just charged with the murder of his wife, another young Oromo, leaving their two-year-old son virtually an orphan. It happened at the height of Toronto's infamous youth gun violence, which became a big election issue that year. While "getting tough on crime" was high on the government agenda, "skills training" programs were also promised. Immigrant youths were particularly targeted as "delinquent youth," "troubled youth," "youth-at-risk," or "marginalized youth" depending on the political agenda. Youth marginalization was rampant in the small Oromo community even before the election. Young Oromos were adversely affected by suicide; intergenerational conflicts; running away, leaving home; substance abuse, teen parenthood; premature disengagement from high schools, colleges, and universities; lack of meaningful employment; and involvement with the correctional system. Some were being charged and locked up for major and petty crimes related to drugs and youth gangs.

From such indicators, this was the proverbial multiproblem community. But I was also aware of social construction and knew that there was no problem inherent in the community. If there was an issue, it was the result of relational processes between the community and wider societal structures. There is no youth violence in a contextual vacuum, unrelated to wider forms of violence. I knew for a fact that most members of the small Oromo community in Toronto were refugees who came to Canada fleeing from the persecution and violence in Ethiopia. I knew that they experienced the violence of poverty and racialization in Canada. I knew that most

Oromo youths also came from traumatic pasts both in Ethiopia and in the refugee camps around Ethiopia. They were born and raised in families and communities of Oromo liberation strugglers. I knew that they had gone through painful experiences of their own and that some had witnessed the torture and execution of parents and close relatives. But I also knew that all who experience violence do not become violent and all cannot be painted with the same brush.

Community concern mounted, however, as families felt solely responsible for the adversity that befell their youth. As a first step in its search for a way out, the community association conducted an informal needs assessment. The survey identified *youth-at-risk* as a major community concern and marked "youth skills training" as its main area of intervention. However, this effort did not come to fruition because youth were left out of the process. Community elders identified needs and planned well-being *for youth without youth*. It was at this point that elders invited me to do another needs assessment because, they said, I had ways with *youth-at-risk*. This was in reference to my previous doctoral research with youth. Confident as an activist academic that this could be a space for the redress of injustice, I joined the community initiative and planned a participatory action research. We had agreed earlier that, by refusing to participate in skills training, youth were sending a strong message: *nothing about us without us!*

MAKING SENSE OF AT-RISK

I took this as an opportunity to unmask the relational construction of the community problem—yes, to implicate wider societal structures but also to claim agency and responsibility as individuals and as a community (for further details on accountability and responsibility, see Butler, 2005). I combined community work and research to redress injustice. I wrote up a tentative proposal for a small grant from my university and taught an overload course to make up for the financial shortfall. I scrutinized the proposal with my sharpest critical lens and, when a team of Oromo youth researchers came forward, I presented it with a caveat: I wrote up tentative beginnings and got the funds but the project was theirs; it was up to them to make it their own. I didn't think anyone believed me. One scratched his head; others looked at me blankly. But I was adamant and asked to be challenged. When the youth obliged, however, it shook the earth from under me.

The youth took the proposal to pieces; I felt *I* was being taken to pieces myself! I defended it vehemently but felt ashamed and fell quiet. *I feel like a child caught stealing. I just asked them to make it their own, and now I'm fighting to keep it mine!?* The first thing they rejected was youth-at-risk. *Why for God's sake?! What's wrong with being at-risk? That's how we mobilize government support! Are they denying they are at risk? Well, they are! They think they know better than everybody? Surely these kids are digging themselves into a hole!* I could not fathom why they resented *youth-at-risk* and I felt it as a personal affront to my own *woman-at-risk* identity. The most persuasive reason for their rejection was that no Oromo youth would participate in this effort if we used that term. There is stigma attached to *youth-at-risk*. It means you are in trouble and no one would want to associate with you. It means you are bad! *Bad? As in inherently bad? I know "in trouble" means I'm in a situation outside of me, but bad is different! It is something about me! Was I inherently bad as a woman-at-risk?*

The youth researchers took issues with several other concepts and we ended up dropping "skills training" and "the refugee" as well. Skills training assumed that youth didn't have skills. What about the skills and gifts youth already have? What about supporting them to develop those? Whose need is "skills training" anyway? That took me by surprise. *How come I didn't think of that? And I thought I was the sharpest critical thinker!?* The refugee was also seen as a space of perpetual unbelonging and nobody wanted to be called refugee. People called you refugee to keep you out— and many years after you'd become a citizen! Well, I had been challenged by youth before on this; obviously I have not learned. *What a shame!*

But the "at-risk" label continued to bother me though I knew it was a relational construct. I took the youth challenge as an invitation to learn. I went in to teach and empower; instead, I got an invitation to relinquish my expertise and sit down to learn. The youth have given me their meaning; the onus is now on me to find out what's bothering me. It's about time I explored my assumptions and uncritical acceptance. How are we constructed as *youth-at-risk* and *woman-at-risk*?

From Youth "At-Risk" to "Risky" Youth

The youth research team committed to a critical engagement of the notions of *youth-at-risk* and we requested our research assistant to do a critical

review of the literature for us. Indeed, the literature turned up rich material. The generic category of "youth" is considered a vulnerable transitional
space, and a host of prevention, intervention, and postvention programs are
suggested for the "proper" transitioning of youth into adulthood (see, for
example, DeVore and Gentilcore, 1999; Kitano and Lewis, 2005; Resnick
and Burt, 1996). Indeed, for those not transitioning "properly," labels like
"troubled youth," "delinquent youth," and "marginalized youth" are proposed to influence policy. We saw such framing of youth transition as problematic because it creates binaries between "good youth" and "bad youth"
and between the human agency of youth and the agency of social structures.

Youth-at-risk seems to break down this binary as it does not locate the
problem anywhere. It is probably an improvement on "troubled" and "delinquent" youth, since "troubled" seems to evoke pathology and invite cu-
rative interventions and "delinquent" seems to evoke deviance and invite
punitive interventions. On the contrary, youth-at-risk seems to only hint at
some tragedy waiting to happen and invite caring interventions to avert the
impending catastrophe. But just what is it that youth are "at-risk" for? So,
youth-at-risk eludes us on this crucial question.

Digging deeper unveils the discursive practices of the nation-state
through which the category of youth-at-risk is produced and reproduced.
There is a particularly intimate affinity between youth-at-risk and the discursive practices of liberal democratic nation-states because they narrate
themselves as caring nations (see, for example, Kelly, 2000, 2001, 2006,
2007; Parton, 1996; Roman, 1996; Stanford, 2008). Immersed in the
"catastrophe talk" of contemporary risk societies (Beck, 1992, 2004; Giddens, 1994) and hinting at an impending catastrophe, the caring nation
creates the category of youth-at-risk to contain and regulate the instabilities
of the rapidly changing world. In a global economy that generates such
deep uncertainties and ontological insecurities, then, youth-at-risk becomes
a synonym for nation-at-risk, and the institutions of the caring nation are
deployed to turn youth into responsible citizens and save the nation from
the impending catastrophe. Within this discourse, being at-risk is an indication of flawed identities and a moral failure to be responsible citizens.

However, we also realized that youth-at-risk is not a homogeneous category and that the caring nation packs different care packages for different
communities of youth. And the experiences of Oromo youth are validated
in studies documenting the double standard and differential deployment of
the state's institutions and regulatory bodies such as schools, police, social

work, health services, justice systems, academics, and researchers (see, for example, Ahmed, 2000; Pratt, 2005; Roman, 1996). But this was no news to the Oromo youth researchers; indeed it was their everyday reality. In the era of heightened globalization, especially in the post-9/11 context of anti-terrorism where fear of the Other is particularly whipped up, many racialized minority youths in the West are being rapidly transformed from *youth-at-risk* in need of caring protection to *risky youth* against whom the nation needs to protect itself and its citizens (see, for example, Pratt, 2005).

When youth are constructed and normalized as embodying risk, risk takes a symbolic leap from some imminent danger out there onto the bodies of *youth-at-risk* and youth *become* the risk itself, the danger. And youth "in trouble" become "troubled youth" and inherently bad youth. Through these iterations, the problem becomes essentially *their problem* and society appears as if it had nothing to do with it. And these are not simple semantic manipulations but elaborations of how risk becomes embodied in social construction. Locating this constitutive process within the discursive practices of the nation-state is still beyond grasp for many of us. However, when they rejected the *youth-at-risk* label with such passion, the Oromo youth researchers seemed to have sniffed the danger of embodying risk intuitively. Indeed intuition is a deeply embodied and sophisticated knowledge that we often dismiss as lack of knowledge. It behooves us then to learn how to honor that intimate intuitive knowledge and validate it as legitimate knowledge.

At Risk or Taking Risk?

I will now bring this learning to the *woman-at-risk* label/identity I wore so happily for so long and take this conversation beyond the bounds of the nation-state into the global family of nations (see Malkki, 2001, for family of nations and national order of things).[5] It was easy for me to state that *woman-at-risk* was created by the United Nations and, therefore, it is a social construction. What I find harder is engaging in critical reflexivity to move beyond the obvious and peel the invisible deeper layer. My encounter with the *youth-at-risk* and the reflexive knowledge we produced relationally opens up just such a space to engage the deeper layers of social construction. So how did *woman-at-risk* ambulate through the family of nations and get woven into my sense of Self? Given the discomforting learning about *youth-at-risk,* what do I make of my comfort with *woman-at-risk?* I see two paradoxical threads in my relation to *woman-at-risk:* being at risk and taking risk.

In being at risk, I embrace *woman-at-risk* so dearly, and it feels so comfortable. My comfort comes from the depth of the human compassion that flowed and soothed me in my deepest moments of need. It comes from the beauty and warmth of the human spirit and the goodness in humanity that wrapped around me and protected me. My new life is a gift that others retrieved from the shadows of death and gave back to me with grace. This prompts me to live it out in the fight for justice. The love others show me fires up my own love for others; the risk others take on my behalf fires up my activism to take risk on behalf of others. To me this is a reflexive and generative relational process. And if *woman-at-risk* happens to be a vehicle for such relationality and mutuality in human kindness and empathy, I will continue to hold it closer to my heart and pass it on to others.

However, I also find another layer of my comfort in being at risk that does not feel as good. Here my comfort is the comfort of victimhood. I have no agency and so don't have to take any responsibility for my actions. The wrongdoers are Others; I am just a passive recipient of their wrongdoing and I can legitimately point to them and curse and complain to the end of time. Public sympathy is with me so I can sit back and enjoy it. *But what a shame!* Being at risk in this way erases my subjecthood as a person and as a people. Were we really passive recipients of others' wrongdoing? What about all that struggle, our overflowing passion about the liberation of oppressed masses and creation of a just society? What about my youthful energy and enthusiasm to change the world? What about my active risk taking rather than staying put and being at risk? All of that goes down the drain when I am constructed as a passive victim. What about my agency as an activist? I deny that part of my Self when I take comfort in *woman-at-risk.*

While my acceptance of a benign victimhood is just a surprise, there is a more shocking layer of *woman-at-risk* that social construction throws at me yet again. And that is the realization that I was just a pawn in the games of the global family of nations. The identity of each nation is constituted in the relational context of Other nations. The global family of good nations is constituted and held together through the banishment of bad Others. For example, in this discourse, America becomes the rescuer in the relational context of irresponsible Others who abuse and abandon. Canada becomes a peacekeeping nation in the relational context of war-making Others.

Savage nations put women at risk and civilized nations rescue the women at risk. Alas! A neoliberal civilizing mission comes embodying a global feminist agenda, ironically to deepen the global oppression of women.

My comfort with *woman-at-risk* becomes deeply unsettling as I see myself taking part in this global injustice even as I ardently fight against it. I realize that I would perish in the Ethiopian dungeons and not even be named *woman-at-risk* if the communist military regime was not the bad Other. I shudder at the thought that *woman-at-risk* is less about the preciousness of human life than about the self-constituting games of good nations through denigrating bad Others. I reflect on the willful silence of the West on the atrocities of the current Ethiopian regime. It does no less evil than its communist predecessor but it is spared because it is put in place by the West. It pains me deeply that *woman-at-risk* was a garb of privilege that I wore comfortably even as I was documenting painful stories of hundreds of women who were at real risk being herded into dungeons and tortured by the current Ethiopian regime, of women who were disappearing and those whose unborn babies were torn out of their wombs. Helpless, I cry my heart out.

At Risk of Taking Risk: Constructing HAC

Tears nurture the seed in the rubbles of my shattered *woman-at-risk* identity, and a reviving activist Self rises up to meet a new sun. I learn that we don't have to eschew "at-risk" in favor of "taking risk," or victimization in favor of agency. Both are inseparably tangled up in our everyday living. Yet it is by participating in such dualisms that we also participate in our own marginalization. The youth researchers also processed their own learning and we were able to break the dualism. We realized that youth needed to embrace the rejected *youth-at-risk* at the same time as they nurtured the courage to take risk and construct their own empowerment. This process gave birth to the Heal and Connect (HAC) project.

HAC is the action phase of the Participatory Action Research we embarked on, but the powerful stories of the research phase that gave rise to HAC also need to be told here. While the research team was wrestling with conceptual issues and running a series of intense consultations on research design and methodology, so much was happening on the practical ground. Two Research Advisory Committees (RACs), one from among community youth (Youth-RAC) and the other from among community elders (Elder-RAC), were created. They were created to assist us in making sense of conceptual, methodological, and ethical concerns. Indeed, RACs proved to be extremely useful in breaking down the dualism surrounding risk. They facilitated the generation of multiple meanings of *youth-at-risk* from which we gleaned a strategic use of the term in constructing Oromo youth empowerment within and beyond the Oromo community.

Inspiring developments were happening alongside deeply distressing ones. A terrible tragedy befell us at the start of data generation when a youth participant was charged with the tragic murder of his girlfriend, a young Canadian. We lost another precious life while working so hard to prevent just such a tragedy. With this, we also lost to prison the life of a traumatized young man who was so in need of healing. Then our youth research coordinator was locked up for some petty charges. He had confided his innocence in several members of our team, so we were waiting for his acquittal. Alas! It was heartbreaking to see such youthful energy and enthusiasm disappear into the prison system. The research straggled on but another terrible tragedy struck again as we were writing our final report. A young Oromo was found dead, and the police reported that it was neither suicide nor homicide. There was no sign of violence. Nor was there any ailment of the medical type. How can a healthy young person just drop and die? Apparently, the violence that took the life of this youth was not of the visible kind.

The small Oromo community was deeply shaken when the tragic news of the murder echoed from the media. It was only a year earlier that another young Oromo took the life of his young Oromo wife. This time it was a young Canadian woman whose life was taken. Images of a devilish young Oromo murderer with a head full of dreadlocks peered back at us from the TV screens, side by side with the beautiful young white Canadian woman whose life was cut short. The name Oromo became a synonym for violence and murder. In such an atmosphere so thick with a sexualized, racialized, ethinicized, and nationalized face of the Other, any association with the murderer became a huge risk. Many Oromos responded by distancing from the evil murderer and denying any association. The initial shock and disbelief turned into rage, rage at the young Oromo charged with the murder. He was a disgrace to his people; he was inherently bad; he was evil. Well, what about our own responsibility as Oromos, as Ethiopians, and as Canadians?

Social construction was thrown out through the window and then invited back through the door in our research team. The disbelief and rage in the community echoed through the team as well and our work was stalled for a while. We felt betrayed by the young man who did just what we were trying to prevent. It came as an attack on us and our efforts. How could he do this to us? The fact that his father was murdered in the Oromo liberation struggle and that the young man was dealing with mental health issues arising from his own traumatic past were forgotten. The fact that he was a homeless youth abandoned by everyone was lost. He was evil; inherently bad. He was the offender. This rigid victim/offender binary made it hard for us to feel the pain of the victim and grieve the lost precious life of the young Canadian woman at the same time as we also supported the healing of the traumatized young Oromo offender.

The rigid binary was made worse by the locking up of our research coordinator. He must have been lying when he shared his innocence. He was guilty all along. He, too, betrayed us in doing just what we were trying to prevent. He was inherently bad. He was an offender. Breaking this rigid victim/offender binary and showing the intimate relationality of agency and victimization were out of reach. And social construction suffered until the quiet death of the young man where police ruled out suicide or homicide. Where is the violence here? Who is the victim, and who is the offender? With this blurring, social construction was invited right back.

While these tragedies marred our research process, they also underscored the crucial importance of the HAC project and solidified the resolve of our team. In a space where any association with violent murderers and offenders was a huge risk, our team took risk to address the issue. Denying the problem or pointing it towards Others was shirking our responsibility. Our resolve was fired up by the poignant findings of our research. The narratives of youth participants indicated that alienation was at the root of the problem. If there was a cause for the silent death of the young Oromo, it was alienation. The violence of dislocation and the ensuing alienation from the homeland and its sociocultural, material, and spiritual resources; the violence of racialization and poverty and the ensuing alienation from mainstream Canadian society; the violence of intergenerational conflicts and the ensuing alienation from family and community; and finally the violence of alienation from their own sense of Self and identity—all these cut deep wounds into the souls of young Oromos, and youth need to heal from all these ailments.

HAC was designed and facilitated with such intimate understanding of social construction to heal the wounds of alienation and reconnect Oromo youths to their sense of Self and identity, to their families and communities and to the wider Canadian and global society. The visibility of the violence that took the precious lives of the young women was considered in relation to the invisibility of the quiet violence that took the precious life of the young man and previous suicide cases. Quiet violence was implicated in the long list of other problems plaguing the community. Violence was seen as social construction; so was healing. Indeed violence and healing were seen as inseparably twined relational processes of Self and Other. If youth are inherently bad there is nothing we can do about it. If *youth-at-risk* is created by embodying risk through the violence of Othering, then we can take risk to go against the grain and instill a strong sense of Self.

HAC was just such a vehicle of healing and connecting youth to the various recourses of Self and identity. When the initial research team disbanded as a result of youth moving to other places in pursuit of schools and jobs, we created a new group called Oromo Coalition against Youth Alienation (OCAYA). OCAYA started HAC by mobilizing human and material resources. Enthusiasm ran low when grant applications were turned down but came swinging right back when OCAYA received a grant close to $100,000 for running the youth healing programs. That was a turning point. A youth program coordinator was hired and youth were actively engaged in enlisting volunteers and organizing homework and tutorial programs to address the staggering rate of premature school leaving. Movie and fun nights as well as soccer and basketball teams were organized to facilitate bonding and engage youth in afterschool activities. Cultural events were organized to connect youth to their elders and ancestral recourses. Recognition events were organized to celebrate youth achievements and to instill hope.

Further Queries

In this chapter, I elucidated two principles of social construction: the relational construction of our world and the denial of its constructedness. This paradox shows how a global family of *good* nations gels together through the banishment of *bad* Others and how the constructed *national* order of things gets reified as the *natural* order of things through a denial of responsibility for the construction. The constitution of Ethiopia through the banishment of its Others, including Oromos, is an example of the relational processes of Self and Other that permeate the discursive practices of nations.[6] It shows how Oromos are put at risk and how risk is embodied via local and global historical, religious, sociocultural, political, economic, and military processes, and how embodied risk follows them through generations and into their countries of asylum. It also shows the paradoxical twist by which the denial of constructing risk turns a people at risk into a risky people.

The Oromo case is but a small dot in the grand scheme of the global family of nations in which we are deeply implicated as social workers. Social work being an institution through which the nation-state deals with its Others, we often find ourselves mediating between the state and its Others. We are comforted by our identity as helpers and take pride in our fight for human rights and social justice. I am comforted by our mediating role as it puts us in a space where we can feel the pain of Others very deeply. But I am also pained because, unaware of our constructedness, we can wreak havoc and pain in Others. We *are* at the cutting edge of local, national, and global transformation. Without losing our empathic *we*, can we also step back, cut through all the rhetoric and ask: How are we constructed as social workers? How do we own our constructedness and the ensuing responsibility? How do we hold ourselves accountable to the Others we put at risk? How do we promote global justice and global responsibility?

In our intimately relational world, the mighty, wealthy, democratic First World Self is constituted only in the relational context of the weak, poor, and undemocratic Third World Other it creates. But this relational construction is deeply hidden in order to hide the organization of privilege and the ensuing responsibility and accountability to the Other. The global family of nations deploys concerted defensive arms at any attempt of making visible such accountability. How do we take risk to hold ourselves and our nations accountable to the many Others we put at risk?

I will close by opening up to the example of Africa and the poignant current situation in Haiti. When we look at the poverty and deprivation in Africa, do we see the problem as inherent to Africans, their geography, their culture, or their corrupt governments? Or do we also see historical and contemporary relational processes of slave extraction, colonial and neocolonial exploitation, and the current structural marginalization in the global market as relations putting Africa at risk? When we see Haiti in such tragic devastation, do we see them as cursed sinners since they made a pact with the devil by fighting for freedom (*remember drapetomania, the DSM diagnosis*)? Do our collective hearts bleed just because Haitians are fellow human beings hit by tragedy? Or do we also see Haitians put at risk from the start by the risk following them from Africa as slaves and by the relational risk they are dealt throughout the years of independence? How do we take risk to hold ourselves and our nations accountable to Haitian Others?

Notes

1. PEN is an international organization of writers fighting for freedom of expression. Initially, PEN stood for Poets, Essayists, and Novelists, but it is now broadened to people promoting all forms of free expression, including journalists and translators.

2. See Foucault 1979, 1980, and Chambon, 1999, for details on the notion of historicizational, archaeological, and genealogical methods of digging in the present in order to excavate the processes that lead to the present. This goes contrary to the dominant historical method of coming into the present from the past.

3. Abyssinians are a people of Arabic origin believed to have come from Yemen, crossed the Red Sea around the first millennium, and mixed with indigenous peoples over the many centuries as they moved south into what is present-day Ethiopia. Over the centuries, they have also branched into two major groups—Tigreans and Amharas. See Melba, 1980, for more details.

4. In ancient Greek, *Ethiop* meant burnt-faced people, and Ethiopia meant the land of burnt-faced people.

5. Here I am using nations interchangeably with nation-states and countries.

6. Here I write in terms of categorical identities of peoples, nations, Oromos, and Ethiopians, fully aware that no two nations are constructed the same way and that no category of peoples or nations is homogeneous.

References

Ahmed, S. (2000). *Strange encounters: Embodied others in post-coloniality.* London: Routledge.

Anderson, B. (1983). *Imagined communities: Reflections on the origin and spread of nationalism.* London and New York: Verso.

Armstrong, J. A. (1982). *Nations before nationalism*. Chapel Hill, NC: University of North Carolina Press.

Beck, U. (1992). *Risk society*. London: Sage.

———. (2004). *Risk society: Towards a new modernity*. London: Sage Publications.

Bhabha, H. (1990). *Nation and narration*. London: Routledge.

Bourdieu, P. (1977). *Outline of a theory of practice* (trans. R. Nice). Cambridge, UK: Cambridge University Press.

———. (1990). *The logic of practice* (trans. R. Nice). Cambridge, UK: Polity.

———. (1998). *Practical reason*. Cambridge, UK: Polity.

Bourdieu, P. and L. Wacquant (1992). *An invitation to reflexive sociology*. Chicago: University of Chicago Press.

Butler, J. (1990). *Gender trouble: Feminism and the subversion of identity*. New York: Routledge.

———. (1997). *Excitable speech: A politics of the performative*. New York: Routledge.

———. (2005). *Giving an Account of Oneself*. New York: Fordham University Press.

Chambon, A. S. (1999). "A Foucauldian approach": Making the familiar visible. In A. S. Chambon, A. Irving, and L. Epstein (Eds.), *Reading Foucault for social work* (pp. 51–81). New York: Columbia University Press.

Connor, W. (1994). *Ethnonationalism: The quest for understanding*. Princeton, NJ: Princeton University Press.

DeVore, D. and K. Gentilcore (1999). Balanced and restorative justice and educational programming for youth at-risk. *The Clearing House*, 73(2): 96–100.

Eley, G. and R. G. Suny (Eds.) (1996). *Becoming national*. New York: Oxford University Press

Fanon, F. (1967). *Black skin, white masks* (trans. C. L. Markman). New York: Grove.

Foucault, M. (1979). *Discipline and punish: The birth of the prison* (trans. A. Sheridan). New York: Vantage.

———. (1980). *Power/knowledge. Selected interviews and other writings 1972–1977* (trans. C. Gordon). New York: Pantheon.

Gellner, E. (1983). *Nations and nationalism*. Oxford: Blackwell.

Giddens, A. (1984). *The constitution of society*. Cambridge, UK: Polity.

———. (1994). *Beyond left and right*. Cambridge, UK: Polity.

Gow, G. (2002). *The Oromo in exile: From the horn of Africa to the suburbs of Australia*. Melbourne, Australia: Melbourne University Press.

Guibernau, M. (1999). *Nations without states. Political communities in a global age*. Cambridge, UK: Polity.

Hall, S. (1996a). Ethnicity: Identity and difference. In G. Eley and R. G. Suny (Eds.), *Becoming national* (pp. 339–349). New York: Oxford University Press.

———. (1996b). Introduction: Who needs identity? In S. Hall and P. DuGay (Eds.), *Questions of cultural identity* (pp. 1–17). London: Sage.

Hall, S. and P. DuGay (Eds.) (1996). *Questions of cultural identity.* London: Sage.

Held, D. (1996). The decline of the nation state. In G. Eley and R. G. Suny (Eds.), *Becoming national* (pp. 407–416). New York: Oxford University Press.

Holcomb, B. K. and S. Ibsa (1990). *The invention of Ethiopia: The making of a dependent colonial state in Northeast Africa.* Trenton, NJ: Red Sea Press.

Kelly, P. (2000). The dangerousness of "youth-at-risk": The possibilities of surveillance and intervention in uncertain times. *Journal of Adolescence, 23*: 463–476.

———. (2001). Youth at risk: Processes of individualization and responsiblization in the risk society. *Discourse, 22*(1): 23–33.

———. (2006). The entrepreneurial self and "youth at-risk": Exploring the horizons of identity in the twenty-first century. *Journal of Youth Studies, 9*(1): 17–32.

———. (2007). Governing individualized risk biographies: New class intellectuals and the problem of youth-at-risk. *British Journal of Sociology of Education, 28*(1): 39–53.

Kitano, M. K. and R. B. Lewis (2005). Resilience and coping: Implications for gifted children and youth at risk. *Roeper Review, 27*(4): 200–205.

Kristeva, J. (1993). *Nations without nationalism.* New York: Columbia University Press.

Kumsa, B. (2009). *Jiruu fi Jireenya: The life and times of Kumsa Boro.* Trenton, NJ: Red Sea Press.

Kumsa, M. K. (2002). Learning not to be Oromo? Chasing the ghosts chasing John Sorenson. *Journal of North East African Studies, 9*(3): 161–192.

———. (2005). The meaning of displacement and the displacement of meaning. In A. Asgharzadeh, E. Lawson, K. U. Oka, and A. Wahab (Eds.), *Diasporic ruptures: Globality, migrancy, and the expressions of identity,* Vol II (pp. 95–110). The Netherlands: Sense.

Malkki, L. (2001). National geographic: The rooting of peoples and the territorialization of national identity among scholars and refugees. In A. Gupta and J. Ferguson (Eds.), *Culture, power, place* (pp. 52–74). Durham, NC: Duke University Press.

Melba, G. (1980). *Oromia: An introduction.* Khartoum, Sudan.

Merleau-Ponty, M. (1999). *Phenomenology of perception* (trans. C. Smith). London: Routledge.

Parton, N. (1996). "Social work, risk and the 'blaming system.'" In N. Parton (Ed.), *Social theory, social change and social work* (pp. 98–114). London: Routledge.

Pratt, A. (2005). *Securing borders: Detention and deportation in Canada.* Vancouver BC, Canada: University of British Columbia Press.

Resnick, G. and M. Burt (1996). Youth at risk: Definitions and implications for service delivery. *American Journal of Orthopsychiatry*, 66(2): 172–188.

Roman, L. (1996). A spectacle in the dark: Youth as transgression, display, and repression. *Educational Theory*, 46(1): 1–22.

Sorenson, J. (1996). Learning to be Oromo: Nationalist discourse in the diaspora. *Social Identities*, 2(3): 439–467.

Stanford, S. (2008). Taking a stand or playing it safe: Resisting the moral conservatism of risk in social work practice. *European Journal of Social Work*, 11(3): 209–220.

Contributors

RUTH GROSSMAN DEAN is a professor at Simmons College School of Social Work in Boston where she teaches courses in clinical practice, narrative therapies, and orientations to knowledge. She has been a practitioner throughout the fifty years of her career, combining community-based family practice as a volunteer at neighborhood health centers with a small private practice. Her most recent publication (with Nancy Levitan Poorvu) was entitled "Assessment and Formulation: A Contemporary Social Work Perspective" (*Families in Society*, 2009).

FIONA GARDNER has been in social work for over thirty years in direct practice, management, teaching, and research. She helped establish the social work program at La Trobe University in Bendigo, Australia, where she is currently Head of Campus. As part of her role at the Centre for Professional Development, she has been running workshops primarily on critical reflection for government and nongovernment agencies for several years. She is the author of *Working with Human Service Organisations: Creating Connections for Practice* and has coauthored two books on critical reflection.

CHRIS HALL is a licensed practitioner and an associate professor of clinical social work at the University of North Carolina–Wilmington where he co-directs the Strengths Collaborative, a group dedicated to encouraging social constructionist-informed and strength-based ways of working. Current publications include, "A Practitioner's Application and Deconstruction of Evidence-Based Practice" (2008), and "Perceptions of Need and the Ethicality of the Male Social Work Practice" (2007). Chris's Web site is www. jchristopherhall.com.

MARIE KEENAN lectures at the School of Applied Social Science, University College Dublin. She is a social worker and registered family and systemic psychotherapist. Her latest book is *Child Sexual Abuse and the Catholic Church: Gender, Power, and Organizational Culture*, 2011.

MARTHA KUWEE KUMSA teaches in the graduate social work program at the Faculty of Social Work, Wilfrid Laurier University. She has been a member of this faculty since 2002. Her teaching and research interests include transformative practice, reflexive learning, nations and nationalisms, home and homelands, issues of identity and belonging among diasporic communities, and explorations of spirituality.

DEBORAH R. MAJOR is the Director of the LOSS (Loving Outreach to Survivors of Suicide) Program at Catholic Charities in Chicago, IL. Formerly, she was an assistant professor at the University of Vermont and has sixteen years of direct practice experience as a therapist with Catholic Charities in Chicago, where she provided services for children and families in the child welfare system.

NIGEL PARTON is the Foundation National Society for the Prevention of Cruelty to Children (NSPCC) Professor in Applied Childhood Studies at the University of Huddersfield, England. A qualified and registered social worker, he has been researching and writing about child welfare and child protection for over thirty years. His most recent books are *Reforming Child Protection* (with B. Lonne, J. Thomson, and M. Harries, 2008) and *Understanding Children's Social Care: Politics, Policy and Practice* (with N. Frost, 2009). He is also the coauthor with Patrick O'Byrne of *Constructive Social Work: Towards a New Practice* (2000).

SALLY ST. GEORGE is an associate professor and Director of Graduate Student Affairs in the Faculty of Social Work at the University of Calgary and a family therapist and clinical supervisor at the Calgary Family Therapy Centre. Practicing marriage and family therapy for the last twenty years, she is dedicated to creating and utilizing social constructionist principles in her teaching and clinical practice. Sally serves on the boards of the Taos Institute and Global Partnership for Transformative Social Work and is also a coeditor of *The Qualitative Report,* an open-access online interdisciplinary journal.

WAI-FONG TING worked as a social worker before becoming a teacher in social work. She is now an associate professor in the department of applied social sciences of the Hong Kong Polytechnic University, teaching theory and practice in social work and narrative therapy. She also writes and edits books on narrative therapy mostly for local practitioners in Hong Kong. Some of her publications (in Chinese) include *Narrative Outreaching Youth Work* (2006) and *All Begins from the Heart* (2009).

TRISH WALSH is a researcher and educator in the School of Social Work and Social Policy, Trinity College Dublin, and an independent social worker and trainer/consultant. Her practice background spans fifteen years in child welfare, family therapy and fostering practice, and child, adolescent, and adult mental health. Her teaching interests are in social work theory, skills, and critical discourses. Her research interests include therapeutic work, social work education, and social constructionism. Her latest book is *The Solution-focused Helper: Ethics and Practice in Health and Social Care* (2010).

STANLEY WITKIN is a professor in the department of social work at the University of Vermont in Burlington, Vermont, and is president and co-founder of the Global Partnership for Transformative Social Work (www.gptsw.net), a worldwide collective of social workers interested in exploring the transforming possibilities of social constructionist and related frameworks. Some recent publications include *Social Work Dialogues* (coedited with D. Saleebey, 2007), *Why Do We Think Practice Research is a Good Idea? Social Work & Society* (2011), and "New Voices in Social Work: Writing Forms and Knowledge Production" (with A. Chambon) in *Qualitative Social Work* (2007).

DAN WULFF is an associate professor in the Faculty of Social Work at the University of Calgary and a family therapist and clinical supervisor at the

Calgary Family Therapy Centre. As a practicing family therapist for thirty-four years in social agencies, mental health centers, psychiatric hospitals, and university marriage and family therapy clinics, his practice and research efforts have centered on an integrative practice of social work and family therapy. Dan serves on the boards of the Taos Institute and Global Partnership for Transformative Social Work and is a coeditor of *The Qualitative Report*.

Index

Mo On Shan St. Joseph's Secondary
School (MOSSJSS), project at,
294–302
modernism, 14
modernity, characterization of,
139–140
mother, deciding what kind to be, 223
mother-daughter conflict, 214–226:
and community support, 215, 224–
226; handling, with philosophical
talk, 215–219; repositioning power
struggles, 215, 219–224
multivocality, emphasis on, 30–31

"name and shame" campaign, 261
narrative approach: client and
professional, exploring, 192;
to externalize problem, 146; in
postmodern and constructionist
perspectives, 144–145; narrative
practice maps, 296
narrative supervision, objectives and
content, 297t
Narrative Supervision and Professional
Development project, 10, 293–302:
new school values created from,
301; objectives of, 295; objectives
and content of, 297t; structure and
organization of, 295–296, 296t;
teachers as companions, 300;
Telling and Re-telling in,
299–300
narrative therapy, 58, 76–98, 193:
applied to teachers' supervision
and professional development,
293–302; challenges and future
directions, 96–99; comparisons
with psychodynamic perspective,
78–81; connections between,
and social constructionism, 78;

decisions about stories to tell, 287;
discovering, 281; externalizing
and re-authoring problem, 84–87;
hallmarks of, 83–84; idiosyncratic
approach to, 84–94; integrating,
with psychodynamic approach, 81–
82; introduction to, 76–78; letter
writing as, 87–93; overview, 287–
289; tools for, 193; usual practice
of, 292. See also conversations with
clients
nation building, in Ethiopia, 311–312
nation-states: caring, and youth-at-
risk, 323–324; discursive practices
of, 311; as social construction, 10,
314–315. See also Ethiopia
national standards, for assessing
state's performance with child
welfare, 181
naturalistic accounts, 258–259
neologisms, 21
neutrality, systemic calling to, 263,
271n16
New Public Management movement,
290
"non-accidental injury." See child
abuse
nonadmitting parents, 163–174: case
resolution without confession,
178; encouraging participation
in research, 168–169; evaluating
treatment of, 174–175; reaching
mutually accepted goals with,
168–170; signs of progress with,
170–174; social constructionist
approach with, 163–168
nonviolent resistance, 228–236:
adapted for families, 212, 220;
as moral and effective position,
236–237; optimism emanating